A
Manifesto
for Theological
Interpretation

A Manifesto

for Theological

Interpretation

EDITED BY

Craig G. Bartholomew
and Heath A. Thomas

B

Baker Academic

a division of Baker Publishing Group
Grand Rapids, Michigan

Published by Baker Academic
a division of Baker Publishing Group
P.O. Box 6287, Grand Rapids, MI 49516-6287
www.bakeracademic.com

Printed in the United States of America

Library of Congress Cataloging-in-Publication Data
Names: Bartholomew, Craig G., 1961– editor.
Title: A manifesto for theological interpretation / edited by Craig G. Bartholomew and Heath A. Thomas.
Description: Grand Rapids : Baker Academic, 2016. | Includes bibliographical references and index.
Identifiers: LCCN 2015050486 | ISBN 9780801030871 (pbk.)
Subjects: LCSH: Bible—Criticism, interpretation, etc.
Classification: LCC BS531 .M34 2016 | DDC 220.601—dc23
LC record available at http://lccn.loc.gov/2015050486

16   17   18   19   20   21   22   7   6   5   4   3   2   1

In keeping with biblical principles of creation stewardship, Baker Publishing Group advocates the responsible use of our natural resources. As a member of the Green Press Initiative, our company uses recycled paper when possible. The text paper of this book is composed in part of post-consumer waste.

More and more "young fogeys" like Oden are discovering the truth that is "ever ancient, ever new" (Augustine of Hippo). It is called the catholic feast, and it is a feast to which he invites us. It is a moveable feast, still developing under the guidance of the Spirit. Oden is like cinema's "Auntie Mame," who observed that life is a banquet and most poor slobs are starving to death. Origen, Irenaeus, Cyril of Alexandria, Thomas Aquinas, Teresa of Avila, Martin Luther, John Calvin, John Wesley—the names fall trippingly from Oden's tongue like a gourmet surveying a most spectacular table. Here are arguments you can sink your teeth into, conceptual flights of intoxicating complexity, and truths to die for. Far from the table, over there, *way* over there, is American theological education, where prodigal academics feed starving students on the dry husks of their clever unbelief.

Richard John Neuhaus, "An Invitation to the Feast"

The waning of Christianity as practiced in the West is easy to explain. The Christian churches have comprehensively failed in their one central task—to retell their foundational story in a way that might speak to the times.

John Carroll, *The Existential Jesus*

The biblical texts *must* be preached—under all circumstances and at any cost. The people for whom we each have a responsibility need them for living (and for dying).

Gerhard von Rad, *Biblical Interpretations in Preaching*

Schweitzer said that Jesus comes to us as one unknown. Epistemologically, if I am right, this is the wrong way round. We come to him as ones unknown, crawling back from the far country, where we had wasted our substance on riotous but ruinous historicism. But the swinehusks—the "assured results of modern criticism"—reminded us of that knowledge which arrogance had all but obliterated, and we began the journey home. But when we approached, as we have tried to do in this book, we found him running to us as one well known, whom we had spurned in the name of scholarship or even of faith, but who was still patiently waiting to be sought and found once more. And the ring on our finger and the shoes on our feet assure us that, in celebrating his kingdom and feasting at his table, we shall discover again and again not only who he is but [also] who we ourselves are: as unknown and yet well known, as dying and behold we live.

N. T. Wright, *Jesus and the Victory of God*

Contents

Preface   ix
Craig G. Bartholomew and Heath A. Thomas

A Manifesto for Theological Interpretation   1

1. The History and Reemergence of Theological Interpretation   27
   Angus Paddison

2. Doctrine of Scripture and Theological Interpretation   48
   Michael W. Goheen and Michael D. Williams

3. The Ecclesia as Primary Context for the Reception of the Bible   72
   Robby Holt and Aubrey Spears

4. Theological Interpretation and Historical Criticism   94
   Murray Rae

5. The Role of Hermeneutics and Philosophy in Theological Interpretation   110
   William P. Olhausen

6. The Canon and Theological Interpretation   131
   Stephen G. Dempster

7. Biblical Theology and Theological Interpretation   149
   David J. H. Beldman and Jonathan Swales

8. Mission and Theological Interpretation 171
   Michael W. Goheen and Christopher J. H. Wright

9. The Telos (Goal) of Theological Interpretation 197
   Heath A. Thomas

10. A Framework for Theological Interpretation 218
    Denis Farkasfalvy

11. Theological Commentary 237
    Mark Gignilliat and Jonathan T. Pennington

12. Theological Interpretation for All of Life 257
    Craig G. Bartholomew and Matthew Y. Emerson

List of Contributors 275
Scripture Index 279
Subject Index 285

Preface

Theological interpretation, which we define broadly as *interpretation of the Bible for the church*, is that most ancient of hermeneutics. Surprisingly and wonderfully, it is also that most recent approach to the Bible witnessed in the renaissance of theological interpretation today. In fact, it is not only that most ancient hermeneutic but also the dominant one during the last twenty centuries. It was only in the past 250 years, with the rise of historical criticism, that theological interpretation became increasingly marginalized. In reaction, we have witnessed a resurgence of theological readings of the Bible in the late twentieth century and on into today.

We welcome this renaissance as a gift, a springtime of biblical interpretation. But how are we to receive this gift, and how are we to contribute toward its maturing? The emergent theological interpretation is a "broad church," which often raises as many questions as it does answers. Our Manifesto is an attempt to identify the key issues in theological interpretation and to propose fruitful ways forward. It is not the first word, nor is it the last word, but we hope it is a good and helpful word. It is written by a diverse group of biblical scholars, theologians, missiologists, and pastors from a range of denominations and universities and seminaries. We celebrate this diversity and welcome the interaction between church, seminary, and academy. We also hope that this work spurs other women and men toward deeper and richer interpretation of God's Word for the church.

Scripture invites us to a feast, to the great feast of the Lamb. For all its insights and rigor, too much modern interpretation has prevented us from hearing God's address in Scripture and feasting at his table through his Word. At its best, theological interpretation offers us a way to recover the feast of Scripture without for a moment sacrificing the insights of modern scholarship.

How should the reader approach the present volume? The first portion of the volume (before the numbered chapters) is the Manifesto itself. The Manifesto is modeled, in part, after the Lausanne Covenant, which was developed to help define theology and practice as the church went into the world for global evangelization. For the cause of Christ, that covenant enabled partnerships and alliances that cut across denominational lines. While the Manifesto does not rise to the level of a "covenant" that swears before God and fellow believers foundational theology and practice, it nonetheless is a document that gathers and presents essential tenets to help orient the church toward theological interpretation today. Because of this, we would like to see others endorse the vision set by the Manifesto as they find it to be a helpful and faithful way forward.

A word should be said about the term "Manifesto." In meetings of the Scripture and Hermeneutics Seminar from 2012–14 (out of which the present volume emerged), some voiced concern about the term, particularly the dangers of hubris or overreach that it may connote. The contributors to this volume (and especially the editors) recognize these dangers and affirm that the term "Manifesto" does not mean the only, first, or final word on theological interpretation.

In a concentrated and concise manner, the Manifesto tries to make public the central tenets that help to orient theological reading of Scripture so as to hear God's address. The Manifesto provides these tenets in order to spur interpreters toward fruitful *practice* of theological reading in various contexts. It is a timely word for the present day as the church charts the way forward.[1] The Manifesto, then, highlights areas informing theological interpretation that may otherwise be ignored or neglected in the reading of Scripture.

Although theoretical conversation may emerge from the Manifesto, it nonetheless is aimed toward faithful practice of reading Scripture so that God might be exalted, the church might be built up, and the saints might be equipped for missional engagement in the world. We recognize that theological interpretation of Scripture in *practice* was the capstone of the Manifesto project in the 2014 Scripture and Hermeneutics Seminar meeting in San Diego, California. "The Son of Man in the Gospels and Daniel" was the focus of the meeting, and the twelve tenets of the Manifesto drove us more deeply into Scripture to hear God's voice and envisage the Son of Man, the Lord Jesus Christ.

Chapter-length expositions on each section follow the Manifesto. Those who produced the concentrated and concise Manifesto sections also provide

---

1. An analogue to our Manifesto is, for instance, the Wiley-Blackwell Manifesto series. Of particular note for the present volume is David F. Ford, *The Future of Christian Theology* (London: Wiley-Blackwell, 2011).

these expositional chapters, which elaborate, with nuance and depth, the affirmations of the Manifesto. Any reader who has a question about particularities of the Manifesto is encouraged to consult the expositional chapter for explication.

This volume is an invitation for women and men to join that company of interpreters who long to hear God's address through Scripture for all of life in the present day. More, no doubt, needs to be said, and more needs to be brought to the banquet to enjoy the feast of Scripture. Yet we hope that, in some small measure, the loaves and fishes that we provide here will be multiplied so that all might feast on Scripture and thereby feast on Christ.

We are grateful for the work of many who have made this project possible. Over a three-year period, the Scripture and Hermeneutics Seminar provided the hospitable space to reflect on what theological interpretation might look like in our day. Various institutional partners helped to fund the work of the seminar, to which we are grateful. We especially acknowledge the generous contributions of Southeastern Baptist Theological Seminary (USA) and Trinity Theological College, Bristol (UK). We are grateful for the wonderful and lively discussions in the seminar during this time, in which we were stimulated, challenged, and encouraged in the Manifesto project. Thanks to all contributors and participants.

Heath would like to thank the administration and faculty of Southeastern for a sabbatical leave that allowed him to work on this project. Heath would also like to thank Craig for his leadership in the Scripture and Hermeneutics Seminar from its inception. His vision remains instrumental for a generation of scholars who strive to work deliberately and faithfully *coram deo*. His life and work models the collaborative, ecumenical, irenic, and hospitable spirit of theological interpretation. May his tribe increase.

A Manifesto for Theological Interpretation

1. The History and Reemergence of Theological Interpretation

Karl Barth's *Romans* commentary of 1919 can be seen as the opening salvo in the twentieth-century's renewed theological engagement with Scripture. Such theological interpretation has reacted against the forces that led to the waning of ecclesial modes of reading the Bible: the professionalization of theology; the disciplinary divide between "theology" and "biblical studies"; a shrill disdain for the church's historical practices of reading; and a secular, disenchanted view of time and history.

Attention to Scripture's life in the context of faith reminds us that the church has always practiced theological interpretation in some form, not least in and through its preaching, sacraments, and acts of charity. An understanding of theological interpretation that restricts it to a conversation between systematic theologians and biblical scholars too easily encourages forgetfulness of the church's enduring and persistent attention to Scripture. Indeed, theological interpretation has never been fully lost in the church.

Tradition, understood as the church's history of indwelling Scripture, needs to be approached as a capacious and broad space in which to explore the biblical texts. Relating to tradition faithfully is not necessarily a task of repeating what was said in the past, but of establishing how to live in communion now with past readers of the text. Reading Scripture in conversation with the church's long history of reading calls at various times for receptivity, generosity, thankfulness, and penitence. Vitally, as we relate to the past

1

in our bid to hear the address of God in the present, we need to be readers characterized by wisdom.

There is much to learn from the history of the church's reading of Scripture. (1) Through the practices of *lectio divina*, we can grow in our appreciation of the shape of the text and its purpose to lead us to God. (2) The church's use of the fourfold sense of Scripture (literal, allegorical, tropological, and anagogical) alerts us to the interlocked and diverse ways in which the text operates in the economy of salvation and in our lives. (3) Typological reading points us to the divine shape of history, our history as part of God's ordering of history, in which Scripture and its texts are suspended. (4) The Rule of Faith provides an indispensable context for plumbing the depth, length, height, and unity of Scripture.

The reading of Scripture as the church's book needs to incorporate the most penetrating insights and scholarly endeavors of our time and the faith of the church as a treasury handed down to us (tradition) and as something we embody now. As such, theological interpretation of Scripture can be cast as *rejoining* an enduring conversation to which modern theology and biblical studies gradually ceased contributing: it is not possible to approach the history of the church and its faith without sensitivity to how both have been formed by and with its reading of Scripture. Scripture comes to all its readers as a text that has been borne through the life of the church.

Theological interpretation comes in many forms and is practiced by Christians across the denominational spectrum. What unites the different approaches is a desire to reconnect biblical reading to the faith and practices of the church catholic and to establish, in a variety of ways, how faithful interpretation should engage with secular ways of reading the text.

It is necessary to say that the reading of Scripture is part of the church's human, and hence fallible, history. Some readings have dehumanized those with whom the church now reads Scripture attentively and prayerfully. Recognizing the church's messy history of engagement with Scripture is part of the task of receiving tradition with humility and, sometimes, penitence. Equally, we need to be alert to the church's history in its broadest sense, with awareness that sometimes we work with a restricted view of what counts as "the church's reading of Scripture." As well as reading the great texts of theological history, we also need to attend to those voices and places that the church or academic theology has marginalized, and to the ways in which Scripture has coursed through the people of God in hymns, prayers, liturgical forms, and sermons. Theological interpretation calls for an irrepressibly ecumenical form of attention, as God's church ever extends beyond particular localization in history or geography.

A healthy crossover between the academy and the church bears within it the promise of enriching theological interpretation. Discovering meaning and purpose in the created order, in relationship with the scriptural texts, calls for an enriching, intense dialogue with the past and the present, with fellow Christians and non-Christians, and with a range of methodologies and approaches. Theological interpretation needs spaces of hospitable generosity.

2. Doctrine of Scripture and Theological Interpretation

To bear fruit within such spaces of hospitality, theological interpretation needs to be informed by a robust, creative theology of Scripture. The Bible is the Word of God and the means by which God addresses his people by leading them to salvation through faith in Christ and by equipping them to live more and more into our creation-wide salvation by leading us to Christ. However, sometimes our doctrinal formulations of Scripture hinder us from hearing God's address in Scripture to this end. Various misunderstandings have contributed to this problem: a rationalism that has caused us to miss the storied nature of the Bible and reduce it to fragments of truth; an individualism that has led to a misunderstanding of the nature of the Bible as a cosmic story of redemption; a severing of the attributes of Scripture—authority, inspiration, infallibility—from their purpose; various dualisms that have reduced the Bible's all-embracing authority; and a false dilemma between the Bible as the Word of God and the words of men. We need a doctrine of Scripture that overcomes these problems and leads us to a fruitful and faithful theological interpretation.

A doctrine of Scripture begins with the insight that the Bible is part of a fuller organism of revelation. An organism has many separate parts, which all have their own particular function but also are bound together in a unity that contributes toward one single purpose. The organism of revelation has many aspects, yet in all of them God discloses himself and his purpose to us. There are various ways to distinguish these diverse components. A twofold distinction between general and special revelation has been common. Some have opted for a threefold distinction: either distinguishing revelation in creation, redemption, and Scripture; or revelation in creation, Scripture, and Christ. We find a fourfold distinction most helpful: creational revelation, redemptive revelation, Christ, and the Scriptures.

This fourfold distinction allows us to see four things clearly: (1) revelation comes in the way of creation, fall, and redemption; (2) redemptive revelation progressively unfolds in history and finds its climactic fulfillment in Jesus

Christ; (3) Scripture is the narrative record and capstone of that revelation; (4) Scripture functions authoritatively as a controlling narrative, with its many genres to lead us to salvation through faith in Christ.

Thus Scripture is not an unrelated collection of divine oracles, theological truths, and ethical principles. Flattening out Scripture in this way reduces the unified story of Scripture into isolated fragments. The Bible is a cohesive and narrative unity that tells the story of God's saving and judging acts, which finds its all-dominating center and concentrated focus in the coming and the work of Christ.

Since this story begins with the creation of the entire world by God and culminates in the renewal of all things as the ultimate consequence of his renewing work, this means that the Bible is nothing less than the true story of the whole world. It is a metanarrative that gives unity and meaning to all creation and tells us the way the world really is. In speaking of scriptural authority, therefore, one must respect the narrative authority of Scripture to narrate the world truthfully over against all other stories that claim to tell us the way the world is.

Scripture is not only a record of God's redemptive work but is also a tool that effectually brings about that redemption in the world. To understand the nature and purpose of Scripture as an instrument, we need to inquire into its role within the very story it tells. Scripture as a whole and in every part finds its place in this narrative through its role of enabling people to take their place in this story, leading us to Christ to know salvation and to live more and more fully into that comprehensive and restorative salvation. And since God's people are always blessed to be a blessing, Scripture equips them throughout redemptive history to take up their missional vocation amid the nations. The various genres of Scripture function as a toolbox with many different tools—law, history, poetry, prophecy, wisdom, gospels, epistles—that are utilized by the Spirit to lead us to faith in Christ so we might embody God's salvation for the sake of the world.

As such, Scripture is the Word of God because in it the Spirit witnesses to Jesus and leads us to salvation. In that statement we see the trinitarian soil of a doctrine of Scripture. The Holy Spirit is the one who witnesses; Christ is the one to whom the Spirit witnesses; and the Father is the source as he sends the Spirit. But to rightly articulate a doctrine of Scripture, we must pay special attention to the work of the Spirit. We can outline a threefold work of the Spirit. Scripture finds its origin in the witness of the Spirit to Christ; the content of Scripture is the witness of the Spirit to Christ; the continuing power of the Scripture is the witness of the Spirit to Christ. As the Spirit witnesses to Christ in this threefold way through human words, we are made wise to salvation through faith in Christ and equipped for every good work.

Speaking of Scripture as making us "wise unto salvation" (2 Tim. 3:15 KJV) does not narrow Scripture's focus to so-called spiritual issues. This would allow Scripture to be molded by an alien sacred-secular dichotomy and would reduce religion to a small compartment of life. Such mistaken understanding is challenged by the comprehensive scope of the biblical story, by the creation-wide breadth of the salvation that is its central theme, and by the cosmic authority of the Lord Christ, who stands at its center as creator and reconciler of all things, ruler of history, and judge of humanity. Scripture's authority is totalitarian in its scope, speaking to every part of human life in its own way and from its own particular standpoint: Jesus Christ.

If the nature and purpose of Scripture is to witness to Christ and his all-encompassing salvation, then authority, inspiration, and infallibility must be defined in terms of its very nature and purpose. Scripture's authority is in its purpose to lead us to Christ; the God-breathed, or inspired, content of Scripture is a story of salvation centered in Christ; infallibility refers to the fact that it does not err in its purpose to lead us to Christ. What Scripture *is* cannot be separated from what Scripture *does*. Scripture is the authoritative, inspired, and infallible Word of God since it is the Spirit's witness to lead us to Christ and his salvation. Asking the Bible to do something else exhibits misunderstanding of the very nature and authority of Scripture. Defining authority or infallibility in terms other than its purpose imposes alien categories on Scripture.

To make confession that Holy Scripture is the Word of God does not in any way diminish its human form. The Spirit's witness to Christ comes precisely through the human witness to Christ, both prophetic and apostolic. Whoever presents a dilemma between the divine and the human introduces a problem that is entirely alien to the Scripture. Organic inspiration best accounts for the fact that the Spirit's witness comes through authors whose full humanity was not overruled and who were fully a part of their culture and environment. This means that to hear the Spirit's witness to Christ, one must carefully attend to the human dimensions of Scripture: historical, cultural, and literary. The church hears God's voice through the human witness to Christ.

3. The Ecclesia as Primary Context for the Reception of the Bible

Because theological interpretation is *from faith* and *to faith*, it is inherently connected with the church. In and through Scripture, God speaks in order to be heard. The church is the primary *context* for theological interpretation of Scripture because she is the bride listening for her Groom's voice. The regular, gathered, and ordered worship of the church is the primary ecclesial *event* when she gathers to listen for his voice. The Groom's proclamation, given through his called and gifted preachers, is vital to the liturgical *acts* whereby he addresses his bride. Christ meets his bride in the proclamation of the Word, Eucharist, and baptism, whereby God's people worship their Lord and are energized and guided for their mission in the world.

God has summoned a people for his purposes through the gospel. The Scriptures reveal God's purposes for his creation, thwarted by human rebellion, but redeemed by God's own Son. The church consists of those who receive the proclamation of this news, as *good news*, before God's purposes are consummated. This faith-full reception is thus always a response to God's summons. Listening while we wait for the Son, who promises to return, makes *our reception* of the Scriptures much like the reception Paul seeks for his letter to "the saints . . . who are in Philippi." Paul gives thanks for their reception of the good news (Phil. 1:3–8), and *then* he prays that they will be shaped by the gospel "more and more" until "the day of Christ" Jesus (Phil. 1:9–11). Like those saints at Philippi, we are the grateful community that has received the gospel. Because we live and worship in the hope of the same Day, we remain deeply open to God's voice in the Scriptures to make our listening more and more fruitful and mature.

Thus *the primary interpretation* of Scripture, taking its place between Christ's inauguration and consummation of his kingdom, is a listening ordered and oriented by faith, hope, and love. This corporate, through-the-ages engagement with Scripture has its own place in God's economy of redemption. While the church is helped by many sources and conversations, by the grace of God the church corporate must humbly submit to this calling to her role in God's economy, to be the primary location of God's address.

The church also receives Scripture when individual Christians, who are themselves members of the body of Christ, practice personal Bible reading. The integral relationship between the corporate and the private reception of God's Word is evident in the Shema (Deut. 6:4–9). The passage begins with and prioritizes the reception of God's address by the gathered community, yet for life in its entirety to be focused on God, the hearing of God's address must extend to the home, to public and private life, to one's rising and lying down. The primary liturgical reception of God's address, therefore, is complemented by the reception of God's Word in all of life.

But how do we go about reading the Bible in private so that the deepest parts of our souls are open to the transformative work of God, who is living and present in his Word? We must approach the Bible with the comportment of a listener. This is a different posture than that of biblical studies and theology, with their analytic orientations. The nature of Scripture as God's address to us and the glory and the goodness of the One who addresses us in Scripture both determine listening as fundamental. This is not to say that analysis is unimportant. Rather, we need to distinguish receptive listening to Scripture for God's address, which can include various acts of analysis, and an analytic approach, which nevertheless should be encompassed by listening for God's address.

Good and fruitful work is being done to address the challenges of analyzing Scripture. The more fundamental approach of listening requires attention too. A basic issue here is the role of silence. The silence required for listening to God's address in Scripture is not a matter of momentarily turning our attention to God, but of bringing our whole selves before God, quieting our inner chatter. The deep-rooted and time-tested way of reading the Bible known as *lectio divina* requires and develops the capacity for just such a disciplined, slow, quiet attentiveness.

Through our ecclesial reception of Scripture—with its corporate and private moments, and its postures of analysis and listening, located between the two advents of Christ—God forms us into the image in which we are created. With Christ as our promise-fulfilling Savior, the whole Scripture story, his story, becomes our story. He now lives his life in us through the Spirit, by whom we are sealed into union with him. His invitation to us is for us to be nourished as dearly loved and so be transformed with ever-increasing glory.

4. Theological Interpretation and Historical Criticism

It is in relation to academic analysis of the Bible, and to historical criticism in particular, that the tension between theological interpretation and modern exegesis is felt most strongly. This tension cannot be avoided. Theological interpretation of Scripture involves acceptance of the theological claim of Scripture itself that the world is created by God. It also involves acceptance of the more specific christological articulation of that claim found in the Epistle to the Colossians: "In him [Christ] all things in heaven and on earth were created; . . . all things have been created through him and for him. He himself is before all things, and in him all things hold together" (1:16–17). This claim, in its various forms throughout Scripture, has far-reaching implications—not least for our understanding of history. As the creation of God, the world and its history are invested with a telos: the world is created for a purpose. History, we might say, is *God's* project. In the terrain of space and time, given as a dwelling place for God's creatures, God seeks to bring about his purpose of drawing all things into reconciliation with himself (2 Cor. 5:19).

If this is true, then every nontheological account of history is bound to be seriously inadequate at best, or simply false. By failing to recognize the essential character of history, nontheological accounts improperly limit the range of categories needed to account for what takes place in history. Most seriously, nontheological accounts omit the category of divine agency. Due to this omission, the eyes of those who operate with nontheological accounts of history are kept from seeing how God is at work in the world. As with the disciples on the road to Emmaus (Luke 24:25–27), this failure can be corrected only by the tutoring of Christ himself. John's Gospel offers a pneumatological elucidation of Luke's claim by explaining that this tutoring is mediated by the work of the Spirit (John 16:12–15).

The involvement of God in history entails that history is an appropriate object of theological inquiry. As distinct from theological approaches that seek an understanding of God through the universal alone rather than through the particularities of history, any theology informed by the Jewish and Christian Scriptures looks to the realm of historical events in order to learn who God is and what God does. It is through history that God identifies himself—archetypally in Hebrew Scripture as the one who "brought you out of the land of Egypt" (Exod. 16:6); then, in the fullness of time, as the one who "sent his Son . . . to redeem those who were under the law, so that we might receive adoption as children" (Gal. 4:4–5); and as the one who, following Christ's crucifixion under Pontius Pilate, raised Jesus from the dead. Consistent with God's self-identification through exodus and redemption, death and resurrection, God acts in many and various ways throughout history as the one who delivers his people from bondage, who dwells amid his people, and who gives new life. History then, to repeat the point, is a proper object of theological inquiry.

A key question arises: How are we in history to apprehend the God who is at work in history? Clearly, it will not be possible to recognize God at work in history if one's method for studying history already excludes the category of divine agency. Yet this is how historical-critical inquiry with respect to Scripture has commonly proceeded, even in the face of the plain intent of Scripture's authors to testify to God's involvement in the world. Theological interpretation, by contrast, seeks to develop and work within an account of history that is itself determined by the reality of God's involvement in history, and seeks to utilize methods of historical inquiry that are alert to the action of God in history. There is no escaping the circularity of this commitment of faith, just as there is no escaping the circularity of historical methods that begin by excluding the category of divine agency and then find themselves unable to recognize the work of God in history.

Because the decisive clue to what history is and how it is to be understood is found in the person of Jesus Christ, in his life, death, and resurrection, both the account of history under which theological interpretation operates and the methods utilized in its investigation of history will be christocentric. Specifically, this means that judgments made about the content and significance of the historical events testified to in Scripture will be made in the light of Christ. The resurrection, of the utmost importance here, is an eschatological event that, in the midst of time, reveals the telos toward which history is directed and also the true nature of history itself. Precisely as such, the resurrection cannot be accommodated within an account of history that begins elsewhere. On account of the resurrection of Jesus from the dead, the fabric of history is altered once and for all. History is now to be understood as the terrain in which God is bringing about his kingdom; it is the place where God's new creation is breaking in! The reality of the resurrection therefore gives rise to a new historiography, a new means of discerning what is actually going on in history.

Although the Bible is comprised of a rich range of literary genres, not all of which are to be interpreted in the same fashion as historical narrative, there is much in the Bible that constitutes a theological account of history and directs us toward the concrete reality of God's work in the world. "Historical criticism" is therefore a necessity, but it will be a historical criticism that is both informed by and indeed *transformed* by Scripture's story. It will test all historical claims, both biblical and extrabiblical, by considering the degree to which the claim in question coheres with the true telos of history made known in Jesus Christ.

5. The Role of Hermeneutics and Philosophy in Theological Interpretation

Theological interpretation presupposes its own hermeneutic, an account of the reading situation that is itself informed by Scripture. Such a hermeneutic rests on an approach to philosophy that not only is self-consciously shaped by the Christian story but also understands the Christian story to be the story in which every other story finds its place. Furthermore, Christian belief gives to this philosophy a series of working assumptions that inform our approach to traditional areas of philosophical inquiry, such as epistemology and ontology.

In turn, philosophy helps us to think through many of the assumptions arising from theological interpretation: the status of the biblical texts, anthropology, language, and history. In other words, theological interpretation assumes a complex philosophical framework and *needs a philosophy practiced in the context of Christian belief.* Fortunately, we are well served by the renaissance of Christian philosophy in our day.

Notwithstanding the sometimes uneasy relationship between philosophy and theology, the resources of philosophy—and by extension of all scholarship—remain essential for maintaining a properly life-affirming and integrated intellectual habitat for theological interpretation. For the task of theological interpretation, philosophy is practiced with an awareness of both its limits and its vocation within God's creational ordinances. The myriad ways in which philosophy has benefited theology include the early Romantic critique of rationalism, postmodernity's healthy suspicion of "idols," accounts of language that helped to resolve long-standing philosophical problems such as skepticism, the exposure of the myth of the lone Cartesian ego, and resistance to the worst excesses of logical positivism. The hermeneutics of Hans-Georg Gadamer has retrieved the best in humanism by demonstrating the importance of tradition, community, and prejudice (prejudgments) for human meaning and understanding. Sensitivity to linguistic genres has also extended our understanding of meaning and truth. Each of these "philosophical" insights can in turn be expressed in terms of Christian wisdom. Indeed, the extent to which these philosophical developments owe their inspiration to convictions learned in the language of faith is a moot point. It therefore becomes somewhat artificial to attempt to draw clear lines of division between theology on the one side and philosophy on the other.

As well as being faithful to Christian belief, the task of theological interpretation must also be evangelistic: it must make its case to the wider world. At its best, philosophical discourse helps us keep our arguments *reasonable* and *persuasive.* For this reason, theological interpretation must be interdisciplinary, learning to speak with multiple conversational partners. The more conversant we become in philosophy, the more adept we will become at identifying relevant fields of knowledge. Philosophy therefore promotes scholarship in a general sense, both in scope and in rigor. At particular junctures in our understanding, philosophy will either point us to a specific field of scholarship or, where no such science currently exists, continue to yield speculative but plausible trajectories of thought and reflection. Those who practice the task of theological interpretation need to know when and where to find help.

Scripture's witness to the loving trinitarian God has far-reaching implications for hermeneutics. As hermeneutics is taken together with biblical anthropology, it is clear that people are made for relationship, with one another and with God. Revelation foregrounds the importance of language and, in turn, the relationships that language makes possible. If "the pearl of great price" of theological interpretation is communion with Christ, then theological interpretation requires a *relational account* of hermeneutics. The impulse for such hermeneutic models proceeds from clues provided by Scripture itself. Prominent passages include the creation narratives, Deuteronomy's insistence that the people of God learn to live on every word that comes from God's mouth (iterated by Jesus in the temptation narrative), the wisdom hermeneutic of Proverbs 1:7, Jesus's parable of the sower, Luke's record of the Emmaus road encounter and his subsequent Pentecostal hermeneutic, and the cruciform hermeneutic in the early chapters of 1 Corinthians. The best research in linguistics and psychology can provide more detailed descriptions of the speech situation of the text as well as the hermeneutical situation.

From time to time the church finds itself in crisis over ethical or doctrinal disagreement. Not all approaches to hermeneutics have managed to integrate a mechanism by which to judge between different positions or interpretations. A relational hermeneutic fit for theological interpretation will transpose the hermeneutic ideals of explanation and understanding into the double hermeneutic of truth and love, in which we are invited to see hermeneutics as part of a Christian praxis, a way of doing discipleship that is at once both compassionate and critical, that is capable of judgment and discernment. By extension such a hermeneutic will also be deeply pastoral.

6. The Canon and Theological Interpretation

The concept and fact of canon is the ground and basis of all theological interpretation. It is because this collection of documents is like no other—it is the Word of the living God—that the canon provides the raison d'être for theological interpretation. It is true that this word is a human word, originating in history and particular ancient cultures, yet as a whole the canon is simultaneously God's Word, which cannot be reduced to or imprisoned by its various historical contexts. Canon grounds theological interpretation. Although this Word originally addressed particular people at particular times in particular cultures, God's ultimate intention is, through the canon, to address all peoples and all cultures throughout all generations. This is one of the reasons the church has called these documents Holy Scripture; they preserve the primary knowledge about God and his purposes for humanity, without which humanity would remain in the dark. Scripture is thus divine revelation. This does not mean that the word of God is exclusively confined to the canon, for that would be impossible, but it does mean that the canon has become a criterion by which all other words are judged.

Thus the canon is not an accident of history. It is not the result of an external force, such as a community of faith, that arbitrarily or willfully made decisions on books to be included and excluded. Rather, in these documents the community of faith has recognized the voice of God and hence gives them its stamp of approval. This stamp of approval ratifies an existing internal force working within the documents and attesting to their divine source.

Since the canon is the ground for theological interpretation, it also provides the context for interpretation. In the canon we do not have the partial counsel of God but the "whole counsel of God" (Acts 20:27 RSV) for salvation and sanctification. Thus we must work not only to understand any particular text of Scripture but also to interpret that particular text in the light of the whole Text. Every word of Scripture occurs in a specific literary context that is part of a larger context, which is part of the ultimate canonical context. The larger canonical context is able to show how the various parts of the canon connect, interrelate, reveal the major accents and emphases, and dialogue with one another. Thus the canon is not flat and one-dimensional but has depth, contour, and texture; it must be understood in its rich and multifaceted totality, what is called *tota Scriptura*.

The one canon consists of two Testaments, which have as their goal and center the Word made flesh, Jesus the Messiah. Thus Jesus Christ is the goal of the canon. "God spoke . . . in many and various ways by the prophets, but in these last days he has spoken to us by a Son" (Heb. 1:1–2). The Old Testament looks forward to him, and the New Testament is a response to his life, death, and resurrection. Jesus Christ is the life-giving Word of God sent for the salvation of humanity: he is the light of the world. The first word spoken in the canon is "Let there be light" (Gen. 1:3); at the end of the canon, Christ is the reason why the sun and moon have become obsolete in the new heavens and new earth, "for the glory of God is its light, and its lamp is the Lamb" (Rev. 21:23). The Old Testament and the New Testament have their own discrete integrity yet must be read together. Without the Old Testament, the New Testament has no meaning. Without the New Testament, the Old Testament has lost its goal.

But there is another sense in which human beings themselves are the goal of the canon. Within the boundaries of canon is a word that is comprehensive and produces life. This word is multifaceted, encompassing a multitude of genres and life situations. There is a text for every situation imaginable, from the utter darkness of Psalm 88 to the light and glory of the New Jerusalem in Isaiah 60. This word is intended not just for information but also to be internalized in the lives of members of faith communities so that they may experience its life-giving blessing. This word is the Word above all words for human beings; it is by this word in particular that human beings receive life (Deut. 8:3). Hence at significant junctures the canon of the Old and New Testaments gives the repeated injunction to internalize the creative word of God (Gen. 1:3) through reading and meditation and thus to experience the life-giving blessing of God (Josh. 1:8–9; Ps. 1:2–3; Rev. 1:3). Part of the goal of canon, then, is to have its words held and pondered in our hearts like they were in the heart of Mary, Jesus's mother, and thereby let them become the pacemakers of our consciousness. This is a word that gives light for the way, medicine for the soul, freedom for the heart, relief for the weary, correction for the wayward, comfort in suffering, and is more precious than gold and sweeter than honey. Thus the canon gives wisdom "for salvation" and "is useful for teaching, for reproof, for correction, and for training in righteousness, so that everyone who belongs to God may be proficient, equipped for every good work" (2 Tim. 3:15–17) through becoming conformed to the divine image.

Every human effort must be used to help us understand the Word of God as it was addressed to its original audience. Because that Word was first addressed to a particular human community in a particular historical period, every tool of historical exegesis must be used, albeit recontextualized within a theology of history. Yet the basic prerequisite for understanding the canon is the attitude of the young boy Samuel in the Old Testament, who says, "Speak, LORD, for your servant is listening" (1 Sam. 3:9), and the attitude of Mary in the New Testament, as she sits at the feet of Jesus and treasures his every word (Luke 10:39).

7. Biblical Theology and Theological Interpretation

Attention to the Bible as canon leads to *tota Scriptura*. But how do we grasp Scripture—and how are we to be grasped by it—in its totality? Biblical theology provides an important answer. Theological interpretation stands on the confession that God speaks in and through Scripture and that he speaks with a unified voice. Although Johann Gabler's inaugural address at the University of Altdorf (1787) is often regarded as the origin of the theological discipline of biblical theology, the practice of biblical theology has its roots at least as far back as the early church fathers. Some of the earliest debates in the first centuries of Christianity centered squarely on how the totality of Scripture is bound up in the person and work of Jesus—a question of biblical theology.

Biblical theology thus engages a key question: How can we discern and articulate the unity of the Bible on the basis of terms and categories derived from the Bible itself? An unfortunate by-product of the past two centuries of modern critical scholarship is that many scholars view the Bible as irrecoverably diverse and fragmented, thus problematizing the very possibility of biblical theology. The recent influence of postmodernism on biblical interpretation has only compounded this challenge, particularly with its suspicion of metanarratives. The reduction of the Bible into fragmentary pieces is not, however, evident only in the academy. Many Christians approach Scripture as a collection of moral instructions, stories, spiritual nuggets, and so forth without a coherent overarching framework. The irony is that biblical theology yields a view of the world (a metanarrative) that is at odds with some of the fundamental assumptions of modern biblical criticism, postmodernism, *and* some pietistic readings of the Bible among Christians.

Biblical theology has always been a task and tool of the church. The New Testament authors, in their intimate knowledge of the Old Testament and their understanding of Jesus as the fulfillment of the Old Testament story, provide a vital foundation for doing biblical theology today. They also demonstrate that one of the primary tasks of biblical theology is to recover the storied shape of Scripture. Out of this narrative approach, many other approaches to biblical theology can and should emerge. In the grand narrative of Scripture, the sovereign God directs history from the beginning, through creation, to the end, the new creation; it all is centered on the good news of the person and work of "Jesus Christ, the Son of God" (Mark 1:1). We are taken up in this story as Jesus the Victor commissions his followers to continue his liberating kingdom mission until he returns. On the one hand, therefore, biblical theology aims to refine and articulate the grand story of Scripture by means of a deep engagement with particular texts, asking, How does *this text* fit into and shape the overarching story of the Bible? On the other hand, the biblical story claims to illuminate all of reality and thus should shape, among other things, the very task of biblical interpretation. Bearing witness to the kingdom of God in biblical studies will mean that our assumptions, methods, and goals of interpretation may—inevitably will—be at odds with those of the modern secular guild of biblical studies. In the recovery of biblical theology, therefore, the stakes are high!

What is the relationship between biblical theology and theological interpretation? If theological interpretation involves listening, biblical theology allows us to hear Scripture as a single (albeit complex) symphony that is made up of many voices, parts, and movements. Biblical theology respects the integrity of each passage in the Bible but also insists that the passage is located within the context of the whole story of Scripture, showing how it contributes uniquely to the whole. Moreover, biblical theology validates the whole project of theological interpretation, calling for a way of reading that coheres with the Bible's view of the world and the text. Yielding as it does a way of seeing and understanding the world, biblical theology summons us to work out an authentically biblical understanding of history, philosophy, literature and language, anthropology, sociology, cosmology, and so forth. This in turn will deeply influence and enhance the riches of theological interpretation on a variety of levels.

Even though biblical theology has received some renewed interest in recent times, much work remains to be done. Surprisingly few attempts at a biblical theology of the whole of Scripture exist. Biblical theology of the Old and New Testaments is a high priority on the agenda for theological interpretation in the present day.

8. Mission and Theological Interpretation

Mission is a central thread in the biblical story and must be taken into account when any part of Scripture is interpreted. By mission we mean the participation of God's people in his mission as narrated in Scripture to restore the whole of the creation, the entire life of humankind, and peoples of all nations from sin and its consequences. A proper theological interpretation of Scripture will therefore attend closely to a missional hermeneutic.

On the one hand, mission is an essential hermeneutical key to reading the whole of Scripture. Mission is not just one of the many subjects that the Bible talks about. Rather, it is a way of reading the whole of Scripture with mission as a central concern. On the other hand, it is not the only lens employed to read the entire canon of Scripture since mission does not constitute the comprehensive subject matter of the biblical narrative. There are three closely related aspects of a missional hermeneutic: the Bible is a *record*, *product*, and *tool* of God's mission to renew his world as he works both in and through his people.

The story of the Bible is first of all a *record* of God's mission in and through his people. The Bible tells a story that begins with God's creation of the world and ends with his restoration of the whole world from sin and its effects, culminating in the kingdom of God. God employs particular means to reach that universal end: the story flows through Israel, Jesus, and the church.

God's way of carrying out his redemptive plan is to choose a people—Israel—to whom he promises a blessing that comes as he rescues them from sin's devastating curse and restores them to the fullness of creational life. However, they are chosen not only to be a recipient of God's redemptive work but also to be a channel of that blessing to others. Participation in God's salvation necessarily entails participation in his mission to the world. God's renewing work is always *in* a people *for the sake of* the whole world. Specifically, they are called to be a display people who exhibit an attractive and holy life that is visible before the nations, as they manifest God's original creational intention for human life, as they are a sign of the coming kingdom of God at the end of history, and as they encounter other idolatrous ways of life that diminish and distort God's creational purpose for human life.

Israel's failure to be a faithful light to the nations brought them under God's judgment. But through the prophets, God promised to gather and renew them by his Spirit so that all nations, and ultimately the whole creation, could be incorporated into God's saving work through them. That promised gathering and renewal are accomplished in the life, death, and resurrection of Jesus, and in his ascension and outpouring of the Spirit. Renewed Israel is sent to all nations in the power of the Spirit to now fulfill God's original intention to gather all the nations into his renewing work through a faithful witness in life, word, and deed. Thus mission is at the heart of the biblical narrative as a record of God's mission in and through his people for the sake of all nations and the whole creation. Reading the Bible missionally, then, means reading it along the grain of its intended story line.

The canon of Scripture is also a *product* of God's mission. The various biblical writings have their origin in some issue, need, controversy, or threat that needed to be addressed in the context of their missional calling. The books of Genesis and Exodus arise out of Israel's need to understand their origins and their covenant vocation in the world. The book of Kings emerges from an acute crisis of faith in God's promises while in exile. The books of Ezra-Nehemiah and Chronicles proceed from a perplexing situation in which Israel struggles with how their postexilic experience matches God's promise of restoration. The various messages of prophetic warning and promise issue from the rebellion of Israel, in which they have lost sight of their covenant calling. Genesis 1 originates in a missionary encounter between ancient Near Eastern myths and Yahweh as Creator. Questions about how to live faithfully in Corinth inspire Paul's letter to that church, and various other threats or crises lead Paul to take up his pen to address missional congregations. In all these cases the point is that the canon of Scripture finds its origin in mission: a crisis or conflict or struggle of God's people in mission calls forth God's word to his people. The Scriptures are a product of God's mission in and through his people.

The Bible is also a *tool* of God's mission. The books of the Old Testament were written to equip Israel for their missional calling in the world. The word "equip" describes the various roles that different genres of Scripture played to enable Israel to be a faithful missional people. It is precisely in order that Israel might be a light to the nations that the law was given to order their national, liturgical, and moral life; that the Wisdom literature was given to help shape the daily conduct of Israel in conformity to God's creational order; that the prophets threatened and warned Israel in their disobedience and promised blessing in obedience; that the psalms nourished Israel's covenantal calling in corporate and personal worship; and that the historical books continued to tell the story of Israel at different points in the overarching story summoning them once again to their missional calling. Christ came and has fulfilled the purpose of the Old Testament canon—forming a faithful people for his mission in the world. Apostolic proclamation and doctrine continue to make Christ present in his saving power to shape and empower a missional people. The New Testament books have emerged precisely as a literary expression of the apostolic preaching and teaching, which continued to make Christ present to form and nourish particular missional communities in different parts of the Roman Empire. Thus the Bible is not only a record and product of God's mission in and through his people but also a tool to effectively bring it about.

A missional hermeneutic not only asks how a particular book of the Bible equipped the original readers for their mission in the world; it also asks how the Scriptures continue to do so today. Contemporary hermeneutics has rightly taught us that our particular interpretive location may open up or close off true understanding of a text. Since missional questions, issues, and problems are what the ancient authors address, then to hear the text today, contemporary readers themselves must be committed to the same mission that the biblical authors pursue. It is only within the hallowed and exhilarating context of the *missio Dei* that theological interpretation finds its place. Only then will we ask the proper questions of the text and experience it as the Spirit's tool to inspire and inform the ongoing mission of the church.

9. The Telos (Goal) of Theological Interpretation

In the context of the *missio Dei*, theological interpretation reads Scripture to hear God's address, so that the church might be transformed into the image of Christ for the sake of the world. A number of points emerge from this simple and yet profound aim. First, theological interpretation aims to hear the voice of God. Readings in the Christian tradition remain helpful and productive insofar as they lead us into Scripture and help us to hear it better. But the aim of theological interpretation is to hear not just the text but also God's voice through the text: God remains the divine "Thou" who addresses his church. Scripture's transformative potency derives from its source: God, the Author and Creator of all things. Scripture is "breathed out by God" (2 Tim. 3:16 ESV) yet written by human hands: these human authors wrote God's words "as they were carried along by the Holy Spirit" (2 Pet. 1:21 ESV). God has given his Sacred Word so that the Scriptures might draw people deeply into the life of God and enact their formative work on those who believe (2 Thess. 2:13).

Second, theological interpretation attends to God's voice in Scripture for the formation of the *whole* person (cognitive, affective, social, and behavioral). Through Scripture, God provides wisdom "for salvation through faith in Christ Jesus" (2 Tim. 3:15) as he reproves, corrects, teaches, and trains God's people in righteousness so they might be "equipped for every good work" in him (3:16–17). The book of Hebrews affirms that Scripture is "living and active" (4:12), able to render judgment, to expose the idolatries of the human heart, to open us to worship of the true God. Scripture builds up the church of God, providing it with an "inheritance among all who are sanctified" (Acts 20:32). This demands cognition, and hence true information remains crucial. *Right information and teaching about God, church, and world* are vital to theological interpretation. However, because of the vast potential of Scripture to address the complexity of what it means to be human, God's Word should not be reduced to knowledge alone. Scripture certainly and importantly teaches doctrine, but it also promises, names, appoints, declares, gives, condemns, binds, delivers, ministers, comforts, blesses, heals, cures, and awakens the human spirit. Right information about God, church, and world remains central in these biblical affirmations, but key to all of them is right doctrine that *transforms* the church. In engaging with God's Word, the Spirit of God does God's work to transform the church into what Christ has already made it: a new creation. Doctrine and praxis complement one another in theological interpretation, so that theological interpretation aims not just at *orthodoxy* but also at *orthopraxy*, correct conduct.

Third, theological interpretation has its roots within the *church*. The church is the true home of Scripture, centrally in its worship of the Triune God, where God communes with Christ's bride in the power of the Spirit: in the Word, the Eucharist, and the waters of baptism. The church is Scripture's home, a home that includes the private reading of Sacred Scripture by believers. Such private reading, aimed at hearing God's address for the transformation of life, is encouraged and fostered. The church's encounter with God speaking in Scripture is holy and majestic, whether the Lord's voice is heard in the thunderous trumpet blast of a Sinai experience (Exod. 19–23); in the still, small voice to a fearful prophet (1 Kings 19); or in the caring words of Christ on a road and preparing a meal (Luke 24 and John 21). In all, the voice of God in Scripture draws the church to worship and enacts real transformation.

Fourth, theological interpretation aims at the transformation of the church into the image of Christ *for the sake of the world*. It may seem that Scripture is only for the church; yet with full seriousness, theological interpretation takes the missional arc of the story of Scripture. Scripture finds its climax and fulfillment in the work of Christ: his life, death, resurrection, and ascension. For this reason, theological interpretation listens for God's *kerygma* (message) in the discrete portions of Scripture (law, letter, poetry, wisdom, parable, prophecy, etc.), yet nonetheless relates these discrete words within the unified testimony of God's salvific work in Christ. Theological interpretation understands Christ as the center of Scripture, the hinge of history, and the clue to creation. Scripture introduces humanity to Jesus Christ. In this way, the transformative potential of Scripture finds its fulfillment as the church sees and hears Christ and is conformed into his image (Rom. 8:29).

But as Scripture's readers are introduced to Christ, those who are his will give themselves for the world. As Christ gave himself for the world, he calls the church to go and do likewise. The church stands as the community that proclaims the good news of the kingdom of God in word and deed. Theological interpretation reads with the aim of the transformative potential of the gospel to be unleashed in *present contexts*, in the whole of life. With each new generation, God's Word must be heard afresh so that God's people might respond to him in worshipful obedience.

10. A Framework for Theological Interpretation

What would a framework for theological interpretation today look like? In the past, the Christian elucidation of doctrine lived from and worked on a theological interpretation of the biblical text. Up to the end of the Middle Ages, the links between Bible and theology were neither questioned nor loosened. In both Catholicism and Protestantism, even the classical schools of theology thought of Scripture as the main source of the theological enterprise. But in the modern era, a genuinely theological interpretation of the Bible was threatened by trends associated with either rationalism or Romanticism. Theological interpretation was imperiled inasmuch as it was viewed either as a "nonscientific" and therefore unjustifiable reading of a text, which instead was to be interpreted exclusively according to the methods of historical exegesis, or as a "dogmatic" imposition on a text, which instead was to be understood merely as a means to an existential experience of faith. In both cases, the theological study of the biblical text was rejected as inadequate for identifying the meaning of that text.

The renewed understanding of the Bible as a work originating within the community of the church implies a claim regarding its theological interpretation: the biblical books may be usefully researched but cannot be validly understood outside of the context in which they were born. That context is *faith*: the biblical documents were written by believers and for believers, to prompt, describe, penetrate, explain, and transmit faith.

A theological study of the biblical text must approach it as God's Word, to which the appropriate human response is *faith*. Faith demands that its meaning be explored in view of the questions that reason-illumined-by-faith raises; theological study orders the biblical meaning in view of priorities emerging for the life of human beings and communities under the guidance of faith. Here we speak of *Christian* faith as we speak of the *Christian* Bible, with a particular understanding of the two Testaments as "Law and Prophets" brought to fullness in Christ—through his words and deeds—reaching out to all humankind through apostolic preaching, consolidated and transmitted in written form to the church.

While a plurality in theological thought and work is a direct result of the human condition, the prerequisites for a theological interpretation must be set in a way analogous to what the canon does for materially defining the Bible. This results in a framework that not only outlines the boundaries but also identifies the focal point of a theological interpretation. The foundational articles of faith in this respect are:

- Belief in one single God, the Creator, from whom all human life takes its origin and meaning, calling human beings individually and collectively to himself, to share his life and happiness.
- One universal plan of salvation, which, although structured in phases, opens the salvation drama with Abraham, continues with Moses and the journey of Israel, carrying the faith in the one God, until it centers on Jesus.
- The acceptance of Jesus as Messiah and God's incarnate Son, in whom the Father addresses humankind as his children to be shaped according to the image of his Son in order to participate in the good pleasure that God finds in the Son through a share in his life and suffering, ending in the glory of his resurrection.

- The expectation of a "new heaven and earth," thus "rebirth" not only for the individual in a mortal life but also leading to a new beginning as of new birth and creation (*palingenesia*) for all humanity when history reaches its final goal.
- An understanding of the human being as an individual person endowed with intellect and freedom so as to be responsible for one's acts, to respond to God individually and collectively when addressed by God, and to be capable of being lifted by God's free grace to the freedom of God's children.
- Working within such a framework obliges the exegete-theologian to engage in dialogue with the philosophical quest, searching for truth about human existence, the cosmos, and the capabilities and responsibilities of human beings.

Theological interpretation neither carelessly expands exegesis into theology nor naively reduces theology to exegesis. Its task is to build bridges between these disciplines without confusing or separating them into a state of isolation. A theological interpretation renders the exegete open to treating a number of concerns that a merely critical or historical interpretation may easily neglect or refuse to consider as legitimate. These concerns may be summarized as follows:

- The issues of the so-called canonical interpretation, or interpretive trajectories that connect all biblical history and all biblical books.
- The issues of inspiration, concerning not only those of human authors but also those of the divine Author. What is the relationship between the divine will that has caused the biblical books to come about by using human beings he inspired? How did historical processes impact how the incarnate Logos emerged in history, both in the flesh and blood of Christ (incarnation) and in the writings of the prophets and the apostles (inspired canon)?
- In particular, theological exegesis must be sensitive in seeing to it that the interpretation will not ultimately compromise the purity of monotheism and a Christology equally free of Nestorian and Monophysite elements. Thus the exegete must be fully dedicated to the truth of the Bible as inspired Word, which in its canonical wholeness never refrains from exposing the incarnate as God's full humanity, but refuses to state as ultimate biblical truth anything unworthy of God.

A theological understanding of God's biblical Word must be undertaken on the basis of believing in its inspired character, which means searching the

Scriptures in the same Spirit in which they were written. The Holy Spirit, through whom the created human spirit obtains an understanding of God's Word, is present in the world through the church, provides the believer with the continued presence of the risen Christ, and leads all human beings through their individual and common journeys through history.

11. Theological Commentary

If theological interpretation works within such a framework, what does this mean for commentary writing? Theological commentary is made possible, indeed obligatory, by the confession that our Triune God reveals himself in canonical *texts*. The character and nature of Holy Scripture flows from this confession. Our hermeneutical approach, therefore, should also be shaped and determined by it. In Holy Scripture, God speaks and witnesses to his own identity as Father, Son, and Holy Spirit. This trinitarian context for reading (the *regula fidei*, Rule of Faith) provides the epistemic basis, interpretive expectations, and prayerful posture for reading and interpreting Scripture. All commentary on Holy Scripture, then, should likewise be shaped and molded by this confessional reality: biblical commentary should ultimately be *theological* commentary; otherwise it interprets the Bible contrary to its nature, origin, and purpose.

A theological commentary recognizes the creaturely and divine authorship of the biblical texts. Although leery of placing a divide between these two, a theological commentary is located within the broad stream of the Christian interpretive tradition that recognizes the dogmatic priority of the divine Author. The divine authorship of Scripture governs our approach to human authorship, and not vice versa: "Men and women moved by the Holy Spirit spoke from God" (2 Pet. 1:21). In this light, the creaturely character of Scripture is not something to shy away from in the task of theological commentary. It is located dogmatically in God's providential oversight of creaturely affairs. The verbal/grammatical sense, along with the historical particularity of texts, is to be examined with all the rigor we can muster, in an effort to understand what the church fathers referred to as the text's *akolouthia*: the way the words go. All the critical tools of biblical scholarship, albeit recontextualized in a theology of history, are welcome in attending to the text's *sensus literalis*. This welcoming entails within it the recognition that such tools can aid the reader's understanding of the text's theological character.

At the same time, the examination of the biblical materials in their historical and literary particularity cannot *exhaust* the text of its theological content. A theological commentary resists the modern historicist tendency to reduce the text's witness to the historical moment of writing and its immediate reception. Christians have always understood that God speaks through Scripture to every generation of readers, so that Holy Scripture is always saying more than what we might determine solely as the intent of the historical author.

Following the interpretive instincts inherited from the Christian tradition, the Scriptures themselves should be understood as their own best interpreter. In this light, the canonical shape of our Christian canon as Old and New Testaments plays a material role in our approach to reading. A combustive interpretive dynamic is at play when the Old and New Testaments are read in dialectic relationship with each other. Ideally, theological commentary reveals the organic relationship between the literal sense of Scripture and its figural sense. Indeed, theological commentary at its best manifests a close attention to the particularity of the biblical texts as they are in broader conversation within the canon and the Christian dogmatic tradition, which is itself shaped by continual reflection on and submission to the canon.

An examination of the history of the biblical commentary in the Christian era is revealing with regard to the different instincts, sensibilities, goals, and practices. There are many good and appropriate types of biblical commentaries, with different emphases and contributions to make. There is no one-size-fits-all way to comment on the biblical texts. But while no time period or singular approach to commentary is perfect, across the history of the church there is a robust way of reading that can be called *theological commentary*. The techniques and methods may vary, but there is a family resemblance in the best kind of trinitarian theological commentary.

A theological commentary is a key location for Christian, theological reflection. In this sense, Christian theology *is* exegesis. Such a statement is initially jarring to interpretive instincts shaped by the legacy of Spinoza's more localized reading strategies or a hermeneutic where *meaning* and *significance* are sharply divided. Nevertheless, a theological commentary seeks to dialogue with and to order our theological grammar by attending closely to the words of the prophets and apostles. This theological ordering is situated in the salvific and liturgical context of Christ's church, where the interpretive community of the church plays a substantive role.

A theological commentary thus engages the biblical text because of the anterior confession that our Triune God has spoken and is speaking in and through the canonical witness. God's own self-determination to be God for humanity places his revelation in the dogmatic location of God's reconciliation of sinners to himself. While affirming the creaturely character of the biblical documents and all that this entails, a theological commentary's goal is to hear God's Word for God's people today, to press through the verbal/ grammatical sense of the text to its theological subject matter. As a result, a theological commentary seeks to aid Christ's church in hearing God's Word for the sake of shaping Christian worship, identity, and mission.

12. Theological Interpretation for All of Life

Acts describes Jesus as "the Author of life" (Acts 3:15), and theological interpretation should embody this creation-wide perspective in its work. If Christ is the Author of life in all its many dimensions, then theological interpretation should work to relate the *kerygma* of the Bible to all of life, and not just "church life." Indeed, Brevard Childs identifies failure in this regard as one of the reasons for the downfall of the biblical theology movement, but it is a critique that can be leveled against too much contemporary biblical interpretation.[1] Scripture deals with "universal history," to use Lesslie Newbigin's poignant phrase, and views Israel, Jesus, and the church in this light.[2] Another way to express this is that creation is the very stuff of salvation.[3] Redemption involves the recovery of God's purposes for the whole of his creation and thus is comprehensive and cosmic in scope. Theological interpretation must be no less.

It is especially in the Old Testament that we witness the comprehensive range of God's *torah* (instruction), whether it is narrative, law, prophecy, or wisdom. While God pursues his redemptive purposes, he chooses a people and forms them into a nation. As an ancient Near Eastern nation in *covenant* with "the LORD," they are called to live under his reign in every aspect of their national life. So, for example, when the Old Testament addresses leadership, it is often not priestly but political or economic or familial leadership that is in view. The Old Testament law deals with all aspects of the life of Israel, and so too does wisdom. The prophets call Israel (and the nations) to account not just for failure in the cultic realm but also for social and political sins.

In the New Testament, the church is no longer a nation as was Israel, but is now scattered among the nations. The church's ethic thus alters—Old Testament torah remains normative but cannot simply be translated and legislated amid cultures that are nontheocratic—and that ethic's outworking becomes more complex while remaining comprehensive in scope: the church is called to

---

1. Brevard S. Childs, *Biblical Theology in Crisis* (Philadelphia: Westminster Press, 1970).

2. Lesslie Newbigin, *The Open Secret: An Introduction to the Theology of Mission* (Grand Rapids: Eerdmans, 1995), 81.

3. Ola Tjørhom, *Embodied Faith: Reflections on a Materialist Spirituality* (Grand Rapids: Eerdmans, 2009), 36.

live all of its life under the reign of Jesus. It is *he* and not Caesar who is *kyrios* (Lord). Amid the nations the ecclesia is called to be a sign of the kingdom. Theological interpretation, if it is true to Scripture and to Jesus, will therefore bring *all of life* within its focus. If a theme like *the kingdom of God/heaven* is as central to theological interpretation today as it was to the ministry of Jesus, then interpreters can do no less.

If we conceive of the Bible as a drama in multiple acts, then we are in the same act as the early church, but our cultural and historical context is vastly different. We need to use all the clues in all the acts of the great, unfolding drama of which we are a part as we work out what these clues mean for *life today*. Mission is lived at the *crossroads* of two stories: the biblical story and our cultural story or stories, a place of extreme tension. Theological interpretation needs to be practiced at this crossroads; in order to do so, we must be familiar with both the biblical story and our cultural story or stories; hence a cultural hermeneutic is an indispensable part of theological interpretation. Rigorous cultural analysis is vital so that, like the Old Testament prophets, we work to relate God's Word to *this* time and *this* place.

All this is not to suggest that theological interpretation will manifest expertise in the detail of all areas of life. There are some areas of life, such as family and social justice, about which Scripture goes into considerable detail, but in many areas of contemporary life, the relevance of Scripture needs to be worked out by practitioners *in those areas*. Theological interpretation, for example, cannot and should not spell out in detail what a biblical aesthetic looks like, but it should alert us to the need for one. Theological interpretation must sound the kingdom note for all of life, but that is not the same thing as being prescriptive in areas foreign to its particular, biblical expertise.

There are few major examples of such work today in biblical studies. Walter Brueggemann stands out as one who has tirelessly and creatively sought to navigate the distance between the Bible and contemporary culture. Oliver O'Donovan's work similarly and repeatedly seeks to make this journey. An older example is the work of Jacques Ellul: alongside his sociological works, he has published a series of important expositions of Scripture. John Stott helpfully spoke about and practiced "double listening": the exegete bends one ear to Scripture and one to contemporary culture in order to connect the two.

Most contemporary theological education does not prepare exegetes for this sort of creative work. To move in this direction, as we must, the comprehensive scope of Scripture will need to be recovered, the time in our culture(s) discerned, and the hard work done of moving back and forth between these two poles, so that Scripture is heard in relation to all of life. Only thus will we hear and transmit Scripture as the great feast that it is.

1

The History and Reemergence of Theological Interpretation

Angus Paddison

Introduction: The Marks of the History and Reemergence of Theological Interpretation

In expounding my contribution to the Manifesto, it is necessary to speak both of the history and the reemergence of theological interpretation. In other words, we need to see what theological interpretation has been in the life of the church, what it is now, *and* what it might be and become. This latter feature is why this book is a Manifesto for theological interpretation: with due humility, the intention is to propose a future for theological interpretation. The history and reemergence of theological interpretation are closely linked: one of the features of the reemergent theological interpretation in recent years has been its desire to be fed by the long history of how the Bible has been read in the church catholic. We therefore can say that theological interpretation of Scripture, as with the Christian life more generally, has a past, a present, and a future orientation.[1]

---

1. "Theological interpretation" as a self-conscious style of theology, perhaps undertaken in response to a wholly secular mode of biblical reading and study, is not a term that premodern

What is to be understood by the term "theological interpretation"? Theological interpretation, theological hermeneutics, and theological reading are all notoriously slippery and porous categories to define.[2] If we consider the topic that is the subject of this particular Manifesto—theological interpretation—only in vain will one look for a single definition of what counts as theological interpretation, which is probably not surprising if we recall that what counts as "theological" is hardly uncontested territory either.[3] Nevertheless, in what many call the most significant development in contemporary theology—the breaking down of what Brevard Childs famously called the "iron curtain" separating theological work and biblical reasoning—it is possible to pick out some recurrent themes, or what I will term "marks" of theological interpretation.[4] After introducing the marks briefly, in this chapter I will unpack them (understanding them as porous one to the other) by highlighting attendant risks and opportunities for the theological interpretation that is reemerging in our time. In this way we will sketch proposals for the future of theological interpretation of Scripture. But before setting out the marks of theological interpretation, it is wise to say something about the *history* of theological interpretation.

When the Manifesto says, "It is not possible to approach the history of the church and its faith without sensitivity to how both have been formed by and with its reading of Scripture," what is being warned against is any notion that theological interpretation is something that relies on professional theologians like Karl Barth to resurrect. Theological interpretation has never been entirely lost in the church. The history of the church is, to a large extent, the history of its engagement with the scriptural text. Theological interpretation is not something that theology has *discovered* in the last half of the twentieth century. Instead, theological interpretation is a

---

theologians would have understood. Many of the concerns that one might presume to be the preserve of theological interpretation—such as the question of how these texts bear divine authority—are characteristically modern, shaped sometimes in defensive response to contemporary challenges.

2. Commentators like Stanley E. Porter have been very keen to distinguish theological hermeneutics from theological interpretation; the latter he judges to be wanting. See his "Biblical Hermeneutics and *Theological* Responsibility," in *The Future of Biblical Interpretation*, ed. Stanley E. Porter and Matthew R. Malcolm (Downers Grove, IL: InterVarsity, 2013), 29–50.

3. Equally worthwhile is Mark Alan Bowald's claim that "all readings of Scripture are theological as all readings occur against a horizon of beliefs about the character of God" ("The Character of Theological Interpretation of Scripture," *International Journal of Systematic Theology* 12 [2010]: 178). This seems to maximize where theological interpretation can be expected to be found.

4. Miroslav Volf, *Captive to the Word of God: Engaging the Scriptures for Contemporary Theological Reflection* (Grand Rapids: Eerdmans, 2010), 14.

conversation with the texts as instrumental to the divine will, a dialogue that theology has started to contribute toward again, a conversation that never truly ceased in the church. Thus, as I say in the Manifesto, "theological interpretation of Scripture can be cast as *rejoining* an enduring conversation to which modern theology and biblical studies gradually ceased contributing." Some examples illustrate how theological interpretation is about rejoining a conversation and extending a history. When Barth undertook his incendiary work in rereading Romans, a key resource for the kind of reading he wanted to adopt was the hermeneutics of John Calvin. In the Brazos Theological Commentary series, a strong emphasis on the figural reading of the Old Testament text is evident: the conviction so important to the history of the church, that the Old Testament texts are to be read christocentrically, has emerged again with clarity.[5] Finally, I could point to my theological interpretation of 1 Thessalonians as a reading of the text that requires an engagement with the historical readings of Thomas Aquinas and John Calvin; I undertook a reading for today by conversing with fellow biblical exegetes such as Cyril of Alexandria and Athanasius, as well as a range of biblical texts.[6]

What unites each of these three examples is not just a desire to be fed by the history of theological interpretation, but also a sense that historical criticism is a resource that, although valuable, is not in itself sufficient for the task of interpreting Scripture theologically. Equally, there is a strong impulse that biblical scholars need to be supplemented by other conversation partners (alive and dead) if we are to understand the texts as divine communication. The theological interpretation that has reemerged in our time has been motivated by a sense that the interests of historical criticism in the genesis of texts needs to be supplemented by a reengagement with the church's history of reading the text. Walter Wink gave powerful metaphorical articulation to this disenchantment with historical criticism when he labeled it a "bankrupt" resource.[7] With a sense that the history of theological interpretation is vital to understanding what is reemerging in our time, we can now try to identify theological interpretation's marks with more precision.

5. To give two examples: Phillip Cary, *Jonah*, Brazos Theological Commentary on the Bible (Grand Rapids: Brazos, 2008); and Robert W. Jenson, *Ezekiel*, Brazos Theological Commentary on the Bible (Grand Rapids: Brazos, 2009).

6. Angus Paddison, *Theological Hermeneutics and 1 Thessalonians*, Society for New Testament Studies Monograph Series (Cambridge: Cambridge University Press, 2005).

7. Walter Wink, *The Bible in Human Transformation: Toward a New Paradigm for Biblical Study* (Philadelphia: Fortress, 1973).

Mark 1. A theological interpretation of Scripture (TIS) approaches Scripture expecting to be *addressed*. This theme of Scripture as address is articulated forcefully in Heath Thomas's contribution to the Manifesto asserting that the aim of TIS is to hear God's voice. God in Scripture speaks, and the church listens for his voice each time it gathers in worship. With no illusions regarding the complex implications of the claim, Rowan Williams reminds us that "the Bible is the territory in which Christians expect to hear God *speaking*."[8] Although Scripture is always mediated through the life of the church catholic, and although Scripture is always webbed in the contexts of its readers, Scripture is never entirely absorbed into our proximate contexts. Scripture always contains the promise of being heard as an exterior word and precisely as an instrument of the gospel; it is good *news*. Yet news to be news needs not to be just exterior to the hearer; it also needs to be communicated and heard. If Scripture is news, it must be communicable.[9]

Mark 2. All theological interpretation is derivative from the confession that God is a living God, communicatively present through the Spirit, who wills to draw readers/hearers into the life of the risen Son. It is this christocentric apprehension of Scripture that lies behind Thomas's statement in his contribution to the Manifesto: "Scripture finds its climax and fulfillment in the work of Christ." Crucial for theological interpretation is a sense that biblical texts must be communicable beyond their original context of production (hence the dis-ease with historical criticism). Yet, to listen to these texts as communicative and to expect to hear the biblical texts as contemporary to us—all this is possible "precisely because their subject matter lives."[10] Theological interpretation recognizes that reading of Scripture cannot rely on our immediate contexts or even the tradition of the church to enliven the text. The fundamental resource for theological interpretation is that Jesus lives, and because he lives and abides with the church, through the Spirit, he is communicatively present—antecedent even—to the community of the faithful. "He is not here. . . . He is going ahead of you" (Matt. 28:6–7). If we listen to these texts expecting to be addressed, this is possible only because Jesus is alive and wills continually to be known. Scripture is not just a series of texts emerging from a variety of different

---

8. Rowan Williams, *Being Christian* (London: SPCK, 2014), 23, emphasis added.

9. See John Howard Yoder, "On Not Being Ashamed of the Gospel: Particularity, Pluralism, and Validation," in *A Pacifist Way of Knowing: John Howard Yoder's Nonviolent Epistemology*, ed. Christian E. Early and Ted G. Grimsrud (Eugene, OR: Cascade, 2010), 40–57.

10. Christopher R. J. Holmes, "Revelation in the Present Tense: On Rethinking Theological Interpretation in the Light of the Prophetic Office of Jesus Christ," *Journal of Theological Interpretation* 6 (2012): 24.

contexts and eras, although it is never less than this. Scripture is also a text that is suspended in an enduring history of divine-human encounter: it is fixed in a field of divine action, in the "domain of the word," which extends out and invites human participation.[11] Theological interpretation wills to be alert to the startling implications that these texts and their readers are bound to a living God. We are wise, Walter Moberly urges, not to dull ourselves to how this theological claim leads to astonishing implications for interpretation: "[Theological interpretation,] while not taking the Bible as *less* than a historical artifact, clearly takes it as *more* than a historical artifact; and that *more* is in some way given content by the notion of the self-communication of the living God—a notion to whose breathtaking implications we are easily dulled."[12]

Mark 3. Theological interpretation has an ecclesial setting. This is a consistent theme throughout the Manifesto, not least in the section authored by Aubrey Spears and Robby Holt. Stephen Fowl helpfully reinforces, stating that "Reading Scripture theologically is first and foremost a practice of the church. It does not depend on the support of academics for its survival."[13] Theological interpretation, self-consciously reading these texts as living and communicative texts, may have been forgotten, neglected, or marginalized in the academy, but as we declared above, it has never been entirely lost in the church, whose vocation it is to read, hear, and preach the Scriptures. It is certainly important to define what theological interpretation is, but this activity of definition and clarification cannot be allowed to displace giving attention to the reality that theological interpretation is what the church *does* in its liturgy and indeed performs in its acts of charity. The church, being like all other social bodies and yet also radically unlike all other social bodies, is rooted in its context and bound to a community of readers suspended across time. Theological interpretation has a home in this communion of saints; accordingly, the reading of Scripture has a past, a present, and a future orientation. The attention to the life of the church catholic is the source of a key feature of theological interpretation: its *ressourcement*, its desire to be nourished by insights and practices of the premodern church in a bid to find a way out of some of the cul-de-sacs of modernity.[14] This reconnection with

11. John Webster, *The Domain of the Word: Scripture and Theological Reason* (London: T&T Clark, 2012).

12. R. W. L. Moberly, "What Is Theological Interpretation of Scripture?," *Journal of Theological Interpretation* 3 (2009): 162.

13. Stephen Fowl, *Theological Interpretation of Scripture* (Eugene, OR: Cascade, 2009), 23.

14. It is preferable to speak of "premodern" exegesis as opposed to "precritical" exegesis. The latter title risks judging premodern exegesis by a presumed superior feature of modern biblical studies. Nor is it entirely accurate. Within their own terms, premodern readers certainly

the church and the wisdom it bears is why we can speak of both the history and the reemergence of theological interpretation: current theological interpreters are not entering into uncharted territory.

Mark 4. Theological interpretation is a moral practice: it is concerned with the character and formation of the reader and with that reader's moral responsibilities toward the neighbor. Scripture wills the transformation of those who read it. In an essay that reminds us of the link between discipleship and reading, Markus Bockmuehl writes, "Without facing the inalienably transformative and self-involving demands that these ecclesial writings place on a serious reader, it is impossible to make significant sense of them."[15] To know the one spoken of in Scripture (John 5:39) is to know the demands this knowing places on the reader. "The commandment we have from him is this: those who love God must love their brothers and sisters also" (1 John 4:21). Augustine says something connected to this mark when he emphasizes that interpretation of Scripture should be distinguished by the love of one's neighbor, to which love of God leads.[16] A theological interpretation of Scripture displays a love for one's neighbor, or, to put it another way, it has as its end that the reader and hearer might grow in their love of the living God and their neighbor.

To varying degrees the reemergent theological interpretation of our time evidences these marks, as we have seen in the indicative quotes above and will unpack further below. These marks share much with the postliberal mood that is undoubtedly conducive to theological interpretation, not least in its predilection for *ressourcement* and its emphasis on the formative role of the church's corporate practices in shaping the character of readers.[17] The burden of what follows is to unpack the marks I have identified and set out some of the opportunities and risks they prompt us to consider. Only if we are alert to both the opportunities and the risks will we be able to chart a route, a Manifesto, if you will, for reemergent theological interpretation. In this way we might begin to imagine new, bold directions in which theological interpretation might be led.

---

bore the capacity to be critically aware readers. Even the term "premodern" is less than perfect. As Darren Sarisky observes, it privileges the modern and can suggest a "progressive" reading of history, as if we were moving from dark to light. See his *Scriptural Interpretation: A Theological Exploration*, Challenges in Contemporary Theology (Chichester, UK: John Wiley, 2013), 10.

15. Markus Bockmuehl, *Seeing the Word: Refocusing New Testament Study* (Grand Rapids: Baker Academic, 2006), 46.

16. Augustine, *On Christian Doctrine* 1.36, trans. J. F. Shaw (Mineola, NY: Dover Publications, 2009).

17. Paul J. DeHart, *The Trial of the Witnesses: The Rise and Decline of Postliberal Theology*, Challenges in Contemporary Theology (Oxford: Blackwell, 2006), 44.

Theological Interpretation and Scripture as Address

Recent advocates of the theological interpretation that has reemerged in our time have emphasized Scripture as divine address. John Webster is indicative in this regard: "God's Word addresses sinful creatures and enters into conflict with them."[18] Scott Swain's essay on theological interpretation is another example.[19] This emphasis is not restricted to Protestant writers. Hans Urs von Balthasar places a strong emphasis on the receptive hearing of "the form and vehicle of God's addressing us here and now."[20] In this register, Scripture is portrayed as slaying herald, piercing annunciation, divine summons, and the *viva vox Dei*. Scripture speaks, and the church listens. Theological interpretation begins with the prayer that God will speak through the human words of its authors. It is possible to detect the influence of Karl Barth, with the significance the Bible played in his revolutionary theology, on reemergent theological interpretation here. The Bible, Barth warns, is not concerned with answering the questions we presume to be significant, but in questioning, destabilizing, and refounding us: "It is not the right human thoughts about God which form the content of the Bible, but the right divine thoughts about men [*sic*]. The Bible tells us not how we should talk with God but what he says to us. . . . The word of God is within the Bible."[21]

This notion of Scripture as address is deeply rooted in how the biblical text speaks of its function in the divine economy and is in rhythm with the prophetic-apostolic shape of Scripture. Here one could appeal to the prophetic commissions (Ezek. 2–3) or Isaiah's declaration that the word that issues from the Lord's mouth "shall not return to me empty, but it shall accomplish that which I purpose" (Isa. 55:11). Paul, modeling himself on the prophet Jeremiah, establishes his authority as one entrusted with a message from God: "The gospel that was proclaimed by me is not of human origin; for I did not receive it from a human source, nor was I taught it, but I received it through a revelation of Jesus Christ" (Gal. 1:11–12). The Revelation of John, a text self-consciously keen to impress on its hearers its authoritative status, declares: "Blessed is the one who reads aloud the words of the prophecy, and blessed are those who hear and who keep what is written in it" (Rev. 1:3). In

---

18. Webster, *Domain of the Word*, 20.

19. See Scott Swain, *Trinity, Revelation, and Reading: A Theological Introduction to the Bible and Its Interpretation* (London: T&T Clark International, 2011).

20. Hans Urs von Balthasar, "The Word, Scripture, and Tradition," in *Explorations in Theology*, vol. 1, *The Word Made Flesh*, trans. A. V. Littledale with Alexander Dru (San Francisco: Ignatius, 1989), 24.

21. Karl Barth, *The Word of God and the Word of Man*, trans. Douglas Horton (New York: Harper & Row, 1956), 43.

accordance with this strain, the notion of hearing a word that is delivered *to the church* runs deep in the history of theological interpretation.[22] Delivering his inaugural lecture at the University of Paris in 1256, Thomas Aquinas emphasized Scripture as divine communication,[23] to which teachers best respond with what John Boyle characterizes as "faithful docility."[24] An emphasis on Scripture as address is an important way to signal that when the church listens to Scripture, it is seeking to respond to a speaker who is radically unlike us, yet who graciously wills that we as creatures may be hearers of his Word. The earlier reference to Barth is a reminder that the emphasis on Scripture as address has a proven track record in helping the church focus on Scripture's disruptive quality, in summoning attention to a word that redirects its hearers, and in resisting the Bible's collapse into contemporary ecclesial life. In the midst of a church at risk of being complicit in the terrors of 1930s Germany, those who appealed to the Word of God found that they were most able to resist the church's co-option. The emphasis on Scripture as address contains a deeply liberating impulse, as Rowan Williams recognizes: "We read *this* text as sacred because it represents the possibility and actuality of relation with more than a competing speaker—a relation, which in so far as it takes us beyond the world of negotiating speakers and rival exercises of power and determination, has the character of grace or liberation."[25] The sheer difference of the speaker and the promise that what is heard might be heard afresh is the reason why, week in and week out, the church listens once more to Scripture, expecting to be addressed. Within itself, Scripture bears a resistance to being absorbed into the life of the church.

Yet for all the helpful emphases on which Scripture as address focuses our attention, there are three emphases in Christian tradition that Scripture as address leaves distinctly unfocused. These can be captured as the wrestling with Scripture, the role played by interpretation, and the contribution of the reader's particular context in a richly layered account of theological interpretation.

First, to talk of Scripture as address is clearly to emphasize a theological mood that can be characterized as imperative or, perhaps better, as responsive to the imperative nature of Scripture. The metaphorical deployment of the

22. Stephen H. Webb, *The Divine Voice: Christian Proclamation and the Theology of the Sound* (Grand Rapids: Brazos, 2004).

23. It is reproduced in *Albert and Thomas: Selected Writings*, trans. Simon Tugwell (New York: Paulist Press, 1988), 353–62.

24. John F. Boyle, "St Thomas Aquinas and Sacred Scripture," *Pro Ecclesia* 4 (1995): 94. See also the account in Donald Wood, "Scripture," in *Sanctified by Grace: A Theology of the Christian Life*, ed. Kent Eilers and Kyle C. Strobel (London: T&T Clark, 2014), 141–55.

25. Rowan Williams, "Historical Criticism and Sacred Text," in *Reading Texts, Seeking Wisdom*, ed. David F. Ford and Graham Stanton (London: SCM, 2003), 224, emphasis original.

grammatical term "moods" is promoted by David F. Ford, who argues that just as the Bible displays a rich variety of moods through its literary genres (a feature pointed out throughout the Manifesto), so a wise theology maintains an "ecology of moods," refusing to let one mood overshadow another.[26] If the theological interpretation of our time is to give space to a variety of theological moods, it needs to reject the kind of zero-sum, either-or logic that can seep into talk of Scripture as address, as typified in Michael S. Horton's injunction that the Bible can be either a "servant of our autonomous self-creation" *or* a "sovereign Word."[27] As with all binary, either-or representations, one can dispute details implied on both sides of the contrast. There will be times when those who indwell Scripture, who feel its pressure on them, will engage with Scripture in the subjunctive or the interrogative mood, adopting a mode of reading that is exploratory, probing, and willing to challenge God. These are the occasions when the reader responds to Scripture not with delight but with distaste, unease, or sheer bemusement. After the church hears, it must speak, and the forms of this speaking will be carried out in a variety of moods. Such reactions are part of the task of incorporating Scripture's story within our story, of hearing it as a living Word that needs to be incorporated into our contexts. Scripture is "the record of an encounter and contest,"[28] and readers may well expect the same feelings to be generated among themselves from time to time. Theological interpretation needs to see a rich variety of reactions not as antithetical to its work, but as part of its task. Contemporary wrestling with Scripture echoes the injunctions of the psalmist, or even the cry of Jesus on the cross. Indeed, the proper home for readings that wrestle with the text is a community of faith, precisely because apart from a wider confidence both in the capacity of Scripture to illumine our lives and its context in the *regula fidei*, such readings are likely to lead to disenchantment or cynicism.[29] In the articulation of Luke Timothy Johnson, where Scripture and Christian practices mutually inform one another, "neither the complexities of the text nor the ambiguities of experience need be feared."[30] Nor need theological interpretation worry that wrestling with Scripture in an interrogative

26. David F. Ford, *The Future of Christian Theology*, Blackwell Manifestos (Chichester, UK: Wiley-Blackwell, 2011), 71.

27. Michael S. Horton, *People and Place: A Covenant Ecclesiology* (Louisville: Westminster John Knox, 2008), 76.

28. Rowan Williams, *Open to Judgement: Sermons and Addresses* (London: Darton, Longman & Todd, 1994), 158.

29. David Fergusson, "The Bible in Modernity," in *The Bible: Culture, Community and Society*, ed. Angus Paddison and Neil Messer (London: Bloomsbury, 2013), 9–29.

30. Luke Timothy Johnson, "Imagining the World Scripture Imagines," *Modern Theology* 14 (1998): 173.

mood—a form of reading that queries the notion that Scripture is purely an address passively received—is somehow "faddish." There is nothing new in the struggle with Scripture. John L. Thompson's historical work has shown the historical precedent for wrestling with strange texts that we would now call "texts of terror."[31]

Second, vigilance needs to be maintained for when talk of Scripture as clear, startling address can serve to marginalize or displace the proper business that is talk of interpretation and hermeneutics. The sense of Scripture is always, Francis Watson urges, "a matter not only of passive reception but also of active construction."[32] Theological interpretation must be committed to the responsibilities of interpretation and all that this entails, precisely because the reading of Scripture as the Word of God must be located within the church's concrete history, rather than as a Word that touches the church's life like a tangent touching a circle, in Barth's famous image.[33] Too many accounts of Scripture as address can assume that interpretation is a competitive, zero-sum game: God speaks, and the reader/hearer passively receives—*or* we have textual indeterminacy and an interpretative free-for-all. The same kind of either-or logic that we saw at work in Horton can be evidenced in parts of Webster, who in a revealing quote speaks of faithful interpretation being about "receiving rather than bestowing meaning."[34] In what can sound like oracular models of how Scripture works, there is the risk of encouraging impatience in the face of learning *how* we read and hear Scripture. Here is where the work of Rowan Williams and his concerns about Barthian conceptions of revelation can be a helpful resource. Our knowledge and awareness of God has a history: it is timeful, not abstracted from history, but part of the church's tradition.[35] Veil-lifting models of revelation bypass any consideration of *how* revelation is received, in *what* particular context, and by *whom*. In some representations of theological interpretation, there is a sense that "hermeneutical inflation" will best be avoided if the emphasis is placed not just on the priority of God as revealing God's self but also on the sufficiency and comprehensiveness of

31. John L. Thompson, "Preaching Texts of Terror in the Book of Judges: How Does the History of Interpretation Help?," *Calvin Theological Journal* 37 (2002): 49–61.

32. Francis Watson, "Hermeneutics and the Doctrine of Scripture: Why They Need Each Other," *International Journal of Systematic Theology* 12 (2010): 118.

33. Karl Barth, *The Epistle to the Romans*, trans. Edwyn C. Hoskins (New York: Oxford University Press, 1933), 30.

34. Webster, *Domain of the Word*, 24.

35. Helpful here are two essays in Rowan Williams, *On Christian Theology*, Challenges in Contemporary Theology (Oxford: Blackwell, 2000): "Trinity and Revelation" and "Word and Spirit." See also the discussion of Williams as theological interpreter in Sarisky, *Scriptural Interpretation*, 159–83.

God's action in revealing God.[36] Dietrich Bonhoeffer is a useful ally in pushing us to recall that God's radical involvement in the world (more on this below) calls for interpretation and engagement with this world rather than what he worries, under Barth's influence, could morph into a "like it or lump it" approach. The opportunity opened up by talk of Scripture as address is its focus on the piercing clarity that Scripture acquires as an instrument of a free God, as indeed it has at countless points within the church's life. The risk courted is that by not allowing space for the complexity and intensity of interpretation, in all its contextual settings, we harbor what Bonhoeffer famously calls, in relation to Barth's theology, a "positivism of revelation."[37] The theological interpretation that is reemerging now needs to ensure that it is not falling into the same kinds of traps against which Bonhoeffer warned in the last century.

Third, readers need to resist any choice between their receptivity and their active engagement with the meaning potential of the scriptural texts. As suggested in the Manifesto, reading the Bible begins with the prayer that God will speak through the texts. But this is not all that needs to be said about the intensities of interpretation that is rooted and fixed in the world precisely because it is theological. As Craig Bartholomew and Matthew Emerson point out in their contribution to the Manifesto, theological interpretation is properly orientated to all of life. Interpreting the biblical texts in the worlds in which readers find themselves located (what I am defining as contextual interpretation) is unavoidable and can, with some justification, be termed a biblical mode of reading. As canon, Scripture is a text in conversation with itself: texts are being reread and reinterpreted in later contexts. The canon's "exegesis of itself" is a process of inviting its readers to see the surprising ways of God's activity in the world.[38] Moreover, this "retrieval of the past" by later canonical texts is a move possible only on the basis that scriptural texts are a form of address capable of being heard by later readers.[39] This text in conversation with itself reminds us that Scripture's human authors point to the shape of God's self-revelation as historical and thus vulnerable to the vagaries of history.[40] Scripture is rooted in the world, orientated to God's ways with

---

36. Webster, *Domain of the Word*, 60. The same could be said for Swain's *Trinity, Revelation, and Reading*.

37. Dietrich Bonhoeffer, *Letters and Papers from Prison*, trans. Isabel Best et al., Dietrich Bonhoeffer Works 8 (Minneapolis: Fortress, 2010), 373. See Sean F. Winter, "Word and World: Dietrich Bonhoeffer and Biblical Interpretation Today," *Pacifica* 25 (2012): 161–75.

38. John P. Bradbury, *Perpetually Reforming: A Theology of Church Reform and Renewal*, Ecclesiological Investigations (London: T&T Clark, 2013), 143.

39. Ford, *Future of Christian Theology*, 196.

40. Von Balthasar, "Word, Scripture, and Tradition," 13.

the world, and addresses every new hearer contextually. The ways in which the biblical authors engage with their contexts is part of the history of theological interpretation and invites reemergent theological interpretation to try to "do something analogous in thoughtful response to God and in the light of God, to the cries and opportunities of our time."[41] Contextual interpretation *is* theological interpretation, precisely because revelation, in the Christian sense, is always "received as that which comes into the midst of the world."[42] The customary appeal to John 1:14 is well rehearsed yet no less important as a vital resource for thinking about God's address to the world as a fleshly engagement. In a haunting phrase, Bonhoeffer speaks of the disciple (whom we can take as the implied reader of Scripture) as following a worldly vocation that allows him or her "to be pulled into walking the path that Jesus walks."[43] To be pulled into the path that Jesus walks invites theological interpretation into a host of different contexts in which Scripture wills to be heard. In these contexts theological interpretation will, of necessity, ask itself how it relates to the worlds in which the text is read. Advocates of Scripture as address do not reserve much space for contextual interpretation, that is, interpretation that self-consciously views our contexts as ingredients for interpreting Scripture. In a tone whose influence can be detected in later theology, Barth warns of the danger of confusing "hearing and our own speaking."[44] Again, John Webster is indicative of a style of theological interpretation that locates the text's resonance within the sphere of Jesus's resurrected presence, without considering in sufficient depth how Scripture resonates with our own contexts. Indeed, in Webster's threefold account of the biblical text, the presence of the risen Christ, and the reader, it is explicitly *only* the readers and their context that seem not to contribute any animation to the business of interpretation: "Interpreters are set in motion by the text; they do not animate it but rather are the audience of its animating utterance."[45] If theological interpretation is about the business of reregionalizing reading of Scripture, one of the regions that wise readers of Scripture need to scrutinize is the particular context in which Scripture wills to be heard. This means refuting the claims of Webster for a restricted region of readerly attention. "The Christian act of reading Holy Scripture is to be characterised by a certain exclusiveness, a deliberate directing of attention to the text and an equally deliberate laying aside of

41. Ford, *Future of Christian Theology*, 201.
42. Winter, "Word and World," 172.
43. Bonhoeffer, *Letters and Papers from Prison*, 480.
44. Karl Barth, *Church Dogmatics*, trans. G. T. Thomson and Harold Knight (Edinburgh: T&T Clark, 1956), I/2:470; cited in Webster, *Domain of the Word*, 28.
45. Webster, *Domain of the Word*, 48.

other concerns."[46] A greater emphasis on what Scripture can do in generating and transforming our contexts, when animated by readers determined not to lay aside other concerns, changes the moral responsibilities of theological interpretation. This is a risky place for theological interpretation: Is it willing to enter into the kinds of conversations that will ensue when talk of "context" is introduced? Yet, as Brian Blount argues, the theological burden of proof should rest on those who refuse to open themselves up to the kind of "communal critique and correction" that arises when we expose ourselves to the messy reality of *how Scripture is read in context.*[47]

In relation to talk of Scripture as address, the three challenges posed here call to mind the stark reality that after the church hears Scripture, it listens to the Word *preached.* Theological interpretation begins with the prayer that God will speak through the human words of Scripture's preachers. The Word is heard in the context of the present church, whose response is to speak in the interpretative form of a sermon. Preaching is an activity in which the "words of Scripture are not simply recounted, but are made present in the immediate context."[48] This making present is possible through both the vivifying energy of the Spirit, who raised Jesus from the dead, and the preacher's engagement with the text in the world.

Theological Interpretation and the Divine Economy

All theological talk of Scripture is bound to the church. And all talk of both the church and of Scripture is bound to what must remain theology's primary preoccupation: God. Theological engagement with the scriptural text longs for encounter with the Triune God, who is the ultimate rationality of the text. To speak of God as the grounding for Scripture is to appeal to the action of a God who orders these seemingly disparate texts to his reconciling purposes. If we imagine the texts of Scripture as a unified collection of texts, such a claim primarily makes sense with reference to God's providential action. When John Webster writes that "setting Scripture in the realm of providence excludes from the beginning the secularization of the history from which the biblical texts emerge,"[49] he is appealing to a set of theohistorical claims, in the context of which Scripture's unity becomes imaginable. The notion that these texts

46. John Webster, *Holy Scripture* (Cambridge: Cambridge University Press, 2003), 90.

47. Brian K. Blount, "Reading Contextually as Reading Reformed," in *Reformed Theology: Identity and Ecumenicity II*, ed. Wallace M. Alston and Michael Welker (Grand Rapids: Eerdmans, 2007), 56.

48. Bradbury, *Perpetually Reforming*, 194.

49. Webster, *Domain of the Word*, 14.

represent a unified whole rests not on claims either about the church's authority or its ingenuity in twisting these seemingly random texts into coherence, nor does it rest on a claim that earlier writers knew what later writers would say.[50] We are declaring that somehow these texts crystallize around the Jesus event (John 5:39–40), the one in whom all things are gathered up (Eph. 1:10). In the proposals of various authors, reemergent theological interpretation has sought to recover a theological notion of history.[51] That history is not confined to the world we can empirically observe is a *skandalon* presented in the Bible itself, for the world presented by the biblical texts is one with which God is irrepressibly engaged and involved.[52] The episode on the road to Emmaus is the clearest witness of the umbilical link between the story of Scripture and the story of Jesus. As indestructibly present to the disciples, Jesus goes through "all" the Scriptures with his disciples (Luke 24:27). Jesus is a "living commentary" on Scripture, in the evocative phrase of Hans Urs von Balthasar,[53] and for this reason all subsequent theological interpretation reads the biblical texts around Jesus. Theological interpretation is a reaction against what I term in the Manifesto "a secular, disenchanted view of time and history." Or, as Murray Rae pinpoints in his contribution to the Manifesto, Christ's tutorial on the road to Emmaus reveals history to be God's "project."

The link between divine action and the biblical text is something that theological interpretation can learn, in its time, from premodern interpreters. For premodern readers, a basic assumption is that the meaning of Scripture is not univocal, precisely because *God*, working with the human authors of the text, is the primary Author of the text. The multilayered spiritual sense of Scripture (sometimes known as its "fourfold sense"), its boundless depth, is part of the claim that these texts are bound to God's purposes. It was Thomas Aquinas who authoritatively established the notion that God is the source of the spiritual sense of Scripture, and that the literal sense is the foundation of the spiritual senses, God being the Author of the literal sense. Human authors use words to signify things, but God can use the things signified to point to future events and meanings.[54] Here we are in a landscape very different from most forms of modern biblical interpretation. The meaning of a text for a premodern such as Aquinas is to be found by close attention to the text and

---

50. Ibid., 18.

51. See, e.g., Matthew Levering, *Participatory Biblical Exegesis: A Theology of Biblical Interpretation* (Notre Dame, IN: University of Notre Dame Press, 2008); and Murray Rae, *History and Hermeneutics* (London: T&T Clark, 2005).

52. Volf, *Captive to the Word of God*, 5.

53. Von Balthasar, "Word, Scripture, and Tradition," 13.

54. Thomas Aquinas, *Summa theologica* 1.10, trans. English Dominican Province (London: Burns, Oates & Washbourne, 1920).

the mind of the author (the human author ultimately guided by God) as rendered by the text itself, not the world "behind" the text. Here there is no need to curate the distinction, so important to modern interpretation, between the author's world and the reader's world, or between one text and another text in the canon. God's action in history is why theological interpretation sees neither discrete biblical texts nor the events of which they speak in isolation from one another. The texts, and the events that they relate, have their ultimate context in God.

The claims that theological interpretation needs to make about the unity of the biblical text, and its multilayered meaning, are therefore sustained by giving attention to the doctrine of God. Inspiration, we can say with von Balthasar, is less about a text being immaculate and free of error and more about the capacity of the Holy Spirit as being always ready to unfold new levels of meaning in the text.[55] But there is another way that the link between God and the text might shape the future of theological interpretation. What would it mean for theological interpretation to take seriously the task that George Newlands lays before all theology: the need to "reappraise its understanding of God as the source of faithful engagement in the world"?[56]

Newlands's statement provokes two questions for reemergent theological interpretation. How does God communicate with his creatures? How might the form of divine communication shape the reemergent theological interpretation? To respond to the first question, God's means of communication with his creatures is persuasive rather than coercive.[57] This is integral to God's determination to reveal God's self through and in history, be it via the textual form, through Israel, or in the life of Jesus of Nazareth. In an essay that reflects on the vulnerability of particularity, John Howard Yoder relates how Christians are always required to communicate the "good news" from within a particular identity and context. That Christians are compelled to be evangels—bearers of good *news*—prompts Yoder to make the following suggestive statements about the category of "news" that Christians bear. First, news always "originates in a particular setting. It is without embarrassment contingent, historical." (Thus the importance of contextual interpretation to theological interpretation, for God reveals God's self in history as a participant in our context.) Second, news is "communicable": far from being esoteric, it is public (thus the Manifesto emphasizes theological interpretation as an

55. Von Balthasar, "Word, Scripture, and Tradition," 14–15.
56. George Newlands, *The Transformative Imagination: Rethinking Intercultural Theology* (Aldershot, UK: Ashgate, 2004), 8.
57. David S. Cunningham, *These Three Are One: The Practice of Trinitarian Theology*, Challenges in Contemporary Theology (Oxford: Blackwell, 1998), 306–9.

activity that is carried out for the sake of the nations). Third, the evangel is willing to submit vulnerably "to the conditions of meaning of the receptor culture."[58] This vulnerability renders the evangel liable to rejection. For Yoder, openness to particularity and vulnerability is ingredient to Christianity because of the shape of Jesus's life.

How might this form of divine communication shape the reemergent theological interpretation? The future of theological interpretation—the temper in which it is carried out, the kinds of readers it incorporates, the questions it will allow, where it draws its borders—will be determined by its response to Scott Swain's claim that the "way we approach and handle Scripture must be determined by the identity of the one whose word Scripture is."[59] If theological interpreters let the life of Jesus of Nazareth define the one whose word Scripture is, then they will be anxious to avoid coercive accounts of Scripture that seek security in making Scripture's agency seem irresistible.[60] Nurturing spaces of hospitable and vulnerable generosity, being pulled into the tension between the texts and our experiences[61]—that *is* theological interpretation responsive to the shape of the divine economy. The place of theological interpretation is one of unbearable tension. Theological interpretation formed by attention to God as the source of its engagement with the world will be eccentric rather than insular and transgressive rather than concerned with preserving its identity. This set of claims takes us forward to unpacking the next mark of theological interpretation.

Theological Interpretation and the Church

An important aspect of reemergent theological interpretation has been its determination to resource what is said now by turning intentionally to insights and instincts from earlier readers in the life of the church.[62] After all, the church is what Thomas calls the "true home" of Scripture. Theological interpretation of Scripture is distinguished by its remembering of former reading practices. How Scripture has been read in the history of the church is of course hugely diverse and complex: there is no one form of premodern interpretation. Yet in attending to the diversity of premodern modes of reading, we are closest to the bond between the theological interpretation that is reemerging in our

58. Yoder, "On Not Being Ashamed," 48–50.
59. Swain, *Trinity, Revelation, and Reading*, 62.
60. See Yoder, "On Not Being Ashamed," 43.
61. William C. Placher, *Narratives of a Vulnerable God: Christ, Theology, and Scripture* (Louisville: Westminster John Knox, 1994), 104.
62. See Swain, *Trinity, Revelation, and Reading*, 10–11.

time and the *history* of theological interpretation. Basic to the reemergent theological interpretation in our time is the sense "that theological interpreters of Scripture should deeply attend to pre-modern interpretation."[63] By attending deeply, one can recover such churchly practices as *lectio divina*, the slow ruminative reading of Scripture, letting Scripture irrigate the mind and will of its reader. *Lectio divina* is a fully engaged encounter in which the living Christ personally addresses his disciple. Eugene Peterson has been a key figure in this emphasis on the spiritual ingestion of the biblical text.[64] If theological interpretation is to be liberated from some of the compulsions and restrictions of modernity, a turn to premodern modes of reading is an entirely explicable move.[65] Thus in my Manifesto section, I strongly emphasize that Scripture needs to be read in communion with those who have carried it faithfully through the church. The appeal to premodern reading of the text is a powerful witness against a theology rooted only in our proximate context: the present church is not the first reader of the text. The turn to premodern exegesis is a timely reminder that theological interpretation is not owned by the academy: it is *a practice* sustained by the life and worship of the church. Theological interpretation is wise to cling to the insight that what it is cannot be defined apart from "close attention to the concrete life of the church."[66] In this sense, Robert Jenson is right to state that, divorced from the life of the church, many of the claims that theology might want to make about the Bible would make no sense.[67]

Yet the enthusiastic turn to premodern modes of reading must work in tandem with ceaseless attention to certain questions: How is the past appropriated? How does the church remember the past in the present for the sake of the future? Thus I claim in the Manifesto, "Relating to tradition faithfully is not necessarily a task of repeating what was said in the past, but of establishing how to live in communion now with past readers of the text." Certainly, for all the value of premodern interpretation, there can be no straight appropriation of premodern voices into our context. In the neat

63. Stephen Fowl, "Effective History and the Cultivation of Wise Interpreters," *Journal of Theological Interpretation* 7 (2013): 155.

64. Eugene Peterson, "Eat This Book: The Holy Community at Table with the Holy Scripture," *Theology Today* 56 (1999): 5–17.

65. Webster, *Domain of the Word*, 17.

66. Nicholas M. Healy, *Church, World and Christian Life: Practical-Prophetic Ecclesiology*, Cambridge Studies in Christian Doctrine (Cambridge: Cambridge University Press, 2000), 50; cited in Bradbury, *Perpetually Reforming*, 3. The original context of Healy's discussion is ecclesiology.

67. Robert W. Jenson, "Scripture's Authority in the Church," in *The Art of Reading Scripture*, ed. Ellen F. Davis and Richard B. Hays (Grand Rapids: Eerdmans, 2003), 27–37.

articulation of Thompson, exegetical insights from the past "cannot simply be transferred from their bank accounts to ours."[68] Saying only what was said in the past is not theology: it is repetition. An appeal only to the past, in a tone that implies the sufficiency of this past, is just as arid as an appeal only to the present. Every theological interpreter is faced with the same question, in his or her own context and time: "How do we become the church in this time and place such that we exist for the sake of the world?"[69] In between references to contemporary experience alone and references to what was said in the past alone, creative engagement with the tradition pulls past and present readers into a conversation, centered around wrestling with the chief question for interpretation: How can this text be read as address "in the context in which God in God's providence has placed us—today in the here and now"?[70] Failing to keep in tension the past readings of the text and the present demands (to allow one or the other to become more dominant) risks denying that God is continually active within history.[71] Theological interpretation that is determined to be ecclesial will be stretched backward into the history of the church's reading with the text and then will be pressed onward to answer: How do we stand in this tradition today?

If the church attends to wise readers of the biblical text like Thomas Aquinas or John Calvin, one of the insights it will learn is that theological readers of the text have always enlisted ways of reading the text developed outside the life of the church. Theological interpretation characterized by wisdom seeks to establish how it can relate to secular modes of knowing and reading the text. Whether it be Aristotle in the case of Aquinas, or the humanist insights adopted by Reformation theologians, wise biblical readers do not shrink from pursuing whatever can be learned from forms of knowledge developed outside the church. Indeed, the church is not a self-enclosed mode of knowing the world: it has always needed to seek out the most penetrating insights and scholarly endeavors of its time. How can the church do now what premodern readers did for the sake of their time? As we seek analogies in our post-Christendom context, one answer is surely to turn to the intensities of different communities of faith, reading one another's

68. John L. Thompson, "At the Margins of the Rule of Faith: Reflections on the Reception History of Problematic Texts and Themes," *Journal of Theological Interpretation* 7 (2013): 193.

69. Bradbury, *Perpetually Reforming*, 206.

70. Tom Greggs, "Being a Wise Apprentice to the Communion of Modern Saints: On the Need for Conversation with a Plurality of Theological Interlocutors," in *The Vocation of Theology Today: A Festschrift for David Ford*, ed. Tom Greggs, Rachel Muers, and Simeon Zahl (Eugene, OR: Cascade, 2013), 33.

71. For some related thoughts about the church's responsibility in and for the present, see Bradbury, *Perpetually Reforming*, 210.

texts together.[72] To engage in interfaith reading relies, of course, on lively communities of faith capable of demonstrating the depths of their reading practices to one another. One of the challenges for church leaders today must surely be how to nurture wise reading communities, capable of relating the text to the complex worlds in which we are placed. Thus I posted a reminder in an earlier contribution to the Manifesto that there is a need in our own time to rethink imaginatively the way we theologically train ministers and clergy for their vocation.

Another challenge awaits theological interpretation as ecclesial interpretation. The time in which we have been placed by God's providence marks a shift of Christianity's center of gravity from the global north to the global south. Attention to the global church must be part of the task of theological interpretation. "Theological interpretation calls for an irrepressibly ecumenical form of attention," I correspondingly state in the Manifesto. In order to attend to the startling implications of this global shift, theological interpretation will have to incorporate sensitivity to the contexts of biblical readers that was mentioned earlier. Pieter Holtrop writes of the challenges that thinking cross-culturally might present to the future of theological interpretation:

> For us the gospel speaks in many tongues. We cannot speak together as Reformed Christians without knowing at once that the gospel has taken root in the various and diverse cultures in which our churches bear witness to the gospel. . . . The incarnation of Jesus Christ demands that we take culture seriously: for there is no "flesh" that is not nourished by a culture. No "word" can be heard that is not the language of a culture. . . . We recognize that the gospel illuminates cultures. . . . Culture also illuminates our understanding of the gospel. Different cultures can perceive in the Gospels that which other cultures have failed to perceive.[73]

Theological Interpretation and the Love of Neighbor

Theological interpretation has a moral dimension. It has as its end that the reader and hearer might grow in their love of the living God and their neighbor. Interpretation in the wake of Augustine's insight, that interpretation should be normed by love of God *and* love of neighbor, will be willing to confess that there are countless theological readings whose effects have been dehumanizing.

72. David F. Ford, "Reading Scripture with Intensity: Academic; Ecclesial, Interfaith, and Divine," in *Shaping Theology: Engagements in a Religious and Secular World* (Oxford: Blackwell, 2007), 59–71.

73. Pieter Holtrop, "Contextuality as Theological Challenge: The WARC at the Threshold of the Third Millennium," *Exchange* 27 (1998): 71; cited in Blount, "Reading Contextually," 44.

"Recognizing the church's messy history of engagement with Scripture is part of the task of receiving tradition with humility and, sometimes, penitence," the Manifesto claims. Adrian Thatcher has helpfully cataloged some of the many ways in which Holy Scripture has been an instrument of terror to different groups of people in history.[74] Scripture's authority has not always been experienced as good news for all. Thus there is a role in theological interpretation for the insights of ideological interpretation, not least if we recall that the church's reading of Scripture is part of a very fallible history. Ideological interpretation can alert the church to the implications that scriptural reading can have, and has had, on those who sometimes were not recognized as our neighbors. Walter Moberly reinforces that ideological readings have a properly theological motivation: "If Christian readers of the Bible, at the heart of whose faith is the inversion of all conventional notions of power in the death and resurrection of Jesus, acquiesce too readily and comfortably in contemporary social, political, and economic distributions of power that happen to favor them, then they are severely failing in their biblical interpretation in a fundamental way."[75]

To lend some concreteness to this discussion, theological interpretation that is normed by love of God and love of neighbor will be aware of the deep connection between the supersessionism of the church (making it hard to see Judaism as a continuing religion in its own right) and its reading of the Old Testament. To put it more starkly, Jewish people and the Jewish faith have not always been beneficiaries of theological interpretation. Here one thinks of the risk that typological interpretation might marginalize the literal and historical sense of the Old Testament, thereby rendering it hard to imagine how Israel can be of *continuing* significance for the identity of the church in the sense that Romans 9–11 compels the church to consider. The response to questions raised by these ethical challenges is not to do less theological interpretation, but to return to Scripture with an expanded set of coreaders and to do *more* theological interpretation. Future theological interpretation, as part of its agapic commitment, will need to ensure that it reads Scripture with those who have sometimes been harmed by theological interpretations.

Conclusion

How might we bring together these reflections on the history and reemergence of theological interpretation? One way to distill what has been said is to offer

74. Adrian Thatcher, *The Savage Text: The Use and Abuse of the Bible*, Blackwell Manifestos (Chichester, UK: Wiley-Blackwell, 2008).
75. Moberly, "What Is Theological Interpretation of Scripture?," 168.

the proposal that theological interpretation is a project of biblical imagination. Theology, Luke Timothy Johnson offers, is ultimately "the name we give to the effort of our minds to grasp the world conjured by God and construed by Scripture."[76] A biblical imagination envisions the ways in which our world is invited to participate in the history of God. Imagination is certainly a virtue demonstrated by the church fathers. Gripped by the Christ event as the center of history and so the center of Scripture, they dared to ponder how one text related to another in the biblical canon and to their own lives, recognizing a unity where we too often see disharmony, rupture, and discord. Imagination is part of the history of theological interpretation. Part of the current task for theological interpretation is to ask what a biblical imagination in our context and time might look like. Allowing our minds, imaginations, and actions to be expanded by a sense of history as God reveals it is theological interpretation's ultimate vocation.

76. Johnson, "Imagining the World Scripture Imagines," 166.

2

Doctrine of Scripture
and Theological Interpretation

MICHAEL W. GOHEEN AND MICHAEL D. WILLIAMS

Introduction

From early times the church has confessed *sacra scriptura est verbum Dei*. This confession that the Holy Scripture is the Word of God demands that the church listen attentively to the Bible to hear God's address there. The problem is, however, that various factors arising within our history have shaped a context in which the church has become a little hard of hearing. This volume is concerned to address such a hearing loss by recovering a theological interpretation of Scripture: listening to the Bible as God's Word addressed to his people.

Although many factors have contributed to this problem, one of the issues is theological reflection on Scripture itself. Sometimes our doctrine of Scripture has not contributed to a posture of listening. In fact, it has often hindered us from hearing and interpreting Scripture as God's address. This is true not only of the more liberal tradition that has more or less abandoned the divine authority of Scripture; it is also true for more evangelical churches.

Indeed, theological reflection on Scripture in the more conservative wing of the church has sometimes fallen prey to a number of crippling assumptions that have misunderstood the nature and purpose of Scripture. This has had a harmful affect on our ability to hear God's address in the Bible.

We notice five such assumptions that appear particularly in Western culture. First, the rationalism of our culture has caused us to miss the storied nature of the Bible. We have reduced it to fragments of theological and ethical truth that give us data for a systematic theology or an ethical system. Moreover, when the many genres of Scripture are pared down to information or doctrine, we miss Scripture's instrumental intent to form us by drawing us more fully into its story in many ways.[1] Second, the individualism of our culture has caused us to misunderstand the nature of the Bible as a cosmic story in which we find our place. It has also eclipsed the covenant community that stands at the center of the story. The cosmic-communal-personal nature of Scripture is blurred. Third, in an admirable attempt to protect the Scriptures from the encroaching naturalism of higher criticism, we have so stressed certain attributes of Scripture—divine authority, inspiration, infallibility—that often they have been cut loose from the purpose of Scripture. What the Bible *is* becomes unyoked from what the Bible *does*. When these attributes are disconnected from the nature and purpose of Scripture, they are isolated from the Bible's framework of meaning, and another framework is provided. They are then defined in ways alien to the Bible. Fourth, Scripture has been forced into the dualisms of our culture—public-private, spiritual-material, sacred-secular—and the comprehensive, all-embracing authority of the Bible as a metanarrative has been greatly reduced. Finally, a tension between the divine authority and the human form of Scripture has led us to stress one over against the other. In so doing, we have established a false dilemma that is entirely foreign to Scripture, and we have not sufficiently understood that it is precisely in listening carefully to the human witness that we attend to God's voice.

It is clear that our cultural assumptions will shape both our doctrine of Scripture and consequently the way we hear it. Of course, sometimes they enable us to hear Scripture aright, but other times they distort God's address. Theological reflection on Scripture may play a role in enabling us to sort this out. The task of theology, Lesslie Newbigin suggests, is "to declare to each generation what is the faith, to expose and combat errors destructive of the

---

1. "The problem with evangelical propositionalism is that it opted out of the drama and took an external, spectator's perspective upon the story," Michael D. Williams writes ("Theology as Witness: Reading Scripture in a New Era of Evangelical Thought—Part II: Kevin Vanhoozer, *The Drama of Doctrine,*" *Presbyterion* 27, no. 1 [Spring 2011]: 24).

faith, to expel from her body doctrines which pervert the faith, and to lead her members into a full and vivid apprehension of the faith."[2] Here the task of theology has both a positive and negative function. On the one hand, in each generation it is a fresh and relevant articulation of the faith, designed to lead the church more and more into a living and vibrant faith. On the other hand, it protects the Bible's teaching from the cultural idolatries that would twist and distort the truth and lead the church astray. Theological reflection on Scripture itself may play this role: on the one hand, it may articulate a doctrine of Scripture that can lead the church into a more careful listening to God's address; on the other hand, it may challenge the cultural idolatries that garble our understanding of Scripture in such a way that our ears are not attuned to God's address.

Scripture as One Component of the Organism of Revelation

To understand the nature and purpose of Scripture, we must grasp its role and function within the larger organism of revelation. The imagery of the organism highlights two things. On the one hand, a living organism is made up of many parts that all have their own particular function. A human being, for example, has eyes, ears, and a mouth. On the other hand, all these diverse parts are bound together in a living unity that works toward a single purpose. Ears hear, eyes see, and mouths speak, but all are part of the singular activity of human life.

So it is with the organism of revelation. Revelation cannot be reduced to Scripture without rejecting Scripture's own testimony. "Long ago God spoke to our ancestors in many and various ways by the prophets, but in these last days he has spoken to us by a Son" (Heb. 1:1–2). "What can be known about God is plain to them, because God has shown it to them. Ever since the creation of the world his eternal power and divine nature, invisible though they are, have been understood and seen through the things he has made" (Rom. 1:19–20). There are many aspects of the organism of revelation, but in all of them God discloses himself, his purpose, and his will to us.

In theological reflection there have been various attempts to account for this diversity of revelation. A twofold distinction between general and special revelation, or creational and redemptive revelation, has been the most common. In this scheme Scripture is considered to be part of special or redemptive revelation. This way of proceeding carries the danger of rupturing God's

2. Lesslie Newbigin, *The Reunion of the Church: A Defence of the South India Scheme* (London: SCM, 1948), 137.

revelation in a dualistic way, forcing it into a supernaturalistic-naturalistic, special-general dichotomy. Yet many have employed this distinction in a way that faithfully aligns itself with Scripture. G. C. Berkouwer, for example, insists that the "distinction between general and special revelation does not posit a rupture in the unity of God's revelation, but points out rather the revealing acts of God in history in the way of creation, fall and redemption."[3]

Others have opted for a threefold distinction. Herman Bavinck, for example, distinguishes between creational, redemptive, and scriptural revelation.[4] For Bavinck, Scripture is the record and capstone of both creational and redemptive revelation. Gordon Spykman offers a different threefold division in terms of revelation in creation, Scripture, and Christ.[5] Spykman enables us to distinguish between the climactic revelation in Christ and the Scriptures that testify to him. Bavinck illumines the distinction between God's redemptive revelation in history and Scripture that records it. Both insights are helpful in giving us a more nuanced understanding of the organism of revelation and in enabling us to formulate it in a way that runs along the narrative grain of Scripture. Drawing on these insights, we propose a fourfold distinction as the most helpful way to draw out the organism of revelation: creational revelation, redemptive revelation, Christ, and Scripture.

Scripture witnesses to God's revelation as it occurs in creation, humanity, and history (Ps. 19:1–4; Acts 14:17; Rom. 1:18–20). In the creation God discloses himself and his will to humankind, inviting a response of trust, obedience, love, and gratitude. However, the rebellion of humankind means that we suppress that revelation and twist it into idolatry (Rom. 1:18–25).[6] Our eyes are blinded to the clear revelation of God in the creation. There is need for sight, new eyes, as well as new light to see in the darkness. God sets out on a long historical journey to restore the creation and humanity back to what he originally intended.

The author of Hebrews summarizes that journey by telling us that God's revelation has come at many times along the way and in various ways (Heb.

---

3. G. C. Berkouwer, "General and Special Divine Revelation," in *Revelation and the Bible*, ed. Carl F. H. Henry (Grand Rapids: Baker, 1959), 23.

4. Herman Bavinck, *Our Reasonable Faith* (Grand Rapids: Eerdmans, 1956), 95–96.

5. Gordon Spykman, *Reformational Theology: A New Paradigm for Doing Dogmatics* (Grand Rapids: Eerdmans, 1992), 76–92.

6. One of the most insightful readings of Rom. 1:18–32 that speaks of creation revelation and its repression and substitution by rebellious humanity is by Herman Bavinck in various places; see *Church between Temple and Mosque: A Study of the Relationship between the Christian Faith and Other Religions* (Grand Rapids: Eerdmans, 1981), 125–6; "Human Religion in God's Eyes: A Study of Romans 1:18–32," in *Scottish Bulletin of Evangelical Theology* 12 (Spring 1984): 44–52; *J. H. Bavinck Reader*, ed. John Bolt and James D. Bratt (Grand Rapids: Eerdmans, 2013).

1:1). Geerhardus Vos, for example, traces the unfolding of this redemptive revelation through the Old Testament, attending to the Mosaic and prophetic epochs of revelation.[7] Bavinck helpfully discusses this redemptive revelation under three heads: manner, content, and purpose.[8] In terms of manner, God's redemptive revelation takes place in his historical acts, through direct discourse, in visions and miracles and dreams, through lots and the Urim and Thummim, among other ways. The content of God's revelation is his covenant. We do not find a string of unrelated revelational moments but an organically unified historical narrative centered in the covenant, with the goal to deal with sin and to renew the creation.[9] The purpose for which redemptive revelation aims is to shape a holy people who will fulfill God's kingdom purposes for the sake of the nations, which leads to the renewal of all things, all for the glory of God.

The Old Testament narrates the covenantal work of God in Israel, which ultimately converges on the person and work of Jesus. Hebrews points to the Son as the climactic moment of redemptive revelation: "In these last days he has spoken to us by a Son" (Heb. 1:2). Indeed, Jesus himself makes clear that the whole Old Testament Scriptures finds their fulfillment and meaning in Jesus Christ. When he opens the minds of the disciples to understand the Scriptures, he says, "Thus it is written, that the Messiah is to suffer and to rise from the dead on the third day" (Luke 24:46; cf. 24:25–27, 44). When he contends with the Jewish leaders, he says to them: "You study the scriptures because you think that in them you have eternal life; and it is they that testify on my behalf" (John 5:39). The New Testament begins with the life and work of Christ, and everything flows from him. The Gospels and the Epistles proclaim and expound what God has done in Jesus Christ. And so Jesus himself reveals to us the organic unity of redemptive revelation, which finds its concentrated center in him.

Redemptive revelation flowing to its climax in Christ is recorded in Scripture. Bavinck helpfully distinguishes revelation in history from Scripture: "Revelation . . . preceded the recording of it by a long way in many instances. . . . Scripture is therefore not the revelation itself, but the description, the record, from which the revelation can be known." To prevent any kind of misunderstanding that might devalue Scripture, he adds: "True, Scripture is to be distinguished from the revelation that precedes it, but it is not to be separated

7. Geerhardus Vos, *Biblical Theology: Old and New Testaments* (Edinburgh: Banner of Truth Trust, 1948).

8. Bavinck, *Our Reasonable Faith*, 61–94.

9. See Michael D. Williams, *Far as the Curse Is Found: The Covenant Story of Redemption* (Phillipsburg, NJ: P&R, 2005); and Sandra Richter, *The Epic of Eden: A Christian Entry into the Old Testament* (Downers Grove, IL: InterVarsity, 2008).

from that revelation. Scripture is not a human, incidental, arbitrary, and defective supplement to revelation but is itself a component part of revelation. In fact, Scripture is the rounding out and the fulfillment, the cornerstone and capstone of revelation."[10]

The Scriptures are the record and canonical deposit of God's covenant journey, which includes redemptive revelation and Israel's response. That record comes from different kinds of people who play their various roles in redemptive history. There are lawgivers who announce laws to order Israel's life to be a just and compassionate community amid the nations, history writers who challenge God's people to find their place in covenant history as they record God's mighty deeds, poets who write songs so God's people can sing their faith so as to nourish covenant faithfulness, wise men who write proverbs and philosophical reflections on the deep questions of life to enable God's people to discern the wisdom of God's creation order and conform themselves to it, prophets who call for covenant obedience with threats of judgment and promises of future blessing, and apostles who call for the obedience of faith to the gospel as they proclaim and witness to the historical events of Christ and teach about their implications for life in the pagan environments. The record of God's redemptive revelation is refracted through the prism of literary form into many genres through which God's voice can be heard.

This fourfold formulation of revelation allows us to see four things clearly. First, revelation runs along the narrative grain of Scripture; it comes in the track of creation, sin, and redemption. Our distinctions do not come from a prior set of categories imposed on Scripture but are molded by the shape of the biblical story itself. Second, we are able to see that revelation forms an organic historical unity that finds its center and climactic fulfillment in Jesus Christ. We do not set the various modes of revelation side by side like so many beads on a string. Rather, redemptive revelation unfolds in a progressive historical unity and culminates in Christ. Third, this formulation enables us to see how Scripture is situated as part of this organism of revelation as a narrative record and capstone of Old Testament redemptive revelation as well as a witness to Jesus as the final revelation. And finally, we can see how Scripture functions authoritatively as a controlling narrative that records God's mighty redemptive deeds in the various literary forms of the canon, which all unite in their purpose to lead us to salvation through faith in Christ.

All of this has great importance for formulating a doctrine of Scripture that carefully attends to its nature yet also its purpose. It marks off the distinctive sound of Scripture in God's symphony of revelation. Only as we rightly see

10. Bavinck, *Our Reasonable Faith*, 95–96.

what Scripture is and what it does will we be able to interpret it faithfully to
hear God's address to his church.

Scripture as One Story Centered in Jesus Christ

Speaking of Scripture as a record of covenantal revelation progressively unfolding in redemptive history makes clear that it is not an unrelated collection
of divine oracles, theological truths, and ethical principles. Leveling or flattening out Scripture in this way reduces the organism of revealed truth into
isolated fragments. Rather, it is a cohesive and narrative unity that tells the
story of God's saving and judging acts and finds its all-dominating center
and concentrated focus in the coming and the work of Christ.

That the Scriptures tell a story is not hard to see. The question is the status of this story and how it might function authoritatively as God's Word.
The basic clue to answer this question comes from noticing where the story
begins and where it ends. It begins with the creation of the entire world by
God and culminates in the renewal of all things as the ultimate consequence
of his renewing work. If one believes this, it means that the Bible is nothing
less than a record that purports to be the true story of the whole world. This
is a very remarkable claim indeed!

To articulate the nature of Scripture in this way breaks with large swaths
of evangelicalism as well as with classical liberalism. Newbigin helps us to
see the way the scientific revolution and the Enlightenment have produced a
dichotomy in Western culture that has had harmful implications for a doctrine
of Scripture. With scientific knowledge installed as the only legitimate arbiter
of truth, all truth claims are judged either to be facts if they line up with this
scientific ideal, or to be values and preferences if they do not. He observes
that often evangelicals have opted for the "fact" side, turning the Bible into
an objectively precise set of theological, historical, and ethical truths. Alternatively, the liberal tradition has opted for the "values" side, diminishing the
biblical story to a mere history of an ancient people's religious consciousness.
To the degree that this has happened, both traditions have failed to see the
most important thing that can be said about the nature of Scripture: it is first
and foremost the true story of the world. N. T. Wright can even make the
striking claim that this defines the very nature of Christianity: "The whole
point of Christianity is that it offers a story which is the story of the whole
world. It is public truth."[11]

11. N. T. Wright, *The New Testament and the People of God*, vol. 1 of *Christian Origins
and the Question of God* (Minneapolis: Fortress, 1992), 41–42.

So the first way we theologically elaborate the nature of scriptural authority is in terms of a controlling narrative that presents God and his relation to the world, that describes the "real" world as it really is, that tells us of its destiny, that reveals the nature and meaning of human life, and that sets forth the vocation of God's people. Scripture is a metanarrative,[12] a comprehensive worldview story,[13] an interpretation of the meaning of universal history.[14]

The word "authority" has rightly been a critical component in theological reflection on Scripture: Scripture carries divine authority. The problem is that sometimes we have not been careful to distinguish the many kinds of authority that are operative. For example, there is a legal authority that commands us what to do; there is the authority of an expert who compels our submission by superior insight; there is the authority of reality or God's creation order that requires our conformity (think, e.g., of gravity at the level of the fiftieth floor!); there is the authority of a story. What kind of authority does a story have?[15] If this is the fundamental nature of Scripture, it is an urgent question.

Much could be said in answer to that question, and much has been written,[16] yet here we can indicate a way forward by making the simple but profoundly important point that a story narrates the world and tells us what the world *really is* like. Wright observes that "a story is the best way of talking about the way the world actually is."[17] The claim of the *biblical* story is that it tells the way the world actually is. And so to accept the authority of the biblical story is "to enter it and to inhabit it. It is to live in the world as the world is portrayed in this story."[18] This means, of course, that it also tells us about God and his relation to this world, and about the meaning of human life.

12. Richard Bauckham, *Bible and Mission: Christian Witness in a Postmodern World* (Grand Rapids: Baker Academic, 2003), 4.

13. Wright, *New Testament and the People of God*, 135.

14. Lesslie Newbigin, *A Walk through the Bible* (Vancouver: Regent College Publishing, 2005), 4; idem, *The Gospel in a Pluralist Society* (Grand Rapids: Eerdmans, 1989), 89.

15. For us, story is fundamentally an interpretation of *history*. Sometimes in narrative theology the status of history in the story is in question. We believe that the historical events in the story are of fundamental significance. That is the only way it can truly become *our* story. Cf. Lesslie Newbigin, *The Open Secret: An Introduction to the Theology of Mission*, rev. ed. (Grand Rapids: Eerdmans, 1995), 66–90.

16. N. T. Wright, "How Can the Bible Be Authoritative?," *Vox evangelica* 21 (1991): 7–32; idem, *New Testament and the People of God*, 139–43; Richard Bauckham, *God and the Crisis of Freedom: Biblical and Contemporary Perspectives* (Louisville: Westminster John Knox, 2002), 64–67; idem, *Scripture and Authority Today* (Cambridge: Grove Books, 1999), 10–13; Michael W. Goheen, "The Urgency of Reading the Bible as One Story," *Theology Today* 64, no. 4 (January 2008): 469–83.

17. Wright, *New Testament and the People of God*, 40.

18. Bauckham, *God and the Crisis of Freedom*, 64.

"The way we understand human life depends on what conception we have of the human story. What is the real story of which my life story is a part?"[19]

Therefore an important question arises: Who gets to narrate the world?[20] To hear this question is an important part of understanding the nature of Scripture. The Bible is not a book that offers abstract truth or even a story that is disconnected from the cultural stories of the world. The biblical story is always engaged in a missionary encounter with, or a subversion of, the idolatrous cultural stories impinging on God's people. This is true in the Old Testament as the various books of the canon engage the Egyptian, Babylonian, and Canaanite idolatrous cultures. It is also true that the New Testament proclaims Jesus as Lord and the kingdom of God over against the lordship of Caesar and the Roman Empire. A clash of kingdoms is reflected throughout the biblical story, and hearing God's address will attend to this encounter. It will not allow the Bible to become a book of abstract doctrine, stories, and ethics. Wright correctly includes this missionary encounter as a component part of his understanding of scriptural authority:

> Here we have the roots of a fully Christian theology of scriptural authority: planted firmly in the soil of a missionary community, *confronting the powers of the world with the news of the Kingdom of God*, refreshed and invigorated by the Spirit, growing particularly through the preaching and teaching of the apostles, and bearing fruit in the transformation of human lives as the start of God's project to put the whole cosmos to rights. God accomplishes these things . . . through the "word": the story of Israel now told as reaching its climax in Jesus, God's call to Israel now transmuted into God's call to his renewed people.[21]

The Role and Purpose of Scripture within the Story

Scripture is not only a record of God's redemptive work but also a tool that effectually helps to accomplish the redemption of which it speaks.[22] The gospel not only announces the kingdom of God but is also an instrument in bringing

19. Newbigin, *Gospel in a Pluralist Society*, 15.

20. Robert E. Webber, *Who Gets to Narrate the World? Contending for the Christian Story in an Age of Rivals* (Downers Grove, IL: InterVarsity, 2008).

21. N. T. Wright, *Scripture and the Authority of God: How to Read the Bible Today* (New York: HarperCollins, 2011), 50, emphasis added.

22. B. B. Warfield affirms also that the Bible is a tool as well as an instrument. The Bible is to be accepted, he wrote, "not merely as the record of the redemptive acts by which God is saving the world, but as itself one of the redemptive acts, having its own part to play in the great work of establishing and building up the kingdom of God" (*Inspiration and Authority of the Bible*, ed. Samuel Craig [Phillipsburg, NJ: P&R, 1948], 161).

that kingdom into the world. The Contemporary Testimony *Our World Belongs to God* rightly confesses, "The Bible is the Word of God, the record and tool of God's redeeming work."[23] How does the Scripture function as a tool or instrument of God's redeeming work? Asking that question means probing the purpose of Scripture. C. S. Lewis says that the "first qualification for judging any piece of workmanship from a corkscrew to a cathedral is to know what it is—what it was intended to do and how it is meant to be used."[24] It is only as we properly formulate a biblical doctrine of Scripture—what it is, what it was intended to do, and how it was meant to be used—that we will be able to clear the way to hear God's address to us.

To understand its instrumental purpose, we must ask about its place *within the very story it tells*. If the Bible is a metanarrative, that means it encompasses and gives integrated meaning to the whole of reality, and this includes the role of the Bible itself. That role can be stated as follows: every part of Scripture finds its place in this narrative to enable us to find our place in this story, to lead us to Christ so we might live faithfully in his kingdom, and so that we might live more and more fully into his comprehensive and restorative salvation.

Paul clearly articulates this role of Scripture when he urges Timothy to continue in the Christian faith as he has learned it from the Holy Scriptures, "which are able to make you wise for salvation through faith in Christ Jesus" (2 Tim. 3:15 NIV). He continues—and this has been the *locus classicus* for a doctrine of Scripture—"All Scripture is God-breathed and is useful for teaching, rebuking, correcting, and training in righteousness so that the servant of God [all God's people] may be thoroughly equipped for every good work" (2 Tim. 3:16–17 NIV). The language of "is able to" and "is useful for" points to the redemptive purpose of Scripture: to make us wise unto salvation through faith in Christ and to equip us to live more fully into that salvation. Herman Ridderbos nicely expresses Paul's intention here: "The purpose and the nature of Scripture lie thus in that qualified sort of teaching and instruction which is able to make us wise to salvation, which gives God's people this 'completeness' and equips them for every good work."[25]

A striking statement by Bavinck makes clear the importance of attending to the particular focus and intent of Scripture if we are to rightly understand it:

23. *Our World Belongs to God: A Contemporary Testimony of the Christian Reformed Church*, paragraph 32 (2008), http://missionworldview.com/resources; under "Worldview—Articles," select "Our World Belongs to God (2008)."

24. C. S. Lewis, *Preface to Paradise Lost* (Oxford: Oxford University Press, 1961 [1942]), 1.

25. Herman Ridderbos, *Studies in Scripture and Its Authority* (St. Catharines, ON: Paideia, 1978), 23.

"Even if a book on geography, say, was inspired from cover to cover and was literally dictated word-for-word [by God], it would not be "God-breathed" and "God-breathing" in the sense of 2 Timothy 3:16. Scripture is the word of God because the Holy Spirit testifies in it concerning Christ, because it has the Word-made-flesh as its matter and content."[26]

The confession that Scripture is the Word of God is not first of all concerned with the process of inspiration or an infallible result. Rather, it is concerned with the content: a cosmic story of redemption centered in Christ. This leads to its purpose: to bring us to faith in Christ so we might be faithfully shaped by that story. The purpose is integrally bound up with its content. Scripture is not a history of Israel, a biography of Jesus, a source for early church history, or a handbook on science. Moreover, it is not a book of theology, or ethics, or a devotional book of spiritual truths. All of these miss the point: the Scripture is the Word of God because therein the Spirit testifies to Christ as the center of kingdom history and the salvation he has revealed and accomplished. The Scripture's purpose and role in this story is to lead us to follow this Christ and embody his salvation.

But if our understanding of Scripture is to be shaped by the biblical story, we must also attend to the missional purpose of Scripture. Jesus opens the disciples' minds to understand the Scripture by giving them not only a messianic key but also a missional key (Luke 24:45–47). It is not only a story of God's redemption finding its fulfillment in Christ; it is also a story in which God has chosen a covenant people to be the means by which his salvation will reach all peoples; this finds its goal in the sending of God's gathered and renewed people to the ends of the earth.

Salvation is never simply a possession of God's people. Scripture records the unfolding of redemptive revelation as it is centered in the covenant. And the covenant always had a missional purpose: to bring God's redemptive work to all people, indeed all creation, through God's covenant people (Gen. 12:2–3; Exod. 19:3–6). Or, as Bavinck states with reference to Exodus 19:5–6, the purpose of redemptive revelation is to incorporate the nations into the covenant so they too might know God's salvation. "Israel did not receive this gracious privilege in order to spurn the nations and exalt itself above them, but rather to be a kingdom of priests who have a priestly task to carry out toward the nations, to bring them the knowledge of the service of God." God's people are always blessed to be a blessing. "This calling Israel can fulfill and will carry out only if it is itself a holy nation, if as a people it consecrates itself entirely

26. Herman Bavinck, *Reformed Dogmatics*, vol. 1, *Prolegomena* (Grand Rapids: Baker Academic, 2003), 443.

to the Lord, hears His voice, and walks in His covenant."[27] And so Scripture always shapes a people, leads them to salvation in Christ, not simply so they can enjoy its benefits, but also so they might be a channel of that salvation to those outside. At various points in the narrative, Scripture equips God's covenant people to take up their missional vocation amid the nations.

The various genres of Scripture show how the Bible functions as a tool in a variety of ways. Perhaps instead of speaking of Scripture as a tool, we might refer to it as a toolbox. It contains various tools to tackle many different jobs needed to shape God's people into a faithful covenant presence amid the nations. The historical books function as the memory of God's people, revealing God's unfolding covenant purpose, always with an eye to invite the readers into the story. The law shapes God's covenant people as a holy nation in their public, moral, and liturgical life on the basis of creation so that they might live amid the nations of the ancient Near East as a distinctive people. The prophetic literature calls God's people to covenant faithfulness in repentance and nourishes hope for the future through warnings and promises. The poetry ignites the imagination and enflames the emotions, drawing forth a covenantally faithful response—praise, lament, thanksgiving, commitment, wisdom, despair—in the many areas of human life, all reminding Israel of the horizon of the nations. Wisdom enabled Israel to understand the wise patterns of God's creation order and conform to them while offering insight into the deepest questions of human existence. The Gospels proclaim and witness to the good news that in Jesus Christ, God's kingdom purpose has come to its climactic moment. The Epistles work out the implications of the Christ event to equip the church to be a faithful presence amid their various contexts in the Roman Empire. The point is that God's redemptive revelation and the response of God's people to that revelation find literary form in the canon of Scripture.[28]

The various literary genres of Scripture again raise the question of the meaning of authority. The Scriptures are divinely authoritative, but what does it mean to say that historical narrative, poetry, wisdom, prophecy, or epistles are authoritative? Clearly the authority of these types of literature differs but must be closely tied to the way God uses them to shape his people for his kingdom purposes.

27. Bavinck, *Our Reasonable Faith*, 89.
28. Speech-act theory has been helpful in articulating the many ways Scripture functions instrumentally to form God's people. A judge who says, "I find the defendant guilty," does more than relay information. That very act of speaking may consign the person to life in prison. Words change things; they perform certain actions. When I say "I do" in a marriage ceremony, it binds me to my wife for life. Words do more than communicate propositional truths. In Scripture, different genres *do* different things.

The task that each of these genres and all of them together are trying to perform—sculpting a faithful covenant people for the sake of the world—is conclusively accomplished by Jesus. "The work which God had done through scripture in the Old Testament is done by Jesus in his public career, his death and resurrection, and his sending of the Spirit. Jesus thus does, climactically and decisively, what scripture had in a sense been trying to do: bring God's fresh Kingdom-order to God's people and thence to the world."[29] Each of these literary genres finds its fulfillment in the work of Jesus Christ.

The Spirit's Witness to Christ in the Scriptures

Above we quoted Bavinck as saying, "Scripture is the word of God because the Holy Spirit testifies in it concerning Christ."[30] In that statement we see that we can speak of the authority of Scripture only with reference to the Trinity. The Holy Spirit is the one who witnesses; Christ is the one to whom the Spirit witnesses; and the Father is the source of that witness. In the Gospel of John, Jesus promises the Holy Spirit, who will come from the Father to witness to Christ through the witness of the apostles (John 15:26–27; cf. 14:16; 16:13–15). Here a doctrine of Scripture is firmly planted in the soil of a trinitarian theology. The Spirit goes out from the Father to witness to Christ.

But the doctrine of Scripture must attend closely to the Spirit.[31] About the Spirit, Peter tells us that "prophecy never had its origin in the human will, but prophets, though human, spoke from God as they were carried along by the Holy Spirit" (2 Pet. 1:21 NIV). Here the word for "carried along" is the same one used in Acts 27:15, 17 to speak of a ship being driven along by the wind. Old Testament prophecy finds its origin in God as the Spirit carries along the human authors. In the Gospel of John, it is the Spirit who will witness to Jesus through the witness of the apostles (John 15:26–27). The Spirit's witness to Christ comes in both the prophetic and the apostolic witness.

Bavinck observes a threefold work of the Spirit in Scripture. Seeing the unity of the Spirit's work is immensely important for understanding what it means to hear God's address to his people in Scripture. "Scripture itself claims that it proceeded from the Spirit of God . . . [in] its origin, content, and power."[32] Scripture finds its *origin* in the work of the Spirit to witness

29. Wright, *Scripture and the Authority of God*, 42.
30. Bavinck, *Reformed Dogmatics*, 1:443.
31. On the Spirit and Scripture, compare the emphasis in John Calvin, *Institutes of the Christian Religion* 1.7, trans. Ford Lewis Battles, ed. John T. McNeill (Philadelphia: Westminster, 1960).
32. Bavinck, *Reformed Dogmatics*, 1:436.

to Christ and his salvation: "No prophecy of Scripture came about by the prophet's own interpretation of things. For prophecy never had its origin in the human will, but prophets, though human, spoke from God as they were carried along by the Holy Spirit" (2 Pet. 1:20–21 NIV). It is instructive to notice that true and false prophecy was distinguished by reference to its origin. False prophets "speak visions of their own minds, not from the mouth of the LORD" (Jer. 23:16). When the issue of Jesus's authority is raised, Jesus asks, "Did the baptism of John come from heaven, or was it of human origin?" (Matt. 21:25). The origin of Old Testament prophecy, Peter says, was not in the human will but "from God." This gives it divine authority. John Calvin makes the same point: "Hence the Scriptures obtain full authority among believers only when men regard them as having *sprung from heaven*, as if there the living words of God were heard."[33]

The *content* of Scripture is also a witness of the Spirit to Christ and his salvation. This is the intent of 2 Timothy 3:16, where Paul says, "All Scripture is God-breathed" (NIV). The Scriptures themselves are the very product of God's breath.[34] This is not a reference to the process by which the authors are inspired by God's Spirit, as is sometimes erroneously inferred when *theopneustos* is translated "inspiration." This was common in earlier translations dependent on the Vulgate and the King James Version. Rather, it refers to the Scriptures themselves as the very content of the Spirit's witness in written form.[35] Theological formulations like verbal inspiration have been used to express that everything is at stake with these words as we have them in Scripture. The terminology of plenary inspiration indicates that there is no part of Scripture that falls outside the Spirit's supervision. Scripture is the Word of God because in its very content, in the very words of Scripture, the Spirit testifies to Christ and his salvation.

And finally, it has ongoing *power* through history until today as the Spirit continues a living witness to Christ and his salvation through Scripture. Paul testifies to this, for example, when he speaks of the power of the gospel unto salvation (Rom. 1:16; 1 Cor. 1:18; 2:4–5). Calvin and Luther speak of Christ or the Spirit coming to us clothed in the words of Scripture.[36] Bavinck says that the Scriptures are God-breathed *and God-breathing*;[37] the Spirit's witness is not only contained in the words of Scripture but also continues as an

33. Calvin, *Institutes* 1.7.1, emphasis added.
34. Warfield, *Inspiration and Authority of the Bible*, 136, 151.
35. Ibid., 133; cf. 275, 286–91.
36. Martin Luther, in Karl Barth, *Church Dogmatics* (Peabody, MA: Hendrickson, 2010), I/2:484; Calvin, *Institutes* 2.9.3, 3.2.6.
37. Bavinck, *Reformed Dogmatics*, 1:385, 425, 596.

encounter with us today in those very words. The following diagram summarizes these three aspects of Scripture.

"Witness to Christ": Nature and Purpose of Scripture

The unity of the Spirit's witness is important for a theological reading of Scripture. We listen to what the Spirit is saying to the churches, knowing that the message we hear in Scripture finds its origin in the Spirit's witness to Christ, that the content we interpret is the Spirit's witness to Christ, and that the Spirit continues to witness to Christ through these human words. Hearing God's address today means listening to his original address through the words of the human author.

The All-Encompassing Authority of Scripture

We have insisted that the nature and purpose of Scripture is to witness to Christ and the kingdom salvation that he reveals and accomplishes. However, there is a potential misunderstanding that we must head off. Our claim may give the false impression that Scripture's focus is narrowed to so-called spiritual issues or religion in some narrow sense. But this would be a mistake.

Two problems produce this misunderstanding. The first is when the purpose of Scripture has been molded by a sacred-secular dichotomy. In particular, a Western cultural context has produced two problematic understandings of Scripture: Biblicism and dualism. Biblicism forces Scripture to speak directly to subject matters that it was never intended to address, whether those be historical or scientific questions or current political, economic, and social issues. Its mirror image is a dualism that reduces scriptural authority to so-called spiritual issues and leaves the rest untouched by its reach. To say that scriptural authority is bound up with its central theme of Christ and salvation is not to limit it to spiritual matters.

Closely related is the second: in the West we have a problematic understanding of religion. We have reduced religion to be one small component of human life among many, sitting alongside the rest as one more part. In this mistaken view, saying that the focus of Scripture is "religious" would restrict it to addressing one aspect of life that is concerned with things like God, the afterlife, religious observances, and so forth. This is not how Scripture views "religion," or for that matter is it the view of all the cultures throughout history and in the non-Western world today.[38] When we speak of religion, we are talking about a foundation on which all other aspects of life are built, or a root that gives life to all other dimensions of human life, or an orienting core that powerfully directs all human life either toward God or toward idols. Religion is a comprehensive directing power that shapes all human life, either toward the service of God or the service of a creational substitute, an idol.[39]

It would be safe to say that only modern, post-Enlightenment people could ever narrow Scripture's authority to some spiritual or so-called religious realm. No Old Testament or New Testament author could ever think this way. For them, Scripture speaks to all of life. It teaches us to see the whole of creation, all of history, and the full spectrum of human life *sub specie Dei* ("under the sight of God"). When Paul tells us, for example, that Scripture is "useful for teaching, rebuking, correcting and training in righteousness so that the servant of God [all God's people] may be thoroughly equipped for every good work" (2 Tim. 3:16–17 NIV), he does not dream of narrowing those good works. Scripture speaks to the whole spectrum of human life: cultural, social, political, economic, academic, and more. But it does so from its own radical and unique standpoint within the history of salvation, centered in the Christ who made all things, rules all things, and is reconciling all things.

The last sentence makes clear why the authority of Scripture cannot be reduced to some kind of spiritual realm. First, the biblical story encompasses all human life. We have argued (above) that this narrative of salvation is

38. Philip Jenkins asks what the "greatest change" that Christianity of the global south will bring to our Western understanding of God and the world. He answers that it is "likely to involve our Enlightenment-derived assumption that religion should be segregated into a separate sphere of life, distinct from everyday reality" (in his *The Next Christendom: The Coming of Global Christianity* [Oxford: Oxford University Press, 2002], 141).

39. Cf. Michael W. Goheen, *Introducing Christian Mission Today: Scripture, History and Issues* (Downers Grove, IL: InterVarsity, 2014), 317–20.

nothing less than a metanarrative, a worldview story, that offers an integrated and comprehensive perspective on the whole of life. If Scripture tells this kind of story, it simply cannot be limited to some spiritual component. Second, the Bible tells the story of salvation and how we can be incorporated into that salvation. If we misunderstand salvation as a spiritual and future escape from creation, then we might plausibly speak of the Bible as addressing spiritual issues. But such is not the case. Salvation is the restoration of the entire cosmos and the whole life of humankind (Matt. 19:28; Acts 3:21; Rom. 8:18–23; Eph. 1:10; Col. 1:20). Salvation is a restoration to live under the lordship of Christ, and there is not a square inch of human life, or a split second of temporal reality, that does not belong to Christ. To be equipped for every good work covers the spectrum of human life, which is all to be done "in the name of the Lord Jesus" (Col. 3:17) and "for the glory of God" (1 Cor. 10:31). And the final reason the Scriptures cannot be diminished to a spiritual authority is because of the Lord Christ, to whom it testifies. If Christ is simply a personal and spiritual Savior who snatches individuals away to heaven, then again we might be justified in speaking of some limited spiritual focus of Scripture. But again it is not so. Christ is Creator of all things, Lord of history, Reconciler of all things, and Judge of all humankind (Col. 1:15–20). The Lord Christ of Scripture has created human life, demands that every part of it conform to his word, is reconciling the whole of human life, and will judge the entirety of human life according to his will. It leads its hearers to a striking confession: "There is one God, the Father, from whom are all things and for whom we exist, and one Lord, Jesus Christ, through whom are all things and through whom we exist" (1 Cor. 8:6).

Thus to speak of Scripture as a story of salvation centered in Christ and the purpose of Scripture to lead us to salvation by faith in this Christ demands that we speak of the all-encompassing authority of Scripture. Nevertheless, it speaks from its own standpoint, the deepest and most comprehensive vantage point possible. The focus of Scripture is Christ, but from this center the light of the gospel beams forth onto the whole creation, illuminating all and every part. Ridderbos states this well in declaring that the authority of Scripture "is totalitarian in its scope, touching every area of human life and knowledge because the salvation of which it speaks is totalitarian. It has that scope, however, *in its own way*, that is, it illumines [hu]man and the world, history and the future, church and nation, the state and society, science and art from one standpoint, the standpoint of the coming, death, resurrection and return of Christ."[40]

---

40. Herman Ridderbos, *Redemptive History and the New Testament Scriptures*, 2nd rev. ed. (Phillipsburg, NJ: P&R, 1988), 58.

Scripture's Attributes and Purpose

The nature and purpose of Scripture is the Spirit's witness to Christ and his all-encompassing, creation-wide salvation. It is from this theological point of view that we must understand Scripture's authority, inspiration, and infallibility. Yet often these characteristics of Scripture have been sundered from the nature and purpose of Scripture, and this has had detrimental effects on our listening to God's address in the Bible.

The severing of Scripture's properties from its purpose has emerged in response to the rise of higher criticism. Critical approaches to Scripture shaped by the encroaching naturalism of Western culture have eroded faith and made it difficult for many to confess that Holy Scripture is the Word of God. To defend the divine authority of Scripture over against this alarming erosion that makes it a mere human document, many have sought to protect the Bible by stressing its authority, inspiration, infallibility, or inerrancy. These words do indeed rightfully protect the divine authority and trustworthiness of Scripture. And they say something very important about Scripture: this document is the Word of God, the very breath of the Spirit, and so is authoritative and reliable.

The motivation for confessing divine authority, inspiration, or infallibility, for example, is clear. If we are staking our lives on the message of Scripture, the question is urgent: Can we trust it for life and for death? Is it the Word of God? We know the weakness and fallibility of human beings. If God has taken fallible humanity into his service, we are right to inquire: Can fallible humans be trusted when the stakes are so high? Moreover, we have been shaken by the power of various criticisms of Scripture that arise from various places in our culture—from science, from higher criticism, from pluralism, and more. To confess the divine authority, inspiration, and infallibility of Scripture is to say, "Yes, we can trust the Bible in life and in death because it is God's Word and tells the truth. It speaks with divine authority. It does not err in its purpose to lead us to salvation in Christ."

Our confession is not simply produced by a desire for certainty. At many points and in many ways, Scripture itself leads us to confess that Scripture is the Word of God. The New Testament authors are unanimous in declaring the Old Testament to be God's Word: they introduce Scripture citations with "God says" or "the Holy Spirit says" (Acts 1:16; 2 Cor. 6:16); Scripture and God's Word are one and the same[41] (Rom. 9:15–16); when citing the Old Testament,

41. "Thus (we may say) God has *invested* himself in his words, or we could say that God has so *identified* himself with his words that whatever someone does to God's word (whether it is to obey or to disobey) they do directly to God himself" (Timothy Ward, *Words of Life: Scripture as the Living and Active Word of God* [Downers Grove, IL: IVP Academic, 2009], 27).

"It is written" introduces the final authority (1 Cor. 4:6; Acts 7:42; Matt. 4:4); the Old Testament contains the oracles of God (Rom. 3:2); the Old Testament is "God-breathed" (2 Tim. 3:16 NIV).[42] The apostles are chosen by God (Acts 10:41–42), commissioned by Jesus (Matt. 10:40), and equipped by the Spirit (John 15:26–27) to authoritatively witness to salvation in Christ.[43] Thus the New Testament writings that contain the apostolic witness are God's Word (1 Thess. 2:13) that has come to the apostles by revelation (Eph. 3:1–13), are binding (Heb. 2:2), and are the foundation for the church (Eph. 2:20).

Moreover, this divinely authoritative Word is reliable and trustworthy. The prophetic message is completely reliable, Peter says, and "you will do well to be attentive to it" (2 Pet. 1:19). Paul urges acceptance of the message that Jesus Christ came into the world to save sinners because it is a trustworthy saying (1 Tim. 1:15). Other theological words not found in the Bible have been used, such as "infallible" and "inerrant."[44] At this stage we will not stop to consider what language is best.[45] The point is that we can rely on God's Word, on the Spirit's testimony to Christ and his salvation, because it speaks the truth; it is utterly reliable and trustworthy. It does not err in its purpose to lead us to Christ.

Yet a problem surfaced in the twentieth century. In the admirable attempt to protect the authority and reliability of Scripture, these words became disconnected from the purpose and nature of the Scripture. Inerrancy, for example, was often defined more in terms of modern standards of precision. Questions of science and post-Enlightenment history writing set the agenda. The result is a separation of Scripture's ontological authority and its instrumental authority.[46]

Ontological authority refers to what the Bible *is*: it is the Word of God, divinely authoritative, inspired, and infallible. Instrumental authority refers to what the Bible *does*: it leads us to salvation by faith in Jesus Christ. The separation of these two leads to a situation where Scripture's characteristics are defined without reference to the purpose of Scripture. This becomes

---

42. Cf. John W. Wenham, *Christ and the Bible*, 3rd ed. (Eugene, OR: Wipf & Stock, 2009).

43. Ridderbos, *Redemptive History*, 12–30.

44. It might surprise some to learn that Warfield preferred the covenantal language of trustworthiness rather than inerrancy. Cf. Michael D. Williams, "The Church, a Pillar of Truth: B. B. Warfield's Church Doctrine of Inspiration," in *Did God Really Say? Affirming the Truthfulness and Trustworthiness of Scripture*, ed. David B. Garner (Phillipsburg, NJ: P&R, 2012), 23–49.

45. All these words have their advantages and disadvantages. In our judgment the best word should be judged both by consideration of Scripture's teaching, content, and purpose, on the one hand, as well as how these are understood in a particular context, on the other.

46. Donald Bloesch, *Holy Scripture: Revelation, Inspiration, and Interpretation* (Downers Grove, IL: InterVarsity, 1994), 133.

especially problematic when the Bible is under attack and one appeals to the divine authority of Scripture to speak to issues it was never meant to address. Moreover, in an age of science and historical precision, the temptation is to define infallibility and inerrancy by standards that are alien to Scripture.

In this matter Ridderbos is a sure-footed guide. He discusses the authority, inspiration, and infallibility of Scripture and then insists that "all attributes which Scripture ascribes to itself stand in close relation to its purpose and nature. And so our way of thinking about Scripture and our theological definitions must also be related to this purpose."[47] Ridderbos, like C. S. Lewis above, tells us that we can rightly judge something only when we know what it is, what it is intended to do, and how it is meant to be used. Our doctrine of Scripture must line up with its purpose. In a similar way, Bavinck insists that the nature and purpose of Scripture should guide the way we formulate our view of Scripture's authority and infallibility: "Scripture does not satisfy the demand for exact knowledge in the way we demand it in mathematics, astronomy, chemistry, etc. This is a standard that may not be applied to it. . . . Scripture has a criterion of its own, requires an interpretation of its own, and has a purpose and intention of its own. That intention is no other than [that] it should make us 'wise unto salvation.'"[48]

Properly reading Scripture to hear God's address requires us to recover a doctrine of Scripture where authority, inspiration, infallibility, reliability, and inerrancy are defined by the very nature and purpose of the book they purport to describe. Divine authority is found, not in its ability to speak to every issue infallibly, but in terms of its purpose to lead us to salvation in Christ. So these attributes must be defined precisely in terms of that particularly unique intention (2 Tim. 3:15–17; 1 Tim. 1:15).

Scripture as God's Word in Human Form

Sacra scriptura est verbum Dei. We have elaborated this confession in terms of the nature of Scripture as the Spirit's witness to Christ in its origin, content, and present power. We have also tied that closely to Scripture's purpose to lead us to faith in Christ so that we might more and more experience the all-encompassing salvation narrated in Scripture. This opens up the way forward to hearing the Bible as the Word of God to the church. But it is also clear that this divine address comes to us in human words: "Prophets, *though human,*

---

47. Ridderbos, *Studies in Scripture*, 22.
48. Bavinck, *Reformed Dogmatics*, 1:444.

spoke from God as they were carried along by the Holy Spirit" (2 Pet. 1:21 NIV, emphasis added).

The relationship between God's authority and human mediation has been the subject of much controversy throughout the church's history. At times the church has so stressed divine authority that the human character was diminished. Authors were regarded as passive receptacles for the oracles of God, and Scripture was leveled out to an assorted collection of divine truths. A good example of this is found in some post-Reformation theology. During this period, theologians rightly stressed divine authority and inspiration of Scripture. For some, however, it was at the expense of its human character. There are evidences of a dictation theory of inspiration in which the human authors were scribes, amanuenses, notaries, the hands and pens of God. Phrases like "the impulse to write" and the "suggestion of matters and words" diminished human agency. The fact that inspiration was considered to include standards of precision in details that even included vowels and accents made clear that the purpose and nature of Scripture had been obscured. Such dictation theories do not take seriously the nature and purpose of Scripture or do justice to its various genres. This formulation of divine authority will not enhance our capacity to hear God's address through the human witness to Christ.

When this happens, there is bound to be a reaction that shifts weight from the divine-authority side to its human character. Careful attention to Scripture immediately confronts the undeniable fact that the various books that make up its canon are firmly embedded in history; they are a wholly human product. Higher criticism arose in the nineteenth century and carefully analyzed Scripture according to its human dimensions. Of course, in itself this is correct: the various books of Scripture are human writings and are located within a certain historical and cultural setting. Yet problems developed in a twofold manner: on the one hand, the analysis of the Scripture proceeded on the basis of a naturalist worldview; on the other hand, this analysis lost sight of the purpose of Scripture to lead us to salvation in Christ.

It is this last issue that is especially important for this volume. Biblical scholars attended to the historical-cultural and the literary-aesthetic dimensions of the biblical text while blinkered to the fact that this is the way in which God addresses his people. Scripture tells the story of covenant history culminating in Christ, history in which God is the primary actor. This theocentric focus continues in the New Testament as it unfolds the implications of Christ for the church in the *kerygma*, *martyria*, and *didachē* of the New Testament. The main theme is God's redemptive work in history. Through this story the Spirit witnesses to God's work culminating in Christ and leads us into the salvation narrated in the story. Whoever misses this fails to grasp the very nature and purpose of Scripture! It is reductionist in the extreme to attend only to the human—the historical and literary aspects of the text—under the guise of scientific neutrality and to eclipse the theological or kerygmatic purpose of the text. Bavinck puts it well:

> Historical criticism has utterly forgotten this purpose of Scripture. It tries to produce a history of the people, religion, and literature of Israel and a priori confronts Scripture with demands it cannot fulfill. It runs into contradictions that cannot be resolved, endlessly sorts out sources and books, rearranges and reorders them, with only hopeless confusion as the end result. . . . That is not what the Holy Spirit had in mind.[49]

Naturalistic higher criticism has been the occasion for another pendulum swing in the twentieth century to fundamentalism, which puts weight again on the divine at the expense of the human. Like its post-Reformation predecessor, there is a rightful stress on divine authority. But it too remains caught up in a divine-human, supernatural-natural dichotomy that is utterly foreign to Scripture. It flattens out Scripture by reducing it to isolated fragments of truth, thereby misunderstanding the organic narrative unity of Scripture and the plethora of genres.

The terminology of organic inspiration is helpful in resolving this dilemma. It is an attempt to elaborate the confession of Scripture as the Word of God that comes to us in human form. Organic inspiration stands over against a dictation or mechanical theory of inspiration that does not take seriously the human form of Scripture. Organic inspiration means that the Spirit's witness has entered fully into the world of human creatureliness and found expression precisely in the limitations of a thoroughly human witness. Scripture is totally the work of the Spirit yet at the same time is totally the work of human authors in history. The Bible senses no tension whatsoever between the voice of God and the human witness through which it comes. It is only post-Enlightenment developments that have set these over against one another.

John makes precisely this connection between the witness of the Spirit in the human witness of the apostles. In the promise of Jesus, it is precisely because the Holy Spirit witnesses to Christ that the apostles must also bear witness to Christ. "When the Advocate comes, whom I will send to you from the Father, the Spirit of truth who comes from the Father, he will testify on my behalf. You also are to testify because you have been with me from the beginning" (John 15:26–27; cf. 14:26; 16:13–15).

49. Ibid.

If the witness of the Spirit to Christ comes to us through human authors, it means that God uses the authors of Scripture in the context of their setting. The theological notion of organic inspiration tries to capture and honor this human dimension. "The doctrine of organic inspiration maintains that God used these authors in their settings and environment with their knowledge, culture, cosmology, view of reality."[50] This means that to hear the address of God, we must pay attention to the historical and cultural setting of the Bible.

A Doctrine of Scripture and the Theological Interpretation of Scripture

Our theological reflection and doctrinal formulations on Scripture itself will play a role in shaping the way we read the Bible. This is because our doctrine of Scripture dictates the terms in which it can speak to us by telling us what it is and what it does. A truncated doctrine of Scripture will establish mistaken expectations and can cause one to approach the text with the wrong questions.[51] Then our ears will not be attuned to God's voice in Scripture.

The destructive power of radical higher criticism has certainly been significant. But the way conservative scholars have rightly sought to protect the Bible as the Word of God has sometimes led to a theology of Scripture that has not helped us. When Scripture is flattened out and reduced to isolated fragments of divine truth, our ears are not attuned to hear God's address. When the divine authority of Scripture is diminished, we will not listen for God's voice. When the human-servant form in which God's Word comes to us is slighted, it is more difficult to do the hermeneutical work necessary to hear God's speech in the ancient text. When inspiration, authority, and infallibility are separated from the nature and purpose of Scripture, it is harder to hear what God is saying.

If, however, we see the Scripture in terms of its organic narrative unity, as a story of God's mission to restore the whole creation and the entire life of humankind, which finds its fulfillment in Christ, we can hear God inviting us into this story to experience his salvation, in order to make it known to all peoples. If we carefully discern the various genres God uses to enable us

50. Bastiaan Van Elderen, "New Perspectives in Biblical Research," *Calvin Theological Journal* 1, no. 2 (1966): 174.

51. "All interpretation is shaped by the frameworks of belief which we bring to it; the hope is that the text—or rather, the Holy Spirit's opening up of the text—will enable us both to use and to transcend those frameworks with ever new insights into the truth of the gospel. . . . Certain things have been missed because the tradition of interpretation has not led us to expect them" (Colin E. Gunton, *Christ and Creation* [Grand Rapids: Eerdmans, 1992], 12).

to find our place in the story, then we are in a proper posture to listen. If we attend to the divine authority of the Bible, we will listen with a hermeneutic of trust and love so that we might joyfully submit to the voice of God. If we fully acknowledge the human form in which God's address comes, we will learn listening habits that attend to all the creaturely aspects of a text: words, grammar, syntax, history, culture, literature, and theology. If we keep the attributes of Scripture together with its nature and purpose, we will recognize that "what it is" serves "what it does."

This is not to confuse the address of God in Scripture and a doctrine of Scripture. God can speak through his Word in spite of our theological confusion—and thankfully he does! However, it remains true that the more our doctrine of Scripture conforms to what Scripture really is, the more we will be in a position to faithfully hear the voice of the living God in the words of the Bible.

3

The Ecclesia as Primary Context for the Reception of the Bible

ROBBY HOLT AND AUBREY SPEARS

> As the Servant speaks to us with God's word, his word becomes our word;
> he draws us into it beside himself; he makes us a community of the word.
>
> Oliver O'Donovan, *The Word in Small Boats*

Theological Interpretation and the Church

The primary context for the reception of the Bible as Scripture, as God's Word to God's people, is the community God has created through his Word, the gospel,[1] for God has spoken to be heard.[2] The church is the ultimate *context*

---

1. See Mark 4:3–20, 26–34; Acts 2:42; 4:4; 6:7; 8:4, 25; 12:24; 13:44–49; 15:7; 19:20; 28:22–31; Rom. 1:1–6, 16–17; 1 Cor. 1:1–4, 9, 21, 26–31; 7:17–24; 14:26–36; 2 Cor. 2:14–17; 4:1–6; Gal. 1:6–16; Eph. 3:7–11; 4:1–6; Phil. 1:3–6; Col. 1:3–8; 1 Thess. 1:2–10; 2:1–4, 13; 2 Thess. 2:13–15; James 1:16–18; 1 Pet. 1:3–25; 2 Pet. 1:3–4, 16–21; Rev. 1:9–20.

2. Given the canonical presentations in passages such as Exod. 20–24; Lev. 1:1 and parallels; Deuteronomy; and Isa. 55, it is no wonder that Paul refers to "the oracles of God" with which Israel has been "entrusted" (Rom. 3:2).

for this theological interpretation of Scripture because she is the body summoned to listen for her Groom's voice in Scripture. The regular, gathered, and ordered worship of the church is the primary ecclesial *event* when she listens for his voice. The Groom's proclamation, given through his called and gifted preachers, is the primary liturgical *act* whereby he addresses his bride.[3]

Theological interpretation of Scripture concerns itself with hearing God's address in the canonical Scriptures of the Old and New Testaments. Theological interpretation of Scripture means treating the Bible as God's chosen means of communication, God's own agent for mediating his presence and communicating his purposes. This chapter asserts that God not only has spoken to be heard, but also that *he creates his own audience with his word.* This audience is the church,[4] making it, with all its warts and bruises, the divinely chosen community for the theological interpretation of Scripture.

Hearing the Word of the Lord: The Audience God Calls

In keeping with his revealed plans to save the nations[5] and renew his creation through Christ,[6] God calls his church into existence through the proclamation of the gospel. The Scriptures reveal God's redemptive plans, including the role God has for God's church, within these plans (for a list of some examples, see Gen. 12:1–3; Isa. 42:1–9; 49; Matt. 28:18–20; Eph. 3:2–13; Col. 1:9–20).[7]

---

3. The idea that the risen and ascended Jesus addresses his people is very ancient. Compare the author of the Epistle to the Hebrews as he places Ps. 22:22 in the mouth of this Jesus: "For he who sanctifies and those who are sanctified are all of one, which is why he is not ashamed to call them his siblings, such as when he says, 'I will proclaim your name to my siblings; in the midst of the congregation I will sing your praise'" (Heb. 2:11–12). Although this chapter is about the ecclesial reception of Scripture, including the reception by believers in private (see below), the authors affirm that God speaks in other ways, such as in creation (Ps. 19), and that all people are accountable to God for his revelation (Rom. 1:18–32). The Scripture translations in the chapter are by the authors unless otherwise noted.

4. This chapter includes reflection on the central importance of individuals receiving the Scripture privately as well. On this and how it is connected to corporate reception of Scripture, see below.

5. Gen. 12:1–3; Isa. 42:1–9; 49:1–7; 56:3–8; Matt. 24:14; 28:18–20; Luke 24:44–48; Acts 1:6–8; Rom. 1:1–6; 15:8–21; 16:25–27; Eph. 3:2–13; Rev. 5:8–10. See (below) the excellent chaps. 7–8, "Biblical Theology and Theological Interpretation," by David J. H. Beldman and Jonathan Swales, and "Mission and Theological Interpretation," by Michael W. Goheen and Christopher J. H. Wright.

6. Isa. 55; Ps. 96; 98; Rom. 8:19–22; Col. 1:15–20; Rev. 5:13–14; 21:1–22:5.

7. Luke 24:44–49 teaches us to read all Scripture christologically and missionally. The message about Christ (24:25–27, 44–46) "is written." Who understands it? The servants whose minds Christ has opened. Further, "It is written . . . that repentance and forgiveness of sins should be proclaimed in his name to all nations" (24:46–47). So who will bear this missional message about Christ to every nation? The christological and missional "reading" of Scripture demands

The apostle Paul recognizes the church as God's people set apart by God's gracious and effective summons, God's new family placed together in Christ and in particular places. This is *reflected in the gratitude Paul so frequently offers to God* for the existence of the earliest churches. To "the church of the Thessalonians in God the Father and in the Lord Jesus Christ" (1 Thess. 1:1), Paul wrote, "we never stop thanking God, that when you [pl.] received God's word which you heard from us, you [pl.] accepted it, not as a human word, but as it truly is, the word of God, which is also at work among you [pl.] who believe" (1 Thess. 2:13).[8]

Paul begins nearly every ecclesial letter similarly.[9] Over and over, Paul thanks God that these churches have formed in response to God's gospel summons[10] and gives thanks for the kind of life they are sharing in Christ.[11] That Paul records this prayerful gratitude to God is more than epistolary convention. This gratitude reflects his insight into the gracious power of God's "call."[12] These communities *are communities* because they have already received the good news of God in Christ by faith when they responded to this call. Our reception-by-faith is a response to God's summons, which opens our ears. Listening while we wait for the promised, returning Son makes our reception of the Scriptures very much like the reception Paul seeks for his letter "the saints in Christ Jesus who [were] at Philippi" (Phil. 1:1). They, like us, share a

---

a people with minds opened by the living Christ. There can be no christological "readings" that fulfill the dominical thrust of Luke 24 apart from ecclesial receptions that hear and bear the received word.

8. Compare what Paul writes in 1 Thess. 1:2–10, especially verses 4–7 as well as significant parallels of expressed gratitude in the Prison Epistles (Eph. 1; Phil. 1; Col. 1; Philem.). We were tempted to use our English dialect of the South for translating these second-person plural pronouns as "y'all" since it could reflect distinctions between singular and plural second-person pronouns, as present in the Greek.

9. Rom. 1:8; cf. 6:7; 1 Cor. 1:4–9; Eph. 1:15–16; Phil. 1:3–8; Col. 1:3–8; 1 Thess. 1:2–10 (doubled in 2:9–13); 2 Thess. 1:3–4; Philem. 4–5.

10. Although Paul does not express his gratitude the same way in 2 Corinthians, he does reflect on the growing gratitude among the churches unto God's glory (4:11–15; 9:10–15), even reversing the frequent direction of prayer requested and thanksgiving offered. In 2 Corinthians Paul elicits prayer from the Corinthian church that many others would give thanks (1:3–11). The difference illustrates the same basic point: the proclaimed gospel, functioning as God's own summons, is creating fruitful communities overflowing with gratitude to the glory of God.

11. In 2 Corinthians and Ephesians, Paul expresses adoration where he frequently expresses gratitude, "Blessed is the God and Father . . ." The blessing in Eph. 1 is closer to the thanksgiving sections in the other letters and is still followed by expressions of gratitude and prayers.

12. The saints "faith in the Lord Jesus" (Eph. 1:15–16) is one of the reasons Paul gives thanks. The grateful prayer in Eph. 1 is the context for Paul's reflection on God's call in Eph. 1:18. The letter records Paul's prayer that they (corporately) may "know the hope" that is theirs due to "[God's] calling." For significant parallels, see Eph. 4:1; Rom. 1:7; 1 Cor. 1:2, 9.

new corporate life as a result of God's good work among them. We, like them, await the day when this gracious work is brought to completion (Phil. 1:6).

Hearing the Word of the Lord: The Audience Whom God Transforms

Once Paul thanks God for calling these churches into existence, he typically reports other specific content of his prayers.[13] Paul prays that their initial reception of the gospel will mature, that those who have listened will listen, together, all the more. For example, Paul reports praying that the church in Colossae would be "filled with the knowledge of God's will, in all wisdom and spiritual understanding" (Col. 1:9). This prayer for *corporate understanding* overlaps with his prayer for the church at Philippi, that their love "would abound more and more in knowledge and all insight" (Phil. 1:9) so that they might have greater ability to "discern" (1:10 NIV) better ways among the various options for living out their new fellowship with one another in and for Christ Jesus. He asks the Father to give the believers at Ephesus a "spirit of wisdom and revelation in the knowledge of him" (1:17), even though the eyes of their hearts have *already* been enlightened (1:18). So he wants them to grasp further, together, the good news they have already received by faith. Moreover, Paul wants them *together* to apprehend the *hope* that settles in because they have been called by God, the *riches* of being the saints he inherits, and the all-surpassing "power for us who believe," that is, the very power that was at work when the King was raised from the dead (Eph. 1:18–21). One wonders what sort of "knowledge" this might be! Paul regularly reports praying for a corporate, participatory apprehension of good news that results in renewed character, reordered affections, and new actions. The "implied reader" of these letters is *a community* of faith-reception, a community that Paul envisions as maturing together.

Thus Paul prayed that the Colossians would be "filled with the knowledge of God's will in all wisdom and spiritual insight" (Col. 1:9). Significantly, this petition for a wise and spiritually insightful grasp "of God's will" is sought that they might discover new patterns of life, "to walk worthy of the Lord," complete with new desires, "with every desire to please" the one who called them (cf. v. 10). Paul spells out what he means by adding that these new desires will bear fruit in "every good work." Drawing on the first canonical account of human flourishing under divine blessing (Gen. 1), the good works he seeks in prayer, which fit this new manner of life, are aimed at "bearing fruit and

13. For the sake of space, we will focus mostly on Paul's prayer in his Letter to the church in Colossae.

increasing in the knowledge of God" (Col. 1:10). Not only has Paul alluded to God's original purpose for the first image bearers (as he has already in v. 6);[14] he has also come full circle to maturing "knowledge" for this church in Colossae. Filled with *the knowledge of his will* (v. 9, emphasis added), this body will live out new desires in new actions that will bring about a fruitful *"knowledge of God"* (v. 10).

Significantly, our reception of the gospel matures according to a similar pattern. Paul gives thanks for the reception of the good news by the believers in Philippi (Phil. 1:3–8), then prays that they will be shaped by the gospel "more and more" until "the day of Christ Jesus" (Phil. 1:9–11).[15] We too live in between our initial reception of the gospel by faith and the return of our Savior. Because we live and worship in the hope of the same Day, we remain open to God's voice in the Scriptures to make our listening more and more fruitful as we mature. Our waiting is a waiting in hope for the things promised *in the Scriptures*, the very Scriptures meant to engender hope.

Hearing the Lord of the (Covenant) Word

One of the primary ways Paul expects the churches to mature into communities who hear God's address is to learn to hear his voice addressing *them* as his people *in the Scriptures of the Old Testament*.[16] As a minister of the new covenant (2 Cor. 3:6), serving those on whom the "ends of the ages have arrived" (1 Cor. 10:11), Paul wants the new-covenant churches to hear themselves addressed by God *in the Scriptures* of the older covenant.

He wants the Jewish *and* gentile church in Rome to know that the words about Abraham's faith from the first book of Scripture apply to them as believers in Christ Jesus. Citing Genesis 15:6, that "his faith was 'counted to him as righteousness'" (Rom. 4:3), Paul asserts that "the words 'it was counted to him,' were *not* written for his sake alone, but *for ours also*" (4:23–24, emphasis added). Thus "it will be reckoned to us" who trust the same God who made and kept the promises to Abraham and his descendants because Jesus was "delivered up

14. Gen. 1:26–28. This double allusion (Col. 1:6, 10, sometimes obscured by ignoring important word order in translation) helpfully guards us against another modernist error: dualism. The wisdom and spiritual insightfulness that Paul desires—rather than resulting in some antimaterialism, or spirit-matter dualism—is "fruited" in lives transformed by *redemptive* grace. God's original purposes for humanity inside God's good creation order are rediscovered and richly desired, even as the entire creation waits (Rom. 8:18–25).

15. See below for the discussion about how we share this horizon of reception.

16. In the Manifesto, see sections on "The Canon and Theological Interpretation," by Stephen G. Dempster and "The Telos (Goal) of Theological Interpretation," by Heath A. Thomas; see also chaps. 6 and 9 below.

for our trespasses and raised for our justification" (4:25). This is important to Paul since he is laying foundations to reconcile fractions inside the new community that the gospel has formed. Later he quotes Psalm 69:9, applies it to Christ, but then adds, "For whatever was written in former days was written *for our instruction*, that through endurance and through the encouragement of *the Scriptures* we might have hope" (Rom. 15:4, emphasis added).[17]

Similarly Paul wants God's largely gentile church in Corinth—"called," as they were "to be saints together with all those who call upon . . . Jesus . . . in every place" (1 Cor. 1:2)—to understand themselves as God's people in a particular sense: genuine heirs to Israel's story and therefore the living, embodied fulfillment of God's redemptive plans. Thus the Jewish Paul addresses the mostly gentile church in Corinth as follows:

> *our fathers* were all under the cloud, and all passed through the sea, and all were baptized into Moses in the cloud and in the sea, and all ate the same spiritual food, and all drank the same spiritual drink. For they drank from the spiritual Rock that followed them, and the Rock was Christ. . . . Now these things took place as *examples for us*, that we might not desire evil as they did. . . .
>
> [Then again] Now these things happened to them as an example, but *they were written down for our instruction*, on whom the ends of the ages has come.[18]

In this argument Paul tells them not to be idolatrous, not to "indulge in sexual immorality," and not to "put Christ to the test," in each case "as some of *them*" did. Quite remarkably, Paul's "us/them" contrast in 1 Corinthians 10 is neither cultural, national, nor even ethnic, but rather *temporal*. Paul, his Corinthian audience, and readers of this Manifesto together *share a redemptive historical horizon*: we live in that time when "the age to come" has *already* erupted (10:11; cf. Heb. 6:5). We also are those people "on whom the ends of the ages has come" for Jesus Christ has *fulfilled* the Scriptures (as central a claim to the New Testament witness as there is).

Eschatological Receptions

The church remains in this shared temporal horizon with Paul and *with the churches* that he addresses (narrates) as included in the fulfillment of God's election of Israel. Paul, along with the other apostles and prophets, submits

17. Compare Jesus's promises of a Comforter, Helper, Spirit of Truth, who will come to teach, guide, and declare truth to the disciples (John 14 and 16). Ultimately the Spirit will glorify Jesus the Christ.

18. From 1 Cor. 10:1–11, with emphasis added.

to, celebrates, and proclaims the way Jesus has fulfilled the role of Israel's Messiah, particularly in his death and resurrection. Like the Corinthians, each particular church throughout the age between the advents of Christ will face its own unique problems and struggles (not least the struggle to understand God's address in the Scriptures). But Paul would have us see our unique struggles in the same horizon he offers the Corinthians, which we share with them! Our struggles are lived between the two advents of our Savior. The struggle to grasp God's Word *together* is anchored in the scriptural witness to the decisive judgment that has already occurred in Christ Jesus and is aimed at the public unveiling of God's verdict when Christ returns. Between this anchor and the assured hope of that shoreline, as a community of reception we live in this stage of the drama of redemption, commissioned with the gift-task of theological interpretation. It is the privilege of the church to listen for God's address while we await the return of the Word. Our ecclesial reception of Scripture, then, is located inside the unfolding redemptive purposes of God. We have *received* the Scriptures after the inaugural events proclaimed in the apostolic gospel and before the Lord of the Word returns to consummate his good purposes.

Creation	Fall	Redemption Inaugurated by Jesus	Our Reception	Redemption Consummated by Jesus

One way to summarize this is to say that Paul reads the Scriptures ecclesially *because* he reads them christologically.[19] Those who believe in the long-promised Messiah of Israel are the present Israel-in-Christ by faith. Since he is the fulfillment of the Scriptures, those who believe in him claim their founding narratives in the stories about him (the Gospels) and the stories filled with the promises, shadows, types, ends, and laws concerning him (the Old Testament). Because the same Savior has summoned us into his kingdom, our faith in him marks us out as people with the privilege and duty to listen for his address in the Scriptures.

Drawn into the Mystery of Christ, Which Is Christ Himself

Paul's pastoral purpose for his churches is evident: he wants them to become like Christ, to be fully formed in him, their living Head.[20] This goal—which

19. In the Manifesto (see section on "Mission" and chap. 8 below), Goheen and Wright demonstrate that faithful ecclesial and christological interpretations are necessarily and fruitfully *missional*. Further, these acts of interpretation should not be played off against one another. The Lord's (Christology) church is his body for his mission.

20. For example, see Paul's desire for new communities to enter deeper into the mystery that is Christ (Col. 1:9–14; 2:1–7), Christ in them (Eph. 3:14–19; Col. 1:24–29), even Christ

he pursues with great struggle, energy, and power (Col. 1:28–29)—fits the whole narrative Paul sees as the story of the churches in Christ. For the good news revealed in the Scriptures centering on Jesus Christ, the Lord of the church, is the center of God's redemptive story concerning God's plan to renew all things.

Moreover, calling and shaping a people for himself to be like his Son is central to God's plans for all things (Rom. 5–8). Calling people into the church is central to his plan for the nations, to draw them to himself, as the church, in his Son (Matt. 28:18–20; Rom. 15–16; Eph. 1–3). This plan for the nations drawn to him in Christ as his living body, his renewed humanity, is central to his plan to renew his whole creation. Indeed, the whole creation groans for this very thing (Rom. 8:19–22, 28–30). God has called a people *for his purposes* through the gospel. Forming a people as the renewed-humanity body of the risen Christ is central to God's revealed purposes. The Scriptures reveal God's purposes for his creation, thwarted by human rebellion, but redeemed by God through his Son. The church consists of those who receive the proclamation of this news, as good news, before God's purposes are consummated, so that we might embody this reconciling message as gracious, renewing power to all people (2 Cor. 5) and the whole creation (Col. 1:15–20).

Hence the Scriptures that Paul reads ecclesially he also and necessarily reads *missionally*—*because* he reads them christologically. Jesus Christ is the head of the church, whose mission is articulated scripturally. The church is his body for God's mission.

The church is the body created by God's summons for God's purposes. Our theological interpretation is anchored in God's saving work and oriented toward the consummation of God's redemptive plan. Inside this church oriented toward God's purposes are individual believers with unique gifts and callings, believers who each contribute to the church and its role to bear witness to God's work in God's world.

Personal Reception of the Bible

Thus the God who addresses his people primarily on a corporate basis also addresses each of us personally. These experiences are related because, individually, all of us are "members of the body of Christ" (1 Cor. 12:12). In the words of Dietrich Bonhoeffer, "Wherever one member happens to be, whatever one member happens to do, it always takes place 'within the body,' within

---

in them in their surprising ethnic distance from those who were looking for a Messiah (Eph. 2:11–3:13).

the church-community, 'in Christ.' Life as a whole is taken up 'into Christ.'"[21] Whether God's address to his people through Scripture occurs in the regular, gathered, and ordered worship or in private Bible reading, the context is always ecclesial, even though not always corporate. And yet the relationship between these two engagements with Scripture needs to be explored.

Deuteronomy 6:4–9 is a good point of entry into the discussion.[22] Verse 4 is a straightforward vocative addressing Israel, "Hear, O Israel!" followed by an identification of Israel's God.[23] Verse 5 identifies the appropriate response to, and consequence of, the declaration of Yahweh's identity: the people of Israel must give him their unreserved love, exclusive faithfulness, and total allegiance.[24] In order to give Yahweh such devotion, verses 6–9 insist that Israel must engage in "concrete practices and symbols as part of regular daily life."[25] Herein lies the relationship of attending to God's address in the liturgy and in private Bible reading. The Shema begins with, and prioritizes the reception of, God's address by the gathered community, but in order for life in its entirety to be focused on God, the hearing of God's address must extend to the home, to public and private life, to one's rising and lying down. For God's "words" (Deut. 6:6) to penetrate to "the innermost core of our being from which life springs forth,"[26] the liturgical reception of the Word is primary, yet private reading complements it.[27] Receiving the Scripture in the context of one's private life is necessary for God's Word to have its intended transformative effect. This is true for several reasons.

The Bible is a big book, and the church's reading of the Bible presupposes a narrative unity.[28] In a coherent story, the meaning and function of any par-

21. Dietrich Bonhoeffer, *Discipleship*, trans. Barbara Green and Reinhard Krauss, Dietrich Bonhoeffer Works 4 (Minneapolis: Fortress, 2001), 234.

22. I (Aubrey) was alerted to the relationship of this passage to the topic at hand by Craig G. Bartholomew, *Introducing Biblical Hermeneutics: A Comprehensive Framework for Hearing God in Scripture* (Grand Rapids: Baker Academic, 2015), especially chap. 2, pp. 17–47.

23. The literature is vast regarding the translation of this notoriously difficult phrase. See, e.g., J. G. McConville, *Deuteronomy*, Apollos Old Testament Commentary (Downers Grove, IL: InterVarsity, 2002), 140; R. W. L. Moberly, *Old Testament Theology: Reading the Hebrew Bible as Christian Scripture* (Grand Rapids: Baker Academic, 2013), 9–24; Daniel Block, "How Many Is God? An Investigation into the Meaning of Deuteronomy 6:4–5," in *How I Love Your Torah, O LORD! Studies in the Book of Deuteronomy* (Eugene, OR: Cascade, 2011), 73–97.

24. For this way of interpreting Deut. 6:5, see Moberly, *Old Testament Theology*, 18–26.

25. Ibid., 26.

26. Bartholomew, *Introducing Biblical Hermeneutics*, 38.

27. "In the liturgy the Word is living and active *maximally* though not *exclusively*" (Mariano Magrassi, *Praying the Bible: An Introduction to Lectio Divina* [Collegeville, MN: Liturgical Press, 1998], 4).

28. Obviously, not all Scripture is of the narrative genre. On the one hand, some of the books that are generically narrative sometimes "contain nonnarrative material with the narrative context

ticular passage is shaped by its location within the larger plot.[29] Most Christians today experience regular, gathered, and ordered worship on Sunday. One reading from the Bible, as in many of the free churches—or even four or more readings, as in churches that utilize one of the several lectionaries—is not enough to gain sufficient knowledge of the large, capacious narrative of Scripture. Breadth, however, is not the only issue. In the vast ocean of Scripture, each passage contains an ocean's depth.[30] Extending the reception of Scripture beyond the liturgy into private devotions enables one to discover more and more of its inexhaustible riches. And yet the private reading of Scripture must push past knowledge acquisition to shape transformation. As we saw, the goal of hearing God's address in Scripture, in terms of Deuteronomy 6:4–9, is for our own deep inner transformation into people who love God completely. And of course we, the listeners, need this deep transformation![31] We are thoroughly disoriented and disintegrated by original sin, indwelling sin, our actual sins and broken patterns, the effects of being sinned against, and by the patterns and powers of the present age. Reading the Bible in private extends and deepens and prepares one for hearing the Bible in regular, gathered, and ordered worship. But exactly how does one go about reading the Bible in private so that the deepest parts of one's soul are open to the God who is living and present in his Word?[32]

(e.g., law in Exodus–Deuteronomy)." On the other hand, "some books contain no narrative material at all." And yet, "the story Scripture tells, from creation to new creation, is the unifying element that holds" all of the generically varying material of the Bible "in an intelligible whole" (Richard Bauckham, "Reading Scripture as a Coherent Story," in *The Art of Reading Scripture*, ed. Ellen F. Davis and Richard B. Hays [Grand Rapids: Eerdmans, 2003], 39). See the Manifesto's section on "Biblical Theology," by David J. H. Beldman and Jonathan Swales, and chap. 7 below. See also Craig G. Bartholomew, Mary Healy, Karl Möller, and Robin Parry, eds., *Out of Egypt: Biblical Theology and Biblical Interpretation*, Scripture and Hermeneutics Series 5 (Grand Rapids: Zondervan, 2004).

29. As the disciples on the road to Emmaus learn, it must be the correct plot. For more on the relationship of the part to the whole, see the Manifesto's section on "Canon," by Stephen G. Dempster, and chap. 6 below.

30. In the words of Augustine, "O Wondrous depth of your words, whose surface presents itself to us and pleases us like children, and yet what wondrous depth, my God, what wondrous depth! It makes one shudder to look into it—a shuddering of awe, but also a trembling of love!" (*Confessions* 12.14.17). Depth not only requires breadth; it also requires repeated readings of the same passage. "Robert Penn Warren once said that the most natural reading of a poem occurs not on the first or the tenth but on the hundredth reading" (Peter Leithart, *Deep Exegesis: The Mystery of Reading Scripture* (Waco: Baylor University Press, 2009], 119).

31. See the Manifesto's section on "Telos (Goal)," by Heath A. Thomas, and chap. 9 below.

32. Not every tradition uses the same vocabulary of spirituality. For example, a traditionally Reformed answer to the question at hand would include faith and repentance, both graces. Reformed spirituality emphasizes engagement with God in Scripture and prayer as among other ordinary means of grace. Thus since God graciously renews us, these means are used by

The French philosopher Jean-Louis Chrétien offers a fecund metaphor:

> Children play with a conch, holding its shell to their ear so as to hear, or imagine
> they hear, the endless roar of the sea. But we, by contrast, can really hear the
> voice of the Bridegroom in person by taking into our hands all those conch
> shells that are the verses of the Bible, those conch-shell words that the powerful
> waves of eternity have heaved about and left on the shores of time where we
> are—and on the sands of inconsistency that are ours when we do not listen.[33]

Here we are alerted not only to the nature of Scripture, as the place in
which God addresses his people, but also to the mode of receiving God's
address through Scripture. Like the child with the conch, we must place our
ear to Scripture and *listen*.

Two Modes of Scriptural Engagement

Before exploring the practice of privately listening for God's address in Scripture, we must first see that this is not the only necessary mode of engagement
with Scripture. In *For Self-Examination*, as Søren Kierkegaard explores the
metaphor of the mirror of Scripture from James 1:22–27, he distinguishes
between looking at a mirror and seeing oneself in a mirror.[34] The former is
more akin to the posture of analysis appropriate to the study of Scripture,
and especially embodied in academic biblical studies and theology: looking
intently at the Bible through historical, critical, philological study. The latter
is closer to the posture of listening: it involves listening intently for God's
address. To develop the distinction, Kierkegaard employs his own metaphor:
a lover receiving a letter from his beloved. If "this letter was written in a language that the lover does not understand, and there is no one around who can
translate it for him," he will take a dictionary and "spell his way through the
letter, look[ing] up every word in order to obtain a translation."[35] There is

---

faith. Since faith here is active, a disciplined commitment to use the means that God graciously
promised to bless with his transforming presence, there is no real conflict with entering into
disciplines by faith. Thus a traditionally Reformed spirituality is not incompatible with concrete
acts of faith and "repentance unto life"; see below in this chapter. The emphasis is on moving
from grace to grace by faith.

33. Jean-Louis Chrétien, *Under the Gaze of the Bible*, trans. John Marson Dunaway, Perspectives in Continental Philosophy (New York: Fordham University Press, 2015), 59–60.

34. Søren Kierkegaard, *For Self-Examination; Judge for Yourself!*, ed. and trans. with introduction and notes by Howard V. Hong and Edna H. Hong (Princeton: Princeton University
Press, 1990), 25–35.

35. Ibid., 26.

much here to unpack, and some of the ways Kierkegaard develops these analogies are problematic,[36] nevertheless two basic insights should be highlighted.

First, while analysis and listening are two different dispositions toward Scripture, both are necessary.[37] As with the lover's work of translating, the last several centuries of academic analysis of Scripture have produced many enduring philological and historical insights. A word of caution is in order here. No one can remain wholly apart from the object of their analysis. The world is no object, something set over against the human subject. Neutrality, in this sense, is a myth. We cannot get outside of the world in order to stand against it. We are subjects inside a reality that cannot be fully objectified. In this sense, reality encompasses both subject and object, constituting humanity as much as humanity constitutes reality. We "are inextricably beings-in-the world who precede the subject-object split."[38] True objectivity, therefore, depends on relating the methods of analysis appropriately to the nature of the inquiry and to the object of interpretation.[39] Unfortunately, ours is a culture in which analysis is often "a cover for simple hostility, or belligerent practices" increasingly incapable of honoring the otherness of the other.[40] Approaching the Bible objectively as an artifact to be studied will distort the Bible if one assumes a "hermeneutic of suspicion, detachment, and *Sachkritik*" that "reduces the divine address to an object for an analysis as if from an Archimedean point outside, by staking a pseudoempirical claim to objectivity."[41] In this case, analysis becomes a kind of "blind barbarism contrary to communication and underlain by a violence 'that does not want to hear anything but itself.'"[42] There is no such thing as a noncommitted academic study of the Bible. As John Paul II wrote, the various approaches to biblical study and analysis "each have their own philosophical underpinnings, which need to be carefully evaluated before they are applied to the sacred texts."[43]

36. See, e.g., Chrétien's critique in *Under the Gaze of the Bible*, 32–34.

37. For the taxonomy of "analysis" and "listening," I (Aubrey) am indebted to Bartholomew, *Introducing Biblical Hermeneutics*, 18–25.

38. Dan Stiver, *Theology after Ricoeur: New Directions in Hermeneutical Theology* (Louisville: Westminster John Knox, 2001), 38.

39. Cf. Rudolph Bultmann's insistence that objectivity can only mean "a knowledge appropriate to the subject" (Rudolph Bultmann, *Essays Philosophical and Theological* [London: SCM, 1955], 255).

40. Gemma Fiumara, *The Other Side of Language: A Philosophy of Listening* (New York: Routledge, 1990), 109.

41. Markus Bockmuehl, *Seeing the Word: Refocusing New Testament Studies*, Studies in Theological Interpretation (Grand Rapids: Baker Academic, 2006), 92.

42. Fiumara, *Other Side of Language*, 111–12; citing Karl Jaspers, *La mia filosofia* (Turin: Einuaudi, 1981), 239.

43. John Paul II, *Faith and Reason: Encyclical Letter* (London: Catholic Truth Society, 1998), 85.

The second insight to highlight is that while listening and analysis are distinct, they exist in an integral relationship, with listening as the primary orientation. The posture of analysis has produced many great benefits in the fields of biblical studies and theology,[44] and yet, as Paul Ricoeur declares, "Beyond the desert of criticism, we wish to be called again."[45] Looking *at* the mirror is different from looking *in* the mirror. But translating the love letter is important for its reading. Much work needs to be done to show how analysis can ultimately be oriented toward God's address in Scripture. Unfortunately, Kierkegaard conceives of scholarly reading as strictly preliminary and thus concedes a strict segregation of the two approaches. In doing so, he allows each to reserve his or her own territory, with the result that the two produce types of readings that, in the words of Chrétien, "fall outside each other and do not communicate, or hardly so; the practitioners of each regard one another with a mutual scorn. . . . Not for a moment does he envision the possibility that Bible reading could be both scholarly and prayerful (that is to say, attentive also, with a different mode of attention)."[46]

Much more work needs to be done to show the role of prayer and being present to God in analysis. After all, the nature of Scripture as God's address to us determines listening as the fundamental mode of receiving Scripture. Building on the work of Gemma Fiumara, Bartholomew opens up this relationship by highlighting our need "to distinguish an approach which is predominantly one of receptive listening [to God's address in Scripture]—which will include analysis—and the predominantly analytical approach of biblical studies, which nevertheless should be rooted and sustained in listening" to God's address in Scripture.[47]

The Difficulty of Listening

A central goal of attending to God's Word is for his Word to be "internalized, integrated, and incorporated in one's very being."[48] And yet, in the words of Mariano Magrassi, Scripture does not "sink immediately into the deeper

---

44. See the Manifesto's section on "Theological Interpretation and Historical Criticism," by Murray Rae, and chap. 4 below. See also Craig G. Bartholomew, C. Stephen Evans, Mary Healy, and Murray Rae, eds., *"Behind" the Text: History and Biblical Interpretation*, Scripture and Hermeneutics Series 4 (Grand Rapids: Zondervan, 2003).

45. Paul Ricoeur, *The Symbolism of Evil*, trans. Emerson Buchanan (Boston: Beacon, 1967), 349.

46. Chrétien, *Under the Gaze of the Bible*, 33.

47. Bartholomew, *Introducing Biblical Hermeneutics*, 22.

48. Block, *How I Love Your Torah*, 87.

part of human life and become a vital part of each one's inner world. Vital hearing requires loving, calm, reflective, personal poring over the text."[49] Various Christian traditions have developed different ways for individuals to practice private Bible reading. Five examples are inductive Bible study, the evangelical quiet time, the Anglican daily offices, the Ignatian meditation, and the monastic *lectio divina*. With each of these approaches, a key issue must be to approach the Bible with a posture of receptive listening. But "what if," Eugene Peterson perceptively asks, "the reader never arrives at listening?"[50]

The failure to listen is a distinct possibility. The proliferation of data in a culture that has exchanged biological time, with its limits and rhythms, for technological time, which has lost all rhythmical flow and erased all boundaries—this welter of data creates a ubiquitous din of words, resulting in widespread benumbment. "Uninterrupted speech deafens" us and "becomes the hum of insignificance."[51] This is partly because listening seems to be "a worthless concern until we are capable of considering as a whole the myriad of subtly opposing accounts that culture constantly produces."[52] But it is not merely a function of technology.[53] As Gemma Fiumara points out, "In the tradition of western thought we are . . . faced with a system of knowledge that tends to ignore listening processes."[54] As the generations pass, those who have "not been sufficiently listened to . . . [become incapable] of listening vigilantly to our resounding culture, but only of becoming its victim."[55] In such a culture, recovering the posture of listening requires attention to silence.

49. Magrassi, *Praying the Bible*, 6.
50. Eugene Peterson, *Working the Angles: The Shape of Pastoral Integrity* (Grand Rapids: Eerdmans, 1987), 89.
51. Jean-Louis Chrétien, *The Ark of Speech*, trans. Andrew Brown (New York: Routledge, 2004), 39.
52. Fiumara, *Other Side of Language*, 113.
53. In this regard, Jacques Ellul has done important work on the issues surrounding technology, as in *The Technological Society* (New York: Knopf, 1964). Also see the works by Willem H. Vanderburg: *Our War on Ourselves: Rethinking Science, Technology, and Economic Growth* (Toronto: University of Toronto Press, 2012); *Living in the Labyrinth of Technology* (Toronto: University of Toronto Press, 2005); and *Perspectives on Our Age: Jacques Ellul Speaks on His Life and Work*, 2nd ed. (Toronto: University of Toronto Press, 2000). Also see George Grant, *Technology and Justice* (Concord, ON: Anansi, 1986).
54. Fiumara, *Other Side of Language*, 1. Along these lines, Peterson partly blames an educational system that habituates our reading as an act of analysis (*Working the Angles*, 93–96). Fiumara describes higher education in the West as "focused upon the development of those linguistic skills associated with great contractual value in a logocentric-logocratic society, and thus intent upon discrediting the values of listening in the most drastic manner: by not even noticing their existence" (*Other Side of Language*, 67).
55. Fiumara, *Other Side of Language*, 82.

The Role of Silence in Listening for God's Address

In Ecclesiastes, Qohelet warns those who approach the temple of God's transcendence; those who draw near to the temple must "draw near to listen" (Eccles. 5:1). In his lectures on preaching, Karl Barth says similarly of Scripture: "The fact of the Canon tells us simply that the church has regarded these Scriptures as the place where we can expect to hear the voice of God."[56] Then he presses the observation into the realm of private Bible reading (for one particular type of reader): "The proper attitude of preachers [depends] . . . on whether or not they expect God to speak to them here."[57] Whether in the regular, gathered, ordered worship of the church or in private Bible reading, the appropriate approach is to listen, and listening begins in silence, not only because of the nature of God but also because of the nature of listening.

Kierkegaard ends his advice on reading the Bible well by commending silence as the starting point. "The first thing, the unconditional condition, . . . the very first thing that must be done is: create silence, bring about silence; God's Word cannot be heard . . . in the hullabaloo. . . . Create silence!"[58] In offering himself to us, God calls us to silence: "Be still, and know that I am God!" (Ps. 46:10).[59] But there are different types of silence. Listening silence is not a matter of momentarily turning our attention to God, but of bringing our whole selves before God, quieting our inner chatter. Such a fruitful, hospitable silence is the proper comportment for reading Scripture so that one's innermost being is open to God's address.

Since 1999, the Irish Jesuits have produced an aid to private Scripture reading titled *Sacred Space*.[60] Especially helpful are the spiritual attitude of trust and the posture of listening for Christ to speak to the reader in his Word.[61]

---

56. Karl Barth, *Homiletics*, trans. Geoffrey W. Bromiley and Donald E. Daniels (Louisville: Westminster John Knox, 1991), 78.

57. Chrétien extends the observation into private Scripture reading: "Belonging to the canon signifies and prescribes that it is for you too that God speaks in this text" (*Under the Gaze of the Bible*, 15).

58. Kierkegaard, *For Self-Examination*, 47.

59. See also Hab. 2:20.

60. They produce a book for each year, e.g., Irish Jesuits, *Sacred Space: The Prayer Book 2014* (Notre Dame, IN: Ave Maria, 2013). They also post their work online: www.sacredspace .ie. Some of the material is so distinctly Catholic that evangelicals may not be able to follow along, but typically this is not so.

61. For the role of trust in hermeneutics, see especially Hans-Georg Gadamer, *Truth and Method*, trans. Joel Weinsheimer and Donald G. Marshall, 2nd rev. ed. (New York: Continuum, 2003); George Steiner, *Real Presence* (Chicago: University of Chicago Press, 1989), 146–65; idem, *After Babel: Aspects of Language and Translation*, 3rd ed. (Oxford: Oxford University Press, 1998), 312–19. For the role of trust in hermeneutics applied specifically to interpreting the Bible, see Bartholomew, *Introducing Biblical Hermeneutics*, 25–33; Richard B. Hays, "A Hermeneutic

We must quiet ourselves, gathering our body, imagination, mind, and heart in order to offer ourselves to God as a temple of listening silence. This is the suspense of speech identified in Ecclesiastes 5:1–3, an eloquent silence that becomes the palace of encounter. It is not an amnesiac or stupid silence; "it is a question of mobilizing my knowledge and my experience, and making them fluid and lively, so that they will serve the attention instead of replacing it."[62] Attentive silence requires effort and patience—repeated, imaginative, vigilant attentiveness! Offering to God the hospitality of listening is not a matter of giving God "the pitiful offering of an instant of our attention" but of relinquishing our arrogance, inclining toward God, offering to him our whole being. "If not, nothing new will have taken place; I will have heard nothing but the incessant murmur of my own idle chatter."[63]

Following a pattern of praying in stages, *Sacred Space* is a disciplined entry into listening, fruitful silence. In the first stage, the listener grows still and quiet, remembering that God is present and waiting for the listener. The *Sacred Space* guide instructs that for the listener: "God always arrives before me, desiring to connect with me even more than my most intimate friend."[64] The listener then greets God, opening oneself to him. In the second stage, the listener asks for God's grace to make one free of one's own preoccupations so that the listener can be open to God's address. The third stage is typically some version of the Ignatian Examen: in the presence of God, one reviews the last twenty-four hours, acknowledging how the listener is really feeling, giving God thanks for his grace, and asking forgiveness for sins.[65] In the fourth

---

of Trust," in *The Conversion of the Imagination: Paul as Interpreter of Israel's Scripture* (Grand Rapids: Eerdmans, 2005), 190–201; Bockmuehl, *Seeing the Word*, 68–74; and Peter Stuhlmacher, *Historical Criticism and Theological Interpretation of Scripture* (Philadelphia: Fortress, 1977).

62. Chrétien, *Ark of Speech*, 15.

63. Chrétien, *Under the Gaze of the Bible*, 10. Ps. 131 offers just such an approach to God. In verse 1, the psalmist declares that his posture before God is one of humility, as shown by what he does *not* do: "O LORD, my heart is not lifted up; my eyes are not raised too high; I do not occupy myself with things too great and too marvelous for me." In verse 2, his humble posture before God is instantiated in the act of quieting himself: "But I have calmed and quieted my soul, like a weaned child with its mother; like a weaned child is my soul within me." Hence silencing oneself is, from a theological perspective, a manifestation of creaturely humility. As Gabriel Marcel states, "At the root of humility lies the more or less unexpressed assertion, 'By myself, I am nothing and I can do nothing except in so far as I am not only helped but promoted in my being by Him who is everything and is all-powerful'" (*The Mystery of Being*, vol. 2, *Faith and Reality* [South Bend, IN: St. Augustine's Press, 2001], 85–86; cited in Bartholomew, *Introducing Biblical Hermeneutics*, 22). Chrétien makes a similar point about the posture of listening: "It is not a matter of assuming a passive attitude, a kind of reading 'quietism,' but of a lively patience and the active self-discipline that consists of relinquishing our arrogance" (*Under the Gaze of the Bible*, x).

64. Irish Jesuits, *Sacred Space*, 330.

65. This is the Ignatian Examen.

stage, the listener reads Scripture in the ancient tradition of *lectio divina*, also known as *lectio sacra*.[66]

Lectio Divina, the Arc/Ark of Silence

At the heart of *lectio divina* is the belief that it is in and through Scripture that Jesus Christ lovingly comes to us and speaks to us. In the words of Martin Luther, "Holy Scripture is the garment which our Lord Christ has put on and in which He lets Himself be seen and found."[67] The essence of *lectio divina* is found in both the Old and the New Testaments,[68] and the church fathers frequently mention it, but Guigo II, prior of Grande Chartreuse in the twelfth century, was the first to systematize the practice of it.[69] He identifies four phases: *lectio, meditatio, oratio,* and *contemplatio.*

Having entered into a fruitful silence, as the reader turns to Scripture, he or she lovingly welcomes the bridegroom: the Christ.[70] The starting point, *lectio,* is a slow, unhurried, disciplined, fully engaged reading of the Scripture.[71] When we approach the Bible to analyze it, we are in charge, looking for information that we can use. This is the way we read an owner's manual and an encyclopedia. When we approach the Bible to listen for God's address, we submit to his authority, remembering everything we have been told, anticipating where the words might lead us, letting God's address use the reader—this is the way we read a poem or a novel or a letter from a beloved one.[72] Such a reading requires rhythm and patience.[73] As Bernard of Clairvaux put it, "The thirsty soul eagerly

66. Magrassi's *Praying the Bible* is a masterful exploration of practice. For a Protestant perspective on *lectio divina*, see Eugene Peterson, *Eat This Book: A Conversation in the Art of Spiritual Reading* (Grand Rapids: Eerdmans, 2006). For an Orthodox perspective on the practice, see John Breck, *Scripture in Tradition: The Bible and Its Interpretation in the Orthodox Church* (Crestwood, NY: St. Vladimir's Seminary Press, 2001), 67–86.

67. Quoted by Karl Barth, *Church Dogmatics* (Edinburgh: T&T Clark, 1936), I/2:208.

68. See, e.g., the comment by Markus Bockmuehl regarding the presupposition of *lectio divina* in his discussion of the implied reader of the New Testament, in *Seeing the Word,* 73.

69. Guigo II, "The Ladder from Earth to Heaven," trans. Jeremy Holmes, *Letter and Spirit* 2 (2006): 175–88.

70. "It is not so much a matter of reading a book as of seeking Someone" (Magrassi, *Praying the Bible,* 52).

71. Application is always already in operation. See Aubrey Spears, *The Theological Hermeneutics of Homiletical Application and Ecclesiastes 7:23–29* (Eugene, OR: Pickwick, forthcoming); as PhD diss., University of Liverpool, 2006.

72. This is the way Eugene Peterson delineates synchronic reading and diachronic reading in *The Jesus Way: A Conversation on the Ways That Jesus Is the Way* (Grand Rapids: Eerdmans, 2007), 65. I find this language and description to be appropriate also to delineate analysis and listening.

73. Cf. Ludwig Wittgenstein's comment, "Sometimes a sentence can be understood only if it is read at the right tempo. . . . My sentences are all supposed to be read slowly. . . . I really

prolongs its contact with Scripture, certain to find there the One for whom it thirsts."[74] In our culture of haste, busyness, and boredom, the capacity for slow reading must be recovered. Such a reading naturally leads into *meditatio*.

This second stage of *lectio divina* is a matter of taking the text into the reader's heart (*meditatio*). Peter Leithart commends God's Word as "sweeter than honey in the honeycomb. His words are the kisses of His mouth, which are better than wine. Immerse yourself in the word, bathe in it, drown in it, drink it until the room starts spinning."[75] It may be the recognition of a direct verbal parallel, a phrase, a theme, or even a mood that suddenly or gradually strikes the reader in a way that leads him or her into the world of the Bible.[76] Jean Leclercq describes how medieval monks, by constantly praying or chanting Scripture, over time, became "a sort of living concordance, a living library, in the sense that the latter implies the Bible."[77] Because the overall story the Bible tells is the unifying element that holds all the snippets of the Bible together, every passage of Scripture depends for its meaning on things that right there are left unsaid.[78] When *lectio* blossoms into an indwelling of the Scripture, one ceases to be a tourist and instead is an inhabitant, roaming freely within the world of the Bible.[79] Such meditation naturally leads to *oratio*, prayer.

In this context, reading, ruminating, and listening are actions that naturally provoke prayer.[80] When prayer spontaneously arises, the soul is leaving "its reading to run to God."[81] Prayer is a reaction to God's presence, to God's

want my copious punctuation marks to slow down the speed of reading. Because I should like to be read slowly (as I myself read)" (*Culture and Value*, trans. P. Winch, ed. G. V. von Wright in collaboration with H. Nyman [Oxford: Basil Blackwell, 1988], 57; cited in Fiumara, *Other Side of Language*, 134).

74. Quoted in Magrassi, *Praying the Bible*, 55.

75. Peter Leithart, "Exhortation for October 5" (2003), www.leithart.com/archives/000157 .php.

76. For an exploration of the significance of intertextuality in terms of echoes, see Richard B. Hays, *Echoes Scripture in the Letters of Paul* (New Haven: Yale University Press, 1989).

77. Jean Leclercq, *The Love of Learning and the Desire for God: A Study of Monastic Culture*, trans. Catharine Misrahi (New York: Fordham University Press, 1961), 77.

78. See Leithart, "The Text Is a Joke: Intertextuality," in *Deep Exegesis*, 109–39.

79. Peter Leithart describes how the patristic commentators "read and copied Scripture; they heard it read; they chanted the Psalms and many had the Psalter memorized; they ate, drank, and breathed Scripture. And as a result, any single Scripture was not a single Scripture but brought a dozen other Scriptures immediately to mind" (*Deep Exegesis*, 138).

80. It would be a mistake to conceive of *lectio divina* as a technique. The four phases are not methodical steps. Eugene Peterson helpfully describes each phase as "calling forth another and then receding to give place to another, none in isolation from the others but thrown together in a kind of playful folk dance. . . . Each of the elements must be taken seriously; none of the elements may be eliminated; none of the elements can be practiced in isolation from the others. In the actual practice of *lectio divina* the four elements fuse, interpenetrate" (*Eat This Book*, 91).

81. Magrassi, *Praying the Bible*, 113.

address. "Behold, I stand at the door and knock. If anyone hears my voice and opens the door, I will come in to him and eat with him, and he with me" (Rev. 3:20). God is seeking us more than we are seeking him. Having been found by Jesus, we offer him "a free outpouring of our soul which has been touched by some of the words it has heard."[82] Scripture and prayer are deeply united. "Having filled those words with all our thought, our love and our life, we repeat to God what he has said to us. The Word is not only the center of our listening; it is also the center of our response."[83]

The summit of the entire process is *contemplatio*, communion with God. *Lectio divina* is an arc/ark of silence. The beginning silence is what Chrétien calls artistic silence: a silence acquired through containing and disciplining the inner noise so that something else can manifest itself. The final silence is what Chrétien describes as mystic silence: our speech is dumbfounded in the encounter with Christ.[84] *Lectio* begins in the silence of hospitality and ends in "a nuptial silence, the silence in which the Beloved and his lover encounter each other in intimacy. . . . Such a silence is at once final and initial: final, because it is the goal of mystical life and constitutes the highest union with God; initial, since it is a sign of future blessedness."[85]

Lectio divina rests on the presupposition that, in the words of Godfrey of Admont, "Sacred Scripture is the breast of Jesus."[86] What a beautiful and true image! When we turn our attention to Scripture, we are like John at the Last Supper, laying our head on the bosom of Christ.

Ideal Listener(s)

God in his grace has "dug ears" for us, his people.[87] Since we are called by grace to listen, the Scriptures sketch pictures of ideal disciples, ideal interpreters.[88] One such sketch is found in Isaiah 50 because the Scriptures present,

82. Ibid., 114.
83. Ibid., 113.
84. Chrétien, *Ark of Speech*, 47.
85. Ibid., 74. "The Hospitality of Silence" is the title of Chrétien's remarkable chapter on silence in *Ark of Speech*, 39–75.
86. Quoted in Magrassi, *Praying the Bible*, 55.
87. Ps. 40:6b, "Ears you have dug for me" (literally). What a crushing metaphor! Where ears should be found, "there is only a smooth, impenetrable surface, granitic bone. God speaks. No response." What a gracious metaphor! "God gets a pick shovel and digs through the cranial granite, opening a passage that will give access to the interior depths, into the mind and heart" (Peterson, *Working the Angles*, 101).
88. Psalms 1 and 119 are obvious examples, along with many of Jesus's parables about true listening.

at the center of the story, an ideal disciple. "The Lord GOD has opened" this disciple's "ear" (v. 5). Morning by morning, his ears are awakened to learn among those who learn. So this ideal disciple has learned to trust Yahweh even in the worst of times, even under severe trial, temptation, and persecution. But having heard his word, this disciple has become the ideal servant, who knows how to sustain the weary with good news. More than that, the theme of the ideal servant-disciple has been fulfilled by the central character of the whole scriptural story. Unlike the first Adam or the original Israel, he is "not rebellious." Rather, he has "set" his "face like flint," offering himself fully to fulfill God's redemptive purposes (see Isa. 50:4–9 for this servant song). Through a centrally significant allusion, Luke infers that the costly devotion of this ideal disciple is the hinge of the whole biblical story.[89] Jesus fulfills the role of Messiah by assuming the life of a genuine disciple (Luke 2:39–52), an obedient son (v. 51), even "the" obedient "Son of God" (Luke 3:1–4:13).[90] As a true disciple and obedient son, he becomes a true teacher (Luke 4:14–22:38) and finally completes his obedience as a suffering servant, fulfilling his own word (Luke 22:39–23:56).[91] Thus all God's promises find their "Yes" and their "Amen" in this Messiah (Luke 24; 2 Cor. 1:18–20). Hence this is good news for every one of his disciples. The life *we* owe God has already been offered to God by Jesus Christ (Luke 22:14–20; 24:44). Now we come to God in worship, fellowship, Scripture, and prayer in and through him (Luke 24:50–53). Now we bear witness to him and his mission, recognizing and hearing him in all of the Scriptures (Luke 24:44–49). Now we are being transformed with ever-increasing glory into his image (2 Cor. 3:18). When Christ returns, "we will be like him, for we will see him as he is" (1 John 3:2). If we listen to his voice, we will not be surprised to see the Master, even in his glorious return, "dress himself for service" (Luke 12:37)![92] Thus we will be renewed according to the image in which we were created (Eph. 4:21–24; Col. 3:9–10). God's plan

89. Thus an allusion to Isa. 50:7 is the structural hinge of his Gospel. Jesus fulfills the role of Messiah by becoming a servant, climactically "setting his face to go to Jerusalem" (Luke 9:51).

90. Luke places his genealogy from Jesus all the way back to Adam, "the son of God," between his narrations of Jesus's baptism and temptation, highlighting a contrast between the first Adam, who rebelled against God in a sumptuous garden, and this Spirit-led Son, who obeyed the Father in a barren wilderness.

91. That Jesus is the true Teacher who obeys the Word crashes powerfully together in Luke 22:37: "I tell you that this Scripture must be fulfilled in me [quoting another Servant Song, in this instance from Isa. 53:12] 'And he was numbered with the transgressors.' For what is written about me has its fulfillment."

92. To move his first disciples to faithful service, Jesus tells them a parable about a returning master (Luke 12:35–40). Because Jesus has first listened to the One who has awakened and opened his ear, and because he obeys him even unto death, he is able to sustain others with a gracious word. The faithful service that he has left to his first disciples, his apostles, is to feed

includes a multinational people, adopted as his children, all becoming like
the Son (Rom. 8:14–17, 29), the Chief Servant (Mark 10:45; Luke 12:37; John
13:1–20), so that the whole creation may obtain the freedom that will result
from the adopted children's glory (Rom. 8:18–25). For when the stewards are
renewed by grace, in this new word of grace we hear an old privilege "to serve
and care" for the rest of God's good creation (Gen. 2:15). Having become
God's new temple in the Spirit (Eph. 2:18–20), we are God's new garden, made
alive in Christ to "bear fruit and increase" just as the gospel "bears fruit and
increases" in us (cf. Col. 1:6, 10). Grace renews nature.

Interpreted by God in Christ: What the Spirit Says to the Churches

We are all interpreters-in-relationship. Given the glory and goodness of the
One who addresses us in Scripture, listening rather than speaking is at the heart
of theological interpretation. When we listen for God's address in Scripture,
when we do the hard and humble work required of all interpreters, all people
in relationship,[93] what we hear is that *we* ourselves *have been interpreted*!
Since God has acted in Christ to draw a people to himself, for his purposes,
and since God addresses us in Scripture, one of the goals of his listeners is
to submit to the otherness of this Other-Who-Speaks. When we, the church,
do this, both corporately and privately, we discover in the Other's voice that
(1) we bear his image and have good work to do as his royal stewards. When
we hear his address, we hear him (2) call out our rebellion and describe its
heinous ripple effects into every part of our persons, our individual and corporate lives, our relationships, his world and all our work in it. When we hear
his voice we hear (3) his promises concerning us and his good world. And by
his grace, when we stop and listen, we hear (4) his verdict pronounced over
us in Christ. We hear him tell us that we are chosen, brought to life, washed,
justified, forgiven, set apart, set free, redeemed, reclaimed, adopted, made
new, fed, served, unified, sent, and empowered. When we listen, we hear, for
his glory and the sake of his world, that we are (5) destined for glory. God in
his grace addresses us with good, sobering, and restorative news about our
identity and purpose.

---

his other servants appropriately. So disciples who feed other disciples must first *listen* and then
speak *the gospel they hear.*

93. Because we are describing a corporate and personal posture rather than a theory, we are
enabled to borrow wisdom from any theory or method that helps us listen and respond well,
including all the help from friends and "enemies" in the academy or elsewhere. Indeed, the God
who speaks fills his world and his image-bearing creatures with such graces that, knowing him,
we are predisposed to expect and humbly accept help from surprising voices.

A genuine hearing of these words tells us that we have been loved by the one who "gave himself up for" us (Eph. 5:25) and told us so in his own Word (5:26; cf. 4:20–21). A genuine hearing tells us that Love will have his way with us. He will ensure that we enter into eternal consummation with him in the shameless beauty of purity and glory (5:27). And love is the clue to the present mystery concerning our hope to be carried from past grace to future glory. We are nourished and cherished in the present by the One who loves us (5:28–29). When Christ, the Word, is present to us in the reading and preaching of the Word, he is feeding us like a wise husband who serves his own wife, like a wise person who takes care of his own flesh. This mystery overwhelms any similitude and accepts that this is indeed what Christ is doing for us, his own "flesh" (5:30–32). Thus we are loved, and this love, communicated in the Spirit, makes us increasingly receptive to this Holy Other. Hearing begets hearing in a communion of faithful Love (1 Cor. 2:6–13; Song 2:10–13).

Thus our ecclesially located interpretation of Scripture, taking its place in between Christ's inauguration and the consummation of God's kingdom,[94] is a listening ordered and oriented by faith, hope, and love. But more than that, according to his promise, we are the body of Christ, addressed by her living Lord. We are the community formed by the gospel, with a destiny to be formed into Christ (Col. 1:28–3:4). This corporate through-the-ages engagement with God in Scripture has its own place in God's economy of redemption. While the church corporate is helped by many sources and conversations, by the grace of God it must humbly submit to this calling to bear a role in God's economy: bearing good news as a people addressed by God. Given this immeasurable gift-task, we rest our hopes in our living Head, being united to him by faith. With him as our promise-fulfilling Savior, the whole Scripture story, his story, becomes our story. He now lives his life in us through the Spirit, by whom we are sealed into union with him. His invitation to us, if we listen, is to be nourished as dearly loved and so be transformed with ever-increasing glory.

---

94. Compare the wonder of the canonical presentation concerning the Pentateuch: Exod. 19:1–23:33; 24:1–18; 31:18; Lev. 1:1–2a; Num. 6:22–27; Deut. 4:9–14; 5:1–6; 6:3–5. Genesis narrates God addressing Abraham, Isaac, Jacob, and others. But according to the canonical presentation as "written by Moses," those stories are presented as Scriptures *written for* the people Israel redeemed from Egypt. There is no written Scripture until there is a redeemed community, called out of Egypt by God's power and according to God's promises to the patriarchs, to receive it. What happened to the patriarchs was written down for "the generation" living in between the exodus from Egypt and entrance into the land of promise. Thus a pattern is established. God's Word as Scripture comes to his people, called out of bondage and waiting for a promised inheritance, just as we observed in Rom. 4:22–25 and 1 Cor. 10:1–11, where such things were written down for the sake of those living between the "exodus" Jesus achieved and his return to usher us into his—and our—inheritance.

4

Theological Interpretation and Historical Criticism

MURRAY RAE

Introduction

One of the defining features of the theological interpretation of Scripture is a commitment shared by its proponents to read Scripture from within the conceptual world of the text itself. Theological interpreters share with the biblical authors the conviction, variously articulated in Scripture, that the world is created by God and is the terrain upon which God is bringing about his particular purposes. The Bible, as it is canonically arranged, begins with an explicit articulation of the conviction that the world is created by God: "In the beginning . . . God created the heavens and the earth" (Gen. 1:1). The canonical arrangement by which the world's creation by God is affirmed at the outset establishes the context in which to understand the story then told and explored through Scripture's diverse collection of texts. The Old Testament affirms and the New Testament witness to Jesus Christ confirms that the world, its character, and its telos are established and preserved by divine intention and will be brought to fulfillment at the last through the divine Word and Spirit.

These are theological affirmations about the nature of history. They entail, to begin with, that history has a purpose. As many have stated, history is not merely "one damn thing after another." Nor is it an endless circularity, leading nowhere and signifying nothing. According to the biblical understanding of things, history is the space and time given by God for the working out of his purposes in covenant communion with his creatures. As expressed in the Manifesto, history is God's project. "In the terrain of space and time, given as a dwelling place for God's creatures, God seeks to bring about his purpose of drawing all things into reconciliation with himself (2 Cor. 5:19)." Throughout Scripture, the biblical authors variously extend and develop an account of how and to what end God is at work in the world. The account includes, to be sure, interpretive glosses and embellishments that are unlikely to correspond in every detail to things that were actually said and done, but these embellishments are subordinate to the purpose of providing "an orderly account of the events that have been fulfilled among us" (Luke 1:1). They serve the author's purpose of making clear to those who have ears to hear the significance of all that has taken place. Far from treating such embellishments as false testimony, therefore, as has been the common practice of historical criticism, we may instead accept the insight they give into what is really going on and thus count them as legitimate parts of the historical record. If it would be demonstrated, for instance, that the "I am" sayings attributed to Jesus in John's Gospel are a Johannine embellishment, that need not undermine their value as historical testimony so long as they shed light on who Jesus really is. John's rendering of the events that have been fulfilled among us, including his interpretive judgments, may be said to tell the truth about what has gone on in history.

The Bible in its rich variety is both a record and an instrument of God's formative work with his people through the course of human history. The detail of this formative work may be found on every page of the Bible, yet certain features of the biblical story, referred to again and again, are especially revealing of God's purpose. These include, for example, the call and the promise given to Abraham through which Israel is appointed as witness to God's intention that all the families of the earth should be blessed (Gen. 12:3). They include God's deliverance of his people from bondage in Egypt; the giving of the law to Moses; experiments with kingship; Israel's exile and return; the promise of a Messiah and true king who will bring God's purposes to completion; the coming of Jesus, his life, death, resurrection, and ascension; and the pouring out of the Spirit, through whom the church is equipped to continue the work of witness and service to the world and is drawn still closer into God's presence. They include as well the promise and the prayer that God's kingdom will one day be fulfilled, on earth as it is in heaven. These are key coordinates in the biblical account of history. Taken together and supplemented by the detail of Scripture as a whole, they constitute a framework within which the whole of history is to be understood. It is within this conceptual framework, furthermore, that theological interpretation of Scripture proceeds.

Before proceeding further to develop this account of history and to consider the role of historical inquiry in theological interpretation of Scripture, it is worth pausing to acknowledge that these affirmations about the nature and purpose of history are claims of faith. They are distinguished from other accounts of what history is, however, not by their fiduciary character but by their content. There is no place from which to determine, independently, as it were, that a theological historiography is more or less legitimate than a secular, Marxist, or idealist historiography, for instance. Every historiography, and more broadly, every view of what life is all about, involves a commitment of faith made by its proponents that cannot be definitively proved but is nevertheless sustained by a constant, and often subconscious, evaluation of its explanatory power. This point will be important as we consider further below the role that historical inquiry may play in the understanding of Scripture.

History Matters

A striking feature of the biblical witness is that God is identified again and again through reference to historical events. God is the one "who brought you out of the land of Egypt," "who spoke through the prophets," "who raised Jesus from the dead," and so on. The Bible does not present us with a set of timeless or universal truths that can be abstracted from history but directs our attention to the God who makes himself known precisely through the particularities of history. On the face of it, therefore, attention to what goes on in history is an imperative of biblical faith. The gnostic tendency to denigrate history and the docetic impulse to shield the transcendent and eternal God from exposure to the vagaries and perils of historical existence—these are, in biblical terms, rightly judged to be heretical. Although, as A. K. M. Adam has shown, Ernst Käsemann's proposal to overcome docetism through the rigorous application of historical-critical method was mistaken, Käsemann was undoubtedly correct in recognizing that docetic denials of the significance of history do indeed pose a threat to the faithful reading of Scripture.[1] The

---

1. See Ernst Käsemann, "Vom theologischen Recht historisch-kritischer Exegese," in *Zeitschrift für Theologie und Kirche* 64, no. 3 (1967): 259–81 (281). Adam's critique of Käse-

God of the Bible is the God who makes himself known through the history of Israel and whose being and action come into sharpest focus through the particular historical figure of Jesus of Nazareth. Contemporary with Käsemann, Wolfhart Pannenberg's efforts to develop a Christology "from below" precisely so as to avoid divorcing the Christ of Christian proclamation from the historical reality of Jesus himself were likewise prompted by a sound theological insight about God's involvement in history, but they faltered on the assumption that divine action may be discerned through naturalistic modes of inquiry.[2]

Despite the biblical imperative, quite properly insisted on by Käsemann and Pannenberg, to be attentive to God's action in history, it will be argued in what follows that the historical-critical method is incapable of discerning where and how God is at work in the world and that it is unable, therefore, to facilitate a faithful reading of biblical texts. This is so, first, because adherence to the standard canons of historical inquiry renders a historical-critical method incapable of reading Scripture on its own terms and of hearing through Scripture the Word of God; second, because the biblical account of the divine economy requires us to rethink what history is; and third, because God is wholly Other, which is to say that God's being and action cannot be detected through the same methods of inquiry that we use to investigate created realities.

The Canons of Historical Inquiry

It has long been an axiom of Western academic culture that scholarly accounts of what goes on in the world have no use for "the God hypothesis."[3] This exclusion of God is often called metaphysical naturalism. As Brad Gregory explains, metaphysical naturalism is the view "that for science to be science, by definition it can pursue, identify, and entertain only natural causes as plausible explanations of natural phenomena, with the universe as a whole

---

mann's proposal can be found in chap. 2 of A. K. M. Adam, *Faithful Interpretation: Reading the Bible in a Postmodern World* (Minneapolis: Fortress, 2006).

2. See Wolfhart Pannenberg, *Jesus—God and Man* (London: SCM Press, 1968).

3. The story is frequently told of a meeting between Napoleon Bonaparte and the French mathematician and astronomer Pierre-Simon Laplace at which Laplace presented a copy of his latest astronomical work to the emperor. It is alleged that when Napoleon asked Laplace why there was no mention of God in his account of how the planets move, Laplace responded, "I have no need of that hypothesis." Reliable accounts of the meeting suggest that Laplace was not proposing the complete exclusion of God from involvement in the operations of the world, but was simply rejecting a Newtonian appeal to divine intervention to correct a particular irregularity in the operations of the solar system; yet it seems likely that Laplace was committed to the sufficiency of naturalistic explanations of reality as a whole.

regarded as if it were a closed system of natural causes."[4] Metaphysical, or ontological, naturalism denies either the existence of God or the action of God in the material universe; it is sometimes distinguished from methodological naturalism.[5] Methodological naturalism holds that while God may exist and may be involved in what goes on in the world, neither the empirical sciences nor the standard methods of historical inquiry can appeal to divine agency as an explanatory category in describing what happens in the world. A physicist pursuing the study of the material world does not have the competence, qua physicist, to determine whether God is involved in the operations of the cosmos. Likewise, a historian operating according to the usual conventions of historical inquiry lacks the competence to determine whether God is involved in history. The methodological naturalist, it is claimed, may be a theist, but the provision of theistic explanations for what goes on in the world lies beyond the competence of scientists acting as scientists or of historians acting as historians. For the sake of scientific endeavor and responsible historical inquiry, the world must be *regarded* as if it were a closed system of natural causes. The metaphysical naturalist, by contrast, insists that theistic explanations have no place in any account of what goes on in the world because the world we live in simply is a closed system of natural causes. God is not involved and so cannot be appealed to in any account of what happens. It is important to be clear that this is a statement of the metaphysical naturalist's own belief about the world. That belief has no scientific basis and can never be proved by the methods that science has available to it. It is a mistake, therefore, to assume that metaphysical naturalism is somehow entailed by "a scientific view of the world."

In an essay introducing a recent volume in which a range of New Testament scholars try to apply the methods of historical inquiry to the exploration of key events in the life of Jesus, Robert L. Webb provides a thorough account of contemporary historiography and sets out three possible approaches. The naturalistic approach, Webb explains, "rejects descriptions and explanations that involve divine causation, because cause and effect within the space-time universe is understood to operate within a closed continuum."[6] Clearly the application of such an approach to the reading of Scripture will require the reader to reject the accounts given by the biblical authors themselves about

4. Brad Gregory, "No Room for God? History, Science, Metaphysics, and the Study of Religion," *History and Theory* 47 (December 2008): 506.

5. A very clear account of this distinction is offered by Robert L. Webb in his essay "The Historical Enterprise and Historical Jesus Research," in *Key Events in the Life of the Historical Jesus*, ed. Darrell L. Bock and Robert L. Webb (Grand Rapids: Eerdmans, 2010), 9–93.

6. Ibid., 40.

what has gone on in history. That decision will be made in advance of any engagement with the texts. It is entailed by the reader's nontheistic view of the world, which precludes that person from reading Scripture on its own terms.

Webb then describes a critical theistic approach. While "not necessarily accepting all claims of divine intervention in descriptions and explanations of events," a critical theistic approach is prepared to use divine intervention as an explanatory category in the description of historical events.[7] Comparing the two approaches, Webb correctly observes:

> The difference between these two poles is not merely a difference of how historical method is understood, but it is, in reality, a difference in ontological worldviews. A naturalistic approach may be . . . associated with a worldview that understands the physical space-time universe to constitute the totality of reality. Whereas a theistic approach, particularly associated with the western religious heritage, arises out of a worldview in which reality includes not only the physical space-time universe but also a supra-mundane, supernatural world that can and does interact with humans in the physical, space-time universe.[8]

Noting that the worldviews undergirding these two approaches are contradictory, Webb proceeds to outline a third approach, which tries to find common ground between the two. Proponents of the naturalistic and of the theistic approaches agree, Webb observes, that reality includes the physical space-time universe and that causal relations operating in the natural and the human worlds can be observed within that universe. Webb then proposes that historical inquiry is concerned simply with the causal relations obtaining in the human realm. "History focuses its inquiry," he says, "on human actions in specific events in the past."[9] An implication of these two principles is that "by definition history is quite focused in this narrow and specific manner."[10] Here the term "history" refers, not to all that has happened in the past, but to the enterprise of investigating the past and formulating narrative accounts that represent, partially and provisionally, what has gone on. This definitional limitation of history to the investigation of human action in the past provides a justification, Webb contends, for the third approach. "This latter view we would call 'methodological naturalistic history'—in other words, for the purposes of doing historical work, the historian is methodologically limited

7. Ibid.
8. Ibid.
9. Ibid., 41.
10. Ibid., 42.

to causation within the physical, space-time universe, but this does not limit the historian's personal ontological worldview, just her/his historical method as a historian."[11] Webb explains one of the advantages of this third approach over the naturalistic and theistic approaches:

> The ontological naturalistic and the critical theistic views of history permit their distinct ontological worldviews to define the type of causation used in historical explanations, whereas the methodological naturalistic view of history attempts to mediate between these two by understanding history as description and explanation of cause and effect of human events within the natural sphere alone, without making ontological claims beyond the natural sphere.[12]

Theological Interpretation and Historical Inquiry

Webb's account of the three historiographical approaches is admirably clear and instructive, providing us with a sound basis on which to consider the relation between historical-critical method and theological interpretation of Scripture. It should be recognized, first of all, that while Webb allows for a theistic approach to history, the study of history in the Western academy is dominated by naturalistic approaches. Within biblical studies too, scholars have commonly felt obliged to function according to one or another of these naturalistic approaches. Some proponents of the ontological naturalistic approach insist that all other approaches should be excluded from the academy, while a good number of Christian biblical scholars have taken refuge in methodological naturalism, mistakenly supposing it to be both academically neutral and devoid of any problematic consequences for their study of the Bible. I suggest, however, that naturalistic approaches of either kind are seriously damaging to our reading and appreciation of Scripture and are inimical, therefore, to truly theological interpretation. The principal reason for this is that naturalistic approaches, whether ontological or methodological, preclude the historian from engaging with the subject matter of the Bible, which is precisely the engagement of God with his creation through the course of human history. The Bible tells of the divine economy. It makes no sense, therefore, to suppose that we can study the Bible well by setting aside the category of divine agency.

Webb explains that when investigating biblical claims about what has gone on in history, the methodological naturalistic historian applies critical faculties to the ancient text's account.

11. Ibid.
12. Ibid., 45.

And just like the other two historians, this historian may make the same types of judgments: reject the text's claim altogether, or provide an alternate natural explanation. If, however, no natural explanation can be found, and yet the evidence for the event itself is strong, then this historian can only lay out what they see as the evidence and their evaluation of it, and then say that they have gone as far as they can go as a historian using historical method. For this historian, the argumentation and evidence for "supernatural" causation, because it is of a different order by its very nature, should be understood within the sphere and discipline of theology, which has its own distinct forms of argumentation and evidence.[13]

For the term "historian" used in this passage, we may substitute "biblical scholar," for it is the work of the historical-critical biblical scholar that Webb is concerned with here. This highlights two difficulties with the historical-critical method as it has commonly been applied in biblical studies during the past two centuries. First, the historical-critical biblical scholar operating under the conditions of naturalistic inquiry falters precisely at the point where the Bible makes its most important claims, namely, its claims about where God is at work in the world. Such a scholar is bound to investigate the Bible as if God is not active in history.

A second difficulty with Webb's portrayal of naturalism, however, is that biblical scholars, very often, have not stopped at the point beyond which naturalistic inquiry cannot go, but have proceeded to offer accounts of the biblical subject matter entirely within categories of immanence. The various quests for the historical Jesus—including, recently, the portraits of Jesus that have emerged from the Jesus Seminar—are the most telling cases in point. There is no need to report in any detail here the proliferation of portraits of Jesus that leave God aside yet suppose themselves to be telling the truth about who Jesus is, or was. The problematic nature of these portraits is captured well by Donald Hagner, one of the contributors to the volume to which Webb's chapter serves as an introduction, who observes: "'The quest of the historical Jesus' is a misnomer. It is not a search that can bring us the real Jesus, . . . but rather a search that provides what necessarily and finally must remain an artificial construct. The fact remains that the historical method, strictly practiced, . . . is ill-equipped to deal with the uniqueness represented by the story of Jesus."[14]

13. Ibid., 47.
14. Donald Hagner, "Jesus and the Synoptic Sabbath Controversies," in *Key Events in the Life of the Historical Jesus*, ed. Darrell L. Bock and Robert L. Webb (Grand Rapids: Eerdmans, 2010), 254.

Sarah Coakley likewise observes that the historical approach "*shrinks* what can be said of Jesus to what secular historians regard as appropriate to their task and duty and so necessarily consigns him to the past."[15] The conventional historical approach, committed as it is to naturalistic forms of inquiry, simply cannot do justice to the reality with which the Bible is concerned.

One further aspect of Webb's account of contemporary approaches to the study of history deserves consideration. We have referred (above) to Webb's observation that historical inquiry is concerned simply with the causal relations obtaining in the human realm. "History focuses its inquiry," he says, "on human actions in specific events in the past."[16] Webb appears to regard this limitation of historical inquiry as theologically neutral, but it is not so. Limitation of the scope of historical inquiry to the realm of human action, conceived naturalistically, already supposes that an intelligible account of human action can be given without reference to God. Thus Webb's exclusion of divine agency from the historian's purview constitutes a very telling limitation of the scope of historical inquiry. It reveals again that naturalistic historians, even those who suppose themselves to be methodological rather than ontological naturalists, are bound in fact to comply with the constraints imposed by ontological naturalism. They must work under the assumption that human agency can be accounted for and rendered intelligible without reference to God. This view is not shared by the biblical authors. Take, for example, the account of Saul's conversion in Acts 9:1–19. It is true that the naturalistic historian will have some things to say about the incident reported here. There is data referred to in the story that is accessible, in principle, to the historian's gaze, but just because the explanatory power of the historian is limited to the causal relations obtaining in the human realm, the explanations offered will be of only marginal interest, precisely because they will fail to penetrate to the heart of what has gone on. What is more, if it really was Jesus whom Saul encountered on the road to Damascus and who was at work within Saul to bring about a dramatic transformation of his heart and mind, then any account given of Saul's "human agency" by the naturalistic historian will fail to get at what really happened.

The theological categories employed in the report of Paul's conversion on the Damascus road are not unusual. They are the stock-in-trade of the biblical writers. A few further examples illustrate the point: "So Abram went, as the LORD had told him" (Gen. 12:4); "Moses and Aaron did just as the LORD

---

15. Sarah Coakley, "The Identity of the Risen Jesus: Finding Jesus Christ in the Poor," in *Seeking the Identity of Jesus: A Pilgrimage*, ed. Beverly Roberts Gaventa and Richard B. Hays (Grand Rapids: Eerdmans, 2008), 306.

16. Webb, "Historical Enterprise," 41.

commanded" (Exod. 7:20); "Jesus said to them, 'Very truly, I tell you, the Son can do nothing on his own, but only what he sees the Father doing; for whatever the Father does, the Son does likewise'" (John 5:19); "Then Peter, filled with the Holy Spirit, said to them . . ." (Acts 4:8); and so on. Human actions are repeatedly explained by the biblical writers with reference to God's guidance and empowerment. The crucial point here is that Scripture repeatedly employs theological categories to make sense of human action. Webb's attempt to distinguish sound historical inquiry from theology by restricting historical inquiry to the realm of human action therefore sets him against the biblical writers themselves. The Bible, quite simply, operates with a different understanding of how reality is constituted than is evident in the ontological naturalism widely taken to be required of scholars working in the modern academy. The *methodological* naturalists might suppose themselves to be leaving the question of divine involvement in history open, but methodologically, and acting as historians, they are in fact consenting to an atheological view of the world.

It is not at all clear why an atheological mode of inquiry should be imposed on the biblical authors when their express purpose is to speak to us of where and how God is at work in the world. The justification often claimed for doing so is that only a naturalistic methodology will be intelligible to or gain the consent of nonbelievers. But that is not a justification that should carry any weight. It requires the biblical scholar to trade a Christian for a non-Christian understanding of the world and assumes that the non-Christian understanding has some superior claim to our allegiance and a higher level of scholarly credibility. If God exists and is involved in history, however, as the biblical writers attest, then a naturalistic historiography will severely inhibit our capacity to understand what is going on in the world. Furthermore, the imposition of naturalistic constraints that preclude the inquirer from discerning what is really going on can hardly be counted as good scholarship. Only with a radically different, nonnaturalistic account of what history is will it be possible for readers of Scripture to apprehend what has gone on in the past in sympathy with, rather than in direct opposition to, the biblical writers themselves.

Thinking Theologically about History

The Manifesto contends that if God is involved in history, then any non-theological account of what history is and of its telos will be "inadequate at best, or simply false." This is not necessarily a negative judgment about the explanatory power of nontheological accounts of the demise of the Roman Empire, for instance, or the impact British colonizers' settlement had on Native Americans, or the causes of World War I, and so on. Many historians will write narratives about these events without paying any attention to God's involvement in these histories or to the ways in which they are incorporated into the working out of God's purpose. This does not mean that their labors yield no insight into the reality with which they are concerned. But it may mean that they miss decisive features of the events they purport to explain.

The claim made in the Manifesto is a negative judgment only on accounts of history that proceed under the assumption that God cannot be appealed to in our representations of history. This naturalistic frame of mind and its attendant historiography are antithetical to that of the biblical authors, and yet, in the form of historical-critical method, they have come to dominate biblical studies in the modern era. The Manifesto proposes not that theological interpretation of Scripture has no use for historical inquiry, but that a renewed, theological conception of history is required if we are to read the Bible well. A renewed, theological conception of history will in turn require a reconsideration of how best to discern where and how God is at work in the world.

The witness of Scripture itself issues the imperative to think again about what history is. As observed in the opening paragraphs of this chapter, the Bible presents us with an account of reality in which history is conceived as a divine project worked out in covenant relationship with his creatures. There is not enough scope here to offer a thorough account of the theological historiography with which the biblical authors operate; hence a brief sketch must suffice, highlighting the christological focus to which the biblical witness eventually comes. It must of course be recognized, to begin with, that although the biblical authors share the assumption that history is to be understood fundamentally in terms of God's purposes for the world and his involvement in the working out of those purposes, these authors do not present a single seamless account of how history is to be understood. Those responsible for the formation of Scripture's texts are participants in an exploration of what the divine economy consists in and to what end it is directed. They do not always agree. They see in part and "through a glass, darkly" (1 Cor. 13:12 KJV), just as does the community of people who, by virtue of God's work in their lives, are likewise drawn to participate in the divine economy and so take Scripture's story as their own. That community reads Scripture with the purpose of hearing the Word of God through it, of discerning more faithfully what is going on in the world, and of sharing in the working out of God's purposes. That is what theological interpretation is concerned with.

Despite the partiality of the biblical witness and the diversity of voices that share in its explorations of the divine economy, a consensus is evident among the writers of the New Testament that in the historical figure of Jesus of Nazareth, the purposes of God are definitively revealed. The claims made about Jesus by the New Testament writers concern his own person and work, to be sure, but they also require us to see the whole of reality in the light of Jesus. Writing to the church in Colossae, for instance, Paul says of Jesus that "in him all things in heaven and on earth were created, things visible and invisible, whether thrones or dominions or rulers or powers—all things have been created through him and for him. He himself is before all things, and in him all things hold together" (Col. 1:16–17). John's testimony to Jesus is likewise cosmic in its scope, beginning with creation (John 1:1) and spanning to the promised day when Jesus will come again (John 21:21–23). The implication of such claims about Jesus is that the whole of reality is to be conceived christologically. In particular, for our purposes here, the witness of the New Testament concerning Jesus requires us to think again about what history is. Seen in the light of Jesus—in the light of his life, death, and resurrection—history turns out to be something other than what it is deemed to be by the long line of modern thinkers who insist that the reality of our world and all that goes on in it can be understood without reference to God.

Biblical scholars and theologians commonly explain that the Gospels were written by people who were convinced that Jesus had been raised by God from the dead. C. F. Evans, for instance, explains, "Of the synoptic gospels it would not be sufficient to say simply that they conclude with resurrection narratives, for it is only in the light of faith in the risen Lord that they were written at all."[17] Faith in the risen Lord, it is further observed, has had a profound impact on the way that the Gospel writers tell the story of Jesus's life up to and including his death. Some scholars take this as a reason (or an excuse) to treat the witness of the New Testament with suspicion. The perspective of faith, it is supposed, somehow problematizes the representations of Jesus's life that are offered to us by the four evangelists. Robert Funk and Roy Hoover, for example, speaking on behalf of the Jesus Seminar, consider it to be a "rule of evidence" that the evangelists "christianized" Jesus by making him conform to what they later came to believe.[18] On the one hand, surely this would be problematic only if "what they later came to believe"

---

17. C. F. Evans, *Resurrection and the New Testament* (London: SCM, 1970), 4.
18. See Robert Funk and Roy Hoover, eds., *The Five Gospels: The Search for the Authentic Words of Jesus* (New York: Macmillan, 1993), 24–25.

were false, only if Jesus were not raised from the dead. On the other hand, if the testimony is true —that on the third day the tomb was left empty and that Jesus, who had been crucified, was alive and appeared to the disciples—then the story of Jesus's ministry among them is quite properly seen in a new light. All sorts of things that Jesus said and did are going to be understood quite differently now than they might have been otherwise. John 12:16 makes this point clear: "His disciples did not understand these things at first; but when Jesus was glorified, then they remembered that these things had been written of him and had been done to him." One would expect that retrospective understanding to be reflected in the way the evangelists relate the history of Jesus before the resurrection, precisely because, as Graham Stanton tells us, the first followers of Jesus believed that "only in the light both of Resurrection faith and of the gift of the Spirit was it possible to understand the full significance of the story of Jesus."[19]

The historiographical legitimacy of the New Testament's faith-full representations of Jesus's history can be denied only if one is certain that the resurrection did not happen. Particular historians may choose to doubt or to deny the reality of the resurrection and to undertake their study of history accordingly, but they cannot deny to others the prerogative to interpret and so present the past in the light of what they hold to be true, namely, that God has indeed raised from death this Jesus who was crucified. In the academy, accordingly, the hegemony of historical-critical method, along with the methodological naturalism that characterizes it, is legitimately challenged by scholars who consider that the utilization of theological categories is essential if we are to understand what went on in the career of Jesus of Nazareth. We cannot read the Bible well by continuing to insist that the theological frame of reference of the biblical authors themselves must be treated as if it were false. A consequence of this view is that a theological reading of Scripture demands also a theological reading of history as a whole. If God raised Jesus from the dead and thereby inaugurated a new creation in which God's purposes will be brought to fulfillment at the last, then there is historiographical work to be done in seeking to discern where and how that new creation is taking shape among us. One might argue that such discernment is a prophetic task rather than a job for historians. It is the work of prophets to read the signs of the times, as it were, and to point to where God is at work in the world. That may be a helpful distinction to make; yet if we accept it, then we should abandon the idea that biblical study should

19. Graham Stanton, *The Gospels and Jesus*, 2nd ed. (Oxford: Oxford University Press, 2002), 299.

be dictated to by historical-critical method. The prophetic and evangelical witness of Scripture should be read and understood on its own terms rather than being confined and diminished by the categories of explanation deemed permissible by naturalistic historians.[20]

Discerning the Work of God

Several times this discussion (above) has recognized the incapacity of any inquiry operating with naturalistic assumptions about the nature of reality to discern where God is at work in the world. That is partly due to the limitations that naturalistic inquiry imposes on itself, but as was mentioned in the opening paragraphs of this chapter, there is a more fundamental theological reason why the empirical sciences, along with historical-critical method, are not competent to discern the being and action of God. Because "God is not part of the furniture of the world,"[21] the operations of God cannot be detected through the same methods of inquiry that are used to investigate created realities. In view of this situation, theological interpretation of Scripture involves a return to practices commended by Scripture itself, particularly the practice of "waiting on the Lord." The appropriate mode of inquiry for reading Scripture theologically and for discerning the work of God in history is revealed in the psalmist's prayer:

> Make me to know your ways, O LORD;
>   teach me your paths.
> Lead me in your truth, and teach me,
>   for you are the God of my salvation;
>   for you I wait all day long. (Ps. 25:4–5)

20. For a recent instance of this confinement, consider the claim of theologian Paul E. Capetz: "In showing the Bible to be *fully explicable as a human product* of the history of religion, historical criticism has made it very difficult for post-Enlightenment persons to continue to regard the Bible as the repository or criterion of all religious and moral truth" (emphasis added). Not content with methodological naturalism's agnosticism about the possibility of divine involvement in the formation of Scripture, Capetz takes it as having been established by historical criticism that God is certainly not involved. See his "Theology and the Historical-Critical Study of the Bible," *Harvard Theological Review* 104, no. 4 (2011): 459–88 (quote from p. 487).

21. This phrase is variously attributed to Karl Rahner or to Donald M. MacKinnon. MacKinnon uses a similar phrase in his lecture "The Problem of the 'System of Projection' Appropriate to Christian Theological Statements," given at the Enrico Castelli Colloquium in Rome in January 1969, first published in French, then in English in MacKinnon's *Explorations in Theology*, Explorations in Theology 5 (London: SCM, 1979), 70–89. I owe the reference to André Peter Muller, "Donald M. MacKinnon: The True Service of the Particular, 1913–1959" (PhD diss., University of Otago, 2010).

Attentiveness to the Word of God does not preclude the use of investigative tools such as literary or textual analysis, or of historiographical tools through which we may discern, for instance, the social and cultural conditions that have contributed to a particular text's formation, or that obtained at the time of the events to which the text bears witness.[22] In the reading of Scripture, however, and in the discernment of where God is at work in the world, these critical tools are subordinate to the practice of prayerful attentiveness to God's self-disclosure through Word and Spirit.

The Manifesto speaks of Christ's tutoring, through which the disciples on the road to Emmaus learn from the risen Lord how to make sense of "the things that have taken place there in these days" (Luke 24:18). Theological interpretation proceeds in accordance with the faith of the Christian community that the risen Lord still speaks in the midst of his people: the Word of God may still be heard through prayerful attentiveness to Scripture, prayer, preaching, and prophetic discernment as God calls attention to his work in the world, both within and beyond the confines of the church. The fruitfulness of these practices of faith depends also on the work of the Spirit, whom Christ sends from the Father to guide us into all truth and to declare to us the things of Christ (John 16:12–15). Put simply, God is involved in our knowing him. We are not left to our own devices in the reading of Scripture, nor in the discernment of God's work among us, and we ought not be constrained therefore by the very severe limits on our understanding imposed by naturalistic modes of inquiry. Just as Peter's recognition of Jesus as the Messiah exceeds the epistemic capacities of "flesh and blood," so theological interpretation depends on revelation from God, who makes visible his being and action in the world (cf. Matt. 16:17).

It may be objected that theological interpretation's appeal—to the insights gained through prayer, through prophetic discernment, and through the guidance of the Spirit—is hopelessly subjective and lacks any critical controls. This is precisely the reason, it might be claimed, why this sort of reading of Scripture has no place in the academy. Indeed, it may certainly be admitted, as is explained in the Manifesto, that the primary though not exclusive locus of theological interpretation is the living community of faith rather than the academy, but it is wrong to suppose that theological interpretation has no critical controls or no objective criteria by which to test its claims. Theological

22. These uses of historical-critical method in the practice of theological inquiry conform to what Joel Green has categorized as "historical criticism$_2$," and "historical criticism$_3$." These are distinguished from "historical criticism$_1$," which purports to reconstruct the history of Israel or of Jesus without reference to God. See Joel Green, *Practicing Theological Interpretation* (Grand Rapids: Baker Academic, 2011), 44–45.

interpretation is bound to the Word of God, made flesh and given concrete and definitive expression in Jesus of Nazareth. Jesus Christ is, for Christians, the criterion against whom all readings of Scripture are to be assessed, and the criterion against whom all claims to discern God's action in history are to be tested. Jewish readers, of course, are more likely to regard the Mosaic law and the exodus as decisive clues to the nature and reality of God's work among us; yet as Christianly conceived, these criteria are not in conflict with the Word of God given to be known in Christ. The christological control on the church's theological reading of Scripture and on its prophetic discernment of where God is at work in the world gives to theological interpretation the scientific integrity that the academy demands, precisely because the theological mode of inquiry is properly suited to the object with which it is concerned: the self-disclosure of God through his Word and Spirit.

Conclusion

The real problem with historical-critical inquiry, subject as it is to the demands of methodological naturalism, is that it imposes limits on the reading of Scripture that are simply not suited to Scripture's own nature as an instrument of God's communicative presence in the world. But this does not preclude there being a form of historical inquiry that takes its point of departure from Scripture itself, that is attentive to the divine economy, and that recognizes the work of God in the world by virtue of that work's conformity to Christ. Any historiography developed along these lines will be alert to the signs of God's kingdom breaking in and transforming our everyday reality. It will be attentive to the Spirit's work of giving life to all things and drawing them in to the praise of God's glory. It will tell of divine judgment against the ways in which humanity through the course of history acts in defiance of God's purposes, and it will recognize where divine grace is at work, forgiving, healing, and reconciling to Godself all that has become alienated from God's good purposes for the world. That is the sort of historiography that has shaped and inspired the biblical witness and in which theological readers of Scripture are themselves being trained.

5

The Role of Hermeneutics
and Philosophy
in Theological Interpretation

WILLIAM P. OLHAUSEN

Introduction

Richard John Neuhaus has suggested that we think of the great theological conversations that continue to unfold in the church as a feast, the catholic feast. Such a feast or banquet is a very inviting metaphor for theological interpretation. At a banquet are various guests, and thus multiple conversations are taking place. One of the conversations concerns the role of philosophy. In recent years there has been something of a renaissance in Christian philosophy, meaning philosophy practiced in the light of Christian assumptions and beliefs.[1]

---

1. Craig G. Bartholomew and Michael W. Goheen have provided an excellent introduction to Christian philosophy as well as an overview of some of the more notable thinkers; see their *Christian Philosophy: A Systematic and Narrative Introduction* (Grand Rapids: Baker Academic, 2013), esp. 199–213.

Within the various theological disciplines, philosophy has been well represented in biblical studies. In particular, the postmodern turn, itself a deeply philosophical development, has had a far-reaching impact on biblical studies. Although postmodernity has presented the church with many challenges, it has at the same time instilled a new awareness of philosophical presuppositions and the multiple hermeneutic variables present in any act of reading. One of the outstanding scholars on the interface of philosophy and biblical studies is Anthony C. Thiselton, who has been both teacher and practitioner. Indeed, Thiselton's work was an important inspiration for the work of the Scripture and Hermeneutics Seminar.[2] By identifying the standout philosophical issues and themes involved in biblical interpretation, the seminar has extended Thiselton's concerns and has proved seminal for further research and reflection in the nexus that is biblical interpretation, philosophy, and theology. And it is precisely within this nexus that this chapter makes a conversational contribution!

In order to honor the primacy of Scripture, my contribution is made in dialogue with passages taken from Paul's First Letter to the Corinthians, an exemplar of applied theology. Consequently, Paul's teaching provides us with all sorts of clues to the nature of theological interpretation. The following example is indicative. In chapter 14 he begins with instruction on the place of uninterpreted tongues in the corporate life of the church. Whatever the exact nature of Paul's concern, he is keen to emphasize the relative importance of prophecy. Three considerations appear to be in play, all of which are necessary for theological interpretation: intelligibility, edification, and missional integrity. I take Paul's understanding of prophecy to be something like this: Spirit-inspired communication to people (believers and, on occasion, unbelievers) about God's character and purposes in Christ, addressing a person, people group, or situation in the world. Understood in this way, prophecy, like theological interpretation, represents a communicative participation in the *koinōnia* of the Spirit.

Buzzwords in this definition include "Spirit," "communication," "people," and "world." Behind each of these words are several overlapping philosophical considerations that bear directly on the task of theological interpretation. In this chapter I set out three theses: First, theological interpretation needs a philosophy to be worked out in the context of Christian belief. Second, theological interpretation needs an understanding of anthropology that fully

---

2. The fruit of this seminar's work has been an 8-vol. Scripture and Hermeneutics series, with contributions from many leading scholars in biblical studies, philosophy, and theology (Grand Rapids: Zondervan; Carlisle: Paternoster, 2000–2008).

honors the capacities and potentialities of human beings. Third, theological interpretation needs a theological hermeneutic. Under each of these theses I also suggest subtheses expressed in a way that is compatible with the idea of this Manifesto.

1. Theological interpretation needs a philosophy to be worked out in the context of Christian belief.

To gather together the broken and partial lights of the special sciences and to evolve a view of the meaning of the whole, is the task of philosophy. . . . To it is committed the office of summing up the insight which has been gained into the various aspects of existence, and, rising above every limited standpoint, to attempt to gain a synthetic apprehension of Reality as a whole.

W. R. Matthews[3]

The field of philosophy can be very confusing for the uninitiated. Each of the traditional concerns of philosophy—such as metaphysics, epistemology, logic, ethics, and aesthetics—generates its own questions and register. Then alongside their local concerns, specialist branches of philosophy—such as the philosophy of language, philosophy of religion, philosophy of science, and so on—make their own contributions to local as well as generic problems. Filling out the scene are broad intellectual traditions of philosophy that bring to bear their own assumptions about the nature of philosophical inquiry. Among the more prominent traditions in Continental philosophy have been rationalism, idealism, existentialism, phenomenology, pragmatism, structuralism, and post-structuralism. Gottlob Frege's work in mathematical logic provided the impulse for analytic philosophy, sometimes called Anglo-American philosophy, which is characterized by rigorous argumentation and a detailed interest in mathematics, logic, and language.[4] In these different ways, philosophical concerns are a part of every area of intellectual thought, including theological interpretation.

The philosophical inquiry most closely associated with theological interpretation is hermeneutics. Hermeneutics can be understood as the philosophy of understanding; in order to do its work, it draws on the findings of other branches of philosophy, such as the philosophies of language and history. The

3. W. R. Matthews, *Studies in Christian Philosophy: Boyle Lectures, 1920* (London: Macmillan, 1921), 3–4.

4. For a taste of such work, see Gottlob Frege, *Collected Papers on Mathematics, Logic, and Philosophy* (Oxford: Blackwell, 1984).

obvious interest in the phenomenon of language means that hermeneutics is increasingly influenced not only by the Continental tradition of philosophy but also by the analytic tradition as well. Thiselton has given five reasons for the importance of philosophy in the hermeneutic task,[5] briefly stated here: (1) It helps to identify the philosophical presuppositions of a particular scholar. (2) It conceptualizes the hermeneutic task. (3) Philosophy assists interpretation of biblical texts. (4) It elucidates the way language functions. (5) Philosophy is important because it is always present even if we imagine we can do without it (itself a philosophical move!). Together these arguments are persuasive.

It will already be clear that philosophy is a contested practice. The philosophy of philosophy, or metaphilosophy, is concerned with defining the purpose and limits of philosophy. Inevitably, each field of intellectual inquiry will take from philosophy what is of relevance and utility. Similarly, theological interpretation will also take what it needs from philosophy, what is demanded of philosophy by the nature and methods of the interpretative task. Theology's metaphilosophy will want to do at least three things: (1) be aware of when theology is doing philosophy, (2) be able to justify a particular philosophical assumption or method, and (3) be aware of the implications of such a move. When we step back from the matter, the ultimate aim of theology, and so of theological interpretation, is not so very different from the aims of philosophy. As Matthews explains, the "attempt to attain an insight into reality is essentially a movement to transcend the limits of the actual self, and reach a life of greater power, harmony, and freedom. . . . In every case the motive is to set the individual in right relationship with the universe."[6] The difference, then, between theological interpretation and other interpretative strategies comes down to what counts as being "in the right relationship with the universe."

The Importance of Philosophy

To illustrate the importance of philosophy for theology, here is an example from the Anglican philosopher of religion W. R. Matthews's Boyle Lectures of 1920. Toward the end of his first lecture, he invites us to consider three influential schools of thought in the church of his own time: the systematics of Albrecht Ritschl, Catholic modernism, and mysticism.[7] Common to each

---

5. Anthony C. Thiselton, *The Two Horizons: New Testament Hermeneutics and Philosophical Description* (Carlisle, UK: Paternoster, 1980), 3–10.

6. Matthews, *Christian Philosophy*, 28–29.

7. Ibid., 9–21.

of these traditions was, and is, a suspicion of philosophy (metaphysics) and hence the belief that any inherent authority or truth of Christian faith must be demonstrated by an appeal to some expression of religious experience: "moral consciousness inspired by the historical Jesus" (Ritschl),[8] "collective consciousness of the historic church" (Catholic modernism), and "religious genius of the mystic." Positively, as Matthews observes, these traditions each "remind us, not that philosophy is irrelevant for religious thought, but of the futility of a metaphysic which leaves the moral and religious aspects of the world out of account."[9]

Negatively, an approach to Christian faith that rests entirely on the authority of religious experience leaves no place for metaphysics or revelation and thus no place for the traditional Christian doctrines of creation, the two natures of Christ, and the Trinity. However, the various phenomena of religious consciousness find their true significance only within "an apprehension of Reality as a whole."[10] It turns out, of course, that Ritschl's approach is equally affected by philosophy. In response to Ritschl's insistence that religion and philosophy should be kept separate, Matthews observes: "It is sufficiently obvious that to maintain the primacy of the practical reason is, in reality, to propound a whole system of philosophy, and to postulate a view of the universe as definite as that which holds sense perception to be the source of real knowledge."[11]

Nearly a century later, readers of Matthews's work can recognize that his insights remain not only valuable but also incisive, especially his critiques of overreliance on religious experience and of theologies that neglect what he calls "an apprehension of Reality as a whole."

The Barthian Challenge to the Role of Philosophy in Theology

Karl Barth's antipathy to natural theology, and so to philosophy, remains influential, though for reasons quite different from those of Ritschl. Working within a Kantian account of philosophy, Barth departed from John Calvin's more positive approach to natural theology to insist that God can be known only by the specific way God chooses to reveal himself: through the revelation

---

8. Trevor Hart has observed that for Ritschl, "'Revelation' (whatever its ultimate source) was effectively reduced to those this-worldly phenomena from Jesus's life which remained once the scholars had done their work on the text of the Gospels." See Hart, "Revelation," in *The Cambridge Companion to Karl Barth*, ed. John Webster (Cambridge: Cambridge University Press, 2000), 40.

9. Matthews, *Christian Philosophy*, 20.

10. Ibid., 4.

11. Ibid., 13.

of himself in Christ, to which Scripture bears witness.[12] On this principle, natural theology is a Trojan horse for autonomous human reason (and by extension, human feeling), and it had led to what he saw as the unhelpful legacy of Friedrich Schleiermacher's philosophical theology, which, according to Barth, "explicitly takes a standpoint or starting-point that lies *outside* Christianity. Hence one cannot expect any *Christian* criticism of the church from it."[13]

However, there is an alternative way to read the contribution of natural theology that does provide it with a Christian "starting-point": by locating it within a biblically informed doctrine of creation. This is how Alister McGrath summarizes T. F. Torrance's response to Barth: "Where Barth tends to see natural and revealed theology as two rival contenders for knowledge of God, Torrance argues that natural theology must be reconceived as an account of nature, undertaken from within the sphere of a revealed knowledge of God. To undertake natural theology, some revealed notions of God are required—above all, a doctrine of creation."[14]

Similarly, Matthews observes, "The conception of creation in some form is a vital element in Christian Theism."[15] As well as overcoming Barth's sharp divide between nature and grace, the old dualism between chaos and creation is also resolved. The personal agency (will) of God is introduced, which in turn finds its fullest expression in Christology and the doctrine of the Trinity.

Belief in creation ex nihilo has far-reaching implications for ontology, epistemology, and anthropology. First, in the area of ontology, creation provides us with what Matthews describes as an "apprehension of Reality as a whole." Second, it alerts us to the ordered nature of things: "Because God is the Creator and because his order is comprehensive in that it relates to all of life, there is not an area of practical human life for which a Christian philosophy will not provide helpful insight."[16] In terms of epistemology, and notwithstanding the

---

12. Barth's reasons are set out most famously in a robust response to his fellow Swiss theologian Emil Brunner. See Karl Barth and Emil Brunner, *Natural Theology*, trans. Peter Fraenkel (London: Bles, 1946).

13. Karl Barth, *The Theology of Schleiermacher: Lectures at Gottingen, Winter Semester of 1923/24*, ed. Dietrich Ritschl, trans. Geoffrey W. Bromiley (Edinburgh: T&T Clark, 1982), 166, emphasis original; see also 148–67. For a brief overview and assessment of Barth's opposition to natural theology, see Alister E. McGrath, *The Science of God* (London and New York: T&T Clark International, 2004), 82–86.

14. McGrath, *Science of God*, 86–87. This conversation is sometimes couched in terms of the distinction between general and special revelation.

15. Matthews, *Christian Philosophy*, 205.

16. Bartholomew and Goheen, *Christian Philosophy*, 10. For their overview of Reformational philosophy, see 243–67.

noetic effects of the fall, the doctrine of creation tells us three things: first, that there is stuff out there in the world that can be known; second, we can know about it; and, third, we can have confidence that we know about it! Third, in the area of anthropology we understand ourselves as created beings, with capacities and potentialities that reflect our status as made in the image of God. Together these are the building blocks for an orientation toward the world that underpins the task of theological interpretation. However, theology does require a conceptual schema for ordering, presenting, and elucidating these deeply theological ideas. One such schema, critical realism,[17] has been advanced by a number of leading Christian scholars.[18] Critical realism preserves epistemological and ontological commitments that are consonant with the doctrine of creation. In turn, these commitments have an important bearing on how we understand anthropology.

Theological Interpretation Must Work with Some Version of Epistemological Realism

In the same way that Paul urged discernment in the interpretation of prophecy (1 Cor. 14:29–33), churches today continue to face the challenge of deciding between ethical and/or doctrinal positions. These challenges have resulted in something of a crisis, especially within Anglicanism. However, Gadamerian hermeneutics, together with the postmodern drift of our Western culture, often means that we struggle to provide a critical horizon in which resolution can be reached. In effect, we learn to live with an easygoing relativism, frozen conflicts, or de facto schism. This is how Thiselton puts it: "A key issue which hermeneutics faces in the wake of Gadamer and Ricoeur concerns the possibility and role of metacriticism: *can we critically rank the different criteria by which we judge what counts as meaningful or productive effects of texts within this or that context in life?*"[19]

---

17. "Critical realism" is a phrase coined by English philosopher Roy Bhaskar. See, e.g., Roy Bhaskar, *The Possibility of Naturalism: A Philosophical Critique of the Contemporary Human Sciences*, 3rd ed. (London: Routledge, 1998); idem, *A Realist Theory of Science*, 2nd ed. (London: Verso, 1997).

18. Prominent advocates include John Polkinghorne, Alister McGrath, Margaret S. Archer, and N. T. Wright. See details of Polkinghorne in McGrath, *Science of God*, 139–52; Margaret S. Archer, "Models of Man: Transcendence and Being-in-the-World," in *Measuring Ireland: Discerning Values and Beliefs*, ed. Eoin G. Cassidy (Dublin: Veritas, 2002), 123–51; N. T. Wright, *The New Testament and the People of God*, vol. 1 of *Christian Origins and the Question of God* (London: SPCK, 1992), 32–37.

19. Anthony C. Thiselton, *New Horizons in Hermeneutics: The Theory and Practice of Transforming Biblical Reading* (Carlisle, UK: Paternoster, 1992), 5–6, emphasis original. Thiselton pursues this concern in his critique of the intralinguistic theorizing of the movement inspired

More succinctly, the German critical theorist Jürgen Habermas has identified the lack of a theory of reference in much hermeneutical philosophy as its "Achilles' heel."[20] A theory of reference requires some version of realism. In light of the postmodern critique of Enlightenment rationalism, critical realism recognizes that human judgments are fallible and hence "critical," but it also insists, with modernism, on a realist ontology so that, together with the judgment of others, experience of the world can yield a posteriori knowledge. Although we proceed with humility, the infinite deferral of judgments is not inevitable.

Critical realism also recognizes that reality is experienced in a variety of ways; it is stratified.[21] McGrath explains: "Critical reason insists that the world must be regarded as differentiated and stratified. Each individual science deals with a different stratum of this reality, which in turn obliges it to develop and use methods of investigation adapted and appropriate to this stratum."[22] McGrath likes critical realism because it promises the possibility of a genuine theological science: "Each stratum—whether physical, biological or cultural—is to be seen as 'real,' and capable of investigation using means appropriate to its distinctive identity."[23]

Bartholomew and Goheen explain that the ordered nature of creation is the inspiration for Herman Dooyeweerd's ontology, which consists of what he calls "modalities" and "individuality structures." Dooyeweerd identifies fifteen ways of being for concrete things in the universe (modalities). Individuality structures are God's order for particular entities.[24] The ontologies of critical realism and Reformational philosophy simply rule out any sort of division of the world into sacred and secular because the task of theological interpretation depends upon and is relevant to the whole of reality.

---

by Martin Heidegger's linguistic turn known as the "New Hermeneutic." Anthony C. Thiselton, "The New Hermeneutic," in *New Testament Interpretation: Essays in Principles and Methods*, ed. I. H. Marshall (Exeter, UK: Paternoster, 1977), 308–33.

20. Jürgen Habermas, "Hermeneutic and Analytic Philosophy: Two Complementary Versions of the Linguistic Turn?," in *German Philosophy since Kant*, ed. A. O'Hear (Cambridge: Cambridge University Press, 1999), 422. Considerations such as these from within the hermeneutic tradition have led to a greater rapprochement with currents within analytic philosophy, especially with speech-act philosophy.

21. McGrath, *Science of God*, 146–47.

22. Ibid., 146.

23. Ibid., 148. To illustrate what is meant by this stratification of reality, McGrath uses the example of illness. Illness has multiple effects and hence realities, from its pathology all the way along the process to a person losing his or her job and requiring rehabilitation. Therefore, different strata of reality are involved in the treatment of a person's illness. No one method or approach can do the job. Similarly, within the field of Christianity, McGrath lists eight possible strata: texts (supremely Scripture), patterns of worship, creedal statements, communities, institutional structures, images, words, and religious experience (ibid., 148–50).

24. For an overview, see Bartholomew and Goheen, *Christian Philosophy*, 243–67.

Summary

It has been suggested that philosophical considerations are involved in any sort of theory construction or intellectual investigation. We have had cause to reflect on the importance of metaphysics, the way in which, for instance, the Christian doctrine of creation provides an account of reality, ontology (e.g., the ordering of creation as the stratification of reality in the case of scientific theology, or the modalities and individuality structures of Reformational philosophy), and epistemology (the possibility of achieving genuine knowledge of reality on the basis of some sort of critical realism).[25] We can express the subtheses of this section as follows:

- Philosophy helps us to discern the intellectual scaffolding of a given theology.
- Theological interpretation proceeds on the basis of a biblically informed metaphysic, an apprehension of reality as a whole.
- Theological interpretation works with some version of realism.
- Theological interpretation proceeds on the basis of an ontology that is informed by a doctrine of creation.

We now turn to the important question of anthropology and the second thesis.

2. Theological interpretation needs an understanding of anthropology that fully honors the capacities and potentialities of human beings.

> It is the importance of what we care about which defines us, but, since we cannot but care, to some degree, for the orders of reality which impinge upon us, then it is the precise patterning of their prioritisation and accommodation which defines the unique personal identity of every individual.
>
> Margaret S. Archer[26]

In the course of his discussion of prophecy, Paul indicates one of the possible outcomes of loving, intelligible, and edifying prophecy: "After the secrets of the unbeliever's heart are disclosed, that person will bow down before God"

---

25. Important work has appeared in the tradition of philosophy known as Reformed epistemology, such as by Alvin Plantinga, *Warranted Christian Belief* (New York: Oxford University Press, 2000); Alvin Plantinga and Nicholas Wolterstorff, eds., *Faith and Rationality: Reason and Belief in God* (Notre Dame, IN: University of Notre Dame Press, 1983).

26. Archer, "Models of Man," 139.

(1 Cor. 14:25). Again, the picture is incomplete since we have no description of exactly what Paul has in mind. However, it is suggestive of an assumed anthropological capacity for divine consciousness and a potentiality for this consciousness to be redirected and thereby transformed. An anthropology fit for theological interpretation will want to draw on the resources that Scripture itself has to offer. Indeed, the passage cited here from 1 Corinthians invites a study in some of Paul's key anthropological terms such as "heart," "body," "flesh," and "image."[27] The depth, richness, and terrible beauty of the picture they provide of the shame and the glory of human being comes into even sharper focus as we survey the ruins of the anthropology bestowed to us first by modernism and then by postmodernism.

There are numerous excellent studies in theological anthropology as well as some excellent resources in the social sciences. However, the focus here is on a contribution made by Roman Catholic sociologist Margaret Archer, in which she brings her scholarship to bear on (1) critiquing the atheistic assumptions in social science and (2) presenting a much more constructive and thus edifying account of our being-in-the-world.

Anthropology in Modernity

Archer is highly critical of the doctrinaire privileging of atheism in social science. Atheism, she says, is "presented as an epistemologically neutral position, instead of what it is, a commitment to a belief in the absence of religious phenomena."[28] The real damage of this atheism has been to rule out, on philosophical grounds, the possibility that humans have the capacity to be addressed by God.[29] Archer offers a critique of the two dominant anthropologies found in her field of social science: the modern ("Enlightenment Man") and postmodern ("Society's Being").[30] Her estimation of the legacy of Enlightenment Man is worth quoting in full:

27. See, e.g., Udo Schnelle, *The Human Condition: Anthropology in the Teachings of Jesus, Paul, and John*, trans. O. C. Dean Jr. (Edinburgh: T&T Clark, 1996).

28. Archer, "Models of Man," 123–24.

29. William P. Alston, *Perceiving God: The Epistemology of Religious Experience* (Ithaca, NY: Cornell University Press, 1991), 240; quoted in Archer, "Models of Man," 125.

30. I suspect that the excesses of modernism (rational-action theory) are more evident in the analytic tradition of philosophy and the social sciences, and the influence of postmodernism (historical and cultural determinism) is more evident in fields of research that have more affinity with the Continental traditions of philosophy and social science. Thus the "model person" posited by Brown and Levinson's original politeness theory is more indicative of modernism, whereas Pierre Bourdieu's social anthropology is much more skeptical toward rational-action theory. See, e.g., Penelope Brown and Stephen C. Levinson, *Politeness: Some Universals in Language Usage* (Cambridge: Cambridge University Press, 1987), 58; Pierre Bourdieu, *Distinction:*

The modern self is universally pre-given. Because all that is contingent can be stripped from this self, he can step forward as a purely logocentric being whose consciousness, freed from any embedding in historical consciousness, can pellucidly articulate the cosmic story. The metaphysics of modernity thus adduced a model of rational man who could attain his ends in the world by pure logos; this was a disenchanted world made up of natural and social reality alone, for it had been ontologically purged of Transcendence. . . . "Modernity's Man" was a model which had stripped down the human being until he had one property alone, that of instrumental rationality, namely the capacity to maximize his preferences through means-ends relationships and so to optimise his utility.[31]

Such a stripped-down human agent is incapable of possessing a range of what Archer calls "normative" and "affective" dimensions of human being. Consequently, such people would be incapable of transcending instrumental rationality in order to engage with "ultimate concerns."[32] But such concerns or beliefs are themselves constitutive of who we are: "It is only in the light of our 'ultimate concerns' that our actions are ultimately intelligible."[33] The ripple effect of this reductionist anthropology has been far-reaching:

> This was the model of man that was eagerly seized upon by social contract theorists in politics, Utilitarians in ethics and social policy, and liberals in political economy. *Homo Economicus* is a survivor. He not only lives on as the anchorman of microeconomics and the hero of neo-liberalism, but he is also a colonial adventurer and, in the hands of Rational Choice theorists, he bids to conquer social science in general.[34]

Anthropology in Postmodernity

In postmodern approaches to anthropology, the lone autonomous self of modernism has been replaced by the irreducibility of society. Everything now has become social: "Human subjects become kaleidoscopically shaped by the flux of historic-cultural contingencies."[35] If Enlightenment Man unnecessarily restricts the potentiality of the human agent, "Society's Being" of postmodernism likewise threatens to dehumanize us by insisting that "our selfhood

---

A Social Critique of the Judgment of Taste (London: Routledge, 2004), 467; cf. idem, *The Logic of Practice*, trans. R. Nice (Cambridge: Polity, 1990), 56.

31. Archer, "Models of Man," 126.
32. Ibid., 127.
33. Ibid.
34. Ibid.
35. Ibid.

is a grammatical fiction," as Archer maintains.[36] How does this happen? According to Archer, Society's Being "impoverishes our humanity, by subtracting from our human powers and accrediting all of them—selfhood, reflexivity, thought, memory, emotionality and belief—to society's discourse."[37] To summarize: "Anthropocentric 'Modernity's Man' makes God and his society in his own image. Sociocentric 'oversocialised' man lets society make him and his God."[38] Regardless of theological considerations, both these accounts of anthropology are reductionist and defective. Theological interpretation must work with a very different understanding of anthropology.

Archer's revision of these reductionist approaches to anthropology begins with a retrieval of a realist ontology because, as she explains, we cannot provide a plausible account of being-in-the-world without taking into account the way the world impinges on our development of personhood: "The way the world is can affect how we are."[39] Accordingly, both anthropocentrism and sociocentrism fall victim to the so-called "epistemic fallacy," on the basis of which reality is reduced to the concerns of instrumental rationality or to social discourse.[40] Similarly, Archer talks in terms of human capacities and potentialities. She insists that a right understanding of anthropology, and certainly one that will make sense of theological interpretation, must begin with a commitment to realism that takes seriously the important notion of practice. According to Archer, religion as a practice is a legitimate experience of reality. It is an important emphasis within this realist ontology that there is always the capacity to revise our beliefs and consequently to be receptive to new ideas.

Archer identifies four orders of reality constitutive of human identity: the natural, the practical, the discursive, and, crucially, what she calls the transcendent.[41] The first three have to do with physical well-being, performative achievement, and self-worth. For people without a religious faith, these constitute their being-in-the-world. Consequently, certain "ultimate concerns"

36. See Archer's argument from ibid., 126–29.
37. Ibid., 129.
38. Ibid.
39. Ibid., 130.
40. From the field of historical pragmatics, Roger Sell has argued for a via media between these two accounts of modern and postmodern anthropology: the former making no allowance for historical processes, the other being overly deterministic. He argues that the philosophical perspective best able to serve pragmatics is one that acknowledges both the historically effected status of human consciousness as well as allowing for the relative freedom of the human agent to act on a new state of affairs. Roger Sell, "A Historical but Non-Determinist Pragmatics of Literary Communication," in *Journal of Historical Pragmatics* 2, no. 1 (2001): 1–32.
41. Archer, "Models of Man," 139.

are not open to them: most important is the experience of the unconditional love of God. She argues that only the experience of transcendent reality as the unconditional love of God enables a person to experience, for instance, "sinfulness" or achieve "detachment" from the emotional demands of the first three orders of reality.[42] As people negotiate ways of prioritizing ultimate concerns from subordinate ones, they experience degrees of struggle. Archer explains: "Struggle is . . . generic to human commitment to any ultimate concern, because subordinate concerns do have naturalistic legitimacy, they are about different aspects of our well-being and the emotional commentaries emanating from them signal the costs entailed to the person by the priorities which they have reflexively determined."[43]

It is notable that the Gospels are characterized by Jesus's struggles with various groupings: the religious order, the crowd, the Roman political order, and the spiritual order of the demonic. It is only against these various "struggles" that Jesus's identity and his mission are understood. Francis Martin talks in terms of "conflict" to elucidate Paul's teaching: "We need only to read . . . the intensity of [Paul's] exhortation in chapters 6 and 8 of the letter to the Romans [and] the exhortation in Ephesians 4:17–24 and elsewhere to see that for Paul and the whole Christian tradition the moment of the indwelling of the Holy Spirit is the beginning of real conflict between the new life of God and the old life of the flesh."[44]

And so, in 1 Corinthians 1:18–2:5 we might view the stake of struggles to be, on one side, the classificatory systems *indicated* by what is deemed "wise" or "spiritual," and on the other, the classificatory schemes implicated by Paul's message about the cross. Importantly, it is the occasion of "struggle" or conflict between Paul's cruciform ethic and the church's fleshly tendencies that provides the community with the opportunity to transform. In a different context, Bourdieu observes: "Only through the struggle do the internalised limits become boundaries, barriers that have to be moved."[45]

Archer concludes: "There are certain ways of being-in-the-world which remain incomprehensible without the admission of transcendence. . . . The relations formed in transcendental 'space' react back upon the world, to which

---

42. Archer characterizes the struggle of human existence as having to "disengage 'ultimate concerns' from subordinate ones" (ibid., 140). In the Christian tradition, this struggle is characterized as one between two kingdoms: the kingdom of the world and the kingdom of God. This is where spiritual exercises play such an important role (ibid., 147).

43. Ibid., 146–47. "Struggle" is also an important concept in Bourdieu's anthropology. See, e.g., Bourdieu, *Distinction*, 479–81.

44. Francis Martin, "Spirit and Flesh in the Doing of Theology," *Journal of Pentecostal Theology* 9 (2001): 5.

45. Bourdieu, *Distinction*, 480.

they are not conformed, by sanctifying it. From these relations ripple out concentric circles of unconditional love."[46]

There is not space here to explore Archer's work further, yet her work is important for the ways in which she manages to integrate philosophy, social science, and the perspective of Christian theology. In particular, her Christian metaphysic not only informs her description of human being but also shapes it in such a way that she can give a convincing account of the processes by which transcendent reality (in this case, the Christian faith) is able to transform humanity's ultimate concerns.

The thesis concerning anthropology has been this: theological interpretation needs an understanding of anthropology that fully reflects the capacities and potentialities of human being. Further subtheses are these:

- Theological interpretation must proceed on the basis of a clear understanding of how different models of anthropology frame our interpretations of Scripture.
- Some important philosophical assumptions are integral to a properly theological anthropology: a realist ontology that allows for transcendence and so can admit the realities of religious practice and experience.
- Theological interpretation will want to press fully the christological implications for anthropology, especially through the work of the cross (1 Cor. 1:18–25), through life in the Spirit (1:7, 12–14), and with the horizon of the resurrection (1 Cor. 15).

3. Theological interpretation needs a theological hermeneutic.

Engagement with contemporary hermeneutical discussion is an essential prerequisite for any attempt to rethink the relationship between exegesis and theology.

Francis Watson[47]

We have seen how the doctrine of creation frames the interface between theology and philosophy by implicating a metaphysic entailing important epistemological, ontological, and anthropological assumptions. This cluster of assumptions now needs to be held together in the development of a

46. Archer, "Models of Man," 148–49.
47. Francis Watson, *Text, Church and World: Biblical Interpretation in Theological Perspective* (Edinburgh: T&T Clark, 1994), 223.

theological hermeneutic. Paul explains that in contrast to those who speak "mysteries in the Spirit," "those who prophesy speak to other people for their upbuilding and encouragement and consolation" (1 Cor. 14:3). Similarly, theological interpretation is an act of understanding divine communication for our upbuilding and encouragement and consolation. We therefore must be committed to deepening our understanding of both the speech situation (in this case the biblical text[s] in view) and the hermeneutic situation (the readers' horizon). In these ways, we honor both axes of the hermeneutic task: the empathetic and the explanatory.[48]

In seeking to describe the conditions under which understanding takes place, hermeneutics is a deeply relational enterprise: by "relational" I mean a hermeneutic that takes account of all those elements of reality that constitute human being and, consequently, from which we determine the coordinates of meaning.[49] If anthropological description is essential for the hermeneutic task, then the window into the anthropological dimensions of the speech situation/text is, primarily, by means of linguistic analysis. The exact character of this horizon will be determined, to a greater or lesser extent, by the text under consideration. As Gordon Fee observes, "By the very nature of things, the Pauline letters serve chiefly not as theological, but as pragmatic, documents; nonetheless, they are full of theological presuppositions, assertions, and reflections of a kind that allow us to describe them theologically."[50]

In the case of 1 Corinthians, only when facts in the extralinguistic world (supremely the cross and resurrection of Jesus), tradition (Jewish Scriptures and apostolic witness), institutional phenomena (pertaining to the church), and the person and work of the Spirit (within the context of the foregoing) are all held together with the insights afforded by philosophy and social science do we have the relevant raw materials with which to do theological interpretation.

48. Much of what has passed for philosophical hermeneutics since at least Gadamer, especially his work on the linguisticality of meaning, has been superseded by developments first in the philosophy of language and later in linguistic pragmatics and related fields within the social sciences. Where hermeneutics retains its importance is its insistence on the historical development of meaning and the ongoing importance of humanist concepts such as *Bildung, sensus communis*, "judgment," "taste," and "tact." See Hans-Georg Gadamer, *Truth and Method*, trans. J. Weinsheimer and D. G. Marshall, 2nd rev. ed. (New York: Continuum, 2003), 9–42. Again, the substantive insights have been developed in sociology and social anthropology.

49. This is not dissimilar to what Wright means by "relational epistemology" (*New Testament and the People of God*, 45).

50. Gordon D. Fee, *God's Empowering Presence: The Holy Spirit in the Letters of Paul* (Peabody, MA: Hendrickson, 1994), 827.

Introducing Pragmatics

Clearly, a theological hermeneutic fit for theological interpretation of Scripture will want to foreground the various elements that make up what we call Tradition: things like the role of the believing community, the Rule of Faith, canonicity, and doctrine. These important themes are addressed elsewhere in this Manifesto, so that enables me here to focus on one especially relevant area of philosophy: language in context. This study of language in context is dealt with now by a branch of linguistics called pragmatics.[51] John Austin's seminal work on speech acts and Paul H. Grice's work on the logic of conversation have, in the words of Jef Verschueren, "provided the frame of reference for the consolidation of the field of linguistic pragmatics."[52] Since the 1960s pragmatics has become a major field of research in its own right. Although Austin, Grice, John R. Searle, and others remain important philosophical touchstones, much of the work has become irreducibly interdisciplinary, reflecting the complexity of interpersonal communication.[53] A strength of Thiselton's work on hermeneutics has been in the ways he has appropriated the resources of the anthropologically oriented philosophy of Ludwig Wittgenstein, speech-act philosophy, and linguistics, especially semantics.[54] Although he has been hesitant to develop a theological hermeneutic, I believe that this is unavoidable if we are to honor both our metaphysical commitments and the particular character of the biblical texts.[55]

Alongside the study of speech acts, pragmatics is concerned with a range of other linguistic phenomena, including implied meanings in conversation, presupposition, deixis, and conversational analysis.[56] It is increasingly clear

51. In the analytic tradition of linguistics, pragmatics has developed into sociolinguistics and psycholinguistics. Here, the field of sociolinguistics is in view.

52. Jef Verschueren, Jan-Ola Östman, and Jan Blommaert, eds., *The Pragmatics of Interaction*, Handbook of Pragmatics, 1995 Installment (Amsterdam and Philadelphia: J. Benjamins, 1995), 3. Both philosophers presented their ideas as their William James Lectures at Harvard University: Austin in 1955, Grice in 1957.

53. There is an analytic and a continental tradition within pragmatics. Both can make a valuable contribution to theological hermeneutics.

54. The following are among the more prominent representatives of this turn: Ludwig Wittgenstein, *Philosophical Investigations*, trans. G. E. M. Anscombe (Oxford: Basil Blackwell, 1989); John L. Austin, *How to Do Things with Words*, ed. J. O. Urmson and Marina Sbisà (Oxford: Oxford University Press, 1978); Paul Grice, *Studies in the Way of Words* (Cambridge, MA: Harvard University Press, 1989); John R. Searle, *Speech Acts: An Essay in the Philosophy of Language* (Cambridge: Cambridge University Press, 1969).

55. Anthony C. Thiselton's argument is worth reviewing; see his "Situating the Explorations," in *Thiselton on Hermeneutics: Collected Works with New Essays* (Grand Rapids: Eerdmans, 2006), 8; cf. idem, "A Reappraisal of Part VII," in *Collected Works*, 802–3.

56. Linguistics traditionally investigates language phenomena under three broad disciplines: syntax, semantics, and pragmatics. For an introduction to analytical pragmatics, see, e.g.,

that the interests of pragmatics have much to offer the more theoretical, and hence speculative, discipline of philosophical hermeneutics. Together with the related tasks of syntax and semantics, a sufficiently nuanced account of pragmatics provides us with a plausible interpretative framework. Another helpful feature of pragmatics is its plasticity: it is a context-sensitive discourse and amenable to further fine-tuning as and when our understanding advances.[57] The following can only be indicative of the sort of approach needed.[58]

Deixis and the Participation Framework

To begin with, the important pragmatic phenomenon of deixis rules out simplistic accounts of the speech/hermeneutical situation in terms of a simple speaker or author (speech situation) or hearer or reader (hermeneutical situation).[59] Stephen C. Levinson defines "deixis" or "indexicality": "Deixis concerns . . . the way in which utterances are semantically or pragmatically anchored to their situation of utterance, by virtue of the fact that certain key words and morphemes have their reference fixed by various (temporal, spatial, participant role and social) parameters of the speech event."[60]

Following Erving Goffman, Levinson has proposed thinking in terms of "production format" in order to offer a more fine-grained analysis of what we mean by a "speaker."[61] Similarly, he suggests that "the hearer" is more

---

Stephen C. Levinson, *Pragmatics* (Cambridge: Cambridge University Press, 1983). Since Levinson's standard introduction, the discipline has developed into a range of interdisciplinary fields, including sociolinguistics, psycholinguistics, and linguistic anthropology. For my doctoral thesis I drew especially on sociolinguistics to develop Thiselton's use of speech-act theory in biblical and theological hermeneutics. William P. Olhausen, "Toward a Relational Hermeneutic: On the Appropriation of Speech Act Theory in the Biblical and Theological Hermeneutics of Anthony Thiselton" (PhD diss., Liverpool University, 2007).

57. A theological pragmatics would proceed on the basis of the particular grammar of the text in view. Methodological assumptions can include a metaphysic that reflects belief in the doctrine of creation. Similarly, Helmut Peukert has argued that a theory of communicative action provides the locus for the meeting of theology and the theory of science. See his *Science, Action, and Fundamental Theology: Toward a Theology of Communicative Action*, trans. J. Bohman (Cambridge, MA: MIT Press, 1984), xxiii; cf. Thiselton, *Two Horizons*, 4.

58. This general approach, a development of the pragmatics of politeness theory, has been suggested by Ken Turner, in "'$W_x = D(S,H) + P(H,S) + R_x$': Notes Towards an Investigation," *Revue de Sémantique et Pragmatique* 13 (2003): 47–67.

59. Here I am thinking of models of communication that operate with a simplistic abstraction of a speaker and a hearer, or a sender and a receiver, text and reader. It was characteristic of early speech-act theory and persists in some approaches to biblical hermeneutics.

60. Stephen C. Levinson, "Putting Linguistics on a Proper Footing: Explorations in Goffman's Concepts of Participation," in *Erving Goffman: Exploring the Interaction Order*, ed. P. Drew and A. Wootton (Cambridge: Polity, 1988), 163; cf. idem, *Pragmatics*, 54–96.

61. Levinson, "Putting Linguistics on a Proper Footing," 161–227.

helpfully transposed into the terminology of "participant role." By extension, the notions of "author" and "reader" can be similarly analyzed in the same way.[62] Together the production format and the participant roles become "the participation framework." Another insight of Goffman is to recognize ways in which speakers/authors shift their topic, register, or mood. He calls this "footing": "A change in footing implies a change in the alignment we take up to ourselves and the others present as expressed in the way we manage the production or reception of an utterance."[63]

Levinson prefers to talk in terms of a shift in participant role. A change of footing, or participant role, affects both production format and the nature of the participation framework. For example, a footing analysis of 1 Corinthians reveals multiple shifts in Paul's discourse: greeting, thanksgiving, pastoral instruction, references to the cross, appeals to Scripture, adopting a position of transcendence (as he narrates his apprehension of reality as a whole), narrative mode, first-person narrative mode, and so forth. A picture builds that enables us to identify the various elements that are integral to Christian discourse.[64]

Anthropological Description of the Text's Participation Framework

The next task is to provide a sociological and anthropological description of the participation framework. First, in addition to second-order anthropology, which posits various universals, a first-order analysis will also need to be made to include an account of the particular anthropology of the speech/hermeneutic situation in view. We have seen how Archer appeals to the important anthropological notion of practice.[65] So in 1 Corinthians, for instance, how do we describe Paul's own practice and habitus, the elements of reality that are constitutive of his being-in-the-world?[66] How does it differ from members of the congregation at Corinth? How does the habitus of members of a church community in a specific context today differ? Second, it will also be part of the

---

62. The application of pragmatics to the analysis of written texts is the focus of historical pragmatics.

63. Erving Goffman, "Footing," in *Forms of Talk* (Philadelphia: University of Pennsylvania Press, 1981), 128.

64. For further details, see William Olhausen, "Elements of Christian Discourse: From Politeness Theory to the Relational Hermeneutics of Paul's Word of the Cross," in *Religion und Sprache—Religion and Language*, ed. Marietta Calderón and Georg Marko, *Sprache im Kontext* 42 (Frankfurt am Main: Peter Lang, 2015), 207–26.

65. Bourdieu has a neat formula for the elements needed to understand what is involved in practice: {(habitus) (capital)} + field = practice (*Distinction*, 101).

66. The notion of habitus is an important concept in Bourdieu's social anthropology: see, e.g., *Logic of Practice*, 52–65.

social and anthropological analysis to describe the dynamics of the particular "fields," or networks of relations, occupied by members of the participation framework (1 Cor. 1:26–27).[67] Third, a relational account of hermeneutics will be sensitive to a number of sociological variables, including the role of power and social distance. Again, these phenomena are marked in language (spoken and written) and thus become the concern of sociolinguistics and discourse analysis.

Anthropological description must also provide an account of the Holy Spirit. Again 1 Corinthians provides us with a number of leads that need to be followed. First, Paul reminds the church that his proclamation has been accompanied by "a demonstration of the Spirit and of power" (1 Cor. 2:4). Exactly what Paul was referring to here is not explained.[68] However, his later teaching on the gifts of the Spirit may help to fill out the possible meanings. Equally, Paul's description of God's love being poured into the believers' hearts through the Holy Spirit (Rom. 5:5) may be at least part of the story. The close relationship between love and the gift of the Holy Spirit would also make good sense of chapter 13 of 1 Corinthians being inserted between Paul's teaching on the gifts of the Spirit in chapters 12 and 14. In any event, what is strongly implied is that the reception of the Gospel impacts the whole person in transformative ways.

Second, because of the noetic effects of sin, Paul explains that the apprehension of cruciform wisdom requires the revelatory assistance of the Spirit (1 Cor. 2:10–11; cf. 14:25). John's record of Jesus's encounter with Nicodemus might make an interesting dialogue partner for interpreting 1 Corinthians 2:6–16.

Third, Paul's description of the believer's body as a temple of the Holy Spirit (1 Cor. 6:19) not only carries important ethical implications but also invites us to revisit the Christian understanding of creation and anthropology. For instance, we might want to ask about the relationship between the first act of creation and the new creation. What might be the implications for prioritizing our "ultimate concerns"? Another important question raised by the Spirit's agency in the believer's life is to ask how the hermeneutical distance of history is mitigated. In the Spirit, the believer belongs to both the temporal order and to eternity. Similarly, the Spirit's presence must also put a

---

67. Pierre Bourdieu, *In Other Words* (Cambridge: Polity, 1990), 110. In this context, Gerd Theissen's sociological exegesis of New Testament studies remains important; see, e.g., his discussion of the plausibility basis for Paul's Christology, in *Social Reality and the Early Christians: Theology, Ethics, and the World of the New Testament*, trans. M. Kohl (Edinburgh: T&T Clark, 1993), 187–201.

68. There may be some important similarities in Paul's thinking here with his comments in Gal. 3:1–5.

limit on our estimations of linguistic and anthropological relativism. In these ways, the Spirit's role in theological interpretation, as part of the production format of the text and as active participant, alerts us to the need to maintain a critical distance from various aspects of philosophical hermeneutics. Indeed, this suspicion would be warranted even without theological considerations. Although there is certainly truth in the ideas of linguistic, historical, and anthropological relativism, the suggestion here is that this hermeneutical hand has been overplayed.

Summary

The thesis that theological interpretation needs a theological hermeneutic includes at least the following:

- Needed is a commitment to the philosophical and anthropological findings outlined under the first two theses.
- Theological interpretation will be open to the work of the Spirit in a wide range of disciplines that can assist the interpretative task. Areas deserving further investigation include the notion of practice and Goffman's appropriation of "face" to explicate the rituals and motivations involved in social interaction.
- Important work remains to be done to develop the shape of a theological pragmatics—a pragmatics that takes full account of the dynamics of the production format and participation framework that Scripture itself assumes. In this respect it is essential to provide a full account of the Spirit's role as participant and as part of the production format. Only then can theological interpretation take into account the necessary coordinates of meaning that bear on human being in the fellowship of God's "Son, Jesus Christ our Lord" (1 Cor. 1:9).
- Theological interpretation is not always well served by philosophical hermeneutics.

Conclusion

Theological interpretation needs a philosophy worked out in, and with, an orthodox Christian view of the world. A Christian metaphysic will insist on the intelligibility of the world and so the existence of criteria by which to come to judgments of fact as well as value. Therefore a Christian worldview will also need to be philosophically self-aware. Like a sword-stick, philosophy helps us to walk and enables us to fend off any threats. In both modernism and postmodernism, reductionist accounts of anthropology prove to be incompatible with theological interpretation, which instead requires a view of the human as capable of being addressed by, and of responding to, Scripture's witness to God's self-revelation in Christ. Finally, a theological hermeneutic needs to work with an expansive view of creation and consequently a more expansive understanding of the Spirit's person and work in the life of the believer, in the church, and in the world. This will include openness to insights from other fields of human endeavor and especially to the totality of human being in God's image, as implicated by the logic of the Christian story.

6

The Canon
and Theological Interpretation

Stephen G. Dempster

Canon as the Word of God and Basis for Theological Interpretation

One of the reasons for the renaissance in the theological interpretation of Scripture has been the growing recognition that something has been dreadfully wrong in the study of the Bible. The increasing gap between two worlds of Scripture reading—(1) the academic study of the Bible as a historical document and (2) its use among believers in the churches—has become a serious problem, a veritable Two Solitudes.[1] This problem has its roots in the Enlightenment and in some ways received classic expression toward the end of the nineteenth century, when Julius Wellhausen resigned his theological professorship at the University of Greifswald for reasons of conscience: "I became a theologian because I was interested in the scientific treatment of the Bible; it has only gradually dawned on me that a professor

---

1. Charles H. H. Scobie, *The Ways of Our God: An Approach to Biblical Theology* (Grand Rapids: Eerdmans, 2003), viii–x.

of theology likewise has a practical task of preparing students for service in the Evangelical Church, and that I was not fulfilling this practical task but was, in spite of all reserve on my part, incapacitating my hearers for their office."[2]

Yet the problem would not go away. As the one solitude of historical study of Scripture grew and had more and more influence over the seminaries, many pastors increasingly felt ill at ease with proclaiming, "Thus says the LORD," from their Bibles.[3] One pastor, steeped in this method through rigorous training, had an intellectual and spiritual breakthrough and discovered the strange new world of the Bible as he studied the Epistle to the Romans. Thus was born neoorthodoxy, and Karl Barth revived genuine theological interpretation, which had stressed the importance of the canon of Scripture: it is especially in these books that the church calls Holy Scripture that God has spoken and continues to speak. They are not just historical artifacts but are truly the Word of the living God.

While neoorthodoxy provided impetus to the biblical theology movement in North America in the mid-twentieth century, the rise and fall of this movement gave way to a renewed interest in various types of interpretation.[4] While historical criticism still had a strong foothold in the academy, it was losing its hegemony. The interest behind the text was being supplemented by an interest in the text itself as well as a focus on the interpreter in front of the text.[5] Each had something to offer as the entire interpretative process was being reconsidered. Interpretation behind the text was often an exercise in doubtful reconstruction, even though supplemented by further disciplines in the social sciences such as sociology, psychology and gender studies; it often depended on decisions made about the text itself, decisions even further dependent on factors influencing the interpreters of the text, such as the contemporary *Zeitgeist* and concerns about class and ethnicity. To make a similar point, Stanley Fish's celebrated book on reader-response

2. See Jeffrey Stackert's discussion of that resignation within the context of a telling chapter: "Locating Biblical Studies in the Academy: From Theology to Religious Studies," in *A Prophet Like Moses: Prophecy, Law, and Israelite Religion* (Oxford: Oxford University Press, 2014), 200–204. It is ironic, though, that Wellhausen was guided by his own theological and philosophical agenda, expressed classically in his *Prolegomena to the History of Israel*, trans. J. S. Black and A. Menzies (Edinburgh: Adam and Charles Black, 1885).

3. See, e.g., some of the points made by Walter Sundberg, "The Social Effect of Biblical Criticism," in *Renewing Biblical Interpretation*, ed. Craig G. Bartholomew, Colin J. D. Greene, and Karl Moller (Grand Rapids: Zondervan, 2000), 66–81.

4. See, e.g., Brevard S. Childs, *Biblical Theology in Crisis* (Philadelphia: Westminster, 1970).

5. Leo G. Perdue, *The Collapse of History: Reconstructing Old Testament Theology* (Minneapolis: Augsburg Fortress, 1994); Roger Lundin, *The Culture of Interpretation: Christian Faith and the Postmodern World* (Grand Rapids: Eerdmans, 1993).

criticism, *Is There a Text in This Class?*, could also have been titled *Is There a Class in This Text?*[6]

Yet the burning question never really asked by many biblical scholars who had often become focused so much on the minute details of the biblical text—the trees in the forest, so to speak—was the question that Barth had asked after World War I: "Is there a word from God in this ancient book?" Much biblical interpretation studied the Bible as if God—never mind his Word—did not exist.[7] Perhaps theoretically God existed, but not practically and certainly not within the pages of the Bible, which essentially had become an ancient artifact, a literary deposit of the national literature of an ancient Near Eastern culture. The frustration of some theologians with these developments can best be illustrated with Jürgen Moltmann's description of one of his theological nightmares:

> I imagine that I step behind the pulpit in a church and preach in order to proclaim the Gospel and, if possible, awaken the faith. But those who sit in the pew don't listen to my words. A historian is there who examines critically facts about which I am speaking; a psychologist is there who analyzes my psyche which reveals itself in my speech; a cultural anthropologist is there who observes my personal style; a sociologist is there who is identifying the class to which I belong as whose representative he believes I am functioning. Everybody is analyzing me and my context, but nobody is listening to what I want to say. And the worst thing is: nobody is disagreeing with me, nobody wants to discuss with me what I have just said.[8]

Moltmann's main point is telling. Interpretation has become one huge exercise in missing the point! Somehow the forest has been lost amid all the trees. Where is the Word of God? Is this not the final end and goal of biblical interpretation, to be addressed by God? This was a question that Brevard Childs raised for the academy and the church after the collapse of the biblical

---

6. Stanley Eugene Fish, *Is There a Text in This Class? The Authority of Interpretive Communities* (Cambridge, MA: Harvard University Press, 1980). The title springs from an anecdote in which a professor misunderstood the question asked by a student at the beginning of the semester (ibid., 305). "The new title, which plays on the word 'class' (classroom versus social stratum), I owe to Ben Faber" (personal communication).

7. Jack Miles, "Between Theology and Exegesis," review of *Jesus of Nazareth*, by Joseph Ratzinger, *Commonweal* 134 (2007): 21.

8. Jürgen Moltmann, "'Do You Understand What You Are Reading?': New Testament Scholarship and the Hermeneutical Question of Theology," unpublished manuscript; cited by Miroslav Volf, *Captive to the Word of God: Engaging the Scriptures for Contemporary Theological Reflection* (Grand Rapids: Eerdmans, 2010), 22.

theology movement, and it became his legacy. The Scriptures are not just any book: they are canon, the Word above all words, the Word of the living God.[9]

The Christian canon refers to the Old Testament and New Testament Scriptures, which are the very word of God: divine revelation. This means that humanity is not left to itself and to its own resources, but that into the midst of the darkness of its sin and lostness, God has illumined the situation with his Word. "In your light we see light," exclaims the psalmist (Ps. 36:9). That light has come through the filters of ancient human languages, refracted through the images and metaphors of a particular ancient Near Eastern culture in a specific historical period, but it nevertheless is light that shines on the darkness of the universal human condition. Time and time again, ancient Israel learned that it needed not just biological life but also a light for a dark place,[10] not just food for the body but also nourishment for the soul (Deut. 8:3). This is what is necessary for the flourishing of human life, for humans to be addressed by God. The canon of Scripture is the primary place where this happens.

Theological interpretation of the canon is based on the fact that this Word of God needs to be heard by human beings in order for them to experience a relationship with their Creator. Although it is important to learn Hebrew, Aramaic, and Greek; to study ancient customs and culture; to become familiar with the particular historical periods and times in which God first addressed Israel; to examine archaeological artifacts to shed light on these ancient societies; to be aware of the influences that affect the interpreters as they go about their task—theological interpretation will not lose its hermeneutical soul in the process. It would do so if it were not finally concerned with the fact that God is speaking in the words of Scripture. This is what Karl Barth learned as he studied the Letter to the Romans, that God is speaking not just to the apostle Paul and to the Roman church but is also addressing Barth himself, now in Safenwil, in the words of Holy Scripture. He was also included in that audience![11] The "then and there" of historical exegesis must serve the "here

9. Childs, *Biblical Theology in Crisis*; idem, *Introduction to the Old Testament as Scripture* (Philadelphia: Fortress Press, 1979); idem, *Biblical Theology of the Old and New Testaments: Theological Reflection on the Christian Bible* (Minneapolis: Fortress, 1993).

10. Ps. 119:105. For a reflection on this verse for theological interpretation of the Old Testament, see Stephen G. Dempster, "'A Light in a Dark Place': A Tale of Two Kings and Theological Interpretation of the Old Testament," *Southern Baptist Journal of Theology* 14 (2010): 18–26.

11. Note Karl Barth's first sentences in the preface to the first edition of his commentary: Paul, as a child of his age, addressed his contemporaries. It is however far more important, that as prophet and apostle of the Kingdom of God, he veritably speaks to all men of every age. The differences between then and now, there and here, no doubt require careful investigation and consideration. But the purpose of such investigation can only be to demonstrate that these differences are in fact, purely trivial.

and now" of hearing the Word of God today.[12] The fact that God has spoken makes the concern to understand that word paramount so that the nightmare of Moltmann does not come true. Analysis and exegesis must serve divine address.

Canon and Community

The standard historical explanation for canon is that at best it is simply a product of the believing community, a fortuitous result of historical circumstances, or at worst a product of political power, the result of the victors in internecine theological struggles.[13] Thus the documents have no inherent transcendent value as such but for various reasons were considered important, and the community or communities gave them a "divine" stamp of approval. External forces operating within the communities produced the canon. This is for the most part the "master narrative" within the academic community.[14] Canon is simply a "human repertoire": documents *considered* sacred and special became canon. Viewed from a distinctly immanent frame,[15] the chief mark of canon is its enumerative nature: it is simply a special list.[16] Thus there is no distinct ontology of canon.[17] Frequently the points are made that canon does not signify *a collection of authoritative documents* but *an authoritative collection of documents*, and that it is wrong to confuse the two. An external process of canonization made a collection of authoritative documents into an authoritative collection through a series of decisions by councils and groups. When the two facts are confused, so it is said, there is historical anachronism since the earlier collection is given an authority it never had, and that later collection owes its authority to human decisions.

Barth proceeds by stating that "the mighty voice of Paul was new to me." He found that he, two thousand years later, had also been addressed by the Word of God (*The Epistle to the Romans* (New York: Oxford University Press, 1968), 1–2.

12. These expressions are taken from Volf, *Captive to the Word of God.*

13. See a similar description in John Webster, "'A Great and Meritorious Act of the Church?': The Dogmatic Location of the Canon," in *Die Einheit der Schrift und die Vielfalt des Kanons*, ed. John Barton and Michael Wolter (Berlin: de Gruyter, 2003), 95–126.

14. See, e.g., Lee M. McDonald, *The Biblical Canon: Its Origin, Transmission, and Authority*, 3rd ed. (Peabody, MA: Hendrickson, 2007); idem, ed., *The Canon Debate* (Peabody, MA: Hendrickson, 2002).

15. For the use of this term, see Charles Taylor, *A Secular Age* (Cambridge, MA: Harvard University Press, 2009), 539–93.

16. See Jonathan Z. Smith, "Sacred Persistence: Toward a Redescription of Canon," in *Imagining Religion: From Babylon to Jonestown* (Chicago: University of Chicago Press, 1982), 36–52; idem, "Canons, Catalogues and Classics," in *Canonization and Decanonization*, ed. A. van der Kooij and Karel van der Toorn (Leiden: Brill, 1998), 295–311.

17. Webster, "'A Great and Meritorious Act of the Church?'"

This immanent explanation is fundamentally a misleading narrative of events since it suggests that the canon as canon did not have a real history and that suddenly it became the result of a council "granting the imprimatur of canonicity in a single shining moment of beatitude."[18] Ironically this creation ex nihilo was done by human beings! The truth of the matter is that there was continuity between the authoritative documents and the later authoritative collection.[19] An open canon of the words of God was later closed.

Although the community was definitely involved in the production of the Word of God (one thinks, e.g., of the prophets and apostles, who spoke and wrote in their very different styles and from their diverse backgrounds), in the editing and transmission of the word by the scribes, and in the acceptance of these texts by the believing community—the community itself is not the final arbiter and definer of the Word of God. Rather, it is the Word and Spirit of God that forms the community and sets it apart. And the community affirms an authority that is already inherent in the documents. Thus there is an internal force within the canon that identifies the material as transcendent, and over a period of time the community eventually recognizes it. Through the historical process there was a canonical evolution, from a basic core, from the original Ten Commandments, to the full two-Testament Bible. The canon is not an accident of history, the result of an external force, such as a community of faith, that arbitrarily made decisions on which books to include or exclude. Rather, in these documents the community of faith through the generations recognized the voice of the living God and gave them its stamp of approval. A final seal of approval that completed the canon simply ratified the self-authenticating voice of God speaking in these texts and attesting to their divine source.

It is the community that is the ideal context for the divine address. In a sense the canon creates community since all who wish to live under its parameters and authority now belong to a particular group of people living in the world, a people who have become part of a new family generated by the divine Word (1 Pet. 1:23; cf. Mark 3:32–35). The community ratifies this divine Word by acknowledging its authority and living by its precepts.

18. The quote is from Andrew Plaks, "Afterword: Canonization in the Ancient World; The View from Farther East," in *Homer, the Bible, and Beyond: Literary and Religious Canons in the Ancient World*, ed. M. Finkelberg and G. G. Stroumsa (Leiden: Brill, 2003), 270. Plaks summarizes a conclusion of scholars studying the concept of canon in the ancient world that a late extrinsic imprimatur of canonicity being placed on a collection of books is a myth not only for biblical canons but also for extrabiblical ones.

19. "The delimitation of a series of sacred texts discernible from other literature only makes sense when based on a canonical or standardizing notion" (Luc Zaman, *Bible and Canon: A Modern Historical Inquiry* (Leiden: Brill Academic, 2008), 25.

Many stages were involved in the evolution of the canon, and it was a complex process, with little external evidence that can point to a clear line of development.[20] At the same time it is certain that a collection of authoritative writings was in the process of becoming an authoritative collection of writings, and some of those signs are found within the documents themselves and in their textual history.[21] But it is also clear that there were two fundamental stages in the formation of the Christian Bible. By the time of Jesus, and certainly by the end of the first century of the Common Era, the question of an authoritative collection, canon in the sense of a final list, had been largely settled within Judaism. Thus the early church was born with a canon in its hands. Although in the first century there were many disputes involving early Christian evangelists in synagogue settings, there was never any dispute over the documents themselves. For example, Paul used a Bible in common with the people he was seeking to evangelize. The Jesus he preached really had nothing to do with much of the noncanonical religious literature of Judaism.[22] The parentage of this Jesus—his genealogy—was found exclusively in the Law, Prophets, and Psalms.[23] As Hans von Campenhausen has observed, "In the early church the problem was not how to square faith with an Old Testament regarded as outmoded but the reverse. How, in the light of Scripture regarded as authoritative and a privileged witness to God and His truth, could it be said that Jesus was in accordance and was one with the Father who sent him?"[24]

20. See, e.g., for the Old Testament, Peter Brandt, *Endgestalten des Kanons: Das Arrangement der Schriften Israels in der jüdischen und christlichen Bibel* (Berlin: Philo, 2001); Stephen G. Dempster, "Canons on the Left and Canons on the Right: Finding a Resolution in the Canon Debate," *Journal of the Evangelical Theological Society* 52, no. 1 (2009): 47–77. For the New Testament, see Hans von Campenhausen, *The Formation of the Christian Bible* (Philadelphia: Fortress, 1972); David Trobisch, *The First Edition of the New Testament* (Oxford: Oxford University Press, 2000).

21. For a fine, careful summary of some of the research and the issues involved, see Ched Spellman, *Toward a Canon-Conscious Reading of the Bible: Exploring the History and Hermeneutics of the Canon*, New Testament Monographs 34 (Sheffield: Sheffield Phoenix, 2014).

22. Some would point to the use of "noncanonical" here as anachronistic. But, first, that is to assume that there is no continuity between a collection of authoritative documents and an authoritative collection. Second, canon in the second sense has been established within the first century CE.

23. Stephen G. Dempster, "From Many Texts to One: The Formation of the Hebrew Bible," in *The World of the Aramaeans: Biblical Studies in Honour of Paul-Eugène Dion*, ed. P. Michèle Daviau, John W. Wevers, and Michael Weigl (Sheffield: Sheffield Academic Press, 2001), 1:19–56.

24. Von Campenhausen, *Formation of the Christian Bible*, 64–65. It is clear, however, that Christian scribes were tampering with the content of the Word of God; this explains some of the Christian additions to the Septuagint and the need for new Greek translations of the Septuagint for Jews, such as those of Aquila and Symmachus. Jews were concerned that Christians had hijacked their Greek Bible and were making changes to it in order to confirm their views. On the issue of a wider scriptural canon used by the church instead of a narrower one by the

With the coming of Jesus, the early church realized that the revelation of God had broken out afresh again, and there was the awareness that a new day had come and that such a time had been the long-awaited goal of the Jewish Scriptures. In the teaching of Jesus himself—orally transmitted at first before being preserved in documents that finally evolved into the Gospels—there is a clear recognition of the authority of the ancient Scriptures as well as Jesus's own transcendent authority, which he contrasts with the Torah. He can speak about the importance of every iota of the Scriptures being accomplished and yet in the great Antitheses immediately elevate his own teaching to a place higher than the commands in the Torah.[25] Sayings such as these were collected and transmitted before being finally produced in the Gospels. In addition, the process of collecting Paul's missionary letters to the churches had also begun. By the end of the first century, these writings were being read in public gatherings of believers; by the middle of the second century, it is clear that the apostles and prophets were being read alongside each other in early Christian services.[26] Thus in the nascent Christian church, writings that became the New Testament had an equal authority with writings from the Old Testament.

The church's responses to both Marcion on the one hand and Montanus on the other hand show the importance of canon for the church.[27] By rejecting Marcion's truncated canon, the church ensured that the Old Testament and Israel would be an integral part of the canon, as well as a larger "Jewish" corpus of writings in the New Testament that included more than the Gospel of Luke and the Pauline letters. Israel was the mother of the church. By rejecting Montanus, the church was rejecting a charismatically inspired revelation that was not tied to the authority of Christ and the apostles. Thus it was not any spirit that was confined to a book but rather the Holy Spirit, the Spirit of Christ. With the terminology the old covenant and the new covenant to describe the two parts of their Bible, the church was using scriptural terminology of ancient Israel to describe the relationship between God and his people. There was the one people of God. In the canon of Scripture, as Gerhard von Rad has phrased it so well, "Christ is given to us only through the double witness of the choir of those who await and those who remember."[28]

---

synagogue, see the pertinent comments by Christopher Seitz, "The Canonical Approach and Theological Interpretation," in *Canon and Biblical Interpretation*, ed. Craig G. Bartholomew et al. (Grand Rapids: Zondervan, 2010), 95–96.

25. Cf. Matt. 5:18–19, 21–48. See, e.g., a contemporary Jewish response to these teachings: Jacob Neusner, *A Rabbi Talks with Jesus* (New York: Doubleday, 1993).

26. See Justin Martyr, *1 Apology* 67.

27. See, e.g., von Campenhausen, *The Formation of the Christian Bible*.

28. Gerhard von Rad, "Typological Interpretation of the Old Testament," in *Essays on Old Testament Hermeneutics*, ed. Claus Westermann (Richmond: John Knox, 1969), 39;

Nonetheless, there is a problem in determining the outer boundaries of the Old Testament in the Christian Bible. The narrow canon of Judaism is the canon of Protestantism; the Roman Catholic and Orthodox canons are wider.[29] This reflects the early church's adoption of the Septuagint and the use within the church of other Jewish Greek writings that were popular. As the church and synagogue moved farther and farther apart, and Latin translations were even produced, there was concern about the limits of canon.[30] Although Jerome was the champion of the narrower canon, Augustine believed that God had also inspired the wider one. This was never really resolved in the church: a wider canon (reflected in the Vulgate) held sway until the Reformation, when the narrower canon of Judaism was adopted by the Reformers. Although the outer limits of the Old Testament canon are blurred to this day, there nevertheless is a comprehensive irreducible core of canonical books common to these main streams of Christendom. The deuterocanonical books can certainly be read for profit by Protestantism and were widely read until relatively recently, while the protocanonical books connect the church strongly to its Jewish roots.[31]

Canon as Context

The canon is not only the ground for theological interpretation but is also intimately bound to the community that the Word and Spirit of God have formed; it provides the interpretative context for that community. The church is thereby protected from being "dominated by alien voices, alien motivations,

---

Bruce Waltke, "Kingdom Promises as Spiritual," in *Continuity and Discontinuity: Perspectives on the Relationship between the Old and New Testaments*, ed. John S. Feinberg (Westchester, IL: Crossway, 1988), 263–88.

29. The wider canon of Roman Catholicism consists of 1 and 2 Maccabees, Judith, Tobit, Baruch, Sirach, Wisdom of Solomon, as well as Additions to Esther, Additions to Daniel, and the Letter of Jeremiah. Beyond these, the Orthodox Old Testament lists 3 and 4 Maccabees, 1 Esdras, and Ps. 151.

30. This can be seen, e.g., in Melito, the Bishop of Sardis, making a trip to the East to determine the exact number of the Old Testament books (ca. 170 CE).

31. A common view is that there were two Jewish canons, a narrower Palestinian canon and a wider Alexandrian canon, which was adopted by the church. This has been decisively shown to be wrong by Albert Sundberg Jr., in *The Old Testament of the Early Church* (Cambridge, MA: Harvard University Press, 1964). Sundberg argues that, because of significant disputes with early Christianity, a wider corpus of Jewish religious writings was narrowed as a result of a council of Jabneh in 90 CE; see idem, "'The Old Testament': A Christian Canon," *Catholic Biblical Quarterly* 30 (1968): 143–55. The Christians were therefore left with the wider corpus when a smaller corpus was canonized by the Jews. This assumes that a council of Jabneh made important decisions about the determination of the Jewish canon, a theory that has been refuted by recent scholarship; see Jack P. Lewis, "What Do We Mean by Jabneh?," *Journal of Bible and Religion* 32 (1964): 125–32. See also note 25 above.

and alien goals in political and social movements,"[32] and it is thereby able to evaluate all of these.[33] The Word of God is to be found within the boundaries of canonical space and can be delivered to any historical context of the church.[34] It is specifically within this space that the divine voice is heard: it is the definitive context! This canonical context provides freedom and protection from the spirits of every age, and within it there is a divine word for any historical context.

Similarly the context of the *whole* counsel of God provides needed balance and correctives for believers. There are many words of God within the canon, and seeing them as a whole helps us to see the various accents and emphases in all their diversity as well as their unity. The larger canonical context is able to show how the various parts of the canon connect, interrelate, reveal the major accents and emphases, and dialogue with one another. Thus the canon is not flat and one-dimensional but has depth, contour, and texture and must be understood in its rich and multifaceted totality, what is called *tota Scriptura*. The four Gospels give a breadth of vision that one Gospel could never give, and these occur right at the beginning of the New Testament, announcing Jesus Christ as the center of the canon.

Consequently, seeing the entirety of the canonical scope can help to determine the central from the peripheral. Thus, for example, Anah's finding the "hot springs in the desert" in Genesis 36:24 (NIV) while seeking pasture for his father's donkeys has a different value than the Shema in Deuteronomy 6:4–9, and the exodus event is viewed as more important than Paul's request for Timothy to come and bring his coat, which was left with Carpus (2 Tim. 4:13). Without the entire canonical context, it is easy to lose sight of the forest for the trees. Thus the prophets are constantly upbraiding their audiences for doing just that by putting undue emphasis on certain elements from the Torah while not emphasizing more their "weightier" elements: justice, mercy, and faith (Hos. 6:1–3; Isa. 5:1–7; Mic. 6:1–8). Jesus makes similar remarks about the religion of his own day (Matt. 23:23). Indeed, Jesus's own understanding of marriage and divorce works within a canonical context, which places the

32. Hans Walter Wolff, *Micah the Prophet*, trans. Ralph Gehrke (Philadelphia: Fortress, 1981), 135.

33. Wolff is speaking from the sad history of his own church's compromise with such alien voices because of a failure to take the Old Testament seriously (ibid.). For this failure to take the entire biblical canon as context for interpretation, see Robert P. Ericksen, *Theologians under Hitler: Gerhard Kittel, Paul Althaus, and Emanuel Hirsch* (New Haven: Yale University Press, 1987).

34. Paul S. Fiddes, "The Canon as Space and Place," in Barton and Wolter, *Die Einheit der Schrift und die Vielfalt des Kanons*, 127–50. This is not to deny the reality of natural revelation but to indicate the priority of canonical revelation; cf. Ps. 19 and Rom. 1:16–32.

law of Deuteronomy 24 against the backdrop of the first chapters of Genesis and connects the historical dots (Matt. 19:1–10). Paul's own understanding of justification works with a similar hermeneutical sweep by noting that the Law came after the promise (Gal. 3:17–29).[35] Thus the prophets, Jesus, and Paul work with an understanding of the text against a wider canonical context, with a narrative shape. Without this wider context, it is possible to make the canon into a dead letter, in which everything becomes flattened into one dimension, in which Scripture is "proverbialized."[36]

All the individual texts must finally be seen in light of the entire text of Scripture so that they receive their proper balance and order. This shows the importance of promise and fulfillment, plus the importance of typology, so that the sacrifices of Leviticus, for example, are no longer practiced but are seen to have their fulfillment in the sacrifice of Christ, or so that the command to circumcise in Genesis is viewed in light of the command not to circumcise in Galatians. At the same time the canonical theology of such early texts is fully in place, and their fulfillment shows a theological depth in the Scriptures that a simple, local exegesis would not be able to appreciate. Similarly, texts that illustrate divine violence in the Scripture can create many problems for individuals who speak of them as intractable biblical problems, part of the "dark side of Scripture," essentially repressive, some of the broken word of God, and needing to be distinguished from the sacred word.[37] Likewise others argue that texts in the canon also legitimize slavery and the subjugation of women, claiming that such repressive and embarrassing texts might better be excised from the canon.[38] Part of the problem, however, is that such texts are not viewed as part of the entire context of Scripture's canon. For example, with respect to the problem of divine violence, the first use of divine violence in the Bible occurs in the story of the flood and is done in order to eliminate rampant human violence; when that attempt fails, God promises to direct the violence against himself in the future (Gen. 6:1–7; 8:20–22).[39] The last

---

35. In this regard, note Jon Douglas Levenson's critique of von Rad as he maintains that Gen. 26:5 should be just as important to consider in Abraham's justification as Gen. 15:6. But the point is that Gen. 15:6 occurs before 26:5. See Levenson, *The Hebrew Bible, the Old Testament, and Historical Criticism: Jews and Christians in Biblical Studies* (Louisville: Westminster John Knox, 1993), 60.

36. See, e.g., the use of Scripture in the Mishnah: Alexander Samely, *The Rabbinic Interpretation of Scripture in the Mishnah* (Oxford: Oxford University Press, 2002).

37. Robert P. Carroll, *The Bible as a Problem for Christianity* (Harrisburg, PA: Trinity Press International, 1991); Kenton L. Sparks, *Sacred Word, Broken Word: Biblical Authority and the Dark Side of Scripture* (Grand Rapids: Eerdmans, 2012).

38. McDonald, *Biblical Canon*, 426–29.

39. I am indebted to Terence E. Fretheim for the observation about the first act of divine violence. See Terence E. Fretheim, "'I Was Only a Little Angry': Divine Violence in the Prophets,"

word on violence is God's ideal for the world, in which the nations come to worship at the temple, hear the word of the Lord, and leave transformed, showing that transformation in practical ways by beating their swords into plowshares and their spears into pruning hooks (Isa. 2:1–5).[40]

It is worth considering some of the so-called texts of terror and even the more marginal texts in the canon.[41] Rather than apologizing for such texts, some pastoral counselors find that such texts particularly speak to people on the margins of life. These people live in the world of the prison, the slum, the shack, the red-light district, the low-rent housing complex, the world of the terrorized and the persecuted. Texts that bother and embarrass so-called conventional churchgoers are the very lifelines that often speak to the disenfranchised.[42]

Finally, the context of canon places limits on interpretation. It might be possible to interpret certain texts in certain ways outside the context of the canon, but the context of canon constrains certain meanings. Thus the Song of Songs cannot be read as a pornographic text that celebrates sexuality outside the context of marriage,[43] nor can the story of the fall be interpreted as a text in which the serpent tells the truth and God ends up the liar.[44] If one just had the immediate text, one might be able to reach this conclusion, but since the text has a larger context and the global context of the canon, such interpretations are ruled out.[45] The canonical context helps to clarify ambiguity.

The provision of a canon to the church means that it must seek to understand the *whole* counsel of God, and this provides it with a breadth of vision

---

Interpretation 58 (2004): 365–75. But the first actual reference to divine violence is Yahweh's killing of animals to provide clothes for fallen humanity (Gen. 3:21). Violence has the goal of love.

40. This shows the importance of Bruce Waltke's consideration of the canonical context for understanding individual texts: "The text's intention became deeper and clearer as the parameters of the canon were expanded. Just as redemption itself has a progressive history, so also older texts in the canon underwent a correlative progressive perception of meaning as they became part of a growing canonical literature" ("Kingdom Promises as Spiritual," 284).

41. Phyllis Trible, *Texts of Terror* (Philadelphia: Fortress, 1984).

42. Bob Ekblad, *Reading the Bible with the Damned* (Louisville: Westminster John Knox, 2005). See also John L. Thompson, *Reading the Bible with the Dead: What You Can Learn from the History of Exegesis That You Can't Learn from Exegesis Alone* (Grand Rapids: Eerdmans, 2007).

43. As it is, e.g., in many modern studies of the text. Thus after the Song's first words (1:2), The Skeptic's Bible can add, "A fitting beginning for a pornographic poem"; http://skepticsannotated bible.com/sofs/sex_list.html.

44. See the following spirited discussion: R. W. L. Moberly, review of *The Garden of Eden and the Hope of Immortality*, by James Barr, *Journal of Theological Studies* 45 (April 1, 1994): 172–75; James Barr, "Is God A Liar? (Genesis 2–3)—and Related Matters," *Journal of Theological Studies* 57 (2006): 1–22.

45. Moshe Halbertal, *People of the Book: Canon, Meaning, and Authority* (Cambridge, MA: Harvard University Press, 1997).

and a depth of insight that a partial canon could never give. Consequently the church must not make a canon within the canon, whether with justification by faith, the Mosaic law, the Sermon on the Mount, or whatever. Individuals not only have their favorite texts; churches and institutions have theirs as well. The battle between the false prophets and the true prophets in the Old Testament was never over the authority of Scripture but rather because parts of Scripture were being emphasized to the exclusion of others. For example, the false prophets in Micah's day emphasized only the first half of the Israelite credo in Exodus 34:5–6, with its focus on God's mercy, grace, and forgiveness; they said nothing about the second half, God's punishment of the guilty (Mic. 2:6–7a). The prophet Jonah, while only too well aware of the second part of that creedal formula, did not want to be reminded of the first part (Jonah 4:2). For many of the false prophets, their canon within the canon was Israel's choice by God, and from that central governing principle they were able to ignore or run roughshod over many other passages that stressed the people's responsibility to keep the Torah and thus be a light to the nations. Hence they misread the Torah. They heard and took to heart the initial half of the covenantal formulary, "I will be your God," but they forgot the conclusion, "And you will be my people."[46]

The Goal of the Canon—Internal

While the total canonical context prohibits a canon within a canon, it does not mean that there is no goal for the canon. Restating von Rad, "Christ is given to us only through the double witness of the choir of those who await and those who remember." Jesus Christ is the focus of those who await and those who remember: he is the goal of the canon. All the words reach their fulfillment in him, the Word made flesh! (John 1:14). "God spoke . . . in many and various ways by the prophets, but in these last days he has spoken to us by a Son" (Heb. 1:1–2). The Old Testament looks forward to him, and the New Testament is a response to his life, death, and resurrection. He is the life-giving Word of God sent for the salvation of humanity, the light of the world; thus the first word spoken in the canon is "Let there be light" (Gen. 1:3), and at the end of the canon he is the reason why the sun and moon have become obsolete in the new heavens and new earth, "for the glory of God is its light, and its lamp is the Lamb" (Rev. 21:23). The Old Testament and the New Testament have their own discrete integrity yet are inextricably bound together. Without

---

46. W. Rudolph, *Micha, Habakuk, Zephanja*, Kommentar zum Alten Testament 13, no. 3 (Gutersloh: Gutersloher Verlagshaus, 1975), 138.

the Old Testament, the New Testament has no meaning. Without the New Testament, the Old Testament has lost its goal.

Although Christ is the goal of the canon, it is important to stress the integrity of both Testaments so that each are given their full canonical weight. The Old Testament keeps the faith of believers grounded in the story of Israel, the importance of creation, the need for redemption from sin, the significance of place and people and worship, the emphases on the holiness and justice of God, the importance of judgment *and* salvation, the concepts of sacrifice and priesthood, and the revelation of God's character at Sinai. It is no wonder that Dietrich Bonhoeffer declares:

> My thoughts and feelings seem to be getting more and more like those of the Old Testament, and in recent months I have been reading the Old Testament much more than the New. It is only when one knows the unutterability of the name of God that one can utter the name of Jesus Christ; it is only when one loves life and the earth so much that without them everything seems to be over that one may believe in the resurrection and a new world; it is only when one submits to God's law that one may speak of grace; and it is only when God's wrath and vengeance are hanging as grim realities over the heads of one's enemies that something of what it means to love and forgive them can touch our hearts. In my opinion it is not Christian to want to take our thoughts and feelings too quickly and too directly from the New Testament. We have already talked about this several times, and every day confirms my opinion. One cannot and must not speak the last word before the last [day] but one.[47]

Moreover, without the Old Testament the last quarter of the Christian Bible, the New Testament, would hang suspended in midair. The first chapter of the first Gospel, Matthew, would be almost incomprehensible. What would be the point of its first phrase, "the book of the birth [genesis] of . . ." (Matt. 1:1, literally)? What would be the point of the genealogy beginning with Jesus the *Messiah*, the son of *David* and then son of *Abraham* (1:1)? What is the Messiah? Who are David and Abraham? Why the unique mention of women in the genealogy?[48] Why the list of three sections of fourteen members representing three historical epochs: Abraham to David, David to the exile,

47. Dietrich Bonhoeffer, *Letters and Papers from Prison*, updated (Austin: Touchstone, 1997), 50. See also Brevard S. Childs: "It is a major function of Old Testament Theology to treat the Old Testament in such a manner as to guard it from being used simply as a foil for the New Testament. Rather it is theologically important to understand the Old Testament's witness in its own right with regard to its coherence, variety and unresolved tensions" (*Old Testament Theology in a Canonical Context* [Minneapolis: Fortress Press, 1985], 17).

48. Matt. 1:3, 5 (2 times), 6. And there is the mother of Jesus in 1:18.

the exile to Jesus (1:17)? What about the meaning of the names "Jesus" and "Emmanuel" (1:21, 23)? But read within the prior context of the Old Testament, it is clearly understood that Matthew is beginning "a new Genesis," establishing a firm bond "between the creation of the cosmos and Adam and Eve on the one hand, and the new creation brought by the Messiah on the other."[49] The genealogy begins with Abraham since his seed is to be the bearer of universal blessing, to reverse the ancient, universal curse. The unique use of the feminine names in a genealogy stresses all the more the universal nature of this blessing since all four are associated with gentiles. The three epochs of fourteen emphasize that Israel's history has ended in exile, but that is not the last word; the last word is the birth of a Savior, whose name means the end of exile—salvation from sin—and that God at last will be home with his people!

One could easily extrapolate the main point of the previous paragraph to the rest of the New Testament. There are countless quotations and allusions that depend on a knowledge of the Old Testament, and not just a superficial knowledge. An entire stock of phrases and images as well as a vocabulary for concepts, stories, and even institutions come from Israel's Scriptures. In terms of the Bible as a story or a play, to have the New Testament without the Old would be like reading the last quarter of a story without the first three-quarters, or to read only the last act of a four-act play. It would be almost impossible to understand. What is the point of the salvation in Christ? Saved from what? Saved to what? Why use Adam-Christ typology? The New Testament remains an insoluble riddle without the Old Testament.

That is why it is so important to work at coming to terms with the discrete witness of the Old Testament. It needs to be understood on its own terms before the New Testament is considered. This is why it is important to keep a Jewish-Christian dialogue open since Christians can learn from studies of the Tanak alone, to which often their Christian eyes keep them oblivious.[50] It is also important to realize that there was no revision of the Old Testament when it was adopted by Christianity. Moreover, it was not placed after the New Testament as a type of appendix; it was situated at the beginning, to provide the essential context for the latter document and as a fundamental dialogue partner.

At the same time, reading the Old Testament without the New would be somehow to miss the main point of it all, like reading the first three acts

---

49. W. D. Davies and Dale C. Allison Jr., *Matthew 1–7* (Edinburgh: A&C Black, 2004), 150. I am indebted to Brian Renshaw and Brian Davidson for this reference.

50. Marvin A. Sweeney, *Tanak: A Theological and Critical Introduction to the Jewish Bible* (Minneapolis: Fortress, 2012). See also Stephen G. Dempster, review of *Tanak: A Theological and Critical Introduction to the Jewish Bible*, by Marvin A. Sweeney, *McMaster Journal of Theology* 14 (2012–13): 203–10.

without the fourth act of a play, the first three-quarters of a novel without the last part. We would still be in the posture of expectation and waiting, to be Annas and Simeons, forever waiting for the experience of saying,

> Master, now you are dismissing your servant in peace,
>> according to your word;
> For my eyes have seen your salvation,
>> which you have prepared in the presence of all peoples:
> a light for revelation to the Gentiles,
>> and for glory to your people Israel. (Luke 2:29–32)

Or it could be like the Ephesians to whom Paul preaches, who know only the baptism of John the Baptist and not that of the Holy Spirit (Acts 19:1–7). But most of all it would be to read the Old Testament like the two disciples on the Emmaus road, without the Master Interpreter walking alongside them to help them make sense of the entire sweep of Israel's story (Luke 24:13–53). Without his instruction, the recent events over which they have been so troubled do not make sense. But with his instruction, they pass from being fools and slow of heart to being able to understand the Law, the Prophets, and the Psalms. The death and resurrection of Jesus have changed everything. The disciples now see that this is the key to and climax of Israel's story. Jesus transforms their understanding so that they are able to make connections between the events, stories, and people in a way that they could never have imagined. As a result they are able to reread the book with a knowledge of the ending, which helps them to see things in a totally different way: instead of waiting for what the one true God has promised to do for Israel at the end of time, they see that action already now in Jesus of Nazareth, in the middle of time.[51] Thus the result of "the resurrection of the Crucified Messiah is the breaking in of the last day,"[52] announced in the Old Testament; as a result it is no longer one day but an era. The old powers of sin and death are still at work, but their decisive hold has been broken, and the good news of this message can be preached to the nations, who are given a chance to repent.[53] Although many Old Testament texts speak of the judgment of the nations, these passages are now to be seen in their proper order. First comes the ingathering of the nations and then judgment on the unrepentant. Thus the New Testament and the Old Testament must be heard together.

---

51. N. T. Wright, *What Saint Paul Really Said* (Grand Rapids: Eerdmans, 1997), 36.
52. Lesslie Newbigin, *The Gospel in a Pluralist Society* (Grand Rapids: Eerdmans, 1989), 110.
53. Ibid.

The Goal of the Canon—External

Interpreting the canon theologically ensures that both Testaments must be heard together and that Jesus Christ as the Final Word of God is the internal goal of the canon. But this also means that the external goal of the canon is soteriological and missiological.[54] The goal of revelation is to illuminate the darkness of the *tōhû wābōhû* at the beginning of creation; after all, the first word of God is "Let there be light!" (Gen. 1:2–3). While the canon is a collection of documents, it is shaped in the form of a comprehensive Story, a metanarrative, that sketches out the history from the beginning of the world to the End. The climax of the Story is found in the fourfold repetition of the Gospels, in which Jesus Christ is seen as the climax of Israel's history. The revelation of the Son of God as the Word of God is the goal of the canon, and this has a fundamental salvific purpose. Key points in the canonical narrative serve to highlight this story-shaped salvation in which everyone is invited to see their story in this larger Story, and thus participate in the salvation that is offered. In this Story, "God creates the world, the world gets lost, [and] God seeks to restore the world to the glory for which he created it."[55] The goal of the canon is that the law of God, heard so powerfully at Sinai, be written in each human being's heart: that God's law be transferred from the tablets of stone, scrolls, and codices of papyrus and leather in the ancient world, or books printed on paper or distributed via digital media in the modern world, and inscribed on human hearts by the Holy Spirit (2 Cor. 3).

> The New Testament documents are largely written for this missiological purpose (cf. Luke 1:1–3; John 20:31), and Jesus's revelation to his disciples on the Emmaus road shows that this was the fundamental purpose of the Old Testament Scriptures, the story of Israel: Thus it is written, that the Messiah is to suffer and to rise from the dead on the third day, and that repentance and forgiveness of sins is to be proclaimed in his name to all nations, beginning from Jerusalem. You are witnesses of these things. And see, I am sending upon you what my Father promised; so stay here in the city until you have been clothed with power from on high. (Luke 24:46–49)

Moreover, in the transmission of the text, the adoption of the codex ensured the missiological, evangelical function of the Scriptures. One reason

54. H. Dan Beeby, *Canon and Mission* (Harrisburg, PA: Trinity Press International, 1999).
55. Frederick Buechner, "The Bible as Literature," in *A Complete Literary Guide to the Bible*, ed. Leland Ryken and Tremper Longman III (Grand Rapids: Zondervan, 1993), 48.

for preferring the codex was its practical value (easier to carry and to find passages) for itinerant evangelists in the spread of the gospel.[56]

The canon is thus not written merely for information but it is written to give life: behind the gift of God's Word lies a philosophical anthropology encapsulated in the words of Deuteronomy: "One does not live by bread alone, but by every word that comes from the mouth of God" (Deut. 8:3). The very formation of the canon shows the importance of putting that Word of God into each human being. Within the boundaries of canon is a word that is comprehensive and produces life. The Word is a multifaceted word encompassing a multitude of genres and life situations. There is a text for every situation imaginable, from the utter darkness of Psalm 88 to the light and glory of the New Jerusalem in Isaiah 60. This word is to be internalized in the lives of members of communities of faith so that they may experience its life-giving blessing. Throughout the canon of the Old and New Testaments is the repeated command at significant junctures to internalize the creative word of God (Gen. 1:3) through reading and meditation, and thus to experience the life-giving blessing of God (Josh. 1:8–9; Ps. 1:1–2; Rev. 1:3; 22:7).[57] The goal of the canon is to have its words transferred to the hearts of human beings, so that they can become minicanons that "anyone can read just by looking at them" (see 2 Cor. 3:1–3 Message). The canon gives wisdom for salvation and is "for teaching, rebuking, correcting and training in righteousness, so that the servant of God may be thoroughly equipped for every good work" (2 Tim. 3:15–17 NIV), becoming conformed to the divine image.[58] In this way the internal and external goals of the canon combine.

Every effort must be used to help us understand the Word of God as it was addressed to its original audience. Since that Word was first addressed to a particular human community in a particular historical period, every tool of historical exegesis must be used, albeit recontextualized within a theology of history. Yet the basic prerequisite for understanding the canon is the attitude of the young boy Samuel in the Old Testament, who says, "Speak, LORD, for your servant is listening" (1 Sam. 3:9), and the attitude of Mary in the New Testament, as she sits at the feet of Jesus and treasures his every word (Luke 10:39).

---

56. Larry W. Hurtado, *The Earliest Christian Artifacts: Manuscripts and Christian Origins* (Grand Rapids: Eerdmans, 2006), 66–78.

57. See further Spellman, *Toward a Canon-Conscious Reading*.

58. The last chapter of Ched Spellman's book (*Toward a Canon-Conscious Reading*), "Identifying and Becoming the Ideal Reader of the Biblical Canon," is well worth reading.

7

Biblical Theology
and Theological Interpretation

David J. H. Beldman and Jonathan Swales

Introduction and Definition

Scripture is "God-Speaking literature."[1] The literature of the Bible, written and compiled over the course of some two thousand years, penned in Hebrew (and some Aramaic) and Greek, composed in a variety of literary genres by authors from different socioeconomic backgrounds, presents the living voice of God to us. Since the one true God, the Father of Jesus the Messiah, speaks in and through Scripture, we expect (rightly) that he speaks with a unified voice. The literature of the Bible is like a large table set out with a variety of dishes of foods; each has its own flavor, texture, color, but each contributes to one delicious and nourishing feast. The Manifesto for Theological Interpretation aims to provide the best tools that will attune our ears for hearing God's address to us with all of its truthfulness, authority, and unity. In the

---

1. See Calvin G. Seerveld, *Rainbows for a Fallen World* (Toronto: Tuppence, 1980), 88–92.

economy of theological interpretation, biblical theology is the practice that helps readers of Scripture grasp God's Word particularly in terms of its unity.

We define biblical theology, therefore, as the discipline that seeks to discern and articulate the unity of Scripture on the basis of terms and categories derived from the Bible itself.[2] At the very foundation of biblical theology is the conviction that the Bible *in its totality* is God's Word.

The Current Context for Doing Biblical Theology

It is one thing to confess that the Bible is a unity, that God speaks with a unified voice in Scripture; it is quite another thing actually to grasp that unity, comprehending it among the diversity of kinds of literature we find in the Bible. Biblical theology is both the task and tool of the church; yet several factors in the academic realm of biblical studies, in our wider culture, and also among believing readers of the Bible make this challenging task even more difficult.

Since the middle of the nineteenth century, modern biblical scholarship has been occupied with paring biblical texts down to their most basic parts. Scholars have focused much attention on theories regarding the forms and sources of the texts that make up Scripture. Thus when consulting many biblical commentaries from this time period, readers may often find them poor resources for biblical theology. Although this kind of approach to biblical study is not categorically wrong, an unfortunate by-product is that it has created a context in which biblical theology is often ignored or rejected altogether.

---

2. Scholars have defined biblical theology in different ways in different times, and no single definition has emerged as universally accepted. Even so, the importance of using the Bible's own terms and categories in biblical theology is articulated in many recent definitions of biblical theology. See, e.g., Richard A. Muller, "The Study of Theology," in *Foundations of Contemporary Interpretation*, ed. Moisés Silva (Grand Rapids: Zondervan, 1996), 595; Brian S. Rosner, "Biblical Theology," in *New Dictionary of Biblical Theology*, ed. T. Desmond Alexander and Brian S. Rosner (Downers Grove, IL: InterVarsity, 2000), 3; D. A. Carson, "Systematic and Biblical Theology," in *New Dictionary of Biblical Theology*, ed. T. Desmond Alexander and Brian S. Rosner (Downers Grove, IL: InterVarsity, 2000), 94; Charles H. H. Scobie, *The Ways of Our God: An Approach to Biblical Theology* (Grand Rapids: Eerdmans, 2003), 91–92; Craig G. Bartholomew, "Biblical Theology and Biblical Interpretation," in *Out of Egypt: Biblical Theology and Biblical Interpretation*, ed. Craig G. Bartholomew, Mary Healy, Karl Möller, and Robin Parry (Grand Rapids: Zondervan, 2004), 1; Mark J. Boda, "Biblical Theology and Old Testament Interpretation," in *Hearing the Old Testament: Listening for God's Address*, ed. Craig G. Bartholomew and David J. H. Beldman (Grand Rapids: Eerdmans, 2012), 122–23; Andreas J. Köstenberger, "The Present and Future of Biblical Theology," *Southwestern Journal of Theology* 56, no. 1 (2013): 19. Similarly, see Peter J. Gentry and Stephen J. Wellum, *Kingdom through Covenant: A Biblical Theological Understanding of the Covenants* (Wheaton: Crossway, 2012), 33–34.

The current postmodern context in which we find ourselves today further complicates the task of biblical theology. A vital insight that biblical theology yields is that the Bible, in its totality, presents to us a view of God, humanity, and the world. This is a cogent and comprehensive perspective on reality, a worldview. As believing readers of Scripture, we maintain that this worldview is not subjective, to be weighed against other worldviews, but that the Bible indeed provides us with *the* true view of the world and God's intentions for it. Postmodernism strenuously rejects this kind of totalizing truth. According to postmodernism, truth is local and subjective: a postmodern view resists claims to universal truth or a comprehensive worldview.[3]

Thus academic study of the Bible and today's wider cultural context present sources of resistance for doing biblical theology. However, even among individual Christians and church communities, ideas about the Bible and regular practices of biblical interpretation tend to work against the practices and principles of biblical theology.[4] Even when we have the best of intentions, we often read the Bible in various ways that fragment and reduce it: as a source of spiritual inspiration, as mere stories of heroic figures to emulate, as a set of abstract ideas on ethics. The Bible certainly works at all of these levels, but it does much more.

N. T. Wright correctly affirms the public and comprehensive nature of the Bible's truth claims:

> If we read the New Testament as it stands, it claims on every page to be speaking of things which are true in the public domain. It is not simply, like so many books, a guide for private spiritual advancement. . . . The New Testament claims to be the subversive story of the creator and the world, and demands to be read as such. . . . It offers itself as the true story, the true myth, the true history of the whole world.[5]

The Bible does present us with "the true story of the whole world,"[6] the account of God's creation of a wonderfully good world that was cast into chaos because of rebellion. It tells of God's determination to restore the world

---

3. For example, this is seen clearly in the French postmodern philosopher Jean-François Lyotard's definition of "postmodern": "I define *postmodern* as incredulity toward metanarratives." See Jean-François Lyotard, *The Postmodern Condition: A Report on Knowledge,* trans. Geoff Bennington and Brian Massumi (Minneapolis: University of Minnesota Press, 1984), xxiv.

4. For the practices and principles of biblical theology, see below.

5. N. T. Wright, *The New Testament and the People of God,* vol. 1 of *Christian Origins and the Question of God* (Minneapolis: Fortress Press, 1992), 471.

6. Craig G. Bartholomew and Michael W. Goheen, *The True Story of the Whole World: Finding Your Place in the Biblical Drama* (Grand Rapids: Faith Alive, 2009).

in and through the work of his Son Jesus Christ. As God's redeemed people, we are taken up into this story, to demonstrate his intentions for humanity and the world until Christ returns and creation is fully restored. Along the way, this story instructs us about what it really means to be human, the true character and ways of God, and the nature and intention of the world in which we live. Each of these sources of resistance to biblical theology (modern academic study, the postmodern culture, and reductionistic Christian readings of the Bible) are themselves founded on and emerge out of larger stories of the world; these conceptual frameworks (i.e., worldviews) become the lenses through which the Bible is understood and read. Since the Bible does yield to us a view of the world as it truly is, then it is imperative that, in light of the biblical story, we understand the tendencies of the modern academy, in culture and in our churches. In other words, instead of using the modern or postmodern worldviews as the lenses through which we read the Bible, the Bible and the view of the world that emerges out of it should be the proper lens by which we understand all things (including the worldviews of our culture).

Biblical Exegesis, Biblical Theology, and Systematic Theology

Biblical theology respects the narrative framework of Scripture as that of storied theology, recognizing that the text does not provide us with "pure" abstract theology. Rather, we find true insights about God (his character, mighty acts, and plans), his world (from creation to new creation), and humanity (beautiful and broken)—all embedded within a narrative that runs from Eden to the New Jerusalem and finds its center and purpose in the story and person of Jesus. Scripture, with its diversity of genres (historical narrative, law, poems, letters, and so on), is a theodrama in which we learn about the ways of God against the backdrop of the true overarching story of the world, rather than an encyclopedia of God that lists in abstract propositional form an A-to-Z compendium of ahistorical principles.

This is not to deny that within the grand narrative there are no loose threads, but to affirm that Scripture has a trajectory in which earlier buds are seen to flower in the progressive revelation of God and his people. As Christopher Wright declares, the Bible is "not just a single narrative, like a river with only one channel. It is rather a complex mixture of all kinds of smaller narratives, many of them rather self-contained, with all kinds of other material embedded within them—more like a great delta. But there is clearly a direction, a flow."[7] By no means does the practice of biblical theology deny or ignore the complexity of the biblical literature; instead, it aims to understand the complex contexts framing the fullness of divine activity and revelation in Scripture.

Since biblical theology is an attempt to grasp and articulate the unity of the Bible, it should always be practiced through a deep engagement with Scripture itself and take with utter seriousness the historical and narrative anchor of the text as well as its historical-grammatical and literary features. Exegesis is the task of drawing out the meaning of a text in its original literary and historical context. Biblical theology should not circumvent sound biblical exegesis. On the one hand, this means that whatever type of biblical theology we are engaged with (see some of the methods below), we must always be immersed in particular texts and be responsible in our handling of these texts. On the other hand, we must also recognize that there is a biblical-theological dimension to all exegesis. Any given biblical passage manifests a complex web of interrelationships with other biblical texts. The biblical authors have many different ways of referring to other texts, and the process of exegesis will have us tracking down references in a particular text to earlier texts. Moreover, biblical exegesis will provide material for tracing how themes, ideas, and motifs play out in later biblical texts. Theological interpretation should produce work that moves from the particular texts to the general themes and/or story of Scripture, and vice versa.

Although biblical theology is an academic discipline practiced by scholars, it is also an essential task and tool of the church. As Archbishop Cranmer wrote, believing readers of the Bible, individually and corporately, need to "read, mark and learn and inwardly digest all Holy Scripture,"[8] yet they should also have a coherent and unified theology. Through the work of God's Spirit, such a theology will function as a tool that can serve in growing disciples and propelling the church in its mission to reach out to a broken world, moving toward the redemption of all things. For example, I (Jonathan) have witnessed firsthand how deep engagement with the biblical-theological theme of the "image of God" opens up avenues of pastoral engagement for those suffering through the chaos of addiction and homelessness. In this context, biblical theology has provided a story, a truth to live by, giving hope to the hopeless and bringing beauty to the broken.

Believing readers of the Bible need more than a *system* of theology. It is important to distinguish systematic theology and biblical theology.

7. Christopher J. H. Wright, *The Mission of God: Unlocking the Bible's Grand Narrative* (Downers Grove, IL: InterVarsity, 2006), 64.
8. This is part of the Collect for the Second Sunday in Advent in The Book of Common Prayer.

Documents like the Westminster Confession of Faith, the Catechism of the Catholic Church, the Heidelberg Catechism, and the Thirty-Nine Articles of Religion are attempts to provide an organized distillation of biblical and Christian truth. These along with Thomas Aquinas's *Summa theologica*, John Calvin's *Institutes of the Christian Religion*, Philipp Melanchthon's *Augsburg Confession*, and many others are examples of systematic (or dogmatic) theology. They are systematic in that they aim to produce a coherent system of doctrine, often providing a shape and using topics that are not necessarily derived from the vocabulary of the Bible itself (e.g., the Trinity). Although the disciplines of systematic and biblical theology overlap at many places, it is common and helpful to distinguish them by recognizing that biblical theology is more descriptive in nature and systematic theology is more prescriptive or normative.[9] To put it another way, biblical theology aims to excavate the theology contained within Scripture, and systematic theology is occupied with "the ongoing theological teaching of the Bible to be lived and applied in the contemporary world."[10] This is not to say that biblical theology is not normative and prescriptive: one of the vital insights of attending to the grand narrative of Scripture is that it invites readers to indwell the narrative as the true story of everything. Moreover, framed in this way, one may get the impression that the proper direction is to move from the Bible, to biblical theology, then to systematic theology. Indeed, there is a natural logic to this movement, but theological interpretation of Scripture involves a process in which biblical exegesis, biblical theology, and systematic theology are held in a dynamic relationship. Brevard Childs is absolutely right to insist that both biblical and systematic theology should help us to attune our ears to God's address in the Bible: "Neither Biblical Theology nor dogmatic theology is an end in itself, but rather they remain useful tools by which to enable a fresh access to the living voice of God in sacred scripture."[11] In our day, fresh articulations of biblical theology should take place in tandem with fresh articulations of systematic theology; some

9. Though see the resistance to this distinction in Trevor Hart, "Systematic—in What Sense?," in Bartholomew et al., *Out of Egypt*, 345–48. For an insightful articulation of the relationship between biblical and systematic theology, see Michael D. Williams, "Systematic Theology as a Biblical Discipline," in *All for Jesus: A Celebration of the 50th Anniversary of Covenant Theological Seminary*, ed. Robert A. Paterson and Sean Michael Lucas (Fearn, Ross-Shire: Mentor, 2006), 167–96.

10. Edward W. Klink III and Darian R. Lockett, *Understanding Biblical Theology: A Comparison of Theory and Practice* (Grand Rapids: Zondervan, 2012), 14.

11. Brevard S. Childs, *Biblical Theology of the Old and New Testaments: Theological Reflection on the Christian Bible* (Minneapolis: Fortress, 1992), 89.

recent publications show the potential of biblical and systematic theology working creatively together for theological interpretation.[12]

The Practice of Biblical Theology

Of course, biblical theology cannot be reduced to a single method, and a number of approaches to biblical theology have emerged in the history of the discipline. Some relatively recent publications have outlined the history of biblical theology; rather than trying to reproduce or improve on them, we commend them to our readers.[13] We are convinced that the New Testament authors offer us important insight into the practice of biblical theology. In what follows, we aim to demonstrate how the apostolic witness, the New Testament, provides a basic framework for doing biblical theology that is worth retrieving for today.

The Apostolic Method

For obvious reasons, modern biblical theology will be distinct from the biblical theology expressed in the New Testament. Christian readers today have the complete canon, which is the working ground for biblical theology. Moreover, we are in a cultural context different than the first-century Greco-Roman context of the New Testament writers. The cultural context changes the focus and shape of biblical theology for each generation by raising new questions and insights and by refocusing the task for the sake of discipleship and mission. This could be illustrated in myriad ways, but we will mention just two. First, the rise of the modern military-industrial complex invites us to explore the biblical witness and find resources to develop a theology of power,

12. See Michael F. Bird, *Evangelical Theology: A Biblical and Systematic Introduction* (Grand Rapids: Zondervan, 2013); Jeremy R. Treat, *The Crucified King: Atonement and Kingdom in Biblical and Systematic Theology* (Grand Rapids: Zondervan, 2014).

13. For an excellent short review of the history of biblical theology, which also sets the ebb and flow of the practice within the larger historical/cultural context, see Gerald L. Bray, "Biblical Theology and from Where It Came," *Southwestern Journal of Theology* 55, no. 2 (2013): 193–208. See also the sketch of the history of biblical theology in James K. Mead, *Biblical Theology: Issues, Methods, and Themes* (Louisville: Westminster John Knox, 2007), 13–59. For biblical theology and the church fathers, see Gerald L. Bray, "The Church Fathers and Biblical Theology," in Bartholomew et al., *Out of Egypt*, 23–40. Both Scobie and Childs examine biblical theology from the early church to the Reformation (and beyond); see Scobie, *Ways of Our God*, 9–28; Childs, *Biblical Theology of the Old and New Testaments*, 30–51; for the history of the academic discipline of biblical theology, see Boda, "Biblical Theology," 123–25.

peace, and violence.[14] Second, the current ecological crisis should cause us to look with fresh eyes at biblical concepts of creation, new creation, and the ethical function of humans as empowered priest-kings, who reign and serve in Yahweh's cosmic temple.[15]

Nevertheless, the apostolic community itself provides us with norms for doing biblical theology today. In the New Testament we observe divinely inspired writers making use of the Scriptures (for them, the substance of the Old Testament) and drawing connections to their own context in the light of the Christ event. Their styles and methods for understanding the Old Testament are diverse, yet with key points of commonality. Although a full discussion of apostolic method is not possible here, we have identified a number of key insights from the New Testament authors that should shape our approach to biblical theology today.[16]

14. For instance, Tremper Longman III and Daniel G. Reid, *God Is a Warrior*, Studies in Old Testament Biblical Theology (Grand Rapids: Zondervan, 1995); Gregory A. Boyd, *God at War: The Bible and Spiritual Conflict* (Downers Grove, IL: InterVarsity, 1997); Willard M. Swartley, *Covenant of Peace: The Missing Peace in the New Testament Theology of Ethics* (Grand Rapids: Eerdmans, 2006).

15. See G. K. Beale, *The Temple and the Church's Mission: A Biblical Theology of the Dwelling Place of God*, New Studies in Biblical Theology (Downers Grove, IL: InterVarsity, 2004); J. Richard Middleton, *A New Heaven and a New Earth: Reclaiming Biblical Eschatology* (Grand Rapids: Baker Academic, 2014); T. Desmond Alexander, *From Paradise to the Promised Land: An Introduction to the Pentateuch*, 3rd ed. (Grand Rapids: Baker Academic, 2012), 119–33.

16. A range of resources examines how the apostolic authors engage in biblical theology and use the Scriptures of Israel. A good one-volume introduction is G. K. Beale's *Handbook of New Testament Use of the Old Testament: Exegesis and Interpretation* (Grand Rapids: Baker Academic, 2012); and a single-volume comprehensive account of how New Testament uses the Old Testament can be found in the volume edited by G. K. Beale and D. A. Carson, *Commentary on the New Testament Use of the Old Testament* (Grand Rapids: Baker Academic, 2007). In addition, the corpus of more specialized studies on this topic is growing. These works include single-volume books that examine how one Old Testament book is taken up in the New Testament; e.g., see the volumes edited by Steve Moyise and Maarten J. J. Mencken: *Psalms in the New Testament* (New York: T&T Clark, 2004); *Isaiah in the New Testament* (New York: T&T Clark, 2005); *Deuteronomy in the New Testament* (New York: T&T Clark, 2007). Also see works that examine how New Testament books use a range of Old Testament Scriptures and motifs: e.g., Dale C. Allison Jr., *The New Moses: A Matthean Typology* (Edinburgh: T&T Clark, 1993); Rikk E. Watts, *Isaiah's New Exodus in Mark*, Biblical Studies Library (Grand Rapids: Baker Academic, 2000); Stephen P. Ahearne-Kroll, *The Psalms of Lament in Mark's Passion: Jesus' Davidic Suffering*, Society for New Testament Studies Monograph Series 142 (Cambridge: Cambridge University Press, 2007); Edmund Little, *Echoes of the Old Testament in the Wine of Cana in Galilee (John 2.1–11) and the Multiplication of the Loaves and Fish (John 6.1–15)*, Cahiers de la Revue biblique 41 (Paris: Gabalda, 1998); David Mathewson, *A New Heaven and a New Earth: The Meaning and Function of the Old Testament in Revelation 21.1–22.5*, Journal for the Study of the New Testament: Supplement Series 238 (Sheffield: Sheffield Academic Press, 2003); Richard B. Hays, *The Conversion of the Imagination: Paul as Interpreter of Israel's Scripture* (Grand Rapids: Eerdmans, 2005).

To summarize in advance, the apostolic writers are (1) saturated in Scripture, and (2) they use the Old Testament in a varied but contextual manner, which includes seeing (a) the person and work of Jesus as directly fulfilling prophecies contained in the Old Testament; (b) Jesus as the fulfillment of aspects of the Old Testament in more subtle and/or typological ways; and (c) the eschatological tension—some events of which the Old Testament speaks are still awaiting fulfillment in the second coming of Jesus, the final defeat of evil, and the arrival of the new creation. Finally, the New Testament writers present (3) a christological reading of the Old Testament.

THE NEW TESTAMENT WRITERS WERE SATURATED IN SCRIPTURE

Although the New Testament writers allude to Greco-Roman writings and extracanonical Jewish literature, they are without exaggeration saturated in what came to be known as the Old Testament. The United Bible Societies' *Greek New Testament* (4th rev. ed., 1993) lists 343 quotations of the Old Testament in the New Testament and over 2,000 allusions. The book of Revelation is unusual in that it never quotes the Old Testament but contains hundreds of allusions.[17] A quotation is "a direct citation of an Old Testament passage that is easily recognizable by its unique and verbal parallelism."[18] An allusion is when the reference to the Old Testament is less obvious and more embedded into the New Testament text. Gregory Beale understands an allusion as "an indirect reference" in which the "Old Testament wording is not reproduced directly as in a quotation."[19] Some scholars have identified a third category of ways that the New Testament refers to the Old Testament: echoes.[20] An

17. Estimates vary due to the nature of allusions. The United Bible Society's 1975 *The Greek New Testament*, ed. K. Aland, M. Black, C. M. Martini, B. M. Metzger, and A. Wikgren (New York) puts the number at 394 (on 901–11), whereas the *Novum Testamentum Graece*, ed. K. Aland, M. Black, C. M. Martini, B. M. Metzger, and A. Wikgren (Stuttgart: Deutsche Bibelgesellschaft, 1979) indicates that the number of allusions is 635 (on 739–94).

18. Beale, *Handbook*, 29. Sometimes the New Testament writers introduce Old Testament quotations with formulas such as "This was/took place to fulfill what was/the Lord had spoken . . ." (Matt. 1:22; 2:15; 8:17; 12:17; 13:35; 21:4; cf. Luke 21:22; John 19:24, 28) or "so/as it is written . . ." (Matt. 2:5; 11:10; Mark 1:2; Luke 3:4; John 12:14; Rom. 1:17; 3:4, 10; 1 Cor. 1:19, 31; 2 Cor. 8:15; Gal. 3:10; 1 Pet. 1:16; etc.). However, many other citations do not contain introductory formulas. Though this is the case, those familiar with the Old Testament passages would have recognized unmarked citations (e.g., Gal. 3:6, quoting Gen. 15:6; Eph. 6:3, citing Deut. 5:16). Given the crucial role in biblical theology that the New Testament use of the Old plays, we recommend the following recent volumes as essential resources: (1) the shorter volume of Beale, *Handbook*; and (2) the larger multiauthor volume edited by Beale and Carson, *Commentary on the New Testament Use of the Old Testament*.

19. Beale, *Handbook*, 31.

20. For example, see Christopher A. Beetham, *Echoes of Scripture in the Letter of Paul to the Colossians*, Biblical Interpretation Series 96 (Leiden: Brill, 2008); Richard B. Hays, *Echoes of Scripture in the Letters of Paul* (New Haven: Yale University Press, 1989).

echo of the Old Testament in the New Testament is perhaps the hardest to identify; it is less deliberate, and the reference to another text is not necessarily conscious.[21] Clearly New Testament quotations of the Old Testament are much easier to identify than allusions or echoes, and some set of criteria is helpful for identifying an allusion.[22] Nevertheless, the New Testament writers' extensive use of these ways of referring to the Old Testament indicates just how much their Scriptures constituted, as it were, the air that they breathed.

By way of example, the account of Jesus's death in Mark's Gospel displays three parallels between the events surrounding Jesus's death and the experiences of the suffering but soon-to-be-vindicated Davidic psalmist of Psalm 22 (21 in the Septuagint [LXX]). The division of Jesus's garments (Mark 15:24 and Ps. 22:18 [21:19 LXX]) and Jesus's cry of God-forsakenness (Mark 15:34 and Ps. 22:1 [21:2 LXX]) offer sustained verbal correspondences that are relatively obvious to those saturated in the Psalms through regular corporate and personal use. Less obvious is the allusion through a thematic correspondence between the mocking of the onlookers and the plight of the psalmist (Mark 15:29 and Ps. 22:7 [21:8 LXX]). It is not sufficient merely to identify these allusions; instead, we ought to comprehend the theological significance of such connections. What Rikk Watts refers to as the "clear and pervasive presence of Psalm 22 in the crucifixion narrative"[23] arguably highlights Jesus as the true David, whose suffering is the necessary prelude to vindication and restoration. The allusion to Psalm 22 provides a further layer of depth and meaning, drawing out the significance of the events of Jesus's passion and death.

The apostolic community was saturated in Scripture, thus challenging anyone committed to theological interpretation and biblical theology to likewise be immersed in Scripture. The challenges of literacy and availability of texts in the ancient world were no doubt real obstacles for the early church, yet they

21. See Beetham, *Echoes of Scripture*, 15–25.

22. Beale says that discovering an allusion will involve identifying an "incomparable or unique parallel in wording, syntax, concept or cluster of motifs in the same order or structure"; see his *Handbook*, 31 (for Beale's fuller discussion, see 29–40). Richard Hayes's highly influential work *Echoes of Scripture in the Letters of Paul* identifies seven criteria for determining "echoes" or "allusions": (1) *Availability*: Was the proposed source of the allusion/echo available to the author and/or original hearers? (2) *Volume*: What is the degree of explicit repetition of words or syntactical patterns? (3) *Recurrence*: How often does Paul elsewhere cite or allude to the same scriptural passage? (4) *Thematic coherence*: How well does the alleged echo fit into the line of argument that Paul is developing? (5) *Historical plausibility*: Could Paul have intended the alleged meaning effect? (6) *History of interpretation*: Have other readers, both critical and precritical, heard the same echoes? (7) *Satisfaction*: Does the proposed reading make sense? (28–32).

23. Rikk E. Watts, "Mark," in Beale and Carson, *Commentary on the New Testament Use of the Old Testament*, 235.

are not problems facing most modern Western followers of Christ. However, our media-rich, sound-bite culture presents new areas of resistance. Christian communities need to develop fresh ways for this generation to be saturated in Scripture and develop a robust biblical theology, one that will undergird and fuel a life of passionate worship, radical discipleship, and world-changing missional activity.[24]

THE NEW TESTAMENT WRITERS' DIVERSE USE OF THE OLD TESTAMENT

The apostolic community used the Old Testament in a variety of ways. They did not arbitrarily cherry-pick Old Testament proof texts to support a point.[25] On the contrary, they developed a sophisticated hermeneutic in which the Old Testament is used in sensitive and contextual ways, although often with fresh christological and eschatological significance. This contextual approach indicates that the apostolic method is more in line with the later Antiochene school of interpretation rather than the Alexandrian school. The Antiochene method focuses on the literal and typological reading of the Old Testament (see below); the school of Alexandria and some Jewish interpreters (e.g., Philo) focus more on allegory, in which the deep truths of the Old Testament are found in a spiritualized meaning not evident from a mere literal reading. How specifically do the New Testament authors draw on the Old Testament? We have identified three of their ways that help us in our practice of biblical theology.

Direct Fulfillment of Prophecy. The New Testament writers often draw on Old Testament passages that point forward to future events. The New Testament reveals how certain events prophesied in the Old Testament have been fulfilled in the life, death, resurrection, and ascension of Jesus and in the outpouring of the Spirit. For example, Matthew shows that Jesus's birth in Bethlehem (Matt. 2:5–6) fulfills the prophecy in Micah 5:2 predicting that

24. Here one is reminded of the connection between story, worldview, and action. Alasdair Macintyre famously said, "I can only answer the question 'What am I to do?' if I can answer the prior question, 'Of what story do I find myself a part?'" (*After Virtue: A Study in Moral Theory*, 2nd ed. [Notre Dame, IN: University of Notre Dame Press, 1984], 216).

25. For a wider discussion of this topic, see Barnabas Lindars, *New Testament Apologetic* (London: SCM, 1961); Christopher D. Stanley, *Arguing with Scripture: The Rhetoric of Quotations in the Letters of Paul* (New York: T&T Clark, 2004); Steve Moyise, "The Old Testament in the New: A Reply to Greg Beale," *Irish Biblical Studies* 21 (1999): 133–34; idem, "Does the New Testament Quote the Old Testament Out of Context?," *Anvil* 11 (1994): 133–43. The essays found in G. K. Beale, ed., *The Right Doctrine from the Wrong Texts? Essays on the Use of the Old Testament in the New* (Grand Rapids: Baker, 1994) set out the arguments and debate well with historical discussion and worked examples.

the Messiah would be born in Bethlehem.[26] This is just one example of many passages in the New Testament where explicit fulfillment of particular Old Testament prophecies occurs in the events of the first century. A basic assumption of the apostolic community is that the hope of Israel, as predicted in the Old Testament, has come to pass and that the Christian community is living, in some sense, in the end times.[27]

Indirect Fulfillment of the Old Testament (Typology). In the New Testament the fulfillment of the Old Testament is not always direct and specific. Sometimes fulfillment language is used of the Old Testament in a more complex and indirect manner. John's Gospel provides a good example of an indirect fulfillment of the Old Testament in the New Testament.

John 19:36 says, "These things occurred so that the scripture might be fulfilled, 'None of his bones shall be broken.'" The Old Testament (whether the Hebrew or the LXX) contains no word-for-word reference that we can point to as an antecedent to John's quote here. The quote does, however, have close thematic and textual similarities to three texts in the Scriptures of Israel and is most likely a composite rendering of all three texts (Exod. 12:46; Num. 9:12; Ps. 34:20 [33:21 LXX]).[28] The references in Exodus and Numbers are quite similar to each other, occurring in the context of the Passover and stating that no bone of the Passover lamb should be broken. Psalm 34 depicts a righteous sufferer and speaks of Yahweh preserving the psalmist in times of trouble ("He keeps all his bones; not one of them is broken" [v. 20, RSV]).

None of these Old Testament texts is "prophetic" in a typical understanding of the term. For this reason some may be led to believe that the New Testament authors, in these and similar cases, employ a noncontextual or even a proof-texting usage of the Old Testament.[29] The reference in John 19, however,

26. Matthew quotes five Old Testament texts in his infancy narrative. This is the only one of the five that can be understood as prediction-fulfillment: the other passages are more complex and use deeper and typological meanings (see below).

27. Other examples include Matt. 3:3; 4:12–16; 8:16–17; 12:17–21; Luke 4:17–21; Acts 2:15–21; 8:31–35; Rom. 9:24–29.

28. Andreas Köstenberger, "John," in Beale and Carson, *Commentary on the New Testament Use of the Old Testament*, 503.

29. Those who see a noncontextual reading of the Old Testament in the New Testament frequently highlight the use of Hosea 11:1 in Matt. 2:15. S. Vernon McCasland notes, "The interpretation of Hosea 11:1 . . . illustrates how early Christians found a meaning entirely foreign to the original" ("Matthew Twists the Scriptures," *Journal of Biblical Literature* 80 [1961]: 143–48). For a robust rebuttal demonstrating that "there are substantial indications already in Hosea 11 itself and its immediate context that Israel's past exodus out of Egypt was an event that would be recapitulated typologically in the eschatological future," see Beale, *Handbook*, 60–64 (quote from 64).

is an example of typological interpretation. This kind of interpretation seeks to show that the New Testament text has a correspondence to and fulfils its earlier counterpart in a way not always immediately obvious to the modern reader. The New Testament writers themselves see indirect fulfillment of the Old Testament in the events surrounding the advent of Jesus, and they employ a vocabulary of terms and phrases to express the legitimacy of their typological approach, thereby defending themselves against the claim of proof-texting. Paul and the author of Hebrews explain that the Old Testament is a "shadow of the good things to come" (Col. 2:17; Heb. 10:1). Old Testament figures, festivals, and events provide a type or pattern of the Christ who was to come (Rom. 5:14; Heb. 9:24). Moreover, the Old Testament presents copies and symbols that correspond to the more recent events in salvation history (Heb. 8:5; 9:9).

Returning to the passage in John 19, based on its Old Testament precedents, the text casts Jesus as the prototypical righteous sufferer (Ps. 34:20), whose death as the Passover Lamb inaugurates the new exodus (e.g., Isa. 40:3–5; 41:17–20; 42:14–16; 43:1–3, 14–21; 48:20–21; 49:8–12; 51:9–10; 52:11–12; 55:12–13). Just as God delivered his people from Egypt through the sacrifice of the Passover lamb, so now he delivers his people from the "Egypt" of sin and evil through the sacrificial death of Jesus. That this is likely the intended understanding of fulfillment language is further strengthened by the fact that John elsewhere states that Jesus's death takes place on the specific day for slaughtering the Passover lambs in the temple (John 19:14).[30]

This approach permits a typological fulfillment of the Old Testament in the person and work of Jesus Christ (e.g., as a type of Adam in Rom. 5:19; of Melchizedek in Heb. 5:5–10; of Moses in 1 Cor. 10:2), in places (e.g., Jerusalem/Mount Zion as a typological forerunner of the church and heaven in Gal. 4:25–26; Heb. 12:22–23; Rev. 21:2), objects and festivals (e.g., the tabernacle as a representative of God's presence in Acts 17:24; the holy days and festivals as figurations of Jesus in Col. 2:16–17; the bronze serpent as a figure of Jesus in his death in John 3:14; 12:32), and events (e.g., the exodus from Egypt and the wilderness wandering as a figure of the Christian experience in 1 Cor. 10:1–14; water from the rock as a prefigure of the living water that Jesus provides in John 4:14). The apostolic witness provides us with many examples of this kind of pattern, in which people, events, objects, and so forth are prefigured in the Old Testament and find their ultimate fulfillment in the events of Jesus's ministry, death, resurrection, exaltation, and the outpouring

---

30. Other places in the New Testament attest the Passover lamb as a type of Christ (e.g., 1 Cor. 5:7; Rev. 5).

of the Spirit. This pattern provides readers today with a template that we can follow in our own practice of biblical theology.

Prophecy Not Yet Fulfilled. The apostolic community saw themselves as living in the eschaton, at the time when the great promises were being fulfilled.[31] However, living in the tension of the already-and-not-yet inaugurated eschatology means that they saw themselves as still awaiting the fullness of the eschaton to arrive. Some of the promises of God had been fulfilled, some had been partially fulfilled, and others are awaiting fulfillment. This is evident among other places in the new-creation passages of 2 Peter 3:11–14 and Revelation 21, which draw on Isaiah 65:17 and 66:22. The notion of a new heaven and earth in Isaiah is taken up in Revelation and Peter as a future-orientated event, which has not yet happened. So Peter writes, "In accordance with his promise, we wait for new heavens and a new earth, where righteousness is at home" (2 Pet. 3:13). On the basis of the scriptural witness and the Christ event, we, like the apostolic community, should discern what aspects of the eschaton are already fulfilled in the present, so that we can live scripturally faithful lives that embrace the eschatological tension and move forward in hope-filled lives of worship, mission, and discipleship.

Christological Reading of the Old Testament

In addition to the three usages outlined above (promise-fulfillment, typology, and future fulfillment), the apostolic community developed a christological hermeneutic for interpreting the Old Testament. According to Luke's Gospel, this method traces its roots back to Jesus himself; on the road to Emmaus with two of his disciples, he began "with Moses and with all the prophets" and "interpreted to them the things about himself in all the scriptures" (Luke 24:27). Just as the traveling companions did not at first recognize Jesus, so we may not always see Jesus immediately when we approach the Law, the Prophets, and the Psalms.

We may not be able to identify Jesus in every proverb or to find Jesus in the book of Esther. Rather, the New Testament witness to the apostolic approach claims that Christ is at the heart of God's redemptive work on earth and that he is the goal of all the work in redemptive history. This christological approach means that the Old Testament refers to Christ and the eschatological life he brings either directly (e.g., messianic hope) or indirectly (typologically). However, it also prepares the way for Christ by laying out the story of Israel as the necessary backstory for understanding the "hope of Israel"

---

31. More on this below.

in the person of Jesus the Messiah. This is not simply to say that the New Testament authors seek Christ in the Old Testament; rather, they understand Christ as the *eschaton*, the destination, the climax of the story of Israel and indeed the story of all history, with each Old Testament text and episode playing a preparatory role. The eschatological fulfillment has come in Jesus the God-Man (Mark 1:15; Acts 2:17; 1 Cor. 10:11; Gal. 4:4; 1 Tim. 4:1; 2 Tim. 3:1; Heb. 1:2; 1 Pet. 1:20; 2 Pet. 3:3; 1 John 2:18; Jude 18).

Although scholars debate whether the apostolic witness sometimes over-read, misread, or developed new meanings that go beyond that of the original intention of Old Testament texts, we affirm that in general the apostolic use of the Old Testament is contextual in nature. Of course, the issues are complex. In some cases it is difficult to understand with absolute clarity the hermeneutical method that the New Testament writers are employing in their use of the Old Testament.[32] Moreover, without a doubt the apostolic community did offer a new fresh reading of the Old Testament in the light of the arrival of both the eschaton and the Messiah.

For instance, Isaiah 40:1–11, in the context of chapters 40–55, is written to those living in exile in Babylon. Isaiah speaks of Yahweh's return to Zion whereby Yahweh will defeat the enemy and lead his people on a glorious new-exodus pilgrimage to Jerusalem, ushering in the eschatological age.[33] In the immediate historical context, Cyrus the Persian was the shepherd and anointed one who would defeat Babylon and thereby end the exile (Isa. 44:28; 45:1–13). However, the fullness of this new exodus never materialized due to the inaction of blind, deaf, and rebellious Israel.[34] Nevertheless, these hopes remained active; with the arrival of Jesus, the apostolic witness came to see that Jesus himself is the embodiment of Yahweh, who did take on the enemy and journey to Jerusalem. In its opening verses the Gospel of Mark identifies Jesus as the fulfillment of this hope that Yahweh would return to his people

32. For example, the use of Gen. 22:17–18 in Gal. 3:16; the understanding of baptism and the flowing rock in 1 Cor. 10:1–4; the allegorical use of Deut. 25:4 in 1 Cor. 9:9; and what appears to be atomistic interpretation of Isa. 40:6–8 in 1 Pet. 1:24–25.

33. Calling attention to ten key texts, Bernard Anderson identifies a typological relationship between the eschatological promise for God's people under Babylonian rule and that of the deliverance achieved in the first exodus: Isa. 40:3–5; 41:17–20; 42:14–16; 43:1–3, 14–21; 48:20–21; 49:8–12; 51:9–10; 52:11–12; 55:12–13. See Bernard W. Anderson, "Exodus Typology in Second Isaiah," in *Israel's Prophetic Heritage: Essays in Honour of James Muilenburg*, ed. Bernard W. Anderson and W. Harrelson (New York: Harper, 1962), 181–82.

34. Israel is called, as Yahweh's servant, to bring justice and torah to the nations, to open the eyes of the blind, and to bring prisoners out from prison (Isa. 42:1–4). However, Israel is blind and deaf; Israel itself is in prison (42:18–22). Israel is called to be a light and a covenant to the world (42:6; 49:8), but instead its people question Yahweh's plan (45:9). They are rebels who are stubborn of heart (46:12).

(Mark 1:1–4; cf. Isa. 40:3).[35] Instead of being welcomed, he was nailed to a tree. In the mysterious and majestic providence of God, this death brought an end to spiritual exile of sin and death. The stunning and startling thing about this apostolic biblical-theological approach is that within about three decades after the death of Jesus, his followers were using the Scriptures to make the bold and world-transforming claim that Jesus, the crucified human Messiah, is no other than the embodiment of the God of Israel himself.[36]

The apostolic witness provides a constructive direction that contemporary biblical theology should follow. Admittedly, we cannot in every case make sense of the New Testament authors' use of Old Testament passages, but in general they provide a basic orientation or framework that is relevant today. Their immersion in Scripture and their commitment to Jesus as the fulfillment, goal, and center of Scripture should inspire the practice of biblical theology today.

Narrative Approach

The apostolic witness provides a helpful framework for doing biblical theology, but within this framework many approaches and methods are appropriate. What are the other methods for biblical theology that are most helpful for theological interpretation? A good biblical-theological method should take seriously the narrative unity of Scripture and the close relationship of the two Testaments.[37] As should be clear by now, a narrative approach to biblical theology must be primary and foundational for all other methods. Here we take our cue from the New Testament authors themselves, who were keenly aware that the Christ event was part of a larger narrative that spanned

---

35. See J. Marcus, *The Way of the Lord: Christological Exegesis of the Old Testament in the Gospel of Mark* (London: T&T Clark, 2004); Watts, *Isaiah's New Exodus in Mark*; and Jonathan Swales, "The Death of the Divine Warrior: A Study of the Gospel of Mark with a Particular Emphasis on the Use of the Scriptures of Israel in Presenting Jesus as the Fulfillment of the New Exodus Hopes of Isaiah" (master's thesis, University of Bristol, 2012).

36. David Capes offers an analysis of how Old Testament Yahweh passages (κύριος [*kyrios*] in the Septuagint) are used within the undisputed Pauline Letters. He recognizes that several of these texts have God as the referent. Seven of these texts have Jesus as the referent (Rom. 4:7–8; 9:27–29; 11:34; 15:9–11; 1 Cor. 3:20; 2 Cor. 6:18). The apostolic community, therefore, is reading the Old Testament in a christological fashion, demonstrating its own christological monotheism—that Jesus is himself part of the divine identity. See David B. Capes, *Old Testament Yahweh Texts in Paul's Christology*, Wissenschaftliche Untersuchungen zum Neuen Testament 2/47 (Tübingen: Mohr, 1992); and also Richard Bauckham, *Jesus and the God of Israel: God Crucified and Other Studies on the New Testament's Christology of Divine Identity* (Grand Rapids: Eerdmans, 2008).

37. This is the view the church assumed from its earliest days and not simply the invention of a niche part of contemporary academic discourse. For instance, Irenaeus in the second century regarded the Bible as a unified narrative; see Robert Louis Wilken, *The Spirit of Early Christian Thought: Seeking the Face of God* (New Haven: Yale University Press, 2003), 63.

back to the beginning of time and had forward implications for the eschaton. At points the New Testament itself contains narrations of the story of Israel (e.g., Stephen's speech before his martyrdom in Acts 7:2–53) and the story of the whole of history (e.g., Rev. 12's symbolic telling of world history). The working assumption of the apostolic writers is not only that the Scriptures of Israel (Old Testament) are authoritative but also that they present the true story of the world that is in search of an ending and that the advent of Jesus has ushered in the final act of this story.

Many different ways of dividing this story into chapters or acts have emerged in the past, including the familiar creation, fall, redemption (consummation).[38] Although space does not permit us to expound these, we think the following categories help to unpack the contours of the biblical story: creation, chaos, calling and covenant, conquest, kingship, catastrophe, consolation, Christ and the church and consummation. These ministories or subplots can help to structure and point to the larger, overarching narrative, a story that comes full circle as the paradise lost becomes a paradise restored: a time of the "renewal of all things" (Matt. 19:28; Acts 3:21; cf. Eph. 1:10; Col. 1:20) in the new creation (2 Pet. 3:13; Rev. 21:1). From a historical point of view, first-century Jews and the early church understood this story or some variation of it. A robust biblical theology will help us draw lines between the Testaments, demonstrating how the eschatological hopes of Israel, which stem from their covenantal story, have been surprisingly fulfilled in the person and work of Jesus.

The story of Israel, climaxing in the person and work of Jesus, provides the apostles and the New Testament with a worldview and a symbolic universe that drive their action and engagement with the world and the Christian community.[39] In his letters, for example, Paul works out the significance of *this*

38. Reformed theology has often advocated a fourfold schema of creation, fall, redemption, and consummation. N. T. Wright improves on this with his five-act play analogy: Creation, Fall, Israel, Jesus, and the Church in "How Can the Bible Be Authoritative?" *Vox evangelica* 21 (1991): 7–32. One recent UK pastor summarized the Old Testament story by using the memorable sequence Eden, Election, Exodus, Empire, and Exile. We should not be embarrassed at the multiplicity of renderings of the biblical story. What Richard Bauckham says for the Gospel writers is not only true but also helpful in thinking about how the story of God's people can be rendered in different yet mutually helpful ways: "While the telling of a story can be true, it can never be adequate to or exhaustive of the reality it renders. In this case, the fact that versions and interpretations multiply—especially in the case of the story of Jesus—is testimony to the importance of not reducing his reality to the limitation of the single rendering" ("Reading Scripture as a Coherent Story," in *The Art of Reading Scripture*, ed. Ellen F. Davis and Richard B. Hays [Grand Rapids: Eerdmans, 2003], 44).

39. In a similar vein, Ben Witherington writes: "(1) Paul's symbolic universe, which entails those things that Paul takes to be inherently true and real, the fixed stars in Paul's mental sky; (2) Paul's narrative thought world, which is Paul's reflection on his symbolic universe in terms of the grand story. This undergirds (3) Paul's articulation of his theology, ethics, and so forth,

story for the fledgling Christian communities he interacts with: for believers in Thessalonica, experiencing persecution; for the church in Corinth, facing the influencing pressures of a thoroughly pagan and pluralistic culture; for Galatian Christians, confused by how the practice of circumcision relates to their new identity in Christ; and so on. Just as Paul thoughtfully and prayerfully brings the gospel story to bear on the issues of the various contexts he finds himself in, so Christians today ought to work out the implications of the biblical story for our contemporary contexts. Again here, the New Testament writers provide us with a pattern that we can follow.

Other Methods for Biblical Theology

A narrative approach to biblical theology must be primary, but from that a number of diverse but legitimate methods can emerge.[40] In what follows we offer a taste of some of these methods.

WHOLE-BIBLE BIBLICAL THEOLOGY

One of the most significant developments in biblical theology in the past century was the emergence of a *canonical approach to biblical theology*. The pioneer of this approach was Brevard Childs. Childs's work breathed new life into the discipline of biblical theology at a time when it was waning and has spawned a new generation of disciples who are developing and working out his approach. Childs was deeply committed to biblical theology that would open up the Bible as the living Word of God for the church today. Crucial to his approach was grasping Scripture in its totality, including the vital relationship between the Old and New Testaments. Childs declares, "Both testaments make a discrete witness to Jesus Christ which must be heard, both separately and in concert."[41] For Childs, biblical theology must start with the discrete witness of the Old Testament and/or the discrete witness of the New Testament, and then broaden out to a theological reflection on the Bible. His magnum opus, *Biblical Theology of the Old and New Testaments*, not only provides a thorough theoretical foundation for his approach to biblical theology, but also

---

in response to the situations he must address" (*Paul's Narrative Thought World: The Tapestry of Tragedy and Triumph* [Louisville: Westminster/John Knox, 1994], 6n7).

40. See Klink and Lockett, *Understanding Biblical Theology*; Childs, *Biblical Theology of the Old and New Testaments*, 11–29; Köstenberger, "Present and Future," 5–18. See also the InterVarsity Press series New Studies in Biblical Theology. The series includes three areas of focus in the study of biblical theology: (1) more theoretical and historical aspects of the nature and practice of biblical theology; (2) studies on the theology of a biblical corpus or author; and (3) the tracing of biblical themes across sections or the whole of the Bible.

41. Childs, *Biblical Theology of the Old and New Testaments*, 78.

engages in the practice of biblical theology, including (1) reflection on what he calls "traditions" within Israel's history and how they are attested in the Old Testament (e.g., prophetic tradition and wisdom tradition); (2) reflection on "traditions" within the New Testament; (3) exegetical analysis in the context of biblical theology; and (4) theological reflection on biblical terms and concepts in the context of the whole Christian Bible. This not only provides fruitful examples of biblical theology; it also hints at some helpful methods for doing biblical theology in the service of theological interpretation.[42]

A common and fruitful approach to biblical theology today is *tracing the central themes of Scripture*. The major whole-Bible biblical theologies of Charles Scobie and Childs utilize this approach. For example, Scobie structures his biblical theology around the central themes of (1) God's order, (2) God's servant, (3) God's people, and (4) God's way.[43] This method involves identifying significant themes (e.g., covenant, kingdom, redemption, God's presence, Messiah, the nations/gentiles, divine warfare, etc.) and examining how these themes unfold throughout the biblical story. For example, Gregory Beale's *The Temple and the Church's Mission* constitutes a biblical-theological study of temple.[44] Beale explores temple theology from Genesis 1–3, through the patriarchal narratives, the exodus, Solomon's temple, the prophetic hope of a new temple, the life of Jesus, the writings of the early church (Acts, Paul, Hebrews), and what will come to pass as set forth in the book of Revelation.[45]

Attempts at a *single-center approach to biblical theology* have emerged, though admittedly this is less common than other methods. This approach is based on the conviction that the unity of the Bible can be articulated around a single theme, center, or big idea. Henning Graf Reventlow defines this approach as "the attempt to discover a particular concept or central idea as a connecting link between the two Testaments or as their 'centre,' around which a biblical theology can be built up."[46] A notable recent example of this approach is the work of James Hamilton. He (rightly) assumes that the Bible is a grand story, and he argues that the center of biblical theology is

---

42. Childs resists a narrative approach to biblical theology; see Childs, *Biblical Theology of the Old and New Testaments*, 18–20; Craig G. Bartholomew and Michael W. Goheen have offered a thoughtful response to Childs's concern in "Story and Biblical Theology," in Bartholomew et al., *Out of Egypt*, 162–64.

43. Scobie, *Ways of Our God*, 105–927.

44. Beale, *Temple and the Church's Mission*.

45. See also Scott J. Hafemann and Paul R. House, eds., *Central Themes in Biblical Theology: Mapping Unity in Diversity* (Grand Rapids: Baker Academic, 2007).

46. Henning Graf Reventlow, *Problems of Biblical Theology in the Twentieth Century*, trans. John Bowden (Philadelphia: Fortress, 1986), vii; cited in James Hamilton, *God's Glory in Salvation through Judgment: A Biblical Theology* (Wheaton: Crossway, 2010), 47–48.

"the glory of God in salvation through judgment";[47] his book constructs a biblical theology around that theme. Graeme Goldsworthy also thinks there is a center of biblical theology, namely the kingdom of God, which he defines as "God's people in God's place under God's rule."[48] Christopher Wright, on the other hand, maintains, "Mission is what the Bible is all about."[49] Wright structures his biblical theology around the triad of (1) the God of mission, (2) the people of mission, and (3) the arena of mission.

Many scholars dismiss the single-center approach to biblical theology because they believe that no single idea or theme is broad enough to hold the whole of Scripture together.[50] It may be stating the obvious, but what occupies the center of the Bible and should occupy the center of our biblical theology is not a concept or theme but a person: Jesus the Messiah, to whom the sweep of the Old Testament finds its culmination and from whom the New Testament orients itself. This christological center naturally assumes a trinitarian center since the ministry of Jesus is part of the triune activity of Father, Son, and Holy Spirit (e.g., Matt. 28:18–20; Mark 1:10–11; John 5:19–29; 16:13–15). This is not to dismiss altogether single-center approaches to biblical theology. Each of these three examples (above) builds its biblical theology on the foundational assumption that the Bible is a grand narrative. Moreover, both Goldsworthy and Wright have built into their biblical theology a triadic structure that includes God, humans, and creation; in our opinion this is very fruitful for doing biblical theology in the service of theological interpretation.

BIBLICAL THEOLOGY OF THE TWO TESTAMENTS, SMALLER BIBLICAL CORPORA, AND BOOKS

As mentioned, upon the foundation of a narrative approach to biblical theology, many other methods can be fruitful. No shortage of theologies

47. Hamilton, *God's Glory in Salvation through Judgment*, 41.

48. Graeme Goldsworthy, *Preaching the Whole Bible as Christian Scripture: The Application of Biblical Theology to Expository Preaching* (Grand Rapids: Eerdmans, 2000), 87. He expounds this theme:
    The pattern of the kingdom is established in the Garden of Eden.
    This pattern is broken when sin enters in.
    The pattern is reestablished in salvation history in Israel but never fully realized.
    The same pattern shapes the prophetic view of the future kingdom.
    The pattern of the kingdom is perfectly established in Jesus in a representative way.
    The pattern of the kingdom begins to be formed in the people of God through the gospel.
    The pattern of the kingdom is consummated at Christ's return. (ibid., 88)
For a more popular articulation of Goldsworthy's approach, see Vaughan Roberts, *God's Big Picture: Tracing the Storyline of the Bible* (Downers Grove, IL: InterVarsity, 2002).

49. C. Wright, *Mission of God*, 29.

50. E.g., Scobie, *Ways of Our God*, 87; Köstenberger, "Present and Future," 12.

of the two Testaments exists, but not all are as rooted in the grand story of the Bible as they should be. Stephen G. Dempster and Bruce Waltke have raised the bar for Old Testament biblical theologies, and G. K. Beale's tome is exemplary for the New Testament.[51] Narrowing the focus somewhat further, there is a need for theologies of biblical sections to be written with biblical-theological sensitivities. Notable examples are T. Desmond Alexander's *From Paradise to the Promised Land*, which offers a theology of the Pentateuch, tracing pentateuchal themes into the New Testament; Craig G. Bartholomew and Ryan P. O'Dowd's theological introduction to *Old Testament Wisdom Literature*; and Thomas Schreiner's *Pauline Theology*.[52] A final approach worth pursuing is developing theologies of biblical books. Andreas J. Köstenberger states that the so-called classical approach to biblical theology "involves studying first the message and theological content of individual books, followed by an attempt at synthesis tracing overarching themes across various corpora."[53] We need fresh and creative theologies of individual books, like J. Clinton McCann's theological introduction to the Psalter, that help us to hear them as movements and/or variations in the symphony of Scripture.[54]

Clearly, many methods for doing biblical theology are appropriate and helpful for theological interpretation. If we build upon the foundational principles that we observe in the apostolic witness and grasp the grand narrative of Scripture, a variety of practices for biblical theology can foster meaningful theological interpretation.

51. Stephen G. Dempster, *Dominion and Dynasty: A Biblical Theology of the Hebrew Bible* (Downers Grove, IL: InterVarsity, 2003); Bruce K. Waltke, *An Old Testament Theology: An Exegetical, Canonical, and Thematic Approach* (Grand Rapids: Zondervan, 2007); G. K. Beale, *A New Testament Biblical Theology: The Unfolding of the Old Testament in the New* (Grand Rapids: Baker Academic, 2011).

52. Alexander, *From Paradise to the Promised Land*, 113–314; Craig G. Bartholomew and Ryan P. O'Dowd, *Old Testament Wisdom Literature: A Theological Introduction* (Downers Grove, IL: IVP Academic, 2011), esp. 231–327; Thomas Schreiner, *Paul, Apostle of God's Glory in Christ: A Pauline Theology* (Downers Grove, IL: InterVarsity, 2006). For theologies of the New Testament corpora, see also George Eldon Ladd, *A Theology of the New Testament*, ed. Donald A. Hagner, rev. ed. (Grand Rapids: Eerdmans, 1993).

53. Köstenberger, "Present and Future," 5. For an example of this type of New Testament theology, see Leon Morris, *New Testament Theology* (Grand Rapids: Zondervan, 1990). See also Gordon D. Fee, *God's Empowering Presence: The Holy Spirit in the Letters of Paul* (Grand Rapids: Baker Academic, 2009); idem, *Pauline Christology: An Exegetical-Theological Study* (Grand Rapids: Baker Academic, 2007).

54. J. Clinton McCann, *A Theological Introduction to the Book of Psalms: The Psalms as Torah* (Nashville: Abingdon, 1993). See also Craig G. Bartholomew, "The Theology of Ecclesiastes," in *The Words of the Wise Are Like Goads: Engaging Qohelet in the 21st Century*, ed. Mark J. Boda, Tremper Longman III, and Cristian G. Rata (Winona Lake, IN: Eisenbrauns, 2013), 369–88.

Conclusion

While theological interpretation is the dynamic and multifaceted activity that best attunes our ears to hear God addressing us today, biblical theology equips us to listen to the whole counsel of God in Scripture. It helps us grasp the Bible's grand, sprawling narrative and to hear Scripture's summons to live out this story. The more we are immersed in the particulars of this story, the more we will recognize the tension between the biblical story and the stories that our culture is telling about the world and humanity's place in it. This chapter has pointed the reader to some helpful examples of biblical theology in academic publications, yet biblical theology is not merely an academic activity. Every Christian should be equipped to narrate the story of the Bible in ways that are appropriate to serve different contexts. This will require a deep engagement and immersion into the texts of both the Old and New Testaments. Biblical theology will then function like a map: it will give us our bearings, help us to navigate the terrain, and keep us focused on the destination.[55] As we are traveling in the biblical landscape, we may need to make adjustments to our map, yet biblical theology is indispensable. We will find the Bible and its story shaping us and our understanding of and approach to vocation, worship, mission, and discipleship.

---

55. For the map analogy, see Christopher J. H. Wright, "Mission as a Matrix for Hermeneutics and Biblical Theology," in Bartholomew et al., *Out of Egypt*, 137–40.

8

Mission and
Theological Interpretation

MICHAEL W. GOHEEN AND CHRISTOPHER J. H. WRIGHT

Starting with Two Controversial Claims

Today there is renewed interest in a theological interpretation of Scripture. At its heart theological interpretation is concerned with recovering a reading of the Bible as Christian Scripture that hears God's address to his people. An essential dimension of a full-orbed theological interpretation will be a hermeneutic that takes seriously the central theme of mission in the biblical story. These opening remarks make two bold claims that certainly are controversial within the guild of biblical studies.

Theological Interpretation Is Essential to Reading the Bible Rightly

The first claim is that biblical interpretation must read the Bible as Christian Scriptures to hear God's address. As a result of the religious conversion of Western culture to the Enlightenment faith, one of the hallmarks of biblical scholarship in the past two centuries is the yawning chasm between a critical reading of Scripture that is considered neutral and a religiously committed Christian reading. Attention to the historical, cultural, literary, and even theological details of the text have been separated from hearing God speak to his people. Although critical scholarship brings much insight, it has often capitulated to the Enlightenment story as its controlling narrative. While it claims to be objective and neutral, it is "a move from one confessional stance to another, a move from one creed to another."[1] In truth, the "Enlightenment did not (as it is sometimes supposed) simply free the scholar from the influence of 'dogma'; it replaced one dogma by another." The compelling power of the Enlightenment story is such that it is difficult to convince many biblical scholars "to recognize the creedal character of their approach."[2] The goal of theological interpretation is to wrest the Bible from an Enlightenment creedal reading and return it to its proper place.

Mission Is Central to Theological Interpretation

The second controversial claim, the primary burden of this chapter, is that mission (as defined below) is essential to faithful theological interpretation. Mission is not just one of the many things the Bible talks about, but rather is thematically central to and historically generative of the scriptural text. Hence reading the Bible in a nonmissional way misses important aspects of what God is saying. Since the Bible is a unified narrative that climaxes in Jesus, a faithful reading interprets all subordinate parts in relation to its center: Jesus Christ. We need a messianic reading of Scripture to rightly interpret the various parts.

Yet a faithful interpretation is not only messianic but is also missional. It is not only Christ but is also the mission of God's people that is a clue to reading the scriptural story. In Luke 24:45–47 Jesus himself articulates this twofold hermeneutical lens. He elaborates what "is written" in the Old Testament story in terms of both its climax in Jesus and in the subsequent mission of the church to the world. Jesus "opened their minds to understand the scriptures," or to put it in contemporary terminology, he gave them a hermeneutical key that is both messianic and missional.

This is not to claim that mission is the only key because mission does not make up the whole plotline of the biblical narrative. However, mission is an essential component of the central story line, and missing it truncates its message.

---

1. Lesslie Newbigin, *Proper Confidence: Faith, Doubt, and Certainty in Christian Discipleship* (Grand Rapids: Eerdmans), 80.
2. Lesslie Newbigin, "The Role of the Bible in Our Church" (remarks at a meeting of the United Reformed Church's Forward Policy Group, April 17–18, 1985), 1.

What Is Mission?

Since the term "mission," and its more recent adjectival form "missional," carries so much mistaken semantic weight, these words must be briefly explained. Mission is often understood to refer solely to activities the church undertakes to bring the gospel to those outside. Certainly these are important: evangelism, service projects, church planting, and cross-cultural missions are essential components of mission. Yet a missional hermeneutic assumes a much broader and deeper understanding of mission. It begins with the assumption that *the whole Bible narrates the story of God's mission in and through his people for the sake of all nations and the whole of God's creation.*

This definition focuses attention on a number of crucial components. First, in its most essential structure, the Bible tells one unfolding story of redemption. All characters and events, books and themes, genres and theological emphases must be interpreted as part of this unified narrative plotline. Thus to rightly understand God, his people, and their relationship to the world, one must see how each is rendered in this story.

But second, this story is, to employ the terminology of postmodernity, a metanarrative. It is not just a story of an ancient people's religious journey, nor salvation history in some narrowly defined sense incidental to world history. It purports to be the true story of the whole world, which gives an integrated meaning to the whole of reality. Thus it encompasses and gives meaning to all other personal or communal narratives, whether ancient or modern.[3]

Third, this story is first of all about God's work to restore the entire creation and rescue a people from all nations, delivering them from all the powers of evil. On the one hand, mission begins with a focus on what God is doing. On the other hand, the scope is comprehensive: it is about the renewal and restoration of his entire creation.

The fourth point is of crucial significance: God as the primary actor carries out his redemptive purpose by choosing a community to partner with him in his work. The story moves through a particular people chosen by God and onward to his universal purpose. The mission of God's people must be understood in terms of participation, at God's calling and command, in God's mission to bring renewal to the world, all peoples, and every part of human life. Mission is about an identity and a vocation that is given to God's people and fulfilled by the role they play in God's story.

3. Since the biblical metanarrative embraces the multiple cultural narratives of humanity and since the cross is at the center—a sign that this story is not coercive—it is not totalizing and oppressive in the way postmodernism accuses all metanarratives of being. On the contrary, it is redemptive—cleansing, liberating and transforming—of all cultures and narratives.

Finally, this means that an important element of the identity of God's people is that they exist for the sake of the world. God has chosen a people not just to experience God's saving love and power but also to be a channel of that salvation to the world.

Recovering the Centrality of Mission to the Biblical Story

In biblical studies, mission has not been recognized as a central category. This highlights one of the distorting presuppositions that shapes biblical scholarship. Our reading of any text is always shaped by what Hans-Georg Gadamer refers to as prejudices, or anticipatory forestructures, established categories that the interpreter necessarily employs to make sense of the text.[4] These prejudices orient our interpretation yet may be enabling or disabling. They may open our eyes to what is in the text but also can blind us to what is there. The problem is that our "missional anticipatory forestructures" have been clouded by a nonmissional self-understanding, closing us off to the missional thread at the heart of the scriptural story.

Today we are moving into a changed context. Our culture is increasingly less influenced by the Christian faith; the church is losing its place of influence. We find ourselves more aware of our missionary setting in the West. Moreover, the church in non-Western parts of the world now dwarfs the church in the West. Their deeper sense of missional vocation brings a challenge to the West. Together these factors are contributing to a "raised consciousness of mission"[5] in the Western church. Will this new situation reopen our missional prejudices? We hope they will, and in this chapter we briefly unfold three aspects of a missional hermeneutic: the Bible is a *record*, *product*, and *tool* of God's mission in and through his people.

The Bible as a Record of God's Mission in and through His People

A missional hermeneutic begins with God and his mission to restore the world and redeem a people from all nations. Speaking of the Bible as a story of God's redemptive work is not new. Referring to this as the *missio Dei* is not so common, and it highlights three related things. First, God is pursuing a cosmic goal to recover the whole creation. Everything that takes place

4. H. G. Gadamer, *Truth and Method*, 2nd rev. ed. (New York: Continuum, 2004), 267–98.
5. Lucien LeGrand, *Unity and Plurality: Mission in the Bible*, trans. Robert R. Barr (Maryknoll, NY: Orbis Books, 1990), xiv.

must be seen in relation to this aim. Second, this renewing work narrated in Scripture is the work of a Triune God. As the narrative unfolds, the Father, who has been at work in Israel, sends the Son in pursuit of his redemptive purpose. Upon the Son's completion of his mission, the Father and the Son send the Spirit to accomplish the goal of healing the world and gathering a people from all nations to himself. God takes the redemptive initiative, and sending is an action within the Triune God to accomplish his salvific purpose. Third, the notion of God's mission also opens up space for the incorporation of a people into his work. This mission of the Triune God is disclosed in a historical narrative in which he chooses and covenants with a people to be part of what he is doing. The sending of Jesus and the Spirit are part of a narrative in which the Triune God journeys toward his destination, including a people as his covenant partners.

This last point is central: at the heart of a missional hermeneutic is the recognition that God includes a *particular people* in his plan to accomplish his cosmic work of restoration. Both the words "particular" and "people" are important. He chooses a *people*. Robert Martin-Achard helpfully distinguishes mission in the Old Testament from kindred ideas: universalism, incorporation of foreigners, and proselytism. In contrast to these three related ideas, mission "involves the belief that the whole community has a task to fulfil on behalf of all mankind."[6] This is what distinguishes a missional hermeneutic: a people chosen by God to play a role in his purpose.

The choice of a certain people assumes a historical *particularity*: a people at a certain time and place. The direction of the biblical story is from the particular to the universal, unfolding both historically and geographically. Historically, the biblical story moves through a particular means to accomplish a universal end, from one nation to all nations. Geographically, the narrative flow is from one place to every place, from a single center to many peripheries, from Jerusalem to the ends of the earth.[7]

The primary focus of most of the biblical story is particular. However, this particularized focus stands between two universal bookends: creation and consummation. The story begins with God's creation of the entire earth and the progenitors of all peoples. The story ends with the new creation and

6. Robert Martin-Achard, *A Light to the Nations: A Study of the Old Testament Conception of Israel's Mission to the World*, trans. John Penney Smith (London: Oliver & Boyd, 1962), 5.

7. Cf. Richard Bauckham, *Bible and Mission: Christian Witness in a Postmodern World* (Grand Rapids: Baker Academic, 2003), 13–16; idem, *Mission as a Hermeneutic for Scriptural Interpretation*, Currents in World Christianity: Position Paper 106 (Cambridge: Cambridge University, 1999), 2–3.

a people from all nations. The church finds its place within this movement of God's redemptive work from the particular to the universal.

Genesis 12:1–3 and Exodus 19:3–6 as Narrative Trajectories

Two crucial texts offer a hermeneutic lens through which to read the role of God's people in the biblical story: Genesis 12:1–3 and Exodus 19:3–6.[8] These texts are not arbitrarily chosen but in the very narratives themselves are offered as narrative trajectories that define the path God's renewing purpose will take. Genesis 12 is at the hinge between primeval and patriarchal history; it tells us why God has chosen Abraham and Israel as well as how he will carry out his plan. Exodus 19 is where God delineates Israel's vocation and place in his purpose. Together these texts define the particular role of God's people in his redemptive program.

Genesis 12:1–3 is a "stupendous utterance,"[9] standing at a crucial intersection in the biblical story. Genesis 1–11 tells the story of the creation of the world, of human rebellion against God, and of the escalating curse of sin across the whole spectrum of the creation and human culture. These early chapters are universal in scope: the entire creation and all peoples are in view. Genesis 1–11 concludes with a list of seventy nations (representing all nations) and the story of Babel. Here is a depiction of all nations under the curse of sin. Against that backdrop, God singles out Abram and promises that he will bless Abram so that all these nations might again be blessed. Already here in the election of Abram at the outset of salvation history we read of the final universal goal of redemptive history.

Blessing is a rich word that describes the flourishing and abundance of creational life as it was meant to be in the goodness of God's original creation (Gen. 1:22–28). Throughout Genesis 3–11 the word "curse" (*'rr*) is used five times to describe the ominous crescendo of sin's effects. But then in 12:2–3 the word "bless" returns five times to make clear that, in Abram, God intends to reverse the curse of sin and restore the blessing of creation.

The grammatical structure of Genesis 12:2–3 shows that God's plan will unfold according to a twofold agenda: first God will restore his creational blessing to Abram and his descendants, and then through that nation God will bless all

8. Many authors see the central significance of these two texts for the story that follows, e.g., William Dumbrell, *Covenant and Creation: A Theology of Old Testament Covenants* (Nashville: Nelson, 1984); Bauckham, *Bible and Mission*.

9. Hans Walter Wolff, "The Kerygma of the Yahwist," trans. Wilbur A. Benware, *Interpretation* 20, no. 2 (1966): 140.

nations.[10] The principal clause of these verses is found in 12:3: "and all peoples on earth will be blessed through you" (NIV). The Hebrew syntax indicates that this clause is the final outcome of all the preceding promises.[11] God will restore to all nations all the good that he generously bestowed in creation, and he will do so through Abram (renamed Abraham in 17:5) and his descendants.[12]

The importance of these verses for the ensuing story cannot be overestimated. "What is being offered in these few verses is a theological blueprint for the redemptive history of the world."[13] This statement rightly grasps the importance of this text for the remaining story: it sets the path that God will travel in his redemptive journey. It establishes the role that God's people are to play: they are blessed to be a blessing.

Exodus 19:3–6 more carefully defines the narrative trajectory given in Genesis 12. Here we find "the unique identity of the people of God."[14] These words are spoken in the covenant at Sinai. God redeems the Israelites from bondage to Egyptian idolatry (Exod. 1–18) and brings them to meet him at Mount Sinai (Exod. 19:4). There he tells them that out of all nations he will make them God's "treasured possession." But this special status is not an end in itself. Rather, it is because "the whole earth is mine" (v. 5). It all belongs to God, and through Israel he is going to take it back.

The unique identity of Israel is found especially in two titles: "a priestly kingdom and a holy nation" (Exod. 19:6). As a priestly kingdom, Israel is

10. A common interpretation in Old Testament scholarship that reduces the Abrahamic covenant to a threefold blessing of people, land, and blessing "fails to pay sufficient attention to the climax of the promise that 'in you all the families of earth shall find blessing,'" Gordon J. Wenham writes ("The Face at the Bottom of the Well," in *He Swore an Oath: Biblical Themes from Genesis 12–50*, ed. Richard S. Hess, Gordon J. Wenham, and Philip E. Sattherthwaite, 2nd ed. [Grand Rapids: Baker Academic, 1994], 203).

11. Dumbrell, *Covenant and Creation*, 65; Wolff, "Kerygma of the Yahwist," 138; Claus Westermann, *Genesis 12–36* (Minneapolis: Augsburg, 1985), 146–52; P. D. Miller, "Syntax and Theology in Gen. 12:3a," *Vetus Testamentum* 34 (1984): 474.

12. Here in Gen. 12:3d the Hebrew verb form for "bless" is reflexive (5 times so in Genesis: it is Niphal 3 times and Hitpael 2 times), and there has been much exegetical debate on its precise meaning. It can imply that the families/nations will *bless themselves by Abraham.* That is, they will use Abraham's name as a model for blessing themselves or others: "May you be blessed like Abraham!" Or it could be "middle": they will "count themselves blessed." However, such usage presumes a knowledge of Abraham and the God who has blessed him, and thus implies that the families/nations will bless Abraham by seeing him as a model of such blessing—and thereby, in the logic of God's promise, enter into blessing themselves. The Septuagint and Paul's reading of the text (Gal. 3:8) certainly assume a passive meaning or implication ("all families/ nations will *be blessed*"). For a fuller discussion, see Christopher J. H. Wright, *The Mission of God: Unlocking the Bible's Grand Narrative* (Downers Grove, IL: InterVarsity, 2006), 216–21.

13. Dumbrell, *Covenant and Creation*, 66.

14. Jo Bailey Wells, *God's Holy People: A Theme in Biblical Theology* (Sheffield: Sheffield Academic Press, 2000), 34–35.

to mediate God's holy presence and blessing to the surrounding nations by being a distinctive people.[15] As a holy nation, "they are to be a people set apart, different from all other people by what they are and are becoming—a display people, a showcase to the world of how being in covenant with Yahweh changes a people."[16] It is as a priestly kingdom and a holy nation that we see "the way in which Israel will continue to exercise her Abrahamic role, and thus to provide a commentary on the way in which the promises of Genesis 12:1–3 will find their fulfilment."[17] As they live before the nations as a model of what God intends for all people, they will be an attractive light to the nations.

These words give us "the most programmatic speech we have for Israelite faith."[18] They set forth the missionary significance of Israel's life and are extremely significant for the following story: "The history of Israel from this point on is in reality merely a commentary upon the degree of fidelity with which Israel adhered to their Sinai-given vocation."[19] Israel's calling to be a priestly kingdom and holy nation for the sake of the nations is the way the Abrahamic promise will be fulfilled. It sets out a hermeneutical framework in which to read the rest of the story in the Old Testament.

Reading the Old Testament in Light of This Narrative Trajectory

Our hermeneutical task, then, is to read the rest of the Old Testament within this interpretive framework.[20] The task includes wrestling with the fit between this program and the various books and literary genres, as well as the central theological themes of the Old Testament. All this sets out an enormous hermeneutical agenda. In this section we simply indicate ways in which the Old Testament can be read missionally.

To this point we have already met three themes central to the Old Testament story: monotheism, election, and covenant. To be rightly understood, all three must be set within a missional framework. When we speak of the mission of God to restore his creation as the central theme of universal history, we are

15. Cf. ibid., 98–129.

16. John I. Durham, *Exodus*, Word Biblical Commentary (Waco: Word, 1987), 263.

17. Dumbrell, *Covenant and Creation*, 90.

18. Terence E. Fretheim, "'Because the Whole Earth Is Mine': Theme and Narrative in Exodus," *Interpretation* 50, no. 3 (July 1996): 229.

19. Dumbrell, *Covenant and Creation*, 80.

20. Both of us have tried to do this in slightly different ways. In *Mission of God* Chris has dealt extensively with large sections of the biblical story in light of a missional reading. In *A Light to the Nations: The Missional Church in the Biblical Story* (Grand Rapids: Baker Academic, 2011), Mike has offered a single narrative that tells the biblical story from this standpoint. Both books show that a missional hermeneutic is fruitful for reading the whole story.

saying that Yahweh is the one and only true God. This was essential to Israel's confession (Deut. 6:4). Yahweh alone has created the world, the world belongs to him, and he rules history. He made the whole creation to glorify himself and made humankind to know him. Thus a fundamental theme in the Old Testament is that the LORD God will displace all rival gods, which are idols, and one day he alone will be acknowledged and worshiped over the whole earth and by all nations (Ps. 96; Isa. 43:9–13; 44:6–20). There is an intrinsic missional thrust to Israel's conviction: their confession must become the confession of all nations—not because of some kind of arrogant Israelite ethnocentricity or imperial ambition, but simply because it is for the good of all nations, all humanity, and all creation, that the one true, living, and loving Creator God should be known, loved, worshiped, and enjoyed for who he is. Biblical monotheism is missional, but that does not make it oppressive. We should not read the misdeeds or faulty cultural assumptions of the worst kinds of modern human missionary zeal into what the Bible clearly portrays as the mission of God: to extend the knowledge and blessing of his love, as Creator and Redeemer, to the ends of the earth.

The *election* of Abraham and Israel cannot be separated from the missional task given to them. The "so that" conjunctions of Genesis 18:18–19 (NIV) make clear that God has chosen Abraham not only so that he might experience God's blessing, but also so that all nations will be blessed through him. Throughout Israel's history, election was constantly misunderstood to be solely soteriological: God was only the God of Israel, and they alone would be blessed with salvation. Certainly Israel's election did mean soteriological blessing. But stopping there shows misunderstanding of biblical election. God is not only the God of Israel but also the God of the whole earth, and election is to the end that the whole earth might know salvation. The Israelites were chosen, not so that they would be the only people to experience salvation, but so they might be the people through whom others from all nations would likewise experience salvation.

The central notion of *covenant* also finds its rightful place in a missional framework. We see this in both the Abrahamic and Sinaitic covenants. The goal of blessing Abraham is so that all nations might be blessed. The reason God makes Israel a special treasure, a holy nation, and a priestly kingdom is because the whole world belongs to him. God's covenantal purpose from the beginning was never simply to limit his blessing to Israel. "The covenant always envisaged a worldwide family; Israel, clinging to her own special status as the covenant-bearer, has betrayed the purpose for which that covenant was made. It is as though the postman were to imagine that all the letters in his bag were intended for him."[21]

---

21. N. T. Wright, *What Saint Paul Really Said: Was Paul of Tarsus the Real Founder of Christianity?* (Grand Rapids: Eerdmans, 1997), 108.

The torah is another critical theme in the Old Testament story. God first gives the law (Exod. 20–23) on the heels of Israel's redemption from Egypt (Exod. 1–18) and call (Exod. 19). The emergence of the law at this point is clear in the literary structure of Exodus: it is given precisely to shape Israel into a new society so they can fulfill their vocation amid the nations. What is implied by the literary structure of Exodus is made explicit in Deuteronomy. If Israel will observe the law carefully, the visibility of their righteous communal life will be observed by the nations, who will conclude that Israel is a wise and understanding people (Deut. 4:5–8). But immediately Moses warns them not to let the law slip from their hearts or turn to idolatry (4:15–31). The prevalent theme of idolatry and the encounter with pagan nations that runs throughout the Old Testament highlights the temptation that Israel will constantly face. Interpreting the continuing role of the law and the seductive power of idolatry must keep this origin in mind even when its connection with mission is not explicit. Israel's life is to be distinctive for the sake of the nations.

Although most of the time the connection between Israel's faithfulness and the nations is not overt, sometimes it is. For example, Jeremiah encourages Israelites to return to God, put their detestable idols out of his sight, and live in the righteous way of the law. *Then*, Jeremiah says, referring to the Abrahamic promise, the nations will be blessed (Jer. 4:1–3).

Another core Old Testament theme is *God's presence* with his people symbolized by the tabernacle and the temple. This must also be interpreted within a missional trajectory. In the book of Exodus, God comes to dwell in the midst of Israel immediately following the consummation of the covenant at Sinai (Exod. 25–40). Again, what Exodus says by way of its literary structure, Deuteronomy makes explicit: God's presence in the midst of Israel would draw the attention of the nations to Yahweh (Deut. 4:6–8). Robert Martin-Achard articulates the missional aim of God's presence clearly: "The evangelisation of the world is not primarily a matter of words or deeds: it is a matter of presence—*the presence of the People of God in the midst of mankind and the presence of God in the midst of His people.*"[22] Gregory Beale argues persuasively for the link between God's presence in the temple and the universal mission of Israel. The temple was to function as "a symbol of their task to expand God's presence to all nations."[23]

22. Martin-Achard, *Light to the Nations*, 79, emphasis original.
23. Gregory K. Beale, "Eden, the Temple, and the Church's Mission in the New Creation," *Journal of Evangelical Theological Studies* 48, no. 1 (March 2005): 19. This is given a full-length treatment (over 400 pages) in idem, *The Temple and the Church's Mission: A Biblical Theology of the Dwelling Place of God* (Downers Grove, IL: InterVarsity, 2004).

The *land* is another vital theme in the Old Testament. In his covenant God promises to give Abraham the land (Gen. 13:14–17; 15:7–21). We have seen that the goal of all the promises to Abraham is blessing to the nations. Thus land as one of those promises is encompassed by the "so that" of being a blessing. The land continues as a prominent theme throughout Israel's story. Yet the missional significance is often missed. This was the place where Israel was to live out its life as a light amid the nations. Ezekiel says, years later, that God set Israel in the center of the nations "with countries all around her" (5:5). Israel was placed at the crossroads of the nations as a display people visible to the nations. "Israel knew that it lived under the constant surveillance of the then contemporary world." Therefore they were to live out their lives "as something enacted before the eyes of the surrounding peoples, ever conscious that the glory of God was at issue."[24] The visibility of Israel on the land was part of its very theological identity in its role as a priestly kingdom.

Throughout Israel's history in the land, various *offices of leadership* emerge. Each of these offices must also be understood within a missional framework; they were gifts of God to enable Israel to fulfill its vocation. The *king* played a decisive role in equipping Israel to be a light to the nations. His task was three-fold: to defeat the idolatrous nations that threatened to corrupt Israel's life with idolatry; to enforce righteousness and justice in conformity with the law; and to promote the temple life, which would nourish faithfulness through worship and repairing the broken covenant through sacrifice.[25] Each task was to enable Israel to experience God's blessing and live distinctively before the nations.

Further, the king also was a symbol of the ultimate horizon of Israel's mission, to be realized in the eschatological future: the universal rule of God over all nations. In the covenant God makes with David, he promises an everlasting and universal kingdom to a descendant of David (2 Sam. 7:11–16). This covenant fits within the larger framework of God's covenant with Abraham to bless all nations. The promise is explicit in Psalm 72: "May all kings bow down to him and all nations serve him. . . . May his name endure forever; may it continue as long as the sun. Then all nations will be blessed through him, and they will call him blessed" (vv. 7, 17 NIV). This last line is an allusion to Genesis 12: when Israel's king reigns over the earth, God's purpose to bless all nations will be fulfilled.

The *priests* also found their role in nourishing Israel for its missional task. They were to teach the law, enabling Israel's life to be attractive to the nations.

24. Herman Bavinck, *An Introduction to the Science of Missions*, trans. David Hugh Freeman (Phillipsburg, NJ: P&R, 1979), 14.
25. This is the threefold role of the king as narrated in 2 Sam. 5–8, where David is portrayed as a faithful covenant-mediator king.

They were to mediate the sacrificial system, by which Israel experienced forgiveness and restoration to its calling. They were to bless Israel so that it might be a blessing to the nations (Num. 6:22–27; cf. Ps. 67).

The selective treatment of major Old Testament themes in this section cannot give full expression to each of these areas of Israel's life. They are necessarily brief and meant to be suggestive, indicating ways in which these important elements of Israel's story may be understood within the framework of a missional hermeneutic. Yet far too often this missional dimension is lost. It is as if God's salvation was meant only for Israel. God's mission *in* Israel is stressed at the expense of God's mission *through* Israel. Then each of these themes is interpreted only in terms of what God is doing for Israel, with little attention to their wider calling.

Often in biblical scholarship these themes are not explicitly connected to Israel's call to bless the nations; this framework established early in the story is left behind. Election and covenant were never meant to be just about Israel. God's presence with Israel was never just so that Israel could enjoy his presence. All the gifts God gives Israel throughout its story—Torah, land, leadership, and more—are meant *not only* to bless Israel *but also* to enable it to bless the nations. From the beginning Israel's life was directed outward to the world. When these theological themes in the Old Testament story lose that perspective, they are severed from the story line of Scripture.

The Prophets and God's Faithfulness to His Missional Path

Israel's mission is universal: the whole world is in view from the outset. Israel's mission is centripetal: its life is to be appealing, to draw the nations to Israel's God. But Israel's mission is also eschatological. Although the promise that Israel will be a blessing to all nations is first set before it as a task, it finds little fulfillment throughout the Old Testament. It seems clear that this will be fulfilled only in the eschatological future. When the Israelites fail to carry out their vocation faithfully and are exiled from the land, God does not abandon his intention to use Israel to bring blessing to the nations. Rather, through the prophets he promises to gather and renew Israel to fulfill its calling.

Ezekiel offers a glimpse of God's eschatological future. Israel has failed in its mission and profaned the Lord's name among the nations (36:16–21). However, God tells Israel that he will act so that "the nations will know[26] that

26. The phrase "then you will know" or "then they will know that I am Yahweh" occurs some 80 times in the book of Ezekiel. Though the book does not have anything comparable to the universal vision and rhetoric of Isaiah, it has not lost sight of the fact that what God did

I am the LORD" when he is "proved holy *through you* before their eyes" (vv. 22–23 NIV). So God will gather the Israelites and cleanse them from their idolatrous impurity. He will replace their heart of stone with a heart of flesh and give them his Spirit so they might live in obedience to God's law (vv. 24–27).

Other Old Testament prophets share the same future vision. Zechariah looks back to the Abrahamic covenant as he paints a picture of the coming salvation. Although Israel has been a curse among the nations, a day is coming when God will restore blessing to Israel and in so doing enable it to be a blessing to all nations. "Just as you have been a cursing among the nations, O house of Judah and house of Israel, so I will save you and you shall be a blessing" (Zech. 8:13; cf. Isa. 19:23–25). So the prophets look forward to "two successive events, first the call to Israel, and subsequently the redemptive incorporation of the Gentiles in the kingdom of God."[27]

This gathering event and the subsequent blessing of all nations will be carried out in connection with the arrival of the kingdom, a work of eschatological salvation enacted by the Messiah in the power of the Spirit. The prophetic link between the coming of the kingdom and the gathering of Israel only increased during the centuries leading up to Christ. However, the additional element that all nations would be blessed was buried by a Jewish ethnocentric exclusivism. Election and covenant had become a matter of exclusive privilege. "Israel, called to be a lighthouse for the world, has surrounded herself with mirrors to keep the light in, heightening her own sense of purity and exclusiveness while insisting that the nations must remain in darkness."[28]

Jesus, the Coming of the Kingdom, and the Gathering and Sending of Israel

Jesus steps onto the stage of redemptive history and announces "the good news" that "the kingdom of God" has arrived (Mark 1:14–15). The kingdom is the central theme of Jesus's mission. The teaching of Jesus makes clear that the kingdom has arrived: God's power to renew is present in history. Yet his teaching also points to a future realization: the power of sin and its effects

---

in and for Israel will have consequences for the knowledge of God, in Israel itself and among the nations. And that is a missional perspective in principle. See the discussion of this dimension of Ezekiel in Christopher J. H. Wright, *The Message of Ezekiel*, The Bible Speaks Today (Downers Grove, IL: InterVarsity, 2001).

27. Joachim Jeremias, *Jesus' Promise to the Nations*, Studies in Biblical Theology 24 (London: SCM, 1958), 71.

28. N. T. Wright, *Jesus and the Victory of God*, vol. 2 of *Christian Origins and the Question of God* (London: SPCK, 1996), 289.

are still very much at work. And so it has become commonplace to speak of the already-and-not-yet era of the kingdom. What is not so commonplace is reflection on *why* God has delayed the final consummation. What stands out in the Gospels is the central activity of gathering, which characterizes this period. God keeps the walls of history open so that an eschatological gathering might take place.

For the Jews of Jesus's day, the arrival of the kingdom meant the time had come for Israel to be gathered. Joachim Jeremias makes the astonishing comment that "the *only* significance of the whole of Jesus's activity is to gather the eschatological people of God." He continues: "Jesus was not the first to attempt to gather God's people of the time of salvation; there was a whole series of attempts in this direction. It is not an exaggeration to say that the whole of contemporary Jewish religious life was fundamentally determined by it."[29] Certainly this corresponds with the prophetic vision for the end of the age.

The pages of the Gospels show that the gathering of a community was central to Jesus's mission. Three images are pervasive: the gathering of sheep into the fold, the gathering of guests to the banquet table, and the gathering of wheat into the barn. All of these can be found in the Old Testament prophets and are developed in the intertestamental period. Gerhard Lohfink correctly links this gathering to missional vocation: "That God has chosen and sanctified his people in order to make it a contrast-society in the midst of the other nations was for Jesus the self-evident background of all his actions." Jesus's gathering activity is God's "eschatological action" to "restore or even re-establish his people, in order to carry out definitively and irrevocably his plan of having a holy people in the midst of the nations."[30]

This clarifies why Jesus restricts his mission to the Jews, which has long puzzled those who wonder why Jesus seems unable to break out of the narrow confines of the Jewish nation. He says that he is sent to gather only the lost sheep of Israel (Matt. 15:24), and he similarly limits the mission of the twelve to Israel as well (Matt. 10:5–6). But his mission only to the Jews is in keeping with the vision of the prophets that first Israel must be gathered and restored so it may be a light to the nations. Indeed, Jesus's "apparent particularism is an expression of his universalism—it is because his mission concerns the whole world that he comes to Israel."[31]

29. Joachim Jeremias, *New Testament Theology*, trans. John Bowden (New York: Scribner, 1971), 170–71.
30. Gerhard Lohfink, *Jesus and Community: The Social Dimension of the Christian Faith*, trans. John P. Galvin (Philadelphia: Fortress, 1982), 123.
31. Johannes Munck, *Paul and the Salvation of Mankind*, trans. Frank Clarke (Atlanta: John Knox, 1959), 272.

But more than gathering is needed. Two things must take place if the newly gathered Israelites are to fulfill their calling. First, they must be liberated from an ethnocentric exclusivism and restored to an outward face. And second, they must be renewed to live distinctive lives. They must, as Ezekiel has promised, be given new hearts; they need God's Spirit to empower them to obey his laws and decrees.

A major part of Jesus's mission is to restore Israel to its missional vocation. We catch a glimpse of this in the Sermon on the Mount. The whole "sermon" is a challenge to Israelites to take up their eschatological calling to be a light to the nations and to reject the nationalistic and separatist way of the other Jewish leaders of the day. "You are the light of the world. A city built on a hill cannot be hid. No one after lighting a lamp puts it under the bushel basket, but on the lampstand, and it gives light to all in the house. In the same way, let your light shine before others, so that they may see your good works and give glory to your Father in heaven" (Matt. 5:14–16). Together, the images of light and city refer to "the eschatological Jerusalem, which the prophets foretell will one day be raised above all mountains and illumine the nations with its light (cf. Isa. 2:2–5)."[32] In the mission of Jesus, Israel is not just being gathered but is also being restored, to be a light to which all the peoples will stream.

Yet this newly gathered eschatological Israel, symbolized by the appointment of the Twelve,[33] is as weak and sinful as the covenant people in the Old Testament. Israel can no more keep the torah than can Old Testament Israel. A new work of God must somehow defeat the power of evil and bring renewing power. This is what is accomplished in the death and resurrection of Jesus (Rom. 8:3–4). Freshly gathered Israel may now participate in the two mightiest acts of God that stand at the center of history: in his death Jesus conquers the sin and evil of the old age and invites his people to share in that victory; in his resurrection he inaugurates the age to come and gives his Spirit that his people might enjoy new life.

So the story of Israel culminates in the death and resurrection of Jesus (Luke 24:46). But these events are intended to be cosmic in scope not only for Israel. Jesus is "the Lamb of God that takes away the sin of the [whole] world" (John 1:29). Hence there is a redemptive-historical logic that runs from the work of Christ to the eschatological mission of God's people. From the beginning of the biblical story, the goal was to incorporate all nations into the blessing of Israel's covenant. That time has arrived! The story of Israel

32. Lohfink, *Jesus and Community*, 65.

33. Ben Meier, "Jesus, the Twelve, and Restoration," in *Restoration: Old Testament, Jewish, and Christian Perspectives*, ed. James M. Scott (Leiden: Brill, 2001), 404; see also Jacob Jervell, *Luke and the People of God: A New Look at Luke-Acts* (Minneapolis: Augsburg, 1972), 75–112.

culminates not only in the work of Jesus but also in the mission of eschatological Israel to all nations (Luke 24:47).

Thus the Gospels end with a commission that leads to a "great change of direction"[34] in redemptive history (Matt. 28:16–20; Luke 24:45–49; John 20:19–23). According to the prophets, the ingathering of the nations was to be an eschatological event in which God would draw them to Israel. The operative word was "come" (Mic. 7:12; Isa. 60:3): it would be a pilgrimage of nations to Jerusalem. The movement is from the periphery to the center. But that is now reversed.[35] Now eschatological Israel is sent to the ends of the earth (Luke 24:47; Acts 1:8). Karl Barth rightly stresses that this commission is given to *gathered, eschatological Israel*: "the Israel of the end time is fulfilling the destiny of historical Israel, as a 'covenant to the people, a light to the nations' [Isa. 42:6; 49:8]."[36]

The Blessing of All Nations: The Story Continues in Acts

The gathering cannot end with the lost sheep of Israel. Jesus has other sheep who are not of this fold (John 10:16). This has been the goal of the biblical story from the beginning. The book of Acts narrates the way the prophetic promise of the incorporation of the nations into Israel is being fulfilled.

In his Gospel, Luke "wrote about all that Jesus began to do and to teach" (Acts 1:1), but now in the Acts sequel he writes about what Jesus continues to do and teach by the Holy Spirit through his sent community. Eschatological Israel will do for the nations what Jesus has done for Israel: through the witness of their life, words, and deeds empowered by the Spirit, they will gather sheep into the covenant fold of blessing. Witness "to all nations": this theme ends the book of Luke (24:47–48) and now begins the book of Acts (1:8).

The already-and-not-yet era of the kingdom continues to open up space for this gathering mission to the ends of the earth (Acts 1:6–7). In fact, this is the meaning and purpose of this present time in redemptive history (1:8). Lesslie Newbigin puts it quite strongly:

> The meaning of this "overlap of the ages" in which we live, the time between the coming of Christ and His coming again, is that it is a time given for the witness

---

34. Johannes Blauw, *Missionary Nature of the Church: A Survey of the Biblical Theology of Mission* (New York: McGraw-Hill, 1962), 85.

35. Charles H. H. Scobie, "Israel and the Nations: An Essay in Biblical Theology," *Tyndale Bulletin* 43, no. 2 (1992): 291–92.

36. Karl Barth, "An Exegetical Study of Matthew 28:16–20," in *The Theology of the Christian Mission*, ed. Gerald H. Anderson (London: SCM, 1961), 58.

of the apostolic Church to the ends of the earth. . . . The implication of a true eschatological perspective will be missionary obedience, and the eschatology which does not issue in such obedience is a false eschatology.[37]

We call attention to four themes in the book of Acts that unfold God's mission at this climactic point in the biblical story. The first is that the gospel is the power of God that brings salvation *first to the Jew, then to the gentile.* In Acts, the gathering of Israel continues in the first section of the book. "The mission to Jews is a necessary stage through which the history of salvation must pass in order that salvation might proceed from the restored Israel to the Gentiles."[38] What unfolds in the narrative of Acts is a division in Israel (cf. Luke 2:34) between those who embrace the Messiah and become the true Israel, and those who reject the gospel and exclude themselves from covenant membership. This mission to the Jews is the necessary prerequisite for the nations to share in the promises. Pauline language in Romans provides imagery for what takes place in Acts: some Jews reject the gospel and are "broken off," while gentiles are "grafted in" (Rom. 11:17–21).[39]

A second theme in Acts is the interplay of the *centripetal and centrifugal* dimensions of mission. On the one hand, the centripetal aspect of mission characteristic of Israel's vocation continues. As the church devotes itself to the means by which the new eschatological life of the Spirit is renewed (Acts 2:42), a distinctive life of power, generosity, justice, and joy is evident: people are drawn to their attractive lives (2:43–47; 4:32–35). On the other hand, there is a centrifugal dynamic that is new. The church in Antioch, inspired by the Holy Spirit, lifts up its eyes and sees many places throughout the Roman Empire where there is no witness to Christ. They send Saul/Paul and Barnabas (Acts 13:1–3), who "preach the gospel where Christ was not known" (Rom. 15:20 NIV), establishing new missional communities.[40]

---

37. Lesslie Newbigin, *The Household of God: Lectures on the Nature of the Church* (New York: Friendship, 1953), 153–54.

38. Jervell, *Luke and the People of God*, 43.

39. David Seccombe, "The New People of God," in *Witness to the Gospel: The Theology of Acts*, ed. I. Howard Marshall and David Peterson (Grand Rapids: Eerdmans, 1998), 371.

40. It is a mistake (though a very common one), however, to speak of that sending of Paul and Barnabas in Acts 13 as "Paul's first missionary journey." In fact, it was his second. In Acts 11:27–30, also led by a word from the Holy Spirit, the church in Antioch responded to famine and poverty in Jerusalem by collecting gifts and "sending" them by the hands of Barnabas and Saul. Paul's first church-initiated missionary journey was for famine relief, and it seems to have made a big impression on him. When he later visited Jerusalem and received the endorsement of the apostles there for preaching the gospel to the gentiles, "they asked only one thing, that we remember the poor, which was actually what I was eager to do" (Gal. 2:7, 10). For Paul, his

A third theme in Acts is the *transformation of the people of God* into a new kind of community. The national form of ethnic Israel was the particular starting point, but God's people were meant ultimately to be a nonterritorially based and multiethnic people. That goal is realized in the book of Acts, but not without painful struggle.

The church at Antioch is a new kind of community. It is truly a multiethnic church that is able to transcend the gentile-Jewish divide both in its fellowship and its leadership. This kind of community is what Paul plants across Asia Minor. This creates no small stir in Jerusalem, where the form of God's people has been Jewish for hundreds of years. Paul's mission to the gentiles does not seem to fit with the prophetic pilgrimage of the nations to Jerusalem, and he is breaking with more than a millennium of divinely authorized tradition.

The question is posed: Do gentiles need to become Jews to become part of the people of God? The Jerusalem Council settles this issue (Acts 15). What becomes clear is that "not even the original, divinely sanctioned culture of God's elect nation has the right to universalize its particular expression of Christianity."[41] The people of God are no longer bound to one land and one cultural way of life; their witness is in every nation.

Our fourth point from the book of Acts is that the account of God's mission through his people is an *unfinished story* in which we are invited to take our place. The book of Acts draws to a close with Paul in Rome. Yet it is an abrupt and puzzling conclusion. Jesus's words indicate that the spread of the gospel will be from Jerusalem to the ends of the earth (Acts 1:8). Acts ends in Rome. But "'the ends of the earth' is not, in fact, a reference to Rome."[42] The sudden ending before it reaches the ends of the earth invites us into a story to complete a task that is not finished. Luke "finishes with the subliminal message, 'to be continued,'"[43] and we might add "with you, the readers, as participants."

Importance for Theological Interpretation

When we read any passage of the Bible, we do so in terms of *some* understanding of the larger canonical story. Often this operative narrative is not

---

mission included preaching the gospel and caring for the poor: both were integral parts of the "obedience of faith" (Rom. 1:5; 16:26) that was the goal of his life's mission.

41. Dean Flemming, *Contextualization in the New Testament: Patterns for Theology and Mission* (Downers Grove, IL: InterVarsity, 2005), 52.

42. Brian S. Rosner, "The Progress of the Word," in Marshall and Peterson, *Witness to the Gospel*, 218–19.

43. Ibid., 231.

recognized. N. T. Wright says, "If I am accused of having in my head a 'large narrative' which I then use as the template for interpreting the Gospels, I plead guilty—and summon the Four Evangelists in my defense. This, demonstrably, is what they are urging us to do."[44] The same is true of every part of Scripture. We need to be aware of the narrative that is shaping our reading of particular texts. If we are to have the right story "in our heads" that functions fruitfully as a template for reading the various parts of the Bible correctly, we will need to recover mission as a central strand. The distorting prejudice of a *nonmissional* self-understanding must be overcome.

Thus a faithful theological interpretation of Scripture will take seriously the theme of mission in the biblical narrative. A faithful theological reading of Scripture, then, will work hard to read any passage in the Bible within this overarching framework, discerning its place in that framework, assessing how the shape of the grand narrative is reflected in the passage in question, and, conversely, how the particular passage contributes to and moves the grand narrative forward.

The Bible as a Product and Tool of God's Mission in and through His People

The biblical canon is not only a *record* of God's mission in and through his people; it is also a *product* and a *tool* to accomplish that mission. Out of the salvation history, various kinds of books arose to form and equip God's people for their mission in the world. These biblical books "were not simply *about* the coming of God's Kingdom into all the world; they were, and were designed to be, part of the *means whereby that happened*."[45] Both perspectives are essential to a missional hermeneutic.

Since the Bible is a metanarrative about God's redemptive journey, the authority of Scripture must be understood in terms of its role in this account. This story is about God's purpose to renew the creation in and through the mission of his people. Thus the issue of biblical authority may be fruitfully explored as a "sub-branch . . . of the mission of the church."[46]

When we ask what role the Bible plays in the biblical story, we receive the answer that God's "self-revelation is always to be understood within the

44. N. T. Wright, "Whence and Whither Historical Jesus Studies in the Life of the Church?," in *Jesus, Paul, and the People of God: A Theological Dialogue with N. T. Wright*, ed. Nicholas Perrin and Richard B. Hays (Downers Grove, IL: IVP Academic, 2011), 131.

45. N. T. Wright, *Scripture and the Authority of God: How to Read the Bible Today* (New York: HarperCollins, 2011), 51, emphasis original.

46. Ibid., 27–28.

category of God's mission to the world, God's saving sovereignty let loose through Jesus and the Spirit and aimed at the healing and renewal of the creation."[47] To understand biblical authority, then, we need to perceive how Scripture powerfully works to shape a missional people. If we miss this role and purpose of Scripture, we misunderstand it.

Scripture as a Means of Grace

To speak of the Scripture as a product and tool has similarities with the traditional language of "means of grace," which has been employed in various theological traditions to indicate the way God uses the Bible, among other means, to equip his people. We wish to connect to this tradition but with an important caveat: Scripture is not merely the means by which God's people are blessed, as if the end of it all is their own salvation. Rather, it is the means that brings salvation to God's people *for the sake of the world*. Understood in this way, Scripture is a *means of missional grace*.

We can bring this into sharp focus by reference to Karl Barth's discussion of the *beneficia Christi* (benefits of Christ) and sacred egocentricity.[48] He asks a basic question: What does it mean to be a Christian? The "classic answer" is to be a recipient and possessor of the *beneficia Christi*. He lists these benefits: regeneration, conversion, peace with God, reconciliation, justification, sanctification, forgiveness of sins, beloved of God, freedom, adoption as God's children, hope of the resurrection, foretaste and heirs of eternal life, and a new obedience. All these come as gifts of God's grace in Christ by the Spirit, in response to repentance and faith. All this, he says, inspires the preaching and teaching, the evangelistic and pastoral efforts, and the hymns, fellowship, theology, and apologetics of the church. It is also the way the New Testament has been read and preached, and the way the means of grace has been understood.

Of course, Barth says, "there can be no disputing that something true and important is meant and envisaged in all this."[49] Yet if we are not careful, it would be easy to make the reception, possession, and enjoyment of these benefits the "essential and central factor" in the Christian life.[50] Can it really be the end of Christian vocation that I should be blessed, that I should be

47. Ibid., 29.
48. Karl Barth, *Church Dogmatics*, trans. G. W. Bromiley (Peabody, MA: Hendrickson, 1961), IV/3.2:554–69.
49. Ibid., 563.
50. Ibid.

saved, that I should receive, possess, and enjoy all these gifts and then attain to eternal life without any regard for others? Does this not smack of a pious or sacred egocentricity? Does this not make us *pure* recipients and possessors of salvation?[51] "Is not every form of egocentricity excused and even confirmed and sanctified, if egocentricity in this sacred form is the divinely willed meaning of Christian existence and the Christian song of praise consists finally only in a many-tongued but monotonous *pro me, pro me,* and similar possessive expressions?"[52]

There is something very seductive about the classic answer, and it seems to have a tenacious grip on the Christian church, as has become increasingly evident in the self-centered nature of many contemporary worship songs. And sadly, this answer most often gives meaning to the means of grace: the Bible becomes the means by which individuals receive the benefits of Christ. But if the scriptural story is our standard, this is at best only half an answer and hence a distortion, betraying the Christian vocation.

This is not to discount the classic answer entirely, of course. The Bible is indeed a tool whereby God's covenant community might know salvific blessing. But it is always so *that* they might be a blessing. Saying that the Bible is a tool of mission challenges both the individualism and the self-seeking nature of the way the means of grace has often been understood. The Scriptures enable the people of God to experience the benefits of Christ's salvation so that they might embody that salvation for the sake of the world.

The Old Testament as a Product and Tool of God's Mission

When we say that the Old Testament is product and tool of God's mission, we affirm that the various books of the Old Testament canon were written to equip Israel to live out its covenantal vocation in the midst of the world. Scripture is a *product* of God's mission: the various biblical writings have their origin in some issue, need, controversy, or threat that needed to be addressed in the context of their missional calling. The Bible is also a *tool*: the various books that make up the canon were written to form God's people for their vocation by addressing the need or threat. So the Bible moves beyond being simply a record of God's redemptive work. It is also a powerful tool to bring it about.

Israel faced many crises and challenges throughout its history. When the Israelites are redeemed from bondage in Egypt, they have lived for four centuries,

51. Ibid., 568.
52. Ibid., 567.

influenced by a pagan worldview expressed in myths of the day. One of the tasks before Moses is to detoxify the Israelites from this pollution. His task is also to help them understand their covenant identity and vocation: why God liberated them from Egypt. The books of Genesis and Exodus arise precisely out of this need. The various historical books meet crises of faith by narrating God's covenant purposes in history. The various messages of the prophets arise in response to the rebellion of Israel, who has lost sight of their covenant calling. They issue a call to return to faithfulness but also promise that Israel's unfaithfulness will not thwart God's plan. The Wisdom literature is intended to shape the daily conduct of Israel in conformity with God's wise creational order. Some of the wisdom books equipped Israel to live in a world that was not so tidy and was full of contradiction and suffering. The psalms nourished the Israelites' covenantal calling in corporate worship in all sorts of ways, giving poetic and musical expression to their deepest needs.

Thus the Old Testament Scriptures were written to "equip" God's people for their missional calling to be a distinctive people. Specifically, they functioned as an instrument of God's loving and powerful presence among his people to shape them for their vocation. Therefore, "a full account of the role of scripture within the life of Israel would appear as a function of Israel's election by God for the sake of the world. Through scripture, God was equipping his people to serve his purposes."[53]

Jesus Christ and the New Testament as a Product and Tool of God's Mission

The apostles proclaim and teach the good news that Israel's Scriptures have been fulfilled in the life, death, and resurrection of Jesus, that Jesus has accomplished what the Old Testament had not. Apostolic proclamation and doctrine continued to make Christ present in his saving power to shape and empower a missional people.

Herman Ridderbos helpfully elaborates the redemptive-historical categories of the apostolic message in terms of *kerygma*, *martyria*, and *didachē*.[54] *Kerygma* is the work of a herald that proclaims the good news of the person and events of Jesus Christ as the climax of the Old Testament story, with an urgent call to faith. *Martyria* is the divinely authoritative witness of the

53. N. T. Wright, *Scripture and the Authority of God*, 35.
54. Herman Ridderbos, *Redemptive History and the New Testament Scriptures* (formerly *The Authority of the New Testament Scriptures* [1963]), trans. H. De Jongste, rev. Richard B. Gaffin Jr., 2nd rev. ed. (Phillipsburg, NJ: P&R, 1988), 49–76.

apostles to what God has accomplished in Jesus, shaping a kingdom people for the sake of the world. *Kerygma* and *martyria* eventually take literary form in the Gospels: written proclamation of and witness to the historical events of Jesus Christ.

Didachē, however, represents a more advanced stage of revelation, which flows from and builds on the proclamation and witness. This will take written form in the Epistles of the New Testament. They build up the church by unfolding the significance of gospel for the church's missionary calling in particular contexts. The imagery of *didachē* arises from the sphere of rabbinic teaching. It is instruction that unfolds the significance of God's mighty acts in history for the covenant community's life. While *kerygma* and *matyria* make known the mighty act of God in Christ, *didachē* works out the missional implications for specific communities.

So, as the apostles proclaim and teach the gospel as God's powerful word, it calls into existence a missional community, shapes that community to be a faithful people, and works through them to draw others to faith.

The verbal preaching and teaching of the apostles take literary form in the canon of the New Testament. Through this written word, the powerful presence of Christ now forms his people for their missional vocation in the way that the living word of the apostles has done so. These New Testament writings carry the same purpose and power as the original proclamation of the apostles.

An obvious example is the group of Paul's Letters.[55] Paul was a missionary who established witnessing communities in places where there were none (Rom. 15:20). As a church planter, he wanted those congregations to bear faithful witness to the gospel in their lives, deeds, and words, in their particular setting. In his letters he seeks to accomplish that end. Thus Paul's Epistles emerge from the heart of a church planter concerned that his newly formed congregations live as a light amid the pagan Roman Empire.

"Paul's understanding of his mission may easily be misassessed," Paul Bowers says, "if for no better reason than the modern conventional equation of mission with evangelism. Given such an equation, nurturing becomes not so much a missionary as a post-missionary function, to be understood as adjunctive rather than integral to Paul's specifically missionary activity."[56] It is not

---

55. Michael Barram, "The Bible, Mission, and Social Location: Toward a Missional Hermeneutic," *Interpretation* 61 (2007): 42–58; cf. idem, *Mission and Moral Reflection in Paul* (New York: Peter Lang, 2005).

56. Paul Bowers, "Fulfilling the Gospel: The Scope of the Pauline Mission," *Journal of the Evangelical Theological Society* 30, no. 2 (June 1987): 189. Cf. Barram, *Mission and Moral Reflection*, 10; and the Third Lausanne Conference on World Evangelization (2010), *The Cape*

only evangelism and church planting that are part of Paul's self-understanding of his missionary task, but also nurturing and upbuilding. To properly read Paul, this missional intent and purpose must be recognized.

A good example of this can be seen in the extensive space Paul gives in his letters to so-called ethical teaching. Pauline scholarship has failed to answer a key question: "On what basis does Paul continue to assert his moral authority over established communities, if his apostolic mission is narrowly construed as an evangelistic and church planting endeavor?"[57] As a missionary, Paul wants to see his congregations live in a way that is not conformed to the idolatry of the Roman world (Rom. 12:2). Paul constantly has in mind the effect of the church's life on the unbelieving world. They are to be careful to do what is right in the eyes of everyone (Rom. 12:17), live in a manner worthy of the gospel of Christ before those who oppose the gospel (Phil. 1:27–28), be wise in the way they act toward outsiders (Col. 4:5), live to win the respect of outsiders (1 Thess. 4:12), and live blameless and pure lives so they may shine in the midst of Philippi as stars holding out the word of life (Phil. 2:16). For Paul, the ethical life of the church is to be a light to draw those outside to the gospel.[58] Thus mission is the key for understanding Paul's ethical teaching. The same point can be made with respect to his theological reflection. "Inasmuch as Paul's thought—theological, moral, or otherwise—contributes to the fulfillment of his apostolic vocation, it is fundamentally missional reflection. Paul's mission provides the crucial link between his theology and ethics."[59]

The book of 1 Corinthians may serve as an example. Various questions about how to live faithfully in the pagan environment of Corinth inspire Paul to pen a letter to the church in that city. The epistle reflects the fact that the church has conformed to the idolatrous world of ancient Corinth. For example, the competition for success characteristic of Corinthian culture has led to jealousy, strife, and splits (1:10; 3:3). Paul counters with a call to humility, love, and recognition of need for one another (3:18–20; 8:1; 12:21–22; 13:1–4). The Corinthian people take pride in their wisdom, knowledge, spirituality, and freedom. Paul employs all these terms but fills them with the new content of the gospel. He "*redefines them* again in accordance with

---

Town Commitment: A Confession of Faith and a Call to Action, Didasko Files, 3rd ed. (Printbridge, UK: Didasko Publishing; South Hamilton, MA: The Lausanne Movement, 2011), 68–69.

57. Barram, "Bible, Mission, and Social Location," 56.

58. Douwe van Swigchem, *Het missionair karakter van de christelijke gemeente volgens de briven van Paulus en Petrus* (Kampen: J. H. Kok, 1955), 78–108.

59. Barram, *Mission and Moral Reflection*, 140.

the received apostolic gospel"[60] (2:6–7, 12, 16; 4:7–14; 6:12; 8:1–2; etc.). The dualism of the Greek worldview has led to problems with understanding the bodily resurrection. Pagan customs have produced questions about eating meat offered to idols. Paul addresses all of these issues by bringing the gospel to bear on life in pagan Corinth.

In all of this, Paul is concerned with the missional import of their lives. Their lives will have either a negative (6:1–12; 15:34) or a positive effect on the gospel (7:12–16; 10:27–29). Paul's own example is to use his freedom so that some might be saved: "I have become all things to all people, that I might by all means save some" (9:22). He tells the Corinthians to consider the effect on outsiders if they use their freedom to eat meat offered to idols. "So, whether you eat or drink, or whatever you do, do everything for the glory of God. Give no offense to Jews or to Greeks or to the church of God, just as I try to please everyone in everything I do, not seeking my own advantage, but that of many, so that they may be saved. Be imitators of me, as I am of Christ" (10:31–11:1). These texts open a window on the motive of Paul: our lives are to be a light to the unbelieving world.[61]

Like all of Paul's Letters, 1 Corinthians finds its origin in mission: a crisis or conflict or struggle or threat to God's people calls forth his word to equip his people. The letters function as powerful tools, enabling the churches to be faithful in their mission: making the gospel known amid an idolatrous culture.

Importance for Theological Interpretation Today

Contemporary hermeneutics has rightly taught us that our particular interpretive location may open up and close off a true understanding of a text. The ancient authors were motivated by mission when they addressed questions, issues, and problems; likewise, contemporary readers who want to hear God's address must come to the text with the same commitments. Only then will we ask the proper questions of the text and experience it as the Spirit's tool to inspire and inform the ongoing mission of the church.

Proper questions rightly orient us to the text. As Darrell Guder puts it: "Studying God's Word is always a process of posing questions to Scripture. The questions we ask will control the answers we receive." He suggests a basic question "that concretely opens up the Bible for us as the written testimony

60. Anthony C. Thiselton, *1 Corinthians: A Shorter Exegetical and Pastoral Commentary* (Grand Rapids: Eerdmans, 2006), 9–19, emphasis original.
61. Barram, "Bible, Mission, and Social Location," 55; idem, *Mission and Moral Reflection*, 35–77.

that God uses to shape us for our faithful witness and service. . . . 'How did this text equip and shape God's people for their missional witness then, and how does it shape us today?'"[62] Guder elaborates the importance of this question for biblical scholarship: "All the resources of historical, critical, and literary research on the biblical testimony can and must contribute to the church's formation by illumining all the dimensions of this fundamental question."[63]

In the case of both the Old and New Testaments, the various genres of literature represent different tools that God has used to form believers into a faithful missionary people. This represents the heartbeat of biblical canon. To properly interpret these books, we must resonate and align ourselves with the missional concern that they carried in their original setting, and then ask how they can equip us today.

Conclusion

Biblical scholarship must ultimately serve the church in its mission. Richard Bauckham points out that often "the academic guild of biblical scholars" has a "largely self-generated agenda [that] increasingly excludes the church from its context and implied audience." But biblical scholarship must "address the church in its mission to the world" and even make the church-in-mission in the West not simply its audience but also its dialogue partner.[64] We have a long way to go, but if we are to read the Bible faithfully along the grain of its message and according to its intent, we must continue to move in the direction of a missional hermeneutic.

---

62. Darrell Guder, "Unlikely Ambassadors: Clay Jar Christians in God's Service," A Bible Study for the 214th General Assembly of the Presbyterian Church (USA) (Louisville: Office of the General Assembly, Presbyterian Church [U.S.A.], 2002), 5.

63. Darrell Guder, "From Mission and Theology to Missional Theology," *Princeton Seminary Bulletin* 24, no. 1 (2003): 48.

64. Bauckham, "Mission as a Hermeneutic," 1–2.

9

The Telos (Goal)
of Theological Interpretation

HEATH A. THOMAS

Hearing God's Address

After years of hard work, expense, and study of the Bible and its world, one is faced with the bracing question: What is the point of becoming a biblical scholar? What is it all for? Many answers emerge: to be able to explain the historical value of the Bible, to revel in its literary qualities, to see its influence on wider culture, or to identify its value as a great piece of classic literature. Each of these answers, no doubt, resonates with many who make the effort to invest their lives in the study of Scripture. Despite the value of each, I am left wondering if there is more by way of an answer. This chapter argues that there is. Whether read by a trained biblical scholar, a minister, or a lay reader of Scripture, this chapter posits a profound point for attending to the Bible, which emerges from the words of a young boy called Samuel: "Speak, for your servant is listening" (1 Sam. 3:10). So the child Samuel speaks in response to God, who has called him. These words open a way forward to answering the question "What is the point of reading this book?" and underline the focus

197

of theological interpretation of Scripture. A broken humanity needs to hear God's words of life for guidance, comfort, confrontation, and transformation. A helpful metaphor for reading Scripture, then, is *listening*.

But addressed by whom? Theological interpretation seeks to listen to God, who has given his word and speaks to humanity through it. So the Manifesto reads: "theological interpretation reads Scripture to hear God's address, so that the church might be transformed into the image of Christ, for the sake of the world." The point of reading Scripture, then, is to be addressed by God. This expositional chapter explores the various points that emerge from this simple, yet profound, claim.

Theological Interpretation Aims to Hear God's Address in and through Scripture

The *theological* dimension of this position remains essential for interpretation. Attending to "God's address" affirms the church's understanding of the Triune God. Scripture's potency derives from its source: God, who is the Author and Creator of all things. What *God* has said in Scripture remains central for those who read his Word. Scripture as *God's address* reminds us that the Triune God desires communion, or "fellowship," with his creatures. The Catholic teaching in *Dei Verbum* rightly affirms that "the invisible God (see Col. 1:15; 1 Tim. 1:17) out of the abundance of His love speaks to men as friends (see Exod. 33:11; John 15:14–15) and lives among them (see Bar. 3:38 [NABRE, 37 NRSV]), so that He may invite and take them into fellowship with Himself."[1] As his creatures, God invites people to participate in the life to which he has called them. Humans are God's *creatures*, but we are loved by God as *friends*. And God extends his invitation (in part) through Scripture, which draws humanity into the obedient life before God.[2] From its advent to its final phase of canonization, Scripture is God's gift that enables humans to adequately know God and to love him in his triune nature.[3]

---

1. Second Vatican Council, *Dei Verbum: Dogmatic Constitution on Divine Revelation* §2. For an extended dogmatic discussion of this idea, see, e.g., John Webster, *Holy Scripture: A Dogmatic Sketch*, Current Issues in Theology (Cambridge: Cambridge University Press, 2003).

2. Although recorded in Scripture, God extended this invitation for fellowship *before* Scripture's formation (e.g., in the Garden of Eden, in the age of the patriarchs, etc.). His divine nature and prior invitation testify to God's desire for communion with the saints, and the ontology of Scripture coheres with this prior testimony. See chap. 2 of this volume, Michael W. Goheen and Michael D. Williams, "Doctrine of Scripture and Theological Interpretation," particularly the section on revelation.

3. Catholic, Orthodox, and Protestant Christians differ somewhat regarding the contours of the sacred writings. See chap. 6, "The Canon and Theological Interpretation," in this volume.

J. I. Packer too agrees that God speaks in Scripture, and interpretation depends on hearing his voice. He describes evangelical interpretation of Scripture, for instance, in this manner:

> Bible writers unanimously and unambiguously testify to a God who *speaks*, in the straightforward sense of that word—that is, a God who addresses verbal messages to people, states facts, tells us things; and therefore Evangelicals affirm, on the basis of the Bible literally interpreted, that cognitive instruction via Scripture is integral to God's self-disclosure and that biblical teaching, as such, is God's teaching, as such.[4]

Scripture reveals the God who speaks to a broken humanity and discloses his messages to them. Readings in the Christian tradition remain helpful and productive, even necessary, as shall be argued below, but the true aim of Scripture reading means attentive listening to *vocem Dei viventis* ("the voice of the living God"; Deut. 5:26 Vulgate).

What God discloses to humanity as he speaks is *himself*. The questions that humans bring to Scripture are good and right, but at root the substance of Scripture—both its subject matter and content—is nothing short of God. For this reason, theological interpretation attends to God and what he says, so that we might be drawn into his life.[5] But as one understands what God says about himself in Scripture, then his association with his creation emerges as a topic for inquiry. In this way, *the whole of life* opens up as deeply connected to the Creator, and thereby theological interpretation attends to the whole of life as well (see section 12 of the Manifesto). Keeping the subject matter of Scripture clear helps faithful readers to maintain their focus on God and thereby, subordinately, to calibrate their inquiries always and ever to what God has already said of himself, his church, and his world.

Listening for God's address in Scripture means that readers negotiate (at least) two levels in their reading. On the one level, the attentive reader hears the message (*kerygma*) or messages of the individual sections and books of the Bible. God has spoken to various peoples at various times through different texts in Scripture. Diverse messages were first given to the group of people called Israel, and their testimony about God and how his magnificent signs and wonders reveal his nature and purposes with his world. These texts were received and appropriated by the children of Israel through the ages and later

---

4. J. I. Packer, *Engaging the Written Word of God* (Peabody, MA: Hendrickson, 1999), 144.
5. Brevard Childs often spoke of the *Sache* (or subject matter) of Scripture as God himself, meaning that the subject of Scripture is *theocentric* rather than *anthropocentric*. On this point, we cannot but agree.

by Jews in the first and second centuries CE, and they were supplemented by narratives, epistles, and apocalyptic texts affirming that the God described in the Hebrew Bible (Old Testament, also in Greek as the Septuagint) was none other than the God and Father of the Lord Jesus Christ. These new writings (the New Testament) disclosed God in ways continuous with those older writings yet also in ways discontinuous with them, even revealing radically new ways. Both the historical creation and reception of these texts testifies to a loving God, who not only desires communion, but also enables it through the giving of his Word. Theological interpretation aims toward attentive and prayed reading that strains to hear what God has said in these books.

On another level, these diverse books have been collected into the full corpus of texts we call Scripture: Old and New Testaments unified in the person and work of Jesus Christ (see section 6 of the Manifesto). On their full testimony, the Old and New Testaments proclaim that God the Father loves a sinful and broken world and has given Christ the Son for the forgiveness of sin and the restoration of all things, for the honor and glory of the Triune God; humans who recognize God's work in Christ and obey God in the power of the Holy Spirit enter into fellowship with the Father and the Son (1 John 1:3). This second level of reading means that the attentive reader who wants to hear God's address will interpret the messages of the individual books within the *kerygma* of the whole corpus. As we have described it, listening for God's address in Scripture, then, means negotiating both microlevels (individual books) and macrolevels (canonical context) of reading.

We do not for one moment assume that this is the *only* way to describe the story of ancient Hebrew Scripture or the story of early Christian writings. It is not dispassionately retelling the story of Scripture's canon (whatever that might be or however one might think that even could be achieved), but rather a distinctively Christian way to relate the Old and New Testaments.

Other groups who claim some or all of these writings narrate the story differently. Observant Jews tell a different story regarding the place and purpose of the Hebrew Scriptures in relation with other Jewish writings (such as the Mishnah or Talmud). Muslims offer another story concerning the Qur'an and its relationship to the Old and New Testaments. And moving from ancient Abrahamic faiths to a modern religious tradition, the Church of Jesus Christ of Latter-day Saints (Mormons) narrates another story, which relates the Old and New Testaments with the Book of Mormon. The point is not that the narrative presented above is the *only* way to tell the story, but rather that it is a distinctively Christian way that claims to be true.

Attempts to narrate the story of the canon from a "dispassionate" or "value-neutral" or "nonconfessional/nonconfessing" position (terms sometimes used to describe the academic retelling of the story of the canon of Scripture) are, in reality, no less traditioned. In his analysis of historical-critical retellings of the story of the Christian canon in biblical theology (e.g., in the work of Julius Wellhausen, Walter Eichrodt, Gerhard von Rad, Albrecht Alt, and George Mendenhall), Jon Levenson rightly, in my view, exposes these scholars' work on the canon as a reconfiguration of historical and literary concerns, so that somehow the history of the biblical texts (and the religions of Israel and the faiths of Christianity), at a higher level of synthesis, coheres to prior Christian convictions.[6]

Dangers immediately appear on the horizon, however, as readers navigate the approach to reading Scripture advocated above. Our approach runs the danger of totalizing theological discourse into a univocal message, story, doctrine, or viewpoint. It may foreclose critical investigation into the text of Scripture. It may present Christian belief and practice like an untethered balloon, floating free in the theological heavens, with no grounding in historical reality. These remain legitimate challenges that warrant more prayer, study, and investigation.

Rowan Williams, for instance, engages some of these dangers by attending to the diverse, even conflicting, testimonies in Scripture. He argues that one must be careful in attempting to foreclose the many things God might say in Scripture in light of its multivocal testimony.[7] Readers with uncritical emphasis on a timeless canonical form in Scripture that leads to one message neglect the many things that Scripture proclaims. Historical study remains essential, Williams avers, both in terms of how Scripture was understood and negotiated in the past, yet also in terms of how Scripture might be understood and negotiated in the future; this is true because historical study enables the text to speak in all its diversity. The Scriptures reveal Christ, to be sure, but he is presented only in the contested history of the church, with its counterclaims and debate.

In addition to Williams, Walter Brueggemann famously affirms theological reading, but only by means of the diverse rhetoric of the Scripture texts that conflict and counter one another. By way of a trial metaphor, Brueggemann posits the Scriptures (particularly the Old Testament) as a series of witnesses that offer testimony, countertestimony (which is often later in history, as a way

---

6. See Jon D. Levenson, *The Hebrew Bible, the Old Testament, and Historical Criticism: Jews and Christians in Biblical Studies* (Louisville: Westminster John Knox, 1993), 1–32, esp. 10–28. If his analysis of these scholars is accurate, then it rightly raises a note of caution when a particular view or method, supposedly dispassionate, promises to yield appropriate results.

7. Rowan Williams, "Historical Criticism and Sacred Text," in *Reading Texts, Seeking Wisdom*, ed. David F. Ford and Graham Stanton (London: SCM, 2003), 217–28, esp. 221–23.

to counter earlier theological commitments in Israel), and advocacy (theological synthesis).[8] Scripture then, in its voices and countertestimony, unsettles and provokes the status quo in the church. In Williams and Brueggemann, totalizing theological readings (past, present, or future) do not do justice to the unsettling and surprising ways Scripture speaks.

The thinking of Williams and Brueggemann, respectively, alerts theological interpretation to the dangers of reductionism and flattening of Scripture, either when reading on the microlevel or macrolevel. It is incumbent on theological interpretation to avoid muzzling Scripture by avoiding its adversarial and confrontational potential. If Scripture is indeed a caged lion, as C. H. Spurgeon has illustrated, then theological reading rightly practiced "lets the lion loose."[9] Readings that either reduce scriptural meaning to a bare minimum, or neglect the historicity and particularity of the texts of Scripture, or collapse texts into one another—these have not wrestled sufficiently with Scripture's diversity of form. Still, diversity, historicity, and particularity in the vast corpus of Scripture do not necessitate an equal claim to dissonance or lack of unity.

Although Scripture may be a coat of many colors, it still is *one* coat. At its best, theological reading, in nonreductive ways, attends to the storied shape of Scripture that centers in Jesus Christ (see sections 2 and 8 in the Manifesto). Reading for God's address at the microlevel, while necessary, remains insufficient by itself. Engaging Scripture's diversity of form is good but, as an individual principle, does not sufficiently wrestle with the centrality of God's unfolding story, which climaxes in Jesus Christ. Attending to the unified and unfolding story of God's works in Jesus does not diminish or flatten the testimony of Scripture. This is so for many reasons, but not least because of the rich and multivalent portrayal of Jesus in the story. He is more than a Nazarene or healer. He is more than the one who died on a cross. He is more than the king of Israel and creation. Jesus is not less than any of these, but he is so much more. If one follows the teaching of Matthew 1; John 1; Colossians 1:15–20; or 1 Corinthians 1:26–31, to identify but a few texts, the central place of Jesus in the story of Scripture does not close down its testimony, but it opens up Scripture in its totality. Understood in these texts, Jesus is the fulfillment of the story of Abraham, Israel, and David. He is the clue that discloses the mystery of creation. He is the wisdom of God. Jesus Christ is the hinge of history. He is the image of the invisible God. He is the

8. Walter Brueggemann, *Theology of the Old Testament: Testimony, Dispute, Advocacy* (Minneapolis: Fortress, 1997).

9. See the description in Eugene Stock, *The History of the Missionary Society: Its Environment, Its Men and Its Work* (London: Church Missionary Society, 1899), 2:343.

means of our salvation and the goal of all redemption. He is hope for the suffering and the Lord of all things new. Viewing Scripture through the lens of Jesus, then, opens up Scripture's testimony in *many* and *surprising* ways. Thus God's address comes to us in all of its dynamic potential.

At its best, theological interpretation uncovers the richness and expansiveness of Jesus as the Messiah and chastens readings that present Jesus as *too small*.[10] Dietrich Bonhoeffer captures the magnitude of Jesus with an image of Christ as the "origin" of the church: "He is the centre and the strength of the Bible, of the Church, and of theology, but also of humanity, of reason, of justice and of culture. Everything must return to Him; it is only under His protection that it can live."[11] In Bonhoeffer's context, Jesus discloses his expansive dominion to the church, especially amid believers' persecution and suffering. But even in these dire straits, Bonhoeffer affirms that the more the persecuted church acknowledges and confesses Christ as Lord, "the more fully the wide range of His dominion will be disclosed to us."[12]

One also gathers a sense of the expansiveness of Christ, as in Irenaeus's *Demonstration of the Apostolic Preaching*.[13] According to John Behr, the purpose of this work is "to relate the content of the apostolic preaching by outlining the history narrated in Scripture [here meaning the Old Testament writings], culminating in the apostles' proclamation that what is prophesied therein is now fulfilled in Jesus Christ, and thereby, in reverse, recognizing the scriptural authority of this preaching of the apostles."[14] In his primer on the apostolic preaching, Irenaeus uncovers the narrative shape to Scripture that reveals God's purposes in Christ and the place of the Spirit-gathered church in that story. For Irenaeus, the storied shape of Scripture, with Christ as its center, is not reductive; rather, it opens up the Word *and* the world. Irenaeus reads the biblical story forward (from the Old Testament to Jesus) and backward (from Jesus to the Old Testament), with Christ as its center and all in all: he is the Son of God the Father, who is received in the church by the power of the Spirit.

With respect to the positions of Williams and Brueggemann (see above), the examples of Bonhoeffer and Irenaeus provide evidence for theological

---

10. So the warning of Grant R. Osborne in his reading of Rev. 4–5, highlighting the majesty of Jesus as God. His fear is that our "Jesus is too small" in modern (esp. evangelical) spirituality. See his *Revelation*, Baker Exegetical Commentary on the New Testament (Grand Rapids: Baker Academic, 2002), 266. The comment also appears in Osborne's commentary on *Matthew*, Exegetical Commentary on the New Testament (Grand Rapids: Zondervan, 2010), 758.

11. Dietrich Bonhoeffer, *Ethics*, trans. N. H. Smith (New York: Macmillan, 1965), 56.

12. Ibid., 58.

13. Irenaeus of Lyons, *On the Apostolic Preaching*, trans. and intro. John Behr, Popular Patristics Series 17 (Crestwood, NY: St. Vladimir's Seminary Press, 1997).

14. Behr's introduction in ibid., 16.

interpretation that wrestles with the storied shape of Scripture, centers on Jesus, and yet remains nonreductive. For Irenaeus, this means that interpretation of Scripture is a great opportunity for the church to engage the world, including addressing heresy. But for Bonhoeffer, it is the centrality of Jesus in Scripture that enables his political position. Nonetheless, in both interpreters we find that seeing Christ as central does not close down close interpretation of Scripture (for Irenaeus, especially, the Old Testament) but opens up close, attentive readings.[15] In both, we see the centrality of Jesus read and embraced through Scripture, but nonetheless he is understood in nonreductive and provocative ways that open up, rather than close down, the Word, church, and world.

Finally, the theological dimension of listening for God's address reminds us that the Bible narrates this story of God's work in Jesus in a familial rather than impersonal way. Hearing God's address in Scripture drives the reader more deeply into relationship with God, to prayer and meditation. Abraham Kuyper captures the idea, following theologians Augustine and Alexander Comrie: "Thus I stand with Augustine, and with Comrie, who entirely along his lines exclaimed: 'When I read the Scripture, I listen to what God speaks to me; and when I pray, God listens to what I stammer.'"[16]

Theological Interpretation Aims at Transformation as Well as Information

The presence of Scripture in the life of faith is a gift that God has bestowed on the church, but it is a gift that implicitly affirms human sinfulness. Humans have forgotten their true Father, their true home, their true identity, and their joy. God provides Scripture to (re)introduce sinful humanity to fellowship with him through Jesus Christ, to discover their purpose in his plans, and to participate fully in them through the Spirit's power. Scripture, then, is God's gift that helps the church re-member itself in relation to the Lord. Scripture also depicts future communion with God in which its very necessity in the life of the believer will be recalibrated: a future time when Scripture itself will be "written on the hearts" rather than printed on the page or scribed

15. See, e.g., Irenaeus on Gen. 1 in *Against Heresies* 4.20; Dietrich Bonhoeffer on the creation accounts, in *Creation and Fall: Temptation; Two Biblical Studies* (New York: Simon & Schuster, 1997). One could also attend to Bonhoeffer's *Prayerbook of the Bible*, in *Life Together: Prayerbook of the Bible*, translated from the German (Minneapolis: Fortress, 1996); or his exposition of the Sermon on the Mount in *The Cost of Discipleship* (New York: Touchstone, 1995).

16. Abraham Kuyper, "The Biblical Criticism of the Present Day (part 1)," *Bibliotheca sacra* 61, no. 243 (1904): 423–24.

on a tablet (Jer. 31). Scripture testifies to this time as an eschatological hope for new creation. The complete interiority of Scripture in the life of God's church at that time discloses how radical will be the church's transformation!

God provides Scripture to the church for its transformation into the image of Christ, by the power of the Spirit. The evocative and unusual phrase used by the apostle Paul in Ephesians 4:20 alerts us to the kind of transformation intended in this Manifesto. Paul instructs the Ephesian Christians to avoid walking in the darkness of their former way of life, before their conversion to Christ. He reminds them that living "as the Gentiles" (here = "unbelievers") is sinful and wrong, and it is not true to their new nature in Christ. He states, "That is not the way you learned Christ!" (Eph. 4:17, 20).

The phrase "learned Christ" is most unusual. Ernest Best rightly observes the oddity of the phrase and proposes some possible meanings.[17] Normally the verb "to learn" evokes gaining knowledge of a body of teaching (like the torah). "Learning Christ" certainly indicates learning the *teaching* of Christ (whether the testimony of the gospel, Jesus's teaching handed down by the apostles, or the Old Testament Scriptures, or all of these). Right information is vital to the church's transformation. Theological interpretation affirms that God provides true and reliable information (orthodox doctrine) that must be acquired: faithful readers of Scripture and theological reading must attend to the "cognitive instruction" that God provides in his Word (as Packer's quote above implies). This point indicates the veracity of the Scriptures and their power to convey revealed truth (Eph. 4:23; Rom. 12:1–2): God's Word testifies to the truth of God because it comes from God. There is no shade of falsity here.

Here Paul's usage moves beyond information gained by catechesis, yet without leaving it behind. His evocative idea of "learning Christ" indicates transformative *communion*, in which the whole church comes to know Jesus and is changed into his disciples.[18] This means that theological reading ought to press toward the *formation of the whole person and the totality of the church*: cognitive, emotional, social, spatial, and psychological.[19] The church

17. Ernest Best, *Ephesians*, International Critical Commentary (London: T&T Clark, 1998), 425–27.

18. The Greek verb "you learned" (ἐμάθετε, *emathete*) in Eph. 4:20 translates as "disciple" (μαθητής, *mathētēs*) when it occurs in its nominative form.

19. A Baptist affirmation of this point comes via George H. Guthrie. Guthrie argues that reading Scripture is important because it conveys truth; gives instruction on living well before God; enables an encounter and experience with God that gives freedom, grace, peace and hope; infuses our lives with joy; fosters spiritual growth; protects us from sin; and builds the church (*Read the Bible for Life: Your Guide to Understanding and Living God's Word* [Nashville: Broadman & Holman, 2011], 5).

needs transformed minds, transformed loves, transformed lives.[20] Rational transformation comprises only a *part* of the entirety of the church's conversion to Christ. Paul describes Christ's church, which has "learned" Christ, as nothing short of "a new creation": "clothed . . . with the new self, created according to the likeness of God in true righteousness and holiness" (Eph. 4:24). When Christ's church takes up and reads Scripture, Christ bids her to come and follow him, to clothe herself in Christ (Rom. 13:14).[21]

Transformation of the saints is not an option but an imperative, as Scripture indicates. The book of Hebrews affirms that Scripture is "living and active" (Heb. 4:12), able to render judgment and expose the human heart in its sinful idolatry or in its dutiful worship to the true God. Scripture builds up the church of God, providing it "the inheritance among all who are sanctified" (Acts 20:32). In his Word, God provides cognitive and practical content, a "wisdom" that is both understood and lived out in Christ Jesus (2 Tim. 3:15). Scripture provides the basis for God's reproof, correction, teaching, and training (3:16). All these texts testify to the transformation of the whole person, mind and body, reason and habits. So theological interpretation aims to acquire right information coupled with real transformation.

In Christian theology, any transformation is always the work of the Holy Spirit. So although theological interpretation "aims" at the transformation of the whole person, it likely is better to say that theological interpretation is a work of the Spirit, where "Christ is formed" in attentive, faithful readers (see Gal. 4:19). In this way, human transformation is spiritual and remains ever grounded on the relational foundation that is "in Jesus Christ."

The Holy Spirit transforms readers who embody certain interpretative virtues, the chief of which is being a good listener. Bonhoeffer is instructive on living the Christian life: "We cannot simply reach our own conclusions about God; rather, we must ask him. He will only answer us if we are seeking after him."[22] The kind of interpreter who reads God's Word and hears his address is one who is seeking God, answerable to God, humble, and hopeful while anticipating communion with God. In short, this is a person who depends on God and listens to his words in Scripture *prayerfully*, attentively, humbly, and tenaciously. We can, with Markus Bockmuehl, call this kind of reader a

20. Jonathan T. Pennington explores this point and applies it to the study of the Gospels in *Reading the Gospels Wisely: A Narrative and Theological Introduction* (Grand Rapids: Baker Academic, 2012), esp. 143–65. See also Timothy Ward, *Words of Life: Scripture as the Living and Active Word of God* (Downers Grove, IL: IVP Academic, 2009).

21. Cf. Augustine of Hippo, *Confessions* 8.12.29.

22. Dietrich Bonhoeffer, *Meditating on the Word*, trans. and ed. David M. Gracie (Cambridge, MA: Cowley, 1986), 44.

disciple, one who is willing and open to be taught by God in and through his Word.[23] The reader who attends to God's address well is one who is answerable to God and searches diligently for him as a person in need.

Theological Interpretation Is an Ecclesial Practice

The Manifesto affirms that the church is the true home of Scripture, centrally in its worship of the Triune God, where God communes with Christ's bride in the power of the Spirit.[24] The church does not predetermine how theological reading should go per se but provides the hospitable space and habitable environment for such reading to be practiced.[25]

Space for theological reading is given in private, corporate, and public contexts of the church's life. Individual use of Scripture outside the local gathering of the church will energize and inform the life of faith. It will fuel and stabilize Christ's church for the rigors of everyday life as a complement to the corporate worship of the church. This is often achieved in private devotion (through something akin to *lectio divina*)[26] or small-group Bible studies. But individual and private interpretation of Scripture upholds, and even reads *toward*, Scripture's central place of corporate worship in the life of the church: the proclamation of the Word, the Eucharist, and the waters of baptism. One could speak here of theological interpretation *performed* as well, as in corporate confession and prayer, with Scripture as the form and content of the church's speech. Scripture is the script and form for the church's worship of its God. It is appropriate to mention that Scripture is central for the church's public witness to the world. As the church acts and works in the world, Scripture informs how the church testifies to Christ and serves Christ (see the Manifesto, section 8). Thus Christ's church needs to hear God's address in Scripture while appropriately gathered for worship but also while scattered for multifaceted witness in God's world.[27]

23. "The implied interpreter of Christian Scripture is a *disciple*, just as that disciple's implied reading of the text is its witness to Christ" (Markus Bockmuehl, *Seeing the Word: Refocusing New Testament Study*, Studies in Theological Interpretation [Grand Rapids: Baker Academic, 2006], 92).

24. For the centrality of the church in theological interpretation, see the Manifesto on "Ecclesia as Primary Context" and its exposition in chap. 3 above.

25. See the delightful discussion of Darren Sarisky, *Scriptural Interpretation: A Theological Exploration*, Challenges in Contemporary Theology (Chichester, UK: Wiley-Blackwell, 2013).

26. Mariano Magrassi, OSB, *Praying the Bible: An Introduction to Lectio Divina*, trans. Edward Hagman (Collegeville, MN: Liturgical Press, 1998).

27. See Abraham Kuyper, *Rooted and Grounded: The Church as an Organism and Institution*, trans. and ed. Nelson D. Kloosterman (Grand Rapids: Christian's Library Press, 2013).

When God addresses his church, the encounter is not always the same. His voice is like many rushing waters, diverse, holy, and majestic: whether the Lord's voice is heard in the thunderous trumpet blast of a Sinai experience (Exod. 19–23); in the still, small voice to a fearful prophet (1 Kings 19); or in the caring words of Christ on a road and preparing a meal (Luke 24 and John 21). In these encounters God meets with his people by means of Scripture and enacts real transformation.[28]

Advocacy of theological interpretation as an ecclesial endeavor, as we have done here, may lead to the charge that such reading is not, indeed *cannot* be, an academic enterprise. Biblical interpretation is (or ought to be) *nonconfessional* and *nonecclesial* in university contexts that stand outside ecclesial interpretation (control?) of Scripture; alternatively, biblical interpretation can be *confessing* and *ecclesial* within the realm of the church.[29] On this line of thought, a difference between confessing readings of Scripture and secular (or academic) readings of the same has to do with readerly goals that emerge in different, nonoverlapping contexts. One is for the church and religious communities (ecclesial), and the other is for the academy and scholarly communities (academic). Rudyard Kipling's line aptly summarizes the idea: "Oh, East is East, and West is West, and never the twain shall meet."[30]

Levenson describes the state of such separation in the 1980s and 1990s and helps to expose what he sees as a problem. His analysis is directed particularly toward Christians who study the Old Testament/Hebrew Bible, and he recognizes that they "are Christians everywhere except in the classroom and at the writing table, where they are simply honest historians striving for an unbiased view of the past."[31] If ecclesial and secular interpretations *do* meet, then conflict inevitably ensues.[32] Clean lines between disciplines and areas of study appear to be a happy result of the proposal.

28. See the discussions of Franklin M. Segler, *Christian Worship: Understanding, Preparing For, and Practicing*, rev. Randall Bradley, 2nd ed. (Nashville: Broadman & Holman, 1996), 109–20; Scott W. Hahn, "Scripture and Liturgy: Inseparably United," *Origins* 35, no. 39 (March 2006): 648–53.

29. So the argument of Philip Davies, *Whose Bible Is It Anyway?*, 2nd ed. (London: T&T Clark, 2004).

30. Rudyard Kipling, "The Ballad of East and West," in *A Victorian Anthology: 1837–1895*, ed. E. C. Stedman (Cambridge, MA: Riverside Press, 1895), 2:596.

31. Levenson, *The Hebrew Bible, the Old Testament, and Historical Criticism*, 29.

32. The reasons for this separation of church and academy are well rehearsed in other projects, such as: Michael Legaspi, *The Death of Scripture and the Rise of Biblical Studies*, Oxford Studies in Historical Theology (Oxford: Oxford University Press, 2011); Jonathan Sheehan, *The Enlightenment Bible: Translation, Scholarship, Culture* (Princeton: Princeton University Press, 2005). See also Scott W. Hahn and Benjamin Wiker, *Politicizing the Bible: The Roots of Historical Criticism and the Secularization of Scripture, 1300–1700* (New York: Crossroad, 2013).

In this proposal for separation, the scholar retains religious beliefs but must "put [them] into brackets" when doing academic study, at least until one can ascertain whether they can be verified. The bracketing-off language is that of James Barr:

> Biblical scholars, therefore, whatever their allegiance in these matters, work usefully in so far as they ask the question: granted that I believe this or that to be in accord with my theological tradition, to be relevant today, to be socially and ethically desirable, my duty to the church or community is to put into brackets, into parentheses, these my own convictions and to ask whether the Bible supports them. If it does, then one can continue as one has been; if not, then a process of theological change may begin.[33]

The rationale behind this is his view that scientific and critical inquiry rests on a clearer standard of "scientific objectivity" than does theology, or more specifically, critical inquiry exhibits a "creative prejudice" against predetermined theological commitments.[34] Barr's mantle has been picked up by John Barton, who avers that biblical criticism at its best sets to the side the question of truth so that the interpreter can see what the text of Scripture means. Only secondarily does the evaluative process of ascertaining truth come into view.[35]

We should note that the laudable goal of bracketing off religious thought, at least in the thinking of Barr and Barton, is to hear the text of Scripture well. I cannot but agree! The problem with this approach, however, is (at least) twofold. (1) There is a question as to the necessity of bracketing off one's religious convictions. Why is this move essential? Is it because religious convictions, doctrines, or whatever *get in the way*? Why would this be *necessarily* so? It seems like a creative, and perhaps arbitrary, prejudice against religious convictions. And then, one must give good warrant *why* these convictions are bracketed and not others! If, however, bracketing off is intended as a kind of "hermeneutic of suspicion," which is matched by a hermeneutic of fidelity in the vein of Paul Ricoeur, then this approach may hold greater promise. (2) The second challenge comes with the first. As one attempts to bracket one's religious convictions, there is always the anxiety, at least in modern hermeneutical theory, of how one knows whether and how one successfully

---

33. James Barr, *The Concept of Biblical Theology: An Old Testament Perspective* (London: SCM, 1999), 208.

34. See James Barr, *Holy Scripture: Canon, Authority, Criticism* (Oxford: Oxford University Press, 1983), 113.

35. John Barton, *The Nature of Biblical Criticism* (Louisville: Westminster John Knox, 2007), esp. 171–75.

brackets *anything* in interpretation! The real challenge is that beliefs and convictions (whatever they may be) tend to slip in through the back door.

Bracketing off religious beliefs may stem from laudable aims, but it is indefensible in light of the fundamental turns in hermeneutics and philosophy in the past sixty years.[36] One of the great benefits of what is often called the "postmodern turn" is the recognition that interests run straight through the whole of life, so that disinterested tools of scholarship (like methods in biblical interpretation) are not as disinterested as they may at first appear. There is a possibility of reading Scripture well without abandoning interests, and so we affirm differences between *thick* and *thin* interpretations and also affirm *validity* in interpretation.[37] Here we do not even mention the theological problems that arise from the notion of bracketing off religious convictions, but John Webster strenuously argues against such a procedure on dogmatic grounds.[38]

The Manifesto avers that it is better to avoid the polarization of academic versus ecclesial interests in reading and interpreting the Scriptures. It recognizes the ways in which the two fields interrelate productively. Nonetheless, the relationship between academic and ecclesial is not equal.

Although the Manifesto recognizes the diverse ways in which the fields of academics and faith relate, it further suggests that theological interpretation at its best will operate under the primacy of ecclesial identity. This is not because the church is better than the academy, or needs a place at the academic table. Rather, it is because the claim of Christ on the church is total. The church affirms the reality that Jesus stands at the center of the whole of creation (Col. 1:15–20). His lordship is supreme over all spheres of life, and it extends, then, outward into all the multifaceted aspects of creation, including the sphere of academics. Bracketing off religious conviction in the process of interpretation effectively quashes the claim of Christ's rule over all. The academic life, therefore, rightly rests under the lordship of Jesus Christ as much as any other sphere in the whole of life. Biblical criticism *can* aid in theological interpretation, but only insofar as it is recalibrated as

36. See, e.g., Steven Seidman, ed., *The Postmodern Turn: New Perspectives on Social Theory* (Cambridge: Cambridge University Press, 1995). See also Craig G. Bartholomew, *Introducing Biblical Hermeneutics* (Grand Rapids: Baker Academic, 2015), chap. 9, "Philosophy, Hermeneutics, and Biblical Interpretation."

37. See the different ways validity in interpretation are presented in Paul Ricoeur, *Interpretation Theory: Discourse and the Surplus of Meaning* (Fort Worth: Texas Christian University Press, 1976), 78–79; E. D. Hirsch Jr., *Validity in Interpretation* (New Haven: Yale University Press, 1967).

38. See, e.g., John Webster, *Word and Church: Essays in Church Dogmatics* (Edinburgh: T&T Clark, 2001); idem, *Holy Scripture*; idem, *The Domain of the Word: Scripture and Theological Reason* (London: T&T Clark, 2012).

a kind of criticism that avoids quarantining Christian faith in the process of interpretation (see Murray Rae's comments in chap. 4 above). To achieve a recalibrated criticism, what is urgently needed is a kind of metacriticism of criticisms for today.[39]

Dietrich Bonhoeffer argues that biblical criticism is of *instrumental* value, and instrumentality is one helpful way to construe its place in theological interpretation.[40] In a letter to his brother-in-law, Dr. Rüdiger Schleicher, Bonhoeffer states that biblical criticism demonstrates its value in exposing the "surface" of the text. But what is of utmost importance lies beneath the surface, in the inner depths "within" it. The reader encounters the depths of meaning "within" Scripture only by attending to the voice of God in it. This is a filial encounter with God in Scripture, which the analysis of biblical criticism is not equipped to provide. Bonhoeffer wonders, "When a dear friend speaks a word to us, do we subject it to analysis? No, we simply accept it, and then it resonates inside us for days."[41] Stephen J. Plant summarizes Bonhoeffer's point: "Bible reading for Bonhoeffer is a matter of attentiveness and faith. The Word of God in the Bible does not lie buried under the alien cultures and foreign languages of the Biblical writers, awaiting the biblical scholar to sweep away the centuries of dust: it is a gift God is free daily to give—or withhold—to each faithful reader in her unique situation."[42] Reading Scripture ecclesially *and* academically, as Bonhoeffer suggests, makes possible its transformative potential to be unleashed in present contexts.

To be fair, one of the reasons for the separation between academic and ecclesial spheres, or so the story goes, derives from a concern among interpreters of Scripture that the church can abuse the plain sense of the Scriptures and build walls of doctrine around the gold mine of God's Word in its originating contexts. Academic approaches to Scripture were designed to tear down the walls, so that the riches of God's Word could be appropriated, unadulterated, for the world. Whether the approach to the concern was indeed the right one, the actual concern to explore the riches of Scripture for the world's good remains salutary.

---

39. Joseph Ratzinger (Benedict XVI), *Wort Gottes: Schrift—Tradition—Amt*, ed. Peter Hünermann and Thomas Söding (Freiburg in Breisgau: Herder, 2005).

40. Still, the term "instrumental" is slippery and must be carefully defined. For one example, see Chen Xun, *Theological Exegesis in the Canonical Context: Brevard Springs Childs's Methodology of Biblical Theology*, Studies in Biblical Literature 137 (New York: Peter Lang, 2010), 234–37. Chen argues that biblical criticism is of instrumental value in the work of Karl Barth and Brevard Childs.

41. Bonhoeffer, *Meditating on the Word*, 44.

42. Stephen J. Plant, *Taking Stock of Bonhoeffer: Studies in Biblical Interpretation and Ethics* (Farnham, UK: Ashgate, 2014), 44–45.

Theological interpretation should be aware of a danger in the church's use and abuse of Scripture, the risk of missing the voice of God and instead (unwittingly) making God's Word a narcissistic echo chamber. For example, J. I. Packer declares, "The possibility of misinterpretation makes Evangelical use of the phrase 'the Bible says' as a formula of authority dangerous, as critics often point out."[43] The danger does not come from Scripture itself but from its abuse by ecclesial interpreters.

Theological interpretation recognizes this danger, that Scripture might be used and abused, bent toward human ends rather than to God's aim of addressing his people.[44] The *regula fidei* historically has been a "shield" to help protect against the abusive or faithless reading practices, as Mark Gignilliat and Jonathan Pennington's expositional chapter (11) in this volume details.[45] The following paragraphs suggest some further helps as well. The metaphor of "guardrail" is useful because it is a way to describe some "guides" that keep the church from "running off the road" while reading Scripture. To guard against (but unlikely to prevent) misuse and abuse of Scripture, theological interpretation of Scripture closely attends to the following:

- The Triune God's disclosure of himself through Scripture, preeminently his disclosure of himself in Jesus Christ.
- What Scripture itself says in its literary, historical, and canonical horizons.
- What the church has believed.[46]
- Private and devotional interpretation shared and tested within the public and corporate worship of the church.

More certainly could be explored or added, but the guardrails above give further help to how the church can proceed with *faith* and *caution* in reading Scripture for today.

43. Packer, *Engaging the Written Word of God*, 144.

44. Note the interesting primer on biblical interpretation by Henry Wansbrough, OSB, *The Use and Abuse of the Bible: A Brief History of Biblical Interpretation* (London: T&T Clark, 2010). The title is evaluative: there *have been* abuses of Scripture that do not do justice to the text.

45. See also Paul Blowers, "The *Regula Fidei* and the Narrative Character of Early Christian Faith," *Pro Ecclesia* 6, no. 2 (1997): 199–208; and Michael J. Kruger, *Canon Revisited: Establishing the Origins and Authority of the New Testament Books* (Wheaton: Crossway, 2012), 138–41.

46. Note, e.g., the structure of a recent Baptist theology for the church. For each doctrine explored, the authors ask, (1) "What does the Bible say?" (2) "What has the church believed?" (3) "How does it all fit together?" See Daniel L. Akin, ed., *A Theology for the Church*, rev. ed. (Nashville: B&H Academic, 2014). Even here, in an Anabaptist tradition, the role of the historic church's voice is taken seriously as a resource for *doing* theology and understanding Scripture.

The first guardrail is metaphysical and theological. It affirms that the Bible remains ever and always *God's* Word—disclosing him and his work, preeminently in Jesus Christ—which is embraced by the church in the power of the Spirit. This is a theological account of Scripture, and attending to its trinitarian affirmation remains vital.[47] Dangers appear when interpretation isolates any one of the three members of the Triune God to the neglect of others.[48] This call for a robust attention to the Triune God is vital for the church today, where "gospel-centered," "christocentric," "Spirit-empowered," or "theological" adjectives attach to many, indeed almost any, ecclesial activity, including interpretation! Hearing God's address must mean hearing and responding to the Triune God in all the fullness of the Godhead. Interpretation that leads away from the Triune God runs the danger of leading the church away from the Scriptures and thereby away from God's voice. To speak of christocentric hermeneutics is *necessarily* to speak in the language of trinitarian hermeneutics: it is God the Father who has given Christ the Son, who was impelled by the Spirit and whom believers recognize by that selfsame Spirit. It is not necessary to invoke all three persons of the Godhead in every interpretation, but rather to be so captured by the *reality* of the Triune God that whatever the passage of Scripture, it is read from a trinitarian theological base.

Misinterpretation and abuse of Scripture can arise from a lack of attention to what the Scripture says in its historical, literary, and canonical horizons.[49] Historically, God's Word came to his people at various times. Attending to the historical, cultural, linguistic, and sociological worlds from which the Scriptures derived helps us to hear his voice. Essentially, this is a philological and grammatical effort that does not neglect or dismiss biblical criticism out of hand, but recontextualizes it within the larger program of hearing

47. For other theological accounts of Scripture, see Sarisky, *Scriptural Interpretation*; Angus Paddison, *Scripture: A Very Theological Proposal* (London: T&T Clark, 2009).

48. The notion of "Christomonism" appears, e.g., where Christ is explored in isolation from God the Father or the Spirit; cf. Sidney Greidanus, *Preaching Christ from the Old Testament: A Contemporary Hermeneutical Method* (Grand Rapids: Eerdmans, 1999), 176–78, 228. In this vein, one could recognize dangers of "theomonism" or "pneumomonism," in which God the Father or the Spirit are isolated from Christ or each other. For helpful and constructive approaches, see Kevin L. Spawn and Archie T. Wright, eds., *Spirit and Scripture: Exploring a Pneumatic Hermeneutic* (London: T&T Clark, 2013). For a constructive trinitarian model, see Craig G. Bartholomew, "Listening for God's Address: A *Mere* Trinitarian Hermeneutics for the Old Testament," in *Hearing the Old Testament: Listening for God's Address*, ed. Craig G. Bartholomew and David J. H. Beldman (Grand Rapids: Eerdmans, 2012), 3–19.

49. Yet see the Manifesto's section on "Historical Criticism" and chap. 4 above, both by Murray Rae.

God's voice. As a historical phenomenon, the canon of Scripture, both in microlevels (e.g., the shape of the Psalms or the Minor Prophets, the correlation between the fourfold Gospels, etc.) and macrolevels (Old and New Testaments), provides the context from which the meaning of Scripture is derived.

The third guardrail advocated above may sound difficult, particularly to Protestant ears. But tradition, or "what the church has believed," is a good thing. Edith Humphrey is certainly correct to say that Scripture itself testifies to the role of tradition in the community of faith.[50] It was good that the apostle Paul received the gospel, passed it down, and then put it into writing (1 Cor. 15:3–5). It was good that the church preserved the Old Testament (*contra* Marcion) and supplemented that Scripture with the New Testament. Some modern theologians are correct (e.g., Rowan Williams) to recognize that this is a book that did not "fall from the sky," as it were, in a completely transparent communicative act.[51] Scripture is not orphaned but historically has been received and carried in the bosom of the church. How the church has believed in the past informs and nourishes the present. It is a sad state, in any age, when the old is castigated for being irrelevant or dangerous simply because of its antiquity or dissimilarity from the new.

The church, in its historic particularity in the world as the called-out people of God, stands in symbiotic relation to the Word of God, however that relationship is construed.[52] God gives his Word to the church; the church receives this Word in the power of the Spirit, nurtures it, and gives it to the world. The people who have carried the Word and have been shaped by it comprise the natural community from which to understand it. Protestant and evangelical traditions place the accent on the primacy of the Word over the church, but sometimes to the neglect of the historic church as the home of Scripture. The Catholic and Orthodox churches, however, can place Scripture and Tradition (i.e., the Great Tradition) as coequals, neglecting the uniqueness of Scripture as God's Word spoken to norm his church. I affirm the primacy of the Scripture as the *norma normans non normata*, "the norm that norms but is

50. Edith M. Humphrey, *Scripture and Tradition: What the Bible Really Says* (Grand Rapids: Baker Academic, 2013).

51. See Rowan Williams, *On Christian Theology* (Oxford: Blackwell, 2000); idem, "Historical Criticism and Sacred Text."

52. For different proposals, see Humphrey, *Scripture and Tradition*, esp. 9–17; also Richard J. Bauckham, "Tradition in Relation to Scripture and Reason," in *Scripture, Tradition and Reason: A Study in the Criteria of Christian Doctrine*, ed. Richard J. Bauckham and B. Drewery (Edinburgh: T&T Clark, 1988), 117–45; Malcom Yarnell III, *The Formation of Christian Doctrine* (Nashville: B&H Academic, 2007).

not normed."[53] Other Christians may see things differently, and thereby the shape of the theological reading will look different as well. The Manifesto recognizes this diversity. But I affirm that Karl Rahner is correct in asserting that historically the codification of Scripture (by the prophets and apostles in the New Testament era) as the governing rule for the life of the church becomes fundamental in its (later) Tradition.[54] That is, the prophets and apostles acknowledged the primacy of Scripture as God's Word and thereby normative for life and faith.

The church carries the Word not because the Word belongs to it. The church carries the Word because through it God has declared the church is his. God's voice in Scripture, then, calibrates the church's association with it. As the church carries the Word in its bosom, it finds that God has already lifted the church and carried it in his bosom, through his self-giving and through Scripture. As a community that is addressed by God, the church is always *responding* to the Word he has already given.[55] Theological interpretation ought to take seriously the question "What has the Church believed?," because in its very construction the question places the interpreter within the stream of the church, which hears and responds to God's call in Scripture. Knowledge of the church's understanding of Scripture should provide (at the very least) a check against novel and unsubstantiated interpretations of Scripture (e.g., by Marcion, Valentinus, Arius). Just because an interpretation is *new* in the Christian faith does not make it *right, coherent,* or *true to the teaching of Scripture.*

Finally, theological interpretation invites reading of Scripture that is personal and devotional, as discussed above. The Orthodox Church rightly states that Christian study of Scripture and the formulation of Christian theology sits rooted in, and generates, *prayer.* The formation of doctrine is not the aim

53. This is due to my belief that the primacy of Scripture is to be always and ever *over* the church in terms of authority. (Some) Catholics affirm this position, understanding the Great Tradition as *norma normata*, "the norm that is normed [by Scripture]." See Karl Rahner, "Scripture and Theology," *Theological Investigations* 6 (Baltimore: Helicon, 1969), 89–97. "For theology, scripture is in practice the only material source of faith to which it has to turn as being the absolutely original, underived source and *norma non normata*" (ibid., 93). Notice that this is a properly *theological* rendering of Scripture.

54. Rahner, "Scripture and Theology," 93–97. This does not sever the tie between Scripture and Tradition, but puts an emphasis on Tradition read through the lens of Scripture (which is already, in his view, traditioned).

55. "It is also true that, even historically, the church's recognition of the canon of Scripture created a real break, which gave the origin of the tradition, in this written form, a uniquely normative status in relation to the rest of tradition. One cannot take the tradition seriously without taking seriously its basically *interpretative* relation to Scripture, which . . . the tradition itself has fully recognized" (Bauckham, "Tradition in Relation to Scripture and Reason," 127).

of theological reading; instead, theological reading aids in "learning Christ" (cf. Eph. 4:20).[56] This is a kind of "prayed reading," to use Jean Leclercq's pregnant phrase.[57] It is a kind of study and meditation of Scripture that is at once personal and prayerful, slow and yet sublime: the individual reads Scripture only to find the Spirit of God reading oneself!

Prayed reading, however, should not be construed merely as a personal, private, and pietistic practice. Private reading that personalizes and energizes the faith of the individual is never for the individual alone. Such interpretation of Scripture, rightly conceived, leads to corporate praise and glory of the risen Christ in Christian worship. So Mariano Magrassi instructs that the private reading of Scripture is a "preparation" for liturgical hearing of the selfsame Word of God.[58] Wherever private interpretation leads *away* from true worship of God in the corporate gathering of the church, it will become apparent that theological interpretation of Scripture has perhaps led down a wrong path.

Theological Interpretation Unlocks Scripture's Transformative Potential for the Sake of the World

Scripture testifies to the God of creation and Jesus the Messiah, Lord of the new creation (see Rev. 21:1–6). The "world" as such needs full redemption in Jesus Christ. Christ redeems a sinful and broken humanity by his power to forgive sin. Those who confess with their mouths that Jesus is Lord and believe in their hearts that God has raised him from the dead will find salvation, as the apostle Paul affirms in Romans 10:9–10. God unites this people by the Holy Spirit, and he fashions them into a new-creation community. In this way, theological interpretation attends to the power of God's message of salvation for those who repent of their sin and believe in Jesus Christ. The missional impetus of the gospel demands that the church is transformed in both its worship and witness for the sake of the world. Worship fuels mission, so that the encounter with the risen Christ in worship focuses the church's eyes to the world that needs him.

56. See the extended exploration of this point in John Behr, *The Way to Nicaea*, Formation of Christian Theology 1 (Crestwood, NY: St. Vladimir's Seminary Press, 2001). Behr opens this work by drawing attention to Jesus's question at Caesarea Philippi: "Who do you say that I am?" (Matt. 16:15). Then he develops the early Christian response to this as theology. See also his later works in this series: *The Nicene Faith*, 2 parts, Formation of Christian Theology 2 (Crestwood, NY: St. Vladimir's Seminary Press, 2004).

57. "Toute cette activité, nécessairement, est une prière: la *lectio divina* est une lecture priée." Jean Leclercq, *L'amour des lettres et le désir de Dieu: Initiation aux auteurs monastiques du Moyen-Âge* (Paris: Éditions du Cerf, 1957), 72.

58. Magrassi, *Praying the Bible*, 5.

In his classic work on intellectual study, A. G. Sertillanges reminds the church of its call to face the world as a missional imperative: "A true Christian will have ever before his eyes the image of this globe, on which the Cross is planted, on which needy men wander and suffer, all over which the redeeming Blood, in numberless streams, flows to meet them."[59] Sertillanges's image of redeeming blood that "flows" to meet a needy world captures the stakes for theological reading. As the church hears God address it through the Word, it turns to face a needy world with the good news of Jesus Christ. In Sertillanges's image, needy people do not run to Jesus; rather, Jesus's blood flows to meet the world. The church should go and do likewise.

Theological interpretation attends to Scripture's delineation of the church's witness. If Christ's reign is as wide as creation, the nature of its witness is as broad. At the blazing center of its witness is the verbal proclamation of the gospel of Jesus Christ. The forgiveness that comes by belief, repentance, and faithfulness to Jesus the Messiah creates a community that proclaims his gospel: that he has lived and died in accordance with the Scriptures, that he was buried, that he rose from death in accordance with the Scriptures, and that he appeared to many (1 Cor. 15:3–5). Everything is through him and for him so that he might be all in all. The church finds life in Christ alone. This must be proclaimed with the church's verbal testimony, without compromise.

But those who *proclaim* the gospel also must *obey* the gospel (2 Thess. 1:8; 1 Pet. 4:12–19, esp. v. 17). Obedience to the gospel demands the church's faithful life of good works in all the spheres of life that God places it: family, friendship, work, business, leisure, worship, and so forth. Obeying the gospel means that there is no arena in God's creation where God's work in Christ is untouched. The transformative potential of Scripture finds its fulfillment as the church sees and hears Christ and is conformed into his image (Rom. 8:29). Fundamentally, as Scripture reveals that Christ gave himself for the world, so also Scripture calls the church to go and do likewise.

Theological interpretation fosters this missional focus. The church stands as the community that proclaims the good news of the kingdom of God in word and promotes the kingdom in deed. Theological interpretation reads with the aim of the transformative potential of the gospel to be unleashed in *present contexts*. With each new generation, God's Word must be heard afresh so that God's people might respond to him in worshipful obedience.

---

59. A. G. Sertillanges, *The Intellectual Life: Its Spirit, Conditions, Methods*, trans. Mary Ryan, foreword by James V. Schall (Washington, DC: Catholic University of America Press, 1998), 13.

10

A Framework
for Theological Interpretation

DENIS FARKASFALVY

The Scriptures Written by Believers and for Believers

The General Thesis

Even a casual but objective assessment of the Old Testament and New Testament shows that the Bible was made by believers and for believers. In this statement the believers involved in composing or using the scriptural texts are no isolated individuals writing down or reflecting on God's word. The persons who have authored these texts invariably saw themselves as part of a community, which God addressed within a historical process. God's word was received and passed on as essential in the formation of a community of believers, who used oral or written testimonies of their encounters with God and shared them in various ways, passing them down to following generations.

Applied to the Old Testament

The Scriptures of the Israelites, regularly referred to at the time of Jesus and his first disciples as "the law and the prophets" (Matt. 7:12; 22:40; Luke 16:16;

John 1:45)[1] were thought of as having issued from a dialogue between God and a people he chose as his own and addressed in a covenantal relationship, manifesting to them his thoughts and will, watching over their history, and demanding from them the fulfillment of his will while promising to carry out in them and through them his salvific plan for the world. The people of God saw themselves not only as God's creation in a general sense, in terms of human origins, but also as the descendants of a particular person, Abraham, selected by God from among his contemporaries to be the forefather of his people. When Moses, a descendant of Abraham and regarded as God's spokesman and lawgiver, attached the history of Abraham and his immediate descendants to the account of human beginnings (Gen. 1–11) in order to set the narrative into the full framework of Israel's formation as a nation, the core of the Hebrew Scriptures became known as the five Books of Moses. This core narrates the beginnings of Israel as both a story and a book of divine legislation, defining, in addition to Israel's way of life and purpose, also a code of norms regulating that way of life and Israel's worship. Thus the Pentateuch presents the record of God's mighty deeds by which he intervened in human history to form a people of his own. Yet it also reveals himself as the one God claiming to rule his people's life and conduct as both individuals and communities, as a nation living in obedience to its God's sovereign will and exclusive worship.

The Pentateuch as written text constitutes a tool for remembering both God's deeds and his will demanding the response of faith, a pattern of life, and acts of worship. In the Pentateuch, Scripture becomes an instrument for retaining the memory of God's self-disclosures, beginning with creation, continuing through the call of Abraham up to Moses's selection and his leadership, mediating God's word and will. Starting with Abraham, the relationship of God and his people is described in the Old Testament by the unique concept of an alliance or covenant; thereby Israel's status in humanity is described as both uniquely exclusive and dynamically aimed toward the benefit and ultimately the inclusion of all humanity. This relationship emphasizes God's absolute sovereignty and inscrutable majesty, yet also his unfathomable and intimate closeness and tender mercy.

The rest of the Old Testament expands the Pentateuch in various ways by Israel's continued history in the land to which Moses led it, tracing the memories and vicissitudes of its subsequent leaders, the judges and kings, and focusing on continuity and discontinuity with the faith of Abraham and the legislation of Moses.

---

1. A threefold division—Law, Prophets, Writings—appears somewhat later; the first of its forerunners may be Luke 24:44. See Stephen G. Dempster's chapter (6) on "The Canon" (above).

Through the various compositions that follow the Pentateuch, we encounter the central theme of God's ongoing presence through his word, by which the lessons of the past are remembered, and failures of faith and obedience are consistently exposed so that the history of Israel becomes a saga of human growth and education just as well as a drama of cultural development, transformation, and deprivation. This history is populated by God's further messengers, who come to express and transmit the word of the same Person whose words Moses transmitted, eventually leaving behind written records for later generations. Prophetic and sapiential literature extends the five Books of Moses and serves as a powerful means by which God creates the record of a Sacred History, with an attached commentary reminding, summarizing, or evaluating, and thereby bringing it about that God's word rings out with a lasting echo and remains recorded through the centuries in the minds and hearts of listeners and readers. In the Hebrew Scriptures, as a consequence, God's words interpret and reinterpret themselves in a rich and complex web of narrative reminders and themes that challenge God's people and call them to reflection, while also providing a certain unity of topics. These Scriptures continuously repeat the people's original call, prompting them to scrutinize the ways of God through the various stories, prayers, and moralizing maxims—an agonizing individual and collective examination of conscience. Long before there is a Jewish canon, there is a concept of Sacred History and Sacred Scripture about the same God, the same people, and a number of recurring themes.

At the same time, Israel's national coherence and independence diminish with growing rapidity. After the disastrous split of Solomon's kingdom, a subsequent chain of deportations and exiles, and the destruction of both the northern and the southern kingdoms together with the first temple in Jerusalem, the nation begins a slow recovery. Some of the people return from exile, and the temple is rebuilt. Yet the small nation of Israel becomes the victim of various empire-building enterprises by Assyrians, Babylonians, Persians, Egyptians, and finally an internationalized Hellenism under Alexander the Great and his successors. In the end, the Roman Empire, the ultimate winner, gobbles up Israel together with the other nations in the region.

The age was awaiting a new signal and initiative from the divine will. The Scriptures accordingly grow: apocalyptic expectations about God's final reckoning with his people and all the earth reach a feverish pitch. Even while new Scriptures are being added to the old, Israel's centuries-old experiences with its God and his will begin to be regarded as the written depositories of God's self-disclosure; yet with regard to the approaching eschatological judgment, those texts need to be further deciphered. In some apocalyptic writings the anxieties of the end times take on a central role. This is the world into which Jesus is born.

An Unexpected Fulfillment of Expectations: The New Testament

Jesus defines his ministry in explicit comparison with Moses, whom he names and quotes from the Pentateuch, while announcing with authority the arrival of the kingdom of God. Through him, God addresses anew his people; through his people, God reaches out to all humanity. His deeds signify a new divine presence coming into the world. Calling his wayward people back to God, Jesus recasts the law in a tone of new seriousness, demanding an all-pervasive response of faith. In particular, while asking for faith in response to the divine word that brings healings and forgiveness, he asks humanity also to forgive in a similar way, without limits, to risk one's life in order to save it, to suffer in obedience to God's will, to carry one's cross as Jesus carries his cross, and to overcome human evil by transmitting divine love.

Jesus speaks to larger and smaller groups, but always to communities. When his own tragic end becomes imminent, he turns the group of the Twelve, whom he has chosen and sent to spread his message over all Galilee, into a foundational group of all his followers that he calls his assembly: "my church" (Matt. 16:18). In the midst of hostile reactions and threats from the powerful, he marches into his most painful act of obedience, to carry out his Father's will by undergoing a shameful and painful death, which he abhors yet wants to undergo willingly, without reservation. At a supper on the last night, he transmits to his disciples the instrument of his obedience to God his Father, his body and blood distributed as lasting food and drink. He efficaciously anticipates that the end of his human existence will soon come, and he dies by crucifixion. As he has foretold to his disciples, who are nonetheless shaken by discouragement and disbelief and run away from him, he rises to a new kind of glorious life, in a renewed human flesh and blood.[2] Then he charges the Twelve to transmit not only his teaching and memory but also his very presence, which, he promises, will accompany them always and everywhere, to the nations of all times and places (Matt. 28:19–20).

---

2. See the expression *anastēnai ek nekrōn* in a statement of Jesus that puzzles his disciples (Mark 9:10), then is part of the risen Lord's speech about himself fulfilling the Scriptures (Luke 24:46), and finally part of the apostolic message in the mouth of Peter (Acts 14:10) and Paul (Acts 17:3). This puzzling concept of the *anastēnai ek nekrōn* evoked in 1 Cor. 15:12–14 receives a careful exposition in terms of transformation of the human body from the realm of flesh and corruption to the realm of spirit in 1 Cor. 12:35–50.

To keep the memory of Jesus's words and deeds and to share them with the world (see Acts 1:2, 8) becomes the lifelong assignment of his disciples under the leadership of the Twelve, regrouped and replenished after the resurrection. In a way similar to the formation of the Old Testament, the message obtains the form of written documents. However, everything happens more quickly. The disciples of Jesus, for whom and by whom the New Testament books were written, reach back and take into possession Israel's ancient books, which in their midst Jesus has brought to completion, as documents written about him and for the community of the believers: "For whatever was written in former days was written for our instruction, so that by steadfastness and by the encouragement of the scriptures we might have hope" (Rom. 15:4).

While taking possession of Israel's Scriptures, the apostolic community finds its identity in Christ's Great Commission (Matt. 28:18–20): he charges them to deliver, to all peoples of all times, what he has taught them. This self-understanding, paired off with the understanding of the role of God's written Word for the old covenant, brings the apostolic community to commit to writing the expression of their faith, solidly documenting and enshrining it in written form. Thus the *graphē* as God's Word in permanently fixed and written human words emerges, channeling preaching and doctrine previously transmitted orally, but now turned into apostolic Gospels as the words and deeds of Jesus, along with other documents as writings guaranteed by the "pillars" of the first community (Peter, James, John, and Paul; cf. Gal. 2:9) and their companions. Thus the Gospels contain Jesus's sayings and speeches, chains of episodic accounts of his deeds, narratives about his origins, the account of his passion and death, and some witness to his resurrection. The rest of the New Testament consists of apostolic epistles, a genre originating with Paul's communications with the churches he founded, and other documents from the "pillars" or their entourage: two Petrine Letters, one letter attributed to James and one to his brother Jude, and three documents of Johannine origin. In addition, the Gospel of Luke was expanded by a second volume, the Acts of the Apostles, which narrates chiefly the activities of two apostles, Peter and Paul, and documents the church's first missionary expansion from Jerusalem to Rome. Finally, the book of Revelation is a prophetic work presenting an apocalyptic perspective on the church's future, within the framework of a cosmic eucharistic celebration with the Lamb of God, who was slain. Although modern critics routinely deny its apostolic authorship by John, it entered the canon on account of this attribution (as Justin Martyr bears witness) before doubts were raised by certain groups in the early church, rejecting the passages about Jesus's thousand-year reign on earth before the final judgment. Through various channels of assumed or attributed[3] apostolic authorship, these documents of the Word of God take the forms of letters, circulars, explanatory and exhortative texts, authored or approved by the leaders of the church in the last decades of the first century CE or the beginning of the second century.

Members of the first two Christian generations following Jesus's immediate disciples were the ones to begin using this new set of holy writings in continuity with the Jewish Scriptures, as a comprehensive set of written documents witnessing to one single salvation plan for Jews and gentiles alike. They equally recognized both Testaments as God's Word about the same work of salvation, centered on his Son Jesus Christ, who, through the active presence of his Spirit, assisted the church in its work of proclaiming the Word of God. The same Spirit also assisted the church by inspiring and interpreting the written documents.

The community of believers embraced this heritage of written words as an extension of the Scriptures of the Law and the Prophets and of Jesus's ministry as taught by the apostles, all translated into the ancient Mediterranean world's language of international communication, Koine Greek.

The church, formed by the Word of God, expanding and developing in response to the same Spirit that inspired the Scriptures, entered history by holding concretely in its hands the Word of God in human words, containing the books of both the Old and New Testament canons. Materially, the canon was in the church's possession already in the second century. Formally, it was closed and stabilized by the fourth century.[4] As we know from Irenaeus and then later with more profound reflection from Origen and Augustine, biblical exegesis was to be a theological enterprise carried out with such an understanding of its origins for about the first fifteen centuries of Christian history.

The Christian Bible: One Book about the One God and the Human Community

One Book

Modern reflection has been slow and remains incomplete about the material and theological unity of the Christian Bible as God's coherent and consistent Word in the sense expressed by the Letter to the Hebrews at its very

3. The so-called pseudo-epigraphic books of the New Testament are regarded in various ways by present-day biblical scholarship. Unless one deals with them as products or instruments of fraud, their existence in the canon may be seen as the result of a multiplicity of respectable causes.

4. Historically, we find the first scriptural Christian canon established by church authority in the East in the list of books contained in the *39th Festal Letter* of Athanasius of Alexandria, January 7, 367, or in the West in the documents of the Council of Rome (382) under Pope Damasus.

beginning: "Long ago God spoke to our ancestors in many and various ways by the prophets, but in these last days he has spoken to us by a Son, whom he appointed heir of all things, through whom he also created the worlds" (Heb. 1:1–2). The plurality of the times and ways in which God speaks to humans is transcended by the essential oneness of God in the way he reveals himself, as well as by the unity of the humanity he has created and redeemed. God puts into effect a unified coherence of the salvation plan:

> There is one God;
>   there is also one mediator between God and humankind,
> Christ Jesus, himself human. (1 Tim. 2:5)

The theological concept of inspiration, which the church inherited from apostolic times and further developed, must therefore overcome every kind of fragmentation that, when used exclusively, the historical-critical method cannot avoid introducing into its program of interpretation. Although the human word of the biblical texts carries within itself the marks of change and multiplicity, characteristic of humanity's historical existence, when God's Word addresses his people, the divine speech reveals the consistency and oneness of the Speaker, manifesting the one God revealing his only Son, the Logos, through the same Spirit that gathers all the believers. The topically and historically multiple human expressions of the encounter with God coalesce into one single, continuous speech as we discover in it the meaning intended by God, who reveals himself in the scriptural Word, thereby transmitting basically one single message in all he tells.

One God

Theological exegesis is, therefore, not the product of an arbitrary postulate that has been superimposed on the biblical texts as a rational construct, providing a single framework of intelligibility, as if theological exegesis were just a product of the system-building human intellect. Rather, it is the necessary presupposition of the Christian concept of the inspired Scriptures, based on the radical monotheism of biblical faith and the unity of the human race, created by God from one ancestor. Humanity is called to share the life of God, who gathers one people as his own and intends by his universal salvific will to incorporate into this one people all human beings.

This vision, challenged early in the second century by Marcion, is foundational to the Christian canon, which came about explicitly on the presupposition that the same Spirit who spoke through the prophets of the first covenant brings this speech to fullness in Jesus Christ, as proclaimed by Jesus himself in his incarnate life on earth and by his apostles. That the one and *same* God is "the Author of the Scriptures" meant originally in Christian parlance that all books of *both* Testaments come from the same divine Author, as the word "Author" is used in the broad sense of a personal initiator, with emphasis lying on the words "same" and "both."[5]

Perhaps more attractive for our contemporary thinking is a less often quoted but striking sentence by Bernard of Clairvaux as he comments on Psalm 61:12 in the Vulgate (cf. 62:11 NRSV): *Semel locutus est Deus*: "God spoke but once: yes, once,—because always. For, indeed, one and uninterrupted is his speech, but continuous and perpetual."[6]

The same divine authority from which all Scriptures derive is the ultimate source and topic of their theological interpretation. The task of biblical interpretation consists of understanding the God of a monotheistic faith as Creator of humanity's historical existence in the way the Old and New Testaments describe it, from the first creation of humankind in Genesis (cf. Gen. 1–2) up to humanity's re-creation in Christ, who is presented in the book of Revelation as "the Alpha and the Omega" (1:8; 21:6; 22:13). Moreover, the task of biblical theology is to explain how the universe, and in it humanity's history, unfolds according to this vision of Scripture that links God and the human creature, the latter made from the earth and with a destiny on earth, yet at the same time fashioned according to God's image and likeness and therefore in relationships of rationality and self-determining freedom of love toward fellow humans. With commitments toward God, oneself, and fellow humans, the individual reaches out, seeking God through acts of obedience and faith, in spite of struggling with urges for self-emancipation from the same Creator and to dominate fellow humans.

The individual and communitarian history of God's chosen people, as well as of humanity at large, reaches the peak in the incarnation of the divine Logos and the proclamation of his kingdom. In addition, God's love is revealed with new depth as God's Son, truly born in the flesh, truly suffers and dies in union with all who unite with him. Humanity's rebirth emerges through the resurrection of God's Son. These become central topics in all

5. This frequently used classical expression comes from Tertullian (cf. *Against Marcion* 4.24.8–9) and resonated throughout the Middle Ages.

6. "Sermones de diversis," in *Opera omnia Sancti Bernardi*, ed. Jean Leclercq, vol. 6.1 (Rome: Editiones Cistercienses, 1970), 99. The general framework of this article is ultimately grounded in the theology of Scripture held by the church fathers and the monastic theology of the twelfth century. Cf. Denis Farkasfalvy, *L'inspiration de l'Écriture Sainte dans la théologie de saint Bernard* (Rome: Herder, 1964).

biblical interpretation insofar as exegesis steps beyond the merely human and historical dimension of the text and searches for the divinely intended meaning of the Bible, presented to humanity in their Creator's grand act of condescension as God approaches us in human terms (human words, flesh and blood) while calling us to himself.

Thus at no point can the exegete's work settle with interpreting mere texts, for they cannot be adequately understood as long as they are regarded in their historically scattered form as merely human documents written for the sake of human self-expression, even if for their religious content they are recognized as scattered expressions of encounters with an unknown God. For in the biblical texts, human speech, presented in written words, obtains the dignity of a vehicle of divine revelation. Due to divine inspiration, its content transcends human thoughts and sentiments. Although the mere possibility of a divinely inspired significance in the human word comes from humanity's "similarity and likeness" with God, a factual insertion of divinely intended meaning comes from the actual event of the incarnation, preparing and extending over all salvation history an ongoing interaction between God and humanity.

Due to the incarnation, all parts of each biblical book are to be referred to the frequent phrase of the prophetic books: "Thus says the LORD." This means that each biblical text reveals its ultimate meaning only if understood as divine intervention addressing some existential situation of human life, including each individual's personal history, hopes, calamities, breakdowns, and tribulations, as well as all the divine promises made and fulfilled, with salvific experiences. In other words, the biblical Word of God is not fully interpreted unless it is heard as transmitting God's speech addressing humans as they are and thus becomes internalized in terms of human experience both individually and collectively.

One Humankind

The Bible deals with the human being as both physical and spiritual in nature, whose existence is derived from both other human beings through acts of reproduction and from God, who initially created humankind and also continues to create each subsequent generation in the chain of human procreation. Whichever way we consider our origins, the biblical books treat the human person as if stretched out between two poles, destined to be born and to die, to wrestle with the temporal and with the infinite, and either to seek God or to flee from him. The human being always remains a creature of earth and time, preoccupied with searching for transcendence. As regarded by the Bible, this human appears prone to fall but also eager to seek rescue, as if suspended between the danger of losing the self and the hope of obtaining redemption.

The book of Genesis begins with the narration of the humans' multiple fall(s) and God's corresponding judgment. This judgment initially exiles the humans from the garden, yet they continue to fall away from God, who sees "that the wickedness of humankind was great in the earth, and that every inclination of the thoughts of their hearts was only evil continually. And the LORD was sorry that he had made humankind on the earth, and it grieved him to his heart" (Gen. 6:5–6). Although through the flood God terminates all human existence except that of Noah and his family, he makes a covenant with them and promises never to repeat this act of universal punishment. Nonetheless, as Genesis continues its narrative, humanity's conceit and wickedness continue to grow, knowing no limit, so that God, in reply to their repeated attempted rivalries with him, deprives humanity of their ability to establish universal community as he confuses their languages and scatters "them abroad over the face of all the earth" (Gen. 11:8). In the Bible, the preamble to human salvation is described not by a narrowly individualized concept of original sin, but by humankind's ongoing advancement toward subjugating the earth as an expression of their conceit, while failing to establish lasting communion with other human beings through culture. In this way, humanity allows their Creator and their own creaturely status to fall into oblivion.

At the same time, the Bible presents humankind as the one project God wants to save, not by saving one individual at a time but by saving humankind as a community that he forms as his own. According to the Old Testament, God's people are an assembly that God gathers through their faith to his word, which thus remains the divine tool initiating and furthering this gathering. Similarly the words of Jesus (and ultimately, the Word that Jesus is) constitute a "last call" to form Jesus's assembly, called in the New Testament by the Greek word *ekklēsia*. The morality of each Testament establishes unbreakable links between the love of God and the love of one's fellow humans: humanity's redemption becomes inseparably connected with the love of God and the love of the neighbor. Consequently, restoring one's union with God cannot happen without re-creating also communion with fellow human beings, nor can one's commitment to the one God validly exist without the search to promote humanity's unity, in both senses of restoring wholeness and integrity in the individual as well as binding ties of understanding and love with other human beings.

Christological Exegesis

Thus one easily comes to see that in the Bible monotheism and commitment to humankind's unity are not mere "presuppositions" implied in the texts but rather are central issues connecting the books of the Bible and challenging humanity to understand and apply them to life.

Hence, a theological exegesis demands an understanding of the Bible as unified in one canon, which was formed on the account of God's one single ultimate message, Jesus Christ, who links the two Testaments together and clarifies that the Bible consists of the unity of two collections of books.[7] This was clear to those who embraced and transmitted the Christian faith at its beginnings, by also embracing the vision of the unity of the Bible, which does not come about by merely rational inquiry or philosophical reflection, but rather belongs to the essential components of Christian faith. This vision is expressed by the book of Revelation in a glorious image of a scroll closed by seven seals, which only the Lamb, who was slain but became victorious, is able to open.

Ultimately this is why the believer cannot agree to an approach to biblical exegesis that restricts itself to dealing with the Scriptures as a mere anthology of ancient texts. The first Christians, of either Jewish or gentile origin, possessed in the person of Jesus Christ the source of their call to be gathered from every corner of the world (see Matt. 8:11; Luke 13:29), or equivalently in the persons of messengers sent by the risen Christ into the whole world to make them disciples, teaching them all what Jesus has taught (Matt. 28:19–20). Therefore the New Testament does not result only in adding new books to the old ones but also in the final definitive invitation God makes by universally expanding salvation history through Christ. His "words and deeds" are to be later collected and included in the Gospels. Yet more than any other episode of Jesus's life or any statement of his teaching, it is by his death and resurrection that he has fundamentally transformed the disciples' understanding of the Scriptures. Paul, when writing to the Corinthians, makes it clear that the Scriptures (of the Old Testament) become fulfilled and thus are fully understood only in context of Jesus's final "deeds," from which Paul also derived his apostleship: "For I handed on to you as of first importance what I in turn had received: that Christ died for our sins in accordance with the scriptures, and that he was buried, and that he was raised on the third day in

7. Again a conceptual difference with regard to Judaism is the fact that in ancient or modern Hebrew there is only an acronym for the word "Bible," in the form of Tanak (Torah + Nebi'im + Ketubim = Law + Prophets + Writings), a tripartite name linked with no conceptual designation of a new word.

accordance with the scriptures, and that he appeared to Cephas, then to the twelve" (1 Cor. 15:3–5).

Similarly two passages in the last chapter of Luke's Gospel may be most relevant here, referring to the same insight, about a new, full understanding of the Scriptures of old: "Then beginning with Moses and all the prophets, he interpreted to them [the disciples of Emmaus] the things about himself in *all the scriptures*" (Luke 24:27). Next, at his appearance to the Eleven, Jesus directly states the same: "'These are my words that I spoke to you while I was still with you—that everything written about me in the law of Moses, the prophets, and the psalms must be fulfilled.' Then he opened their minds to understand the scriptures" (Luke 24:44–45). In his Letter to the Romans, Paul boldly claims that it is in the hands of Christ's disciples—first the Jews and then the gentiles—that the Scriptures are, ultimately, handed over to their divinely meant owners (cf. Rom. 15:4, quoted above).

The Scriptures' new understanding is correlative with and coextensive with a change in the disciples, when their eyes are opened. The change is both objective (for Christ is truly risen) and subjective (the eyes when opened are endowed with a new understanding of the Scriptures). Thus, in Christian faith, the New Testament is not only inseparable from the Old, but also the Bible's understanding cannot come about without a response of faith in Christ. For the apostolic church, similarly, understanding Christ had to encompass also a penetration of the Scriptures of old, which then eventually brought about— during a few decades of proclamation of Christ's words and deeds—the new written documents representing apostolic preaching.

Christian theological exegesis is, therefore, nothing else than an ongoing search of the Scriptures of old, yet in the sense in which the Johannine Gospel recommends it: "It is they [the scriptures] that testify on my behalf" (John 5:39).

The Patristic Heritage of Christological Exegesis

The roots of early Christian exegesis are found in the New Testament. Already Paul uses Old Testament texts with direct christological references, as when he identifies the "spiritual rock" yielding water in the desert with Christ (1 Cor. 10:4) or speaks of the two children of Abraham, by Hagar and Sarah respectively, in terms of an "allegory" (Gal. 4:24).

In the early days of the twentieth-century's patristic *ressourcement* (return to the church fathers as sources), the study of ancient theological exegesis attracted growing attention among biblical scholars, especially Catholics. However, the embrace of the historical-critical program in biblical studies, accelerated after the

Second Vatican Council, brought about interesting reversals of orientations so that a considerable number of Protestant exegetes became students of patristic exegesis, while significant groups of Catholic biblical scholars and professors distanced themselves from the church fathers' method of theological exegesis.

In recent studies, however, interest in patristic and medieval exegesis does not follow denominational divisions. Nowadays the study of ancient methods, combining biblical exegesis with theological interpretation, is taking place on an ecumenical basis and brings contemporary biblical students of diverse backgrounds into closer relationship with the patristic heritage.

The most important positive characteristic of this ancient exegesis is its clear christocentric character. Even those disturbed by the church fathers' lack of historical consciousness remain aware that as exegetes they can teach us about the center and purpose of the biblical Word of God, aiming at transmitting his truth and his salvation to a human race unified in its need for and desire of God. This is why all studies of ancient exegesis cannot help but underline its clarity of vision regarding the unity of the two Testaments in Christ, a unity that remains the most important principle in the lasting legacy of their exegesis, even if in detailed applications their heritage needs a serious overhaul.

Inspiration and Incarnation

Since early patristic times the concept of biblical inspiration and christological reflection showed a certain convergence. Our newly acquired appreciation of the parallels between God's entering into history and his entering into the finite dimensions of individual human existence mean the discovery of Scripture as both *the context of and a parallel with* the incarnation of the Son. Human speech proceeds first from the "mouth of God" to reach humans, first in words of revelation (Matt. 4:4 quoting Deut. 8:3), and then in the process through which, in the fullness of time, God's Word becomes flesh. Thus Scripture and the humanity of Christ share a common structure of being created in order to transmit God's personal Word: we see, on the one hand, the divine Word in permanently registered human speech, and on the other hand, God's self-giving in his eternal Word when he becomes flesh. This perception, present in patristic theology, has reentered modern theological reflection through the concept of *Schriftwerdung* ("becoming Scripture"), coined in German theology on the analogy of *Menschwerdung*,[8] and through a modern French theological idiom

---

8. Cf. Hugo Rahner, "Das Menschenbild des Origenes," *Eranos-Jahrbuch* 15 (1947): 197–248; Hans Urs von Balthasar, *Verbum Caro: Skizzen zur Theologie* (Einsiedeln: Johannes Verlag, 1955), 12–27.

for biblical monophysitism and Nestorianism.[9] Later *Menschwerdung* was used in an American publication trying to describe how (1) divinely inspired Scriptures and (2) the incarnate God-Man of salvation history making his arrival in the fullness of time[10] are two ways to conceptualize the theandrical (divine and human) structures of our history of salvation.

A more extensive study of ancient exegesis could reveal why and how the insights quoted above from three different cultural backgrounds are ultimately reducible to a common source, the New Testament's view of the unity of the two Testaments, carefully developed in patristic and medieval times. According to this view, as God approaches humanity by manifesting himself in "human vestments," he not only "appears" in human form, but also humiliates himself to leave behind his divine *morphē* ("form," way of appearance in glory) and becomes truly subject to mortality, even death—the death of a criminal. His condescension is not only truthful in terms of the human experience of life but, in addition, involves full emptying of the self and its complete assimilation to the human condition. This is the peak of the journey by which God approaches humanity and makes *himself* heard, expressed, and revealed in fully human terms, not merely in terms of words and speech, analogies or simple metaphors, but in human acts and being subject to human destiny, the Son of God made flesh. In the words of Augustine, commenting on Matthew 5:2, "He who used to open the mouth of Moses and the Prophets, opened his own mouth."[11]

It is such a vision of the incarnate Word that has recently come to expression with a demand to reformulate the theology of biblical inspiration at a time when scriptural exaltation of the "literal sense," with its Marcionite leanings, has repeatedly frustrated efforts for a Christian actualization and interiorization of the Old Testament. Peter Enns's book[12] begins in chapter 1 with "The Incarnational Analogy" and then, after surveying the theological

---

9. Louis Bouyer, "Où en est le mouvement biblique?," *Vie chrétienne* 18 (1956): 7–21.

10. Peter Enns, *Inspiration and Incarnation: Evangelicals and the Problem of the Old Testament* (Grand Rapids: Baker Academic, 2007). My own views on this topic are based on and further develop the Second Vatican Council's *Dei Verbum: Dogmatic Constitution on Divine Revelation*. Cf. Denis Farkasfalvy, *Inspiration and Interpretation: A Theological Introduction to Sacred Scripture* (Washington, DC: Catholic University of America Press, 2012), 188–202, 233–35.

11. "Now he is said to have opened his own mouth, because in the Old Testament he used to open the mouths of the prophets" (*Nunc eum dictum est aperuisse os suum, quod ipse in Lege veteri aperire soleret ora Prophetarum*), writes Augustine, *Sermon on the Mount* 1.2 (Patrologia latina 34:1231). The Greek text of Matt. 5:2 (*kai anoixas to stoma autou edidasken autous legōn*), when undergoing modern translations by dynamic equivalents, makes Augustine's comment inaccessible because in these versions we read something like this: "He began teaching them, and saying" (cf. NKJV, NABRE, NEB, NJB, etc.).

12. Enns, *Inspiration and Incarnation*.

diversity of Old Testament Scriptures, arrives with apparent ease to the point of sketching the outline of an "apostolic hermeneutics" (chap. 4); it concludes in the last chapter (5) with an outline he calls "The Big Picture," blazing a viable road from Genesis to Romans, in the imitation of the apostolic church's understanding of the Old Testament.

The Body of Christ and the Sacramentality of Scripture

The analogy of inspiration and incarnation might appear only as a flash of light that illuminates divine condescension as the way God reaches out to humanity in his postlapsarian condition and from where as the point of departure God begins to lead humankind to himself by revelation and the connected gift of inspiration.

However, incarnation as a defined single-point event would not fully represent the *reality* that the Bible teaches because incarnation means more: it signifies God approaching humankind in the closest conceivable way. The incarnate Son's human life, as he ministers in Galilee and in Jerusalem, dies at Golgotha, and rises from the tomb—all this tells only an unfinished story. The event of the incarnation, according to its full meaning, stretches beyond its initial realization in the earthly span of Jesus's life as he comes from and returns to his glory because it continues to extend beyond the resurrection, to be offered for the participation of all humankind and so fulfill its goal by effectively drawing all human beings into the ecclesial community, as the Son has said: "When I am lifted up from the earth, I will draw all people to myself" (John 12:32). God's people are led to participation in the incarnation, yet this is fully achieved only at the end of time, when God's eschatological people fully and truly reach creation's purpose as a humankind redeemed and unified in grace. They no longer will be divided by collective hunger for power and wealth, the individuals' rebellious self-will, self-seeking lifestyle, and prideful intellect because all who respond by faith to God are effectively introduced to the vision of God and become, at the general resurrection, incorporated into the risen Christ as a "new creation."

The believer's life on earth means being "on the way," on a journey in real companionship with Christ through his Word and sacraments, yet not fully arriving to the status of full knowledge by which we "know as we are known," when our will is fully one with the divine will and we are granted the experience of seeing God face-to-face.[13] Although God's biblical revelation speaks

---

13. "At present we see indistinctly, as in a mirror, but then face to face. At present I know partially; then I shall know fully, as I am fully known" (1 Cor. 13:12 NABRE).

of this final end and goal only in terms of earthly knowledge and language, it also calls for an ongoing theological inquiry, by both reflection and debate, on the part of every person searching the Scriptures.

Thus the Word of God continues to be "living and active, sharper than any two-edged sword, piercing until it divides soul from spirit, joints from marrow; it is able to judge the thoughts and intentions of the heart" (Heb. 4:12), to be used as a tool for building the body of Christ, extending God's voice into history as it calls all persons to conversion, to virtue, to a Christlike way of life, and unites them with the redeeming sufferings of Christ.

God's Word Leads Humankind to His Own Truth

The first summary of Jesus's preaching in the Gospels consists of the sentence "Repent, for the kingdom of heaven has come near" (Matt. 4:17).[14] In the first place, this proclamation invites the hearer to face him- or herself for the sake of performing an internal change, which the concept of *metanoia* ("repentance") implies. If explained fully as "conversion," this internal change in mind also entails a radical change in conduct. Thus in this proclamation, turning to God is inseparably linked to undertaking a radical transformation of the self. Augustine sums up this biblical truth in his dictum *Noverim te, noverim me* ("May I know you, may I know myself"), which indissolubly links knowing God and knowing the self. In the passages of the Synoptic Gospels about "the greatest commandment" (Matt. 22:36–40; Mark 12:29–31; Luke 10:26–28), we meet the well-known and almost commonplace element in Jesus's teaching that love for one's neighbor, both in will and in action, is inextricably linked to love for God. We also see that this same love, as an immediate result of one's love for God, is to be commensurate to one's love for self, the basic cognitive function of a rational and free being who, although not always in terms of reflexive or conceptual knowledge, is yet necessarily ordered internally to embrace and promote his or her God-given existence.

Thus the main biblical commandment for human behavior, which entails loving God in inseparable union with loving the neighbor and in the measure one loves oneself, is not merely an axiom of a moralistic value system, but the deepest expression of God's demand that his creatures, made according to his image and likeness, imitate him by loving themselves with all those he loves in the way he loves. Thus theological exegesis cannot bypass reflection on the human being's conduct, nor can humanity's reflection on sin and sinfulness

14. "The time is fulfilled, and the kingdom of God has come near; repent, and believe in the good news" (Mark 1:15).

(and liberation through redemption) omit the subjects usually listed as topics of personal and social ethics or the moral dimension of "being in Christ," a response to Christ's free and undeserved love expressed in acts of obedience and gratitude, even if alienation from God and from one another reigns in the world.

That the Bible supposes and/or imposes ethical norms on the believer is hardly an issue of dispute.[15] What has been and still is an issue concerning the Scriptures' moral teaching is how Christian conduct, the Christian life of virtue, Christian prayer, and the Christian experience of spiritual life are to be understood and promoted as God's gift streaming from faith rather than a system of human efforts in the form of a humanly designed and executed project of perfection. This difference appears most clearly in the exegetical tradition insisting that "the moral sense" of a scriptural text must be examined after, rather than before, a christological reading of the text takes place. The purpose is so that "morality" will not be treated as humanity's self-sufficient response to the literal sense of the text, but rather as a discovery of the moral challenge that Christ's coming in the flesh reveals as a call to conversion, or as a series of sayings and events inviting hearers to imitate God: "Be perfect, therefore, as your heavenly Father is perfect" (Matt. 5:48).

The Biblical Word in Worship

God's Word teaches us to understand him and ourselves, to form our conscience, to become aware of our needs, and to ask to learn how to pray. In this context, God teaches the faithful to worship. This transcends the prayer of petition for daily needs by seeking God's presence, recognizing our dependency on him, and expressing our essential creaturely dependence on him by giving thanks. In many texts, especially in the Psalms, God teaches us to worship amid human misery, physical suffering, anguish, and doubts, approaching him as the source of all joy and success. The psalms are eye-openers for believers, helping them to enjoy and admire the world, and while doing so to participate in God's own all-surpassing joy in his everlasting being and the lasting existence of his creation. At the end of Psalm 104, a surprising line reveals this association between God and humanity in their joint delight at the beauty of all creation: the psalmist exclaims, "May the LORD rejoice in his works!" (v. 31). Besides the psalms, the Bible provides other prayerlike passages in many prophetic and sapiential texts that are not doctrinal in a strict sense of the word but rather invitations

15. The recently rediscovered system of patristic exegesis included among the so-called four senses of biblical texts, and usually in third place, a "moral meaning," a demonstrably permanent dimension of the exegetical enterprise for 10–12 centuries of scriptural interpretation.

to prayer, both private and collective. Such texts that teach us to pray are in particular asking for theological exegesis in order to enrich our understanding of how God expects his people to approach him; this aim was also made explicit by the incarnate Word in the Lord's Prayer (Matt. 6:9–13; Luke 11:2–4).

Ecumenical and Pastoral Dimensions

It would be a false path to pursue a theological exegesis of biblical texts in order to follow an apologetic agenda. Each branch of Christianity has much experience of ambiguous value with what we may call, for a lack of better expression, a confessional or denominational interpretation of biblical texts. In some periods of the past, this kind of arguing about doctrinal issues, based on biblical texts, might have been unavoidable. Although it promoted inter-denominational controversies and sometimes employed a demeaning tone, Christians could not help experiencing that they were still connected by a common Bible, especially the New Testament, whose common canon survived without damage as one of the commonly held institutions among Christians.

Yet a confessional exegesis is often distorting and even destructive. Its worst aspect comes about from its selectivity as it chooses texts by exporting them from their context and neglects those texts from which it cannot fashion weapons, disregarding in either case the author's intention and the literary genre used. Meanwhile it may emphasize a particular doctrinal link, often imposed as a tool for denominational alienation or an uncharitable preoccupation to prove one's opponent wrong.

Contrary to such abuses of the commonality of a shared Bible, an ecumenical biblical exchange should address a text with explicit awareness that the same Spirit who inspired the biblical authors and texts connects the participants of the exchange even if in many matters they remain separated from one another by their fragmented or distorted understanding of God's Word. At such occasions, the participants can realize that, in spite of divergent interpretations, the inspired Word of the divine Author is always larger and broader than what an individual reader is able to fully express. Therefore our disagreements might be vehicles by which we may finally arrive, as if by surprise, at meanings that no participant in an exchange could have anticipated at the beginning.

Conclusion

Theological exegesis grows and broadens with the exegetes' intellectual or moral readiness, spiritual attentiveness, and desire to hear God speaking through the biblical text. Nevertheless, it is not by erudition, learnedness, or the mastering of a bibliography alone that theological exegesis develops and unlocks both the mind of the reader and the content that God intends to communicate through a text.

Until we reach a readiness to approach the text and its human authors as vehicles carrying to us what God intends to tell through the Scriptures, the scene of the book of Revelation remains as an eloquent expression of our desire to unlock the Scriptures:

> I began to weep bitterly because no one was found worthy to open the scroll or to look into it. Then one of the elders said to me, "Do not weep. See, the Lion of the tribe of Judah, the Root of David, has conquered, so that he can open the scroll and its seven seals." (Rev. 5:4–5)

Yet the intervention of grace can change this scene:

> Then I saw between the throne and the four living creatures and among the elders a Lamb standing as if it had been slaughtered, having seven horns and seven eyes, which are the seven spirits of God sent out into all the earth. He went and took the scroll from the right hand of the one who was seated on the throne. When he had taken the scroll, the four living creatures and the twenty-four elders fell before the Lamb, each holding a harp and golden bowls full of incense, which are the prayers of the saints. They sing a new song:
>
> > "You are worthy to take the scroll and to open its seals,
> > for you were slaughtered and by your blood you ransomed for God
> > saints from every tribe and language and people and nation;
> > you have made them to be a kingdom and priests serving our God,
> > and they will reign on earth." (Rev. 5:6–10)

11

Theological Commentary

MARK GIGNILLIAT AND JONATHAN T. PENNINGTON

Introduction

Qoheleth warns, "Of making many books there is no end" (Eccles. 12:12a). This discouraging wisdom is certainly true of the creation of biblical commentaries. How often in the halls of the guild and the church are lamentations heard about the appearance of yet another commentary. Do we really need another? Is not the impulse to write a commentary born out of Romanticism's sentiments about the necessity of originality or individual expression? "Yes, I know of the three commentaries on John that appeared last year, but none are marked by the singularity of my voice and vision." These questions raise for the present authors a sense of wonder and self-doubt about their own ongoing involvement in the writing of yet more commentaries. Perhaps we too are romantics!

As often as complaints arise about the glut in the field of biblical commentary, pastors and priests also remark about the general unhelpfulness of biblical commentaries when it comes to what they care most about, aiding in sermon preparation. For all the commentaries out there on a said book of the Bible, few are deemed useful for the pastor who is preparing sermons that move beyond descriptions of the text into its subject matter as a living

Word for the people of God. In his *Sickness unto Death*, Søren Kierkegaard's pseudonym Anti-Climacus (Kierkegaard's better self) insists that for Christian scholarship to be Christian, it must be beneficial.[1] Admittedly, what counts as "usefulness" is not always immediately self-evident. Nevertheless, for a commentary to be Christian, its usefulness must certainly be taken into account. And this usefulness, understood from within the Bible's own view, must ultimately be *theological*, about God himself as the subject matter.

The question that this essay raises and seeks to clarify thus is straightforward: What deems a biblical commentary theological? Or from another angle, given the plethora of extant commentaries, what warrant is there for new commentaries that are self-identified as "theological"? Moreover, given the ascendancy of historicist approaches for the establishment of the text's "literal sense," what methodological claims does a theological commentary make vis-à-vis modern criticism's governing, interpretive instincts? These are the kinds of questions this chapter takes first steps toward answering, while fully recognizing that the genre of theological commentary is a matter of some dispute.

The structure of this chapter's exploration into theological commentary is twofold. First, in facing the question of writing commentary theologically, we will offer a survey of the history of biblical commentary. Second, we will explore this issue theologically itself, reflecting on the nature of Holy Scripture and how the trinitarian reality affects the task of biblical commentary.

Part 1: A Brief History of the Biblical Commentary in Light of Theological Exegesis

The history of Christian doctrine is itself an exercise in the history of biblical interpretation. This section will offer a brief account of the history of the commentary genre. This admittedly truncated survey serves a simple purpose: in the history of the tradition, identifying the breakdown between (1) theological commentary and (2) detached, academic commentary, where interpreters tend to dislocate the verbal/historical character of Scripture from its theological subject matter (the *res*).

The genre of the commentary under discussion here is distinguished from the sermon, "rewritten Bible,"[2] and intracanonical intertextuality. Each of

---

1. Søren Kierkegaard, *The Sickness unto Death: A Christian Psychological Exposition for Upbuilding and Awakening*, ed. and trans. Howard V. Hong and Edna H. Hong (Princeton: Princeton University Press, 1980), 5–6.

2. "Rewritten Bible" describes the phenomenon discovered from Second Temple literature wherein authors "expressed exegetical and theological opinions by presenting a new version of scriptural narratives and laws," Molly Zahn explains (*Rethinking Rewritten Scripture:*

these forms of the use and reappropriation of Scripture is related substantially to the commentary genre, and each is important for a full treatment of the history of interpretation. Our aim here, however, is more modest. We are referring to the specific genre of the systematic commenting on a set text of Scripture.[3]

Theological Commentary in Early Christianity

The earliest Christian commentaries on Scripture in the patristic period were not created out of a vacuum. Rather, they naturally flow from a long tradition of Greek and Roman commenting on the classic texts—Homer, of course, and later the great tragedians and comedians of the Greek tradition, along with the work of the philosophers.

Not surprisingly, Alexandria, the home of the great library and of scholarly output, appears to be the source of much Greek commentary, starting in the early third century BCE and continuing strongly through the fourth century CE. These provide a solid tradition and habit of commenting on classic texts. For our purposes we notice that such commentary writing included a great variety of notes on the text, ranging from comments about breathing marks, the meaning of specific terms, historical information, onward to scientific, religious, and philosophical notes. Also noteworthy, it appears much of the commentary writing in this tradition was not done as a strictly scholarly pursuit but instead to offer "sapiential, moral, and aesthetic interpretation, sometimes derived by means of allegory."[4]

This observation will prove to be of great importance as we scan the long history of the commentary. Specifically, we will see that it is only from a modern viewpoint that distinctions between "scholarly" and "devotional" arise; modernity will come to define "scholarly" and "academic" commentary as

Composition and Exegesis in the 4QReworked Pentateuch Manuscripts [Leiden: Brill, 2011], 2). The past several decades have heard no small debate about the proper definition and application of these terms. See Moshe J. Bernstein, "'Rewritten Bible': A Generic Category Which Has Outlived Its Usefulness?," *Textus* 22 (2005): 169–96; Anders Klostergaard Petersen, "Rewritten Bible as a Borderline Phenomenon—Genre, Textual Strategy, or Canonical Anachronism?," in *Flores Florentino: Dead Sea Scrolls and Other Early Jewish Studies in Honour of Florentino García Martínez*, ed. Anthony Hilhorst et al., Journal for the Study of Judaism: Supplement Series 122 (Leiden: Brill, 2007), 285–306.

3. Markus Bockmuehl helpfully defines the commentary as "a work consisting primarily of sequential, expository annotation of identified texts that are distinguished from the comments and reproduced intact, whether partially or continuously" ("The Making of Gospel Commentaries," in *The Written Gospel*, ed. Markus Bockmuehl and Donald Hagner [Cambridge: Cambridge University Press, 2005], 274).

4. Ibid., 277.

somehow objective and nonpersonal, nonsapiential, and nonexhortational. Such a definition would make no sense to ancient scholars.

The overriding concern for the personal and spiritual effects of a text does not mean that the Alexandrian and later Roman tradition of commentary was not rigorous and intensive; it was. In fact, it was from very close and detailed readings of texts that the need to read texts allegorically became so apparent in the Alexandrian tradition as well as in the Jewish tradition as found in Philo. As commentators read carefully and sought to apply the classic text to the contemporary reader, they found it obvious that the deepest reading of a text would "discover under the rough surface of the literal text the polished gems of an interpretation for the life of the readers."[5] This allegorical tradition was not a function of fast and loose, but quite the opposite: it flowed from the exercise of thoughtful commentary on the text.

The earliest Christian commentaries, typically on the Gospels,[6] begin to appear in the mid-second century. Not surprisingly, they largely follow the well-established Alexandrian models of commentary, including the universally accepted multiple levels of meaning approach.[7] Commentaries such as those by Origen, Clement, and others quote the text and then make wide-ranging comments. Their strategy for textual comment, however, resists a uniform schema. The variance in textual comment ranges from philological, text-critical, and philosophical ideas to a freer homiletical style, betraying their genesis as sermons. Nonetheless, in every case, the driving purpose is always moral and spiritual edification.[8]

As the Alexandrian and Antiochene approaches develop (and do indeed diverge at points), we find different emphases within both the schools and individual interpreters across the schools. For the authors who provide less allegorical commentary and focus more on simpler readings, the commentary becomes more accessible to the masses of believers.[9] But the difference between Antiochene and Alexandrian commenting was not so much in *method* as in

---

5. Ibid., 278.

6. For an argument asserting the central role the Gospels played in the early years of the established church, see Jonathan T. Pennington, *Reading the Gospels Wisely* (Grand Rapids: Baker Academic, 2012), chap. 12. Because the Jesus traditions in both oral and written form were so widely used it is understandable that most early commentaries exposited the Gospel texts.

7. We are now hopefully in a place in our understanding of patristic exegesis that the old line, "Alexandrian exegesis was allegorical, and Antiochene was literal/grammatical-historical [miraculously like modern exegesis]," is forever repudiated. See Frances Young, "Alexandrian and Antiochene Exegesis," in *A History of Biblical Interpretation*, vol. 1, *The Ancient Period*, ed. Alan Hauser and Duane Watson (Grand Rapids: Eerdmans, 2003), 334–54.

8. Bockmuehl, "Making of Gospel Commentaries," 283–84.

9. Ibid., 294.

results or *ends*, which were considered to be the most useful and beneficial readings.

At the height of mature, balanced commentary in early Christianity is certainly Augustine of Hippo.[10] His various commentaries[11] and sermons manifest the balance of the *sensus literalis* and the deeper, cross-canonical associative, theological, and sapiential readings that are the best of the patristic habit. It is this vision that he himself lays out in his highly influential hermeneutics book *Christian Instruction*.

Early Christian commentary, whether Alexandrian or Antiochene, focused on the world of the Bible, its vision and understanding of the created world. Patristic commentary did not start with the world or life and then go to the Bible for understanding, whether it be historical or theological, as later modern commentators will do. This difference, which represents a major shift in modernity, is what John O'Keefe and R. R. Reno have called the "sanctified vision." Early Christian commentators understood Holy Scriptures *as indeed* the revelation of God, not the thing that points to revelation. Their commenting on the Bible, therefore, sought meaning *within* the text, not *from* it. Early commentators saw all Scripture as relevant, even the seemingly mundane details, because of the Christian assumption that "the text is the verbal form of divine pedagogy," all of it aiding in the development of the Christian life.[12] As a result, in practice this looked like an intensive reading that focused on connections between words, images, and phrases, associating them with one another and building up a world of cross-links that evoke many layers of meaning.[13] This moving *across* the text of the Bible, not past it, is what makes early commentary feel so different and foreign to modern readers. It is based on an entirely different worldview, one of universal interconnectedness, and a higher theology of Scripture than later readers will possess.

10. A helpful survey of Augustine's hermeneutical arguments and interpretive practices can be found in Richard Norris, "Augustine and the Close of the Ancient Period of Interpretation," in Hauser and Watson, *History of Biblical Interpretation*, 1:380–408.

11. One of Augustine's most influential commentary-like works on the Gospels, his *Harmony of the Gospels*, must be set aside and seen as *not* typical for good commentary writing. This is because the sharply apologetic purpose of this work, designed to offer a response to attacks on the historical accuracy of the Gospels, makes his approach and comments too narrowly focused on defensive explanation. See also the separate comments by Francis Watson on how, unintentionally, the approach of Augustine's *Harmony* will eventually play into the hands of Enlightenment critics who use the same approach (minus the theological convictions) to undermine the faith—as he explains in *Gospel Writing: A Canonical Perspective* (Grand Rapids: Eerdmans, 2013), chaps. 1–2.

12. John O'Keefe and R. R. Reno, *Sanctified Vision: An Introduction to Early Christian Interpretation of the Bible* (Baltimore: Johns Hopkins University Press, 2005), 22.

13. Ibid., 48–49.

Theological Commentary in the Medieval Period

We have spent significant time on early Christian commentary because it lays the foundation for how most Christians have commented on Scripture throughout the church's history. This is not to suggest that there were no developments and identifiable habits in the medieval and Renaissance eras. But in many ways these are the natural flowering of the garden planted in the patristic period. The rise of humanism and the philological turn of the Renaissance show a notable development, but even this is a rediscovery (rebirth) of certain emphases of the ancient world, including the radically personal accent found in Augustine.

When considering theological commentary in medieval Christianity, we must first distinguish sequential commentary writing from the later *scholia* and *catena* traditions. *Scholia* are generally defined as commentary notes on classic authors that are written in the margins of medieval manuscripts. Sometimes we know the authors of these notes and sometimes not. We cannot assume that these notes found in medieval manuscripts originated in that time period; many are likely records of earlier teachers.[14] As notes on scriptural manuscripts grew in use and fashion, the result was eventually a more uniform design and set of notes, called a glossed Bible. The most famous, standardized version of this was the *Glossa ordinaria*.[15] Starting in the early sixth century, with the massive amount of commentaries that by then had been produced, scholars began to produce *catenae*, chains of "verbatim extracts from existing commentaries [compiled] into a large new single commentary."[16] The most famous of these was Thomas Aquinas's *Catena aurea*, or *Golden Chain*. At the same time, in connection with the school of St. Victor, there developed a number of works that helped to clarify the distinction between the "historical" and "spiritual" meanings, according to the principles of Augustine and explained in Hugh of St. Victor's *Didascalion*. This tradition was eventually codified as the *Historia scholastica*, which sat alongside the *Glossa ordinaria*.[17]

The genre of scriptural reflection that correlates most clearly to the commentary developed in the mid-thirteenth century was called the *postilla*. The *postilla* was a running commentary, produced especially in the schools of the mendicant orders.[18] Among the most famous and influential versions of

14. Nigel Wilson, "Scholiasts and Commentators," *Greek, Roman, and Byzantine Studies* 47 (2007): 40.

15. Christopher Ocker, "Biblical Interpretation in the Middle Ages," in *Dictionary of Major Biblical Interpreters*, ed. Donald McKim (Downers Grove, IL: IVP Academic, 2009), 15.

16. Wilson, "Scholiasts and Commentators," 47.

17. Ocker, "Biblical Interpretation," 15–16.

18. Ibid., 16.

the *postillae* were those produced by the erudite commentator Nicholas of Lyra.[19] Like all premodern interpreters, Nicholas believed in the multiple senses of Scripture, at the most basic level at least a *sensus literalis* and a spiritual sense. What makes Nicholas especially interesting and important is his great emphasis on the literal sense. Nicholas was interested in and sensitive to the literary structure and plan of the text's author. Background information about Jewish customs and the Hebrew language plays a significant role in his commentaries. He certainly is a very theological commentator, yet his work represents a robust and thoughtful balance of literal and spiritual readings. In this he serves as an important segue into the Renaissance and the Protestant Reformation.

Theological Commentary in the Renaissance and Reformation Age

The age of the Renaissance and the rise of humanism affected commentary writing in significant ways. The biggest change is that the Renaissance placed great emphasis on philology and establishing and translating the texts of Scripture. The *sensus literalis*, understood as what the words say, becomes the foundational focus in this era. This is both an *effect* from the Renaissance turn toward language and texts and simultaneously *affects* more of the same. Translations and the production of new editions (and the beginnings of what will later be called textual criticism) become the focus of attention and much energy. It is appropriate to discuss the Renaissance and Reformation eras together in this regard because it is these emphases from humanism that have the greatest effect on how commentary writing is done by the Reformers.

In terms of the form of commentary writing, Protestants in particular move away from the medieval interlinear gloss and *scholia* approach toward more discursive comment. For some commentators the focus is strongly on philology, while others emphasize certain loci or topoi that give understanding to a whole book.[20] There is also the novel genre of Erasmus's paraphrases, but this approach was an outlier.[21]

---

19. See Philip D. W. Krey and Lesley Smith, eds., *Nicholas of Lyra: The Senses of Scripture* (Leiden: Brill, 2000); especially helpful are the essays by Kevin Madigan and Lesley Smith.

20. Richard Muller, "Biblical Interpretation in the Sixteenth and Seventeenth Centuries," in McKim, *Dictionary of Major Biblical Interpreters*, 27.

21. See Judith Rice Henderson, ed., *The Unfolding of Words: Commentary in the Age of Erasmus* (Toronto: University of Toronto Press, 2013), and especially the essay by Jean-François Cottier, "Erasmus's *Paraphrases*: A 'New Kind of Commentary'?," 27–54. Cottier argues that Erasmus was seeking to do more than instruct as a commentary or scholion would, but to move and please as well by rewriting Scripture.

In terms of content, commentary writing manifests great continuity with medieval exegesis. The main differences are the natural outworking of the Renaissance's philological and textual emphases. Yet Reformation commentary writing is still thoroughly theological. In continuity with all premodern reading of the Bible, its interest is in the meaning of the text for the Christian understanding and life, for the building up of faith, love, and hope. These interpretive instincts are all based on a belief in the divine authorship of Scripture. In this sense, as Richard Muller points out, the Reformation and the post-Reformation period has more in common with medieval and patristic exegesis than with the modern higher-critical interpretation of the Bible.[22]

As we should expect, the different Reformers (and counter-Reformers) are not uniform in their approach or emphases. Some put more or less emphasis on the fathers, others write long treatises, and yet others seek to follow the pattern of John Calvin's valuing of brevity. Some commentators are more directly homiletical and personal, while others offer their exposition for the learned. All the Reformers express concern about and even opposition to the traditional *quadriga*, or fourfold sense. But for many of them, this is really a rejection of the staleness of scholasticism and the dominance of *sacra doctrina* over *sacra pagina*, rather than a different hermeneutical view or practice. This is certainly the case for Martin Luther.[23]

Luther represents how medieval interpretation of Scripture is wedded to a renewed and radical reassessment of the centrality of Scripture's authority; Calvin, then, is the model for how this same view of authority is combined with Renaissance humanism. Regarding theological commentary, which he produces on most books of the Bible, Calvin represents a premodern turn toward the commentary as brief and focused on the *sensus literalis*. Calvin's attention to the *sensus literalis* entails a concern for brevity, clarity, and textual intentionality. The latter is governed by how Calvin understood the operative work of the Spirit in the text's composition and transmission, and the singularity of the divine economy between the Testaments. His approach was to understand the "mind of the [human] author" as inspired by the Holy Spirit, with a great emphasis on the historical situation of the text and the reader.

Calvin—along with other interpreters who valued historical context, such as many of the Antiochenes, Nicholas of Lyra, Martin Bucer, and John Oecolampadius—particularly prioritized the historical sense of a text, and thus his commentaries manifest "special attention to the historical situation and

---

22. Muller, "Biblical Interpretation in the Sixteenth and Seventeenth Centuries," 22–23.

23. See Kenneth Hagen, "Luther, Martin," in McKim, *Dictionary of Major Biblical Interpreters*, 687–94.

stylistic peculiarities of the various biblical writers."[24] As a result, Calvin was often accused by other Reformers, especially Lutheran contemporaries, for "Judaizing exegesis" that focused too much on the historical context of a passage.[25]

Calvin was no modernist, however, nor a modern historical critic. For him, the humanistic emphasis on the historical setting and authorial intent still served the greater purpose of edifying and nurturing the faithful.[26] In this sense his commentaries, though very different in feel from earlier commentaries, are still theological, even if the ability to apply an ancient text to a current reader is not always as smooth; in some sense there is a gap to be crossed by way of historical analogies.

Theological Commentary and the Modern Turn

The scope of our discussion here is already vast and remains a surface account. Rather than trying to describe and explain the effects of modernity on the commentary, it may be most helpful, by way of contrast, to elucidate how premodern interpretation differs from modernity once the latter becomes the dominant force. In this we will follow the helpful analysis of Richard Muller and John L. Thompson, who identify four differences. First, premodern exegetes understood the *historia*, or story, of Scripture to reside not in something behind the text but as the *sensus literalis* itself, what the words say. Second, the meaning of a text is governed not by a reconstructed *Sitz im Leben* behind the text but by the scope of the canonical Scriptures. Third, premodern readers understood the primary audience of the text to be not its historical community but "the believing community that once received and continues to receive the text."[27] This means that the text is a divinely inspired message, speaking to the contemporary believing reader. Finally, no premodern exegete considered himself to be an isolated scholar providing the definitive answer to the meaning of a text, but rather "understood the interpretive task as an interpretive conversation in the context of the historical community of belief."[28]

24. Barbara Pitkin, "Calvin, Theology, and History," *Seminary Ridge Review* 12, no. 2 (Spring 2010): 4.

25. Ibid. See also David Puckett, *John Calvin's Exegesis of the Old Testament* (Louisville: Westminster John Knox, 1995).

26. Pitkin, "Calvin, Theology, and History," 6.

27. Richard Muller and John L. Thompson, "The Significance of Precritical Exegesis: Retrospect and Prospect," in *Biblical Interpretation in the Era of the Reformation*, ed. Richard Muller and John L. Thompson (Grand Rapids: Eerdmans, 1996), 340–41.

28. Ibid., 341.

The effect of these epistemic and exegetical changes on modern commentary writing are not hard to see. In short, commentaries—at least "real" or "academic" commentaries—become by definition historically distant, descriptive, and nontheological. John Barton, for example, claims that bracketing off theological beliefs is a key ingredient for modern criticism.[29] For the first time, one can discern commentaries that are "devotional" or "homiletical," adjectives that need scare quotes to explain how they deviate from what becomes the standard kind of nontheological commentary.

While most of Christianity in the West adopts these methods of commentary, even amid this major hermeneutical shift many Christians continue to read the Bible differently. For some, such as the Puritans or many in the Reformed tradition, this is because they do not adopt the epistemic shift and continue to read and comment on Scripture theologically. For others, such as much of the evangelical tradition, a bifurcation arises between their academic work on the Bible and their more devotional or homiletical reading, the true wedding of which is made impossible by their hermeneutical stance.

Even as the hegemony of the modernist and rationalist era reaches its height, many commentators recognize the problem of the nontheological commentary and begin to object. Kierkegaard is a notable example, as is the most famous and influential critical-of-criticism theologian, Karl Barth. The questions raised by these and other Christian thinkers problematizes the modern bifurcation between a text's verbal/literary quality and its theological subject matter. The objections and alternatives to modernity begin to develop, but it will take a few generations and broader cultural, literary, and epistemic shifts before commentary writing will take another turn.

One example of a current theological commentator is Frederick Dale Bruner, whose commentaries on Matthew and then on John serve as an early outlier example of theological commentary. Bruner offers a traditional section-by-section commentary on Matthew, but all framed and integrated with the categories and concepts of systematic theology. The result is a fresh and challenging commentary that deals with the *sensus literalis* grammatically, historically, literarily, and critically, yet it is also immediate with application and theological integration. In this sense, Bruner's commentating is genre-bending work.[30]

A more widespread and systematic attempt is being made to offer fresh theological commentary through a number of multiauthored commentary

29. See John Barton, *The Nature of Biblical Criticism* (Louisville: Westminster John Knox, 2007).

30. Frederick Dale Bruner, *Matthew: A Commentary*, rev., enlarged ed., 2 vols. (Grand Rapids: Eerdmans, 2007); idem, *The Gospel of John: A Commentary* (Grand Rapids: Eerdmans, 2012).

series. These include the Brazos Theological Commentary on the Bible series, the Concordia Commentary (described as "A Theological Exposition of Sacred Scripture"), the Two Horizons Commentary, and most recently, the International Theological Commentary, which is designed as an intentionally theological counterpart to the famous International Critical Commentary series by the same publisher (T&T Clark).

The form and method differ between the various attempts at theological interpretation on offer today. Only time will tell what shape these commentaries will take and how they will fare in the large world of commentary publishing. In their own ways, each seeks to serve both the academic community and the church. In this they represent a remarriage of two kinds of reading made uncomfortable to each other in modernity. Historical-critical/ grammatical commentaries will continue to serve an important purpose. How theological commentaries enter into the commentary market is a phenomenon worth tracking and yet to be determined. There is little doubt that these major works, produced by leading scholars, will have an impact.

Conclusion

In her elegant and significant little study of early Christian hermeneutics, Margaret Mitchell convincingly argues that the rhetorical schools of the ancient world set the tone and goal for how to interpret classic texts and thereby how they are commented on.[31] The issue of interpretation was not allegory versus literal, but reading in such a way that one adapts and applies what a text is saying to the specific case at hand; appropriation to the current reader is the focus. All early Christian commentators read in this way as well.

This does not mean, however, that texts become arbitrary wax noses for the interpreters' whims. Quite the contrary: intensive, close reading was highly valued. But it does mean that the focus of reading and commenting on texts is not on using a proper *method* but on achieving the best *end*, so that the interpretation might be *useful* or *beneficial* (*pros ophelimon*). This "agonistic paradigm of interpretation" is what drives patristic exegesis.[32]

On this basis, then, Mitchell suggests that the task of biblical scholarship today should learn from this model and seek to maintain "a carefully calibrated balance among three cardinal virtues of ancient textual interpretation." These are *akribeia* ("precision," "keen attention"), a close examination of

---

31. Margaret Mitchell, *Paul, the Corinthians, and the Birth of Christian Hermeneutics* (Cambridge: Cambridge University Press, 2012).
    32. Ibid., 107–8.

what the text says in whole and in part; *opheleia*, an awareness of the *benefit* for present readers; and *epiekeia* ("clemency"), which seeks to keep the first two in balance.[33]

Mitchell's suggestion is apropos and can prove very beneficial for the contemporary, believing commentator and the believing reader. Because the Christian Scriptures are about God (*theos*), faithful commentary on Scripture must ultimately be *theo*-logical commentary. Yet we cannot go backward, ignoring our own tradition-history or acting as if there is no benefit to each stage of commentary, including modernism's historical/literary turn. Rather, faithful theological commentary will seek to maintain this *epiekeia* (balance) between intensive reading (including use of modern tools of inquiry) and focus on the spiritual and moral benefit to the commentary reader.

Muller and Thompson write,

> Precritical exegesis was *not* always correct in its assertions, nor certainly *univocal* in its views; but it was always concerned to locate biblical exegesis within the community of those who valued the text as more than a curiosity, indeed, as inspired Scripture. For moderns and postmoderns alike, then, the traditionary path of "precritical" exegesis may well be the only track that joins the present-day interpreter to the sacred text and that brings the sacred text forward again to us as having significance, not only for the dead but also for the living.[34]

Part 2: Theological Reflections on the Nature of Biblical Commentary

Holy Scripture's Character

Though expounded on in chapter 2 (above), the character of Holy Scripture and the hermeneutical significance of its character bears repeating here. A theological commentary operates within the confessional space that Holy Scripture originates in the self-determination of God to reconcile humanity to himself. In the providence of God, whose name is Father, Son, and Holy Spirit, the Triune God reconciles the whole cosmos by means of his Word: *Fiat lux* ("Let there be light," Gen. 1:3 Vulgate). Within trinitarian confessional language, the Word of God exists in the eternal unity of our Triune God as the Second Person of the Trinity: Jesus Christ. God *is* his Word. Such a basic theological observation has enormous import for the interpretive posture of Scripture's readers. We understand Scripture within this theological sphere,

---

33. Ibid., 108.
34. Muller and Thompson, "The Significance of Precritical Exegesis," 345.

dogmatically located in the context of God's own self and God's self-determination to create and redeem. Scripture's character as Word is derivatively related to God's own character as Word. God speaks.

T. F. Torrance's understanding of the scientific nature of Christian theology makes its rounds in print quite often. Torrance understands scientific inquiry as "scientific" when the method of study is commensurate with its object. Over the past century, for example, quantum physics as a discipline has been forced to recalibrate its methods of inquiry because seemingly antonymous realities were taking place at the submolecular level, such that unobserved phenomena could be at two places at once. As physicists followed the material evidence to the conclusion that multiple universes are not only possible but probable, the whole field of physics has had to adjust methodologically because of the character of the subject matter under investigation.[35]

Admittedly, quantum physics is beyond the pay grade (not to mention mental capacity) of this chapter's authors. But the analogy to biblical studies works. When confession regarding the nature of Scripture and its primary divine source becomes matters of first principles on the hermeneutical level, then object and method are correlate. When Scripture as an object of study and as a self-differentiated reality from the reading subject is located dogmatically within the saving actions of God *ad extra* ("toward the outside"), then our hermeneutical efforts from beginning to end need to situate themselves within this sphere. Doing otherwise becomes interpreting something other than Holy Scripture.

The theological claims made above in no wise castigate the creaturely reality of Scripture, a matter to which we will return in due course. Both authors here affirm without reservation the enormous benefit received from biblical exegetes who do not work within this confessional frame of reference—thus refuting a straw-man charge sometimes leveled against practitioners of theological exegesis.[36] Our shelves are weighted down by many excellent books and reference materials that restrict their biblical engagement to literary/historical matters. At the same time, a theological commentary rooted in the wide stream of the Christian, interpretive tradition recognizes the creaturely reality of Scripture as an important stop along the way, but not the final destination. Scripture's identity as "an eternally youthful Word" drives the interpretive mechanism from beginning to end, including the utilization of

35. See Heinrich Päs, *The Perfect Wave: With Neutrinos at the Boundary of Space and Time* (Cambridge, MA: Harvard University Press, 2014), chap. 3.

36. R. R. Reno's dismissal of Claus Westermann's Genesis commentary in the preface to his Brazos *Genesis* commentary shows the need for this concern: Reno, *Genesis*, Brazos Theological Commentary on the Bible (Grand Rapids: Brazos, 2010), 24.

tools from nonconfessional approaches born out of the great boon of textual inquiry in the modern period.[37]

Scripture's Source: Human and Divine

As mentioned above, a theological commentary of the sort identified herein does not shy away from the human or creaturely character of Scripture. Much has been made of the Chalcedonic or incarnational analogy in recent attempts to give the historical or human dimension of Scripture its due: as Jesus was fully human and fully divine, so too Scripture is divine and human. While we find the appeal to the incarnational analogy unhelpful at its most basic level—Holy Scripture is not divine even though its source is—the appeal to it may prove helpful heuristically.[38] The use made of the analogy is telling.

For biblical scholars making use of the analogy (e.g., Peter Enns, Kenton L. Sparks, and Paul Williamson), the Chalcedonic christological formula provides the warrant for historical-critical study of Scripture. We are to treat the Scriptures as historical documents lest they fall prey to the docetic tendency to remove Scripture (or Jesus) from the historical nexus of time and space. The "fully human" nature of Scripture is the green light for the use of critical tools on offer within the guild, especially as these tools have been honed and refined in the modern period. The result of this humanizing tendency is more often than not a resistance to univocal and cross-associative readings of biblical texts. Instead, the results tend toward an atomizing of the biblical forms or traditions to their basic level for the sake of identifying the religious-historical plurality that gave rise to the biblical traditions. This is, for example, redaction-criticism's basic contribution to the reconstruction of Israel's or the early church's religious pluriformity.

The tightrope on which we are walking begins to sway precisely at this point: the achievements of modern, critical study of Scripture cannot be easily jettisoned, regardless of where one falls on the grid between confessional and nonconfessional approaches to Scripture. The Bible is a creaturely document from beginning to end, and this inescapable reality (and confession) makes demands on modern readers.[39] Our students realize these demands quite

37. Herman Bavinck, *Reformed Dogmatics*, vol. 1, *Prolegomena*, ed. John Bolt, trans. John Vriend (Grand Rapids: Baker Academic, 2003), 384.

38. John Webster raises this basic concern about the incarnational analogy in his *Holy Scripture: A Dogmatic Sketch*, Current Issues in Theology (Cambridge: Cambridge University Press, 2003), 22–23.

39. Webster warns about the potential danger in the Protestant scholastic notion of accommodation precisely at this point. With the understanding that God stoops low in the divine economy and uses human language to communicate himself, the overly formal distinction

quickly as they learn Hebrew and Greek. The pressing question, then, is not whether critical tools are useful in the work of exegesis: the Bible's creaturely character is unavoidable. The question concerns the proper location of these tools in the singular act of reading Christian Scripture.

If we turn our attention back to the incarnational analogy, again for heuristic purposes because on final analysis the analogy breaks down at every level, then the engagement of the creaturely/historical dimension of Scripture as a single reality amounts to a Nestorian Christology that was ultimately rejected at Chalcedon. Guided by Cyril's insistence on single-subject Christology, the Nestorian tendency to treat the human nature of Jesus as a single *prosōpon* was rejected in the early fifth century. In other words, the human nature of Jesus Christ as a *separate* entity cannot be predicated. Only the single subject, Jesus Christ, fully God and fully man, can be predicated. In time, the technical term for this christological claim is the *anhypostatic* character of Jesus's humanity. Put simply, Jesus's human nature does not exist apart from its hypostatic union with his divine nature in a single subject.[40]

A theological commentary of the type prescribed in this chapter resists the Nestorian tendency of biblical scholars to treat the human character of Scripture in isolation from its divine source, import, and overarching voice. The historical-critical dimension of biblical inquiry, with all of its achievements notwithstanding, remains in John Webster's terminology en passant ("in passing") toward its final divine end.[41] Again, and for the sake of a charitable engagement with colleagues who are not persuaded, such a claim does not diminish the value of these Nestorian contributions. The fact remains, however, that theological commentary of the Christian kind treats the Scriptures as a single reality, whose source is both human and divine. Moreover—and this is perhaps where the Chalcedonic analogy breaks down yet again or at least where theological controversy over Chalcedon's proper interpretation thickens—it is our contention that the creaturely character of Scripture is

---

between form and content runs the risk of externalizing or instrumentalizing the creaturely character of Scripture in the process (ibid., 22).

40. Admittedly, this rehearsal of Chalcedon is pedestrian in nature. That Chalcedon creates as many problems as it resolves remains a topic of theological controversy to this day. See Oliver D. Crisp, "Desiderata for Models of the Hypostatic Union," in *Christology: Ancient and Modern Explorations in Constructive Dogmatics*, ed. Oliver D. Crisp and F. Sanders (Grand Rapids: Zondervan, 2013), 19–41. Robert Wilkin provides an accessible account of the Council of Ephesus in 431 (where Cyril of Alexandria bested his theological rival, Nestorius); Chalcedon in 451; the two subsequent councils it spawned, Constantinople II in 553 and Constantinople III in 680–681; and the monothelite controversy. See Robert Louis Wilkin, *The Spirit of Early Christian Thought* (New Haven: Yale University Press, 2003), chap. 5.

41. John Webster, *The Domain of the Word: Scripture and Theological Reasoning* (London: T&T Clark, 2012), 10.

understood from the governing standpoint of the divine perspective. Such an understanding allows notions of canonical intentionality to broaden beyond the human author's purview to a divine intentionality whose sense comes from thick and cross-associative reading patterns that are so integral to the Christian reading tradition.[42] Put in other terms, the commitment to the theological priority of the Bible's divine source elicits a commitment to divine providence, even when attending to the creaturely character of Scripture.

The Literal Sense and Scripture's Triune Subject Matter

A Christian theological commentary operates with two ontological commitments. We have already engaged one: the Scripture's nature derives from its dogmatic location within God's reconciling movement toward humanity. Such a commitment impinges on our interpretive method as mentioned above. The second commitment rests on the confession that God's triune nature derives from the biblical witness itself. God's triune character is not located developmentally in the fourth century as a later clarifying "extra" in the history of Christian doctrine. While the coming to terms with trinitarian grammar vis-à-vis competing options resides especially in the fourth century, the epistemic and ontological distinctions regarding this subject matter are requisite at this point. The trinitarian precision that Nicaea offers is an extracanonical concept born of Scripture's internal judgments about the unity of God in the plurality of personhood. But the theoepistemic clarity graced on us by the fourth-century trinitarian debates does not mean God was not yet triune.

While such a claim, we imagine, strikes most readers as obviously as the nose on their face, the hermeneutical implications for keeping the epistemic and ontological dimensions of God's triune self-disclosure distinct have not always been clear. God's identity as triune is exactly that: his identity. And his identity as triune undergirds the identity of the one God of the two Testaments, both Old and New. Such is the ontological or metaphysical claim about the identity of the one God of the two Testaments.[43] And this commitment to the triune nature of God both in his work *ad intra* and *ad extra* ("inwardly and outwardly") has hermeneutical significance for the theological commentator.

Karl Barth provides a twentieth-century example of the epistemological significance of trinitarian confession. In his *Church Dogmatics* (IV/1), Barth identifies Jesus Christ as the epistemological principle of Christian belief.

---

42. See O'Keefe and Reno, *Sanctified Vision*; and Michael Graves, *The Inspiration and Interpretation of Scripture: What the Early Church Can Teach Us* (Grand Rapids: Eerdmans, 2014).

43. Neil MacDonald, *Metaphysics and the God of Israel: Systematic Theology of the Old and New Testaments* (Grand Rapids: Brazos, 2007).

Within the context of this insight, Barth wards off the incipient danger of the Christian church to treat Jesus Christ as the source of Christian faith, while at the same time keeping him somewhat removed from the warp and woof of churchly life. He clarifies:

> But the Christian message does say something individual, new and substantial because it speaks concretely, not mythically, because it does not know and proclaim anything side by side with or apart from Jesus Christ, because it knows and proclaims all things only as His things. It does not know and proclaim Him, therefore, merely as the representative and exponent of something other. For it, there is no something other side by side with or apart from Him. For it, there is nothing worthy of mention that is not as such His. Everything that it knows and proclaims as worthy of mention, it does so as His.[44]

The theological force of Barth's comment registers quickly. The hermeneutical significance should follow en suite.

The authorizing presence of Jesus Christ constrains our reading of the biblical text. Paul's affirmation that Jesus Christ "is before all things" (Col. 1:17) has both temporal and theological implications. If there is a prophetic edge to this chapter, it is as follows: the compartmentalization of our exegesis of Scripture from the lordship of Jesus Christ in all spheres runs the very real danger of disobedience. "Christians are Trinitarians," Gerhard Sauter affirms.[45] And our trinitarian confession resides at the center of Christian belief, not merely as a theological lens that clarifies but as retina that allow us to see in the first place.

A detractor to the kind of theological exegesis suggested here might retort as follows: A theological commitment such as you are suggesting stacks the deck in such a way as to render the exegetical task itself superfluous. John Barton's lucid *Modern Biblical Criticism* makes this particular matter one of his three key ingredients of modern criticism: the necessity of bracketing off theological commitments on the front end of the exegetical enterprise. How can the bracketing suggested here aid the interpreter rather than put up a stumbling block to the complex and diverse material the Bible contains?

This question pertains to the *regula fidei* and its relationship to the verbal givenness of the biblical text. Over the past decade much scholarly attention directs itself toward sorting through the nature of the *regula fidei* and its

---

44. Karl Barth, *Church Dogmatics*, trans. G. W. Bromiley (Edinburgh: T&T Clark, 1956), IV/1, 21.

45. Gerhard Sauter, *Protestant Theology at the Crossroads: How to Face the Crucial Tasks for Theology in the Twenty-First Century* (Grand Rapids: Eerdmans, 2007), 38.

hermeneutical significance. Without providing a detailed taxonomy of the various understandings of the Rule of Faith here—narratival, precreedal, and so forth—it is our understanding that the Rule of Faith functions as a shield and not a sword.[46] In other words, the Rule of Faith guards the interpretive enterprise, providing the proper context (*hypothesis*) for reading the Scripture, but it is not the gist of Scripture or a heavy-handed hermeneutical tool.[47] It is difficult to identify a single or stable form of the Rule of Faith in the early church. The probable reason behind the rule's unfixed form resides in this context. The rule, as it pertains to the identity of the one God who is Father, Son, and Holy Spirit, was not intended as a heavy overlay on the biblical text or the theological outcome of the text in condensed form. The "sword" of Christian theology was and remains the exegesis of Scripture itself.

In Irenaeus's oft-repeated image, the rule helps one to put the various tiles of Scripture together so the resultant mosaic is a king and not a fox. This metaphor pertains to the triune identity of God and an understanding of the order (*taxis*) of Scripture. But it does not pertain to a monochromatic biblical reading that dispenses with the task of exegesis itself. Mark Elliott helpfully clarifies the function of the rule and its relation to Scripture in the early church:

> Those who think that "theological interpretation" is salutary for any profit-
> able reading of the Bible often make reference to Irenaeus and other patristic
> exegetes as employing a "rule of faith." However, Irenaeus was in fact more
> concerned that texts did not get distorted by heretical leanings leading to a heavy
> ideological "spin" than he was suggesting, positively, that scripture needed to
> be understood in terms of a creedal statement. . . . The term "regula fidei" as
> such does not appear in Irenaeus, whose motto might more have been: let the
> scriptures speak for themselves.[48]

The rather straightforward claim the rule makes is that in their totality the Scriptures have to do with the one God who is Father, Son, and Holy Spirit. More specifically, the rule insists that readers of Scripture locate Jesus Christ in the very life of God himself, along with the Holy Spirit, who testifies to him:

46. We are consciously borrowing Mark W. Elliott's helpful metaphors on the subject, as in *The Heart of Biblical Theology: Providence Experienced* (Surrey, UK: Ashgate, 2012), 6–7.

47. See Christopher Seitz, *The Character of Christian Scripture: The Significance of a Two-Testament Bible* (Grand Rapids: Baker Academic, 2011), chap. 7.

48. Elliott, *Biblical Theology*, 6–7. Such an understanding of the rule is affirmed by John Behr (*The Way to Nicaea: Formation of Christian Theology* [Crestwood: St. Vladimir's Seminary Press, 2001], 1:35–36) and Christopher R. Seitz (*The Character of Christian Scripture: The Significance of a Two-Testament Canon*, Studies in Theological Interpretation [Grand Rapids: Baker Academic, 2011]).

this Scripture includes the Old Testament.[49] A rather significant disjunctive follows this claim about the rule's function. The rule itself never displaces the actual exegetical engagement with Scripture, nor does it stack the deck when wrestling with the particularities of texts. The rule simply identifies, on the basis of the internal claims of Scripture itself, the identity of the God whose authorizing voice resonates in the totality of the biblical witness.

Barth's clarion call of "exegesis, exegesis, and yet more exegesis" retains its force in this context.[50] The threefold ringing of "exegesis" is Barth's understanding of the theologian's primary role. The Christian tradition from Paul through Irenaeus to Augustine and down the vast haunts of the Christian tradition would in principle agree, and this despite differences in exegetical outcomes. The heart of the Christian theological discipline is the exegesis of Holy Scripture. And such exegesis requires hard work. As B. F. Westcott surmises:

> The Bible does not supersede labour, but by its very form proclaims labour to be fruitful. . . . There is, no doubt, a restless desire in man for some help which may save him from the painful necessity of reflection, comparison, judgment. But the Bible offers no such help. It offers no wisdom to the careless, and no security to the indolent. It awakens, nerves, invigorates, but it makes no promise of ease.[51]

Christian exegesis works within the frame of the triune identity of the one God of the two Testaments alongside a commitment to the verbal character of the text in relation to its triune subject matter. All critical tools are welcome in the establishment of the text's verbal character, but such critical tools are not separated from the singular reading task that takes into account the nature and identity of the one God of the two Testaments.

Conclusion

Theological commentary as a genre operates within the hermeneutical space suggested in this essay. We hope the reader recognizes the constraining and unleashing character of this hermeneutical space. It constrains because exegesis works with ontological commitments regarding the character of the text,

---

49. Seitz, *Character of Christian Scripture*, 198; see his engagement with John Behr in the notes.

50. Eberhard Busch, *Karl Barth: His Life from Letters and Autobiographical Texts*, trans. John Bowden (Grand Rapids: Eerdmans, 1976), 259.

51. Quoted in Rowan Williams, *Anglican Identities* (Lanham, MD: Rowman & Littlefield, 2003), 76.

God's providential ordering of creaturely affairs, and the triune identity of this selfsame God. At the same time, the notion of a theological commentary on offer here unleashes the text's potential because the given verbal character of the text is not hemmed in by the text's compositional history or historical provenance. The text's "canonical intentionality" does not work against the grain of Scripture's verbal profile and its attendant creaturely reality. At the same time, the text's verbal profile is generative and expansive, given the divine Author and the intracanonical conversation Scripture has with itself.

Because this is the case, two concluding factors should be taken into account. First, as the Reformers understood implicitly, no one interpreter (or ecclesial tradition, for that matter) has the corner on the market of the text's theological potential. This outlook tempers our introductory paragraph's basic complaint about the plethora of commentaries on the market. No one commentary can (or should!) be a final period. And as this pertains to theological commentaries that operate in the hermeneutical space laid out herein, may their tribe increase. Second, because the literal sense of Scripture remains ensconced within ontological commitments regarding the character of God, and moreover because Scripture is the speaking voice of God to his church, then the task of exegesis *is* the necessary ongoing activity of the church's theological vocation. Every generation of the faithful both relies on the exegetical labors of the church's past and actively engages in their own exegetical labors for the current moment. All this is done in the hope for God's strange and inviting Word to break forth again in our midst.

12

Theological Interpretation for All of Life

CRAIG G. BARTHOLOMEW
AND MATTHEW Y. EMERSON

We like to think of the Bible as that field in which is hid the pearl of great price, so that while theological interpretation will be sweaty, rigorous, hard work, it will have us emerging time and again in the presence of the living Christ. If we are handling the Word through which God addresses his people, then there ought to be a deeply existential ethos to theological interpretation. In our view there is no antithesis between prayer and the most rigorous exegesis, and these elements will be inseparable in theological interpretation. Thomas Aquinas was exemplary in this respect. When he encountered an obstacle in his work, he would hasten to the altar and pray and cry out to God for illumination, and then return strengthened to his labors. Shortly after his death, one of his secretaries, Reginald of Piperno, commented:

> Always, before he studied or disputed or lectured or wrote or dictated, he would pray from the heart, begging with tears to be shown the truth about the divine

257

things that he had to investigate. . . . And when any difficulty arose, he . . . had recourse to prayer, whereupon the matter would become wonderfully clear to him. Thus, in his soul, intellect and desire somehow contained each other, the two faculties freely serving one another in such a way that each in turn took the lead: his desire, through prayer, gained access to divine realities, which then the intellect, deeply apprehending, drew into a light which kindled to greater intensity the flame of love.[1]

The most rigorous biblical study and the most profound spirituality are allies and ought to be so in theological interpretation.

However, as Dietrich Bonhoeffer would ask: Who is this Jesus for us today,[2] in whose presence we hope to emerge again and again? Acts 3:15 evocatively describes Jesus as "the Author of life," and a theologian friend used to tell Craig that when we gather around Jesus, he stands with his face to his world. The Jesus we will encounter is, as John tells us, the Word become flesh, the incarnate one, but the Word who came to that which is his own, for apart from him, nothing came into existence that has come into existence.

Thus when John tells us that Jesus is "the light of the world," we ought to understand the illumination of Jesus in a comprehensive and cosmic sense. As the *archē* ("point of origin") of the world, it is only natural that by entering the world in human flesh, Jesus would illumine *the whole*. This is not falsely to assert that Scripture provides us with all the answers we need to every question we have, but it is to assert, in Lesslie Newbigin's memorable words, that Christ is *the clue* to all that is.[3] This clue is the key to *all creation*, and it needs to be pursued in all areas of life, with all the rigor we can muster, including in biblical interpretation.

One would therefore expect that it is the norm in biblical interpretation to read the Bible for all of life. Sadly, this is not the case; even amid the welcome renaissance of theological interpretation, it is common to read the Bible for the institutional church or for Christian doctrine, but often without opening up the comprehensive range of Scripture's witness. Brevard Childs identifies failure in this area as a reason for the downfall of the once-vibrant biblical theology movement,[4] but it is a critique that can be leveled against large

1. Kenelm Foster, trans. and ed., *The Life of Saint Thomas Aquinas: Biographical Documents* (London: Longmans, Green, 1959), 70n44.

2. See, e.g., Bonhoeffer's comments in "Letter to Eberhard Bethge, 30 April 1944," in *Letters and Papers from Prison: The Enlarged Edition*, ed. Eberhard Bethge (New York: Touchstone, 1971), 279.

3. Lesslie Newbigin, *The Gospel in a Pluralist Society* (Grand Rapids: Eerdmans, 1989), 103–15.

4. Brevard S. Childs, *Biblical Theology in Crisis* (Philadelphia: Westminster, 1974).

swaths of academic biblical interpretation on both the liberal left and the conservative right.[5]

How, then, do we recover Scripture's comprehensive witness in our theological interpretation?

1. We need to consciously embrace an adequate Christology.

For Christians, Christ is the center of the Bible, the pearl of great price. J. B. Phillips wrote a provocative book titled *Your God Is Too Small*. One fears that in biblical studies, too many Christians work similarly with a diminished Christology. The New Testament is chock-full of christological data that should leave us gasping before a huge view of Jesus, but alas, one suspects that for some readers even the proposal that we ought to enlarge our Christology in order to read the Bible aright will be offensive, such has the secular ethos pervaded biblical studies.

We have already referred to the rich Christology in the Gospel of John. Such references could be multiplied across the New Testament. In terms of the Gospels, we will discuss (below) Jesus as the King who ushers in the kingdom of God/heaven, clearly the main theme of his teaching in the Synoptic Gospels. Jesus's kingdom is comprehensive in scope, and its realm embraces the whole of the creation. We have already referred to one short phrase from Acts of the Apostles, yet that book is full of rich christological data. Likewise, Paul's Epistles yield a rich Christology and not least in books like Ephesians and Colossians. Paul's long sentence in Ephesians 1 concludes in verse 10 by describing God's purpose "to gather up all things in him [Christ], things in heaven and things on earth." Colossians 1:15–20 is a rich text in terms of ecclesiology, but it is crystal clear that the one who is "the head of the body" (1:18) is the same one who is "the firstborn of all creation; for in him all things in heaven and on earth were created, things visible and invisible, whether thrones or dominions or rulers or powers—all things have been created through him and for him. He himself is before all things, and in him all things hold together" (Col. 1:15–17).

In Philemon, that gem of an epistle, such is the transformative power of Christ that the gospel implicitly shatters the institution of slavery. And so we could continue on into the General Epistles. Few books have such an exalted Christology as Hebrews, and in Revelation 11:15 we find that extraordinary proclamation from heaven: "The kingdom of the world has become the kingdom of our Lord and of his Messiah, and he will reign forever and ever."

5. At their worst the liberal left closes down the relevance of the Bible for today, and the conservative right reduces Scripture to a "spiritual" book. Both tendencies prevent us from hearing the comprehensive witness of Scripture.

Amid its diversity of authors and genres, the New Testament bears relentless witness to the Christ as befits its purpose. Thus, as Lesslie Newbigin states, "We go to the Bible to meet Christ, our present and Living Lord."[6] He is indeed the Redeemer, and we are brought to faith in him and baptized into his body by the Spirit, but the one to whom we are brought is Lord of all and everything. In the justly celebrated words of Abraham Kuyper, who understood with crystal clarity the comprehensive range of Christ's lordship and God's sovereignty, "There is not a square inch of the entire creation of which Christ does not say, 'That is mine!'"[7] Similarly, in terms of the relationship between Word and world, Herman Bavinck rightly declares:

> Christ—even now—is prophet, priest, and king; and by his Word and Spirit he persuasively impacts the entire world. Because of him there radiates from everyone who believes in him a renewing and sanctifying influence upon the family, society, state, occupation, business, art, science, and so forth. The spiritual life is meant to refashion the natural and moral life in its full depth and scope according to the laws of God.[8]

Hence we remind ourselves that this Christ's claim to sovereignty includes biblical interpretation. Here too he is the clue that must be pursued. As Jerome says, we should interpret Scripture with the help of the same Spirit who inspired Scripture.[9] In our view it is greatly to the credit of Tom Wright that he has rehabilitated what one might call an Emmaus-road hermeneutic,[10] which helps us to see how we can take seriously the disciples' encounter with Jesus on the road to Emmaus: "Beginning with Moses and all the prophets, he interpreted to them all the things about himself in all the scriptures" (Luke 24:27).

Thus in truly "Pentecostal" biblical interpretation we are led by the Spirit to read Scripture with a view to Christ, and the Christ we find again and again is the one who claims sovereignty over the entire creation. This means that his life and teaching have implications for all of life as he has made it. Therefore, few things are as important in renewing theological interpretation as the recovery of an adequate Christology.

6. Lesslie Newbigin, *The Sending of the Church—Three Bible Studies* (Edinburgh: Church of Scotland Board of World Mission and Unity, 1984), 131.

7. Abraham Kuyper, *Abraham Kuyper: A Centennial Reader*, ed. James D. Bratt (Grand Rapids: Eerdmans, 1998), 488.

8. Herman Bavinck, *Reformed Dogmatics*, vol. 4, *Holy Spirit, Church, and New Creation*, ed. John Bolt, trans. John Vriend (Grand Rapids: Baker Academic, 2008), 437.

9. Jerome, *Epistula* 120, 10, as quoted by Vatican II, *Dei Verbum* §12.

10. See, e.g., N. T. Wright, *The Challenge of Jesus: Rediscovering Who Jesus Was and Is* (Downers Grove, IL: InterVarsity, 1999), 169.

2. We need to recover a full-orbed doctrine of creation.

We have already seen how an adequate Christology backs us into the doctrine of creation.[11] The Word came to that which was his own; without him nothing came into existence that has come into existence. John 1 clearly articulates a doctrine of creation ex nihilo, which is essential for any doctrine of God's sovereignty.

If we are concerned to read the Bible for all of life, then a robust doctrine of creation certainly is of fundamental importance. Sadly, much theology and church life did not perform well in this respect in the past century or so. It is well known that Gerhard von Rad made creation subsidiary to redemption in some of his influential work,[12] and Gordon Spykman has pointed out how too many evangelicals bypass the first article of the Apostles' Creed in their haste to get to the second one, about Jesus.[13] This is fatal because, as we have seen above, it is only in the context of the grand story of Scripture rooted in the doctrine of creation that we are able to grasp the immense significance of Jesus and his salvation.

Fortunately we live amid a good deal of creative work being done to retrieve a biblical doctrine of creation for today. As Paul Ricoeur has observed,[14] one of the most crucial issues facing theology and biblical interpretation is the relationship between redemption and creation.

3. We need to recover the theological and biblical-theological connection between creation and redemption as an overarching heuristic informing our interpretation.

In masterly fashion Colin Gunton uses Irenaeus to good effect for this in his *Christ and Creation*.[15] There are many other nodes in the tradition that lend themselves to such retrieval; one thinks of Maximus the Confessor,[16] the Re-

11. See Craig G. Bartholomew and Bruce Ashford, *The Doctrine of Creation* (Downers Grove, IL: IVP Academic, forthcoming).

12. Gerhard von Rad, "The Theological Problem of the Old Testament Doctrine of Creation," in *The Problem of the Hexateuch and Other Essays* (New York: McGraw-Hill, 1966), 142; idem, *Weltschopfung und Menschenschopfung untersucht bei Deuterojesaja, Hiob und in den Psalmen* (Stuttgart: Calwer, 1974), 174. See Richard J. Clifford, SJ, "The Hebrew Scriptures and the Theology of Creation," *Theological Studies* 46 (1985): 507–23.

13. Gordon J. Spykman, *Reformational Dogmatics: A New Paradigm for Doing Dogmatics* (Grand Rapids: Eerdmans, 1992), 176.

14. Paul Ricoeur, "Thinking Creation," in *Thinking Biblically: Exegetical and Hermeneutical Studies*, Paul Ricoeur and André LaCocque, trans. David Pellauer (Chicago: University of Chicago Press, 1998), 31–70.

15. Colin Gunton, *Christ and Creation* (Eugene, OR: Wipf & Stock, 2005).

16. See Craig G. Bartholomew, *Where Mortals Dwell: A Christian View of Place for Today* (Grand Rapids: Baker Academic, 2011), 202–5.

formers, Dietrich Bonhoeffer, Karl Barth, Jürgen Moltmann, and others. Oliver O'Donovan builds on insights from Galatians to set up the heuristic for his evangelical ethics (*Resurrection and Moral Order*), with resurrection as the reaffirmation of creation.[17] Biblical interpretation needs to find ways to rehabilitate this connection through the inner structure of Scripture itself. Fortunately some of the best theology and biblical exegesis come together at this point. Although there are a plethora of ways in which the infrastructure of Scripture can be foregrounded, in our view two motifs stand out in particular: covenant in the Old Testament and the kingdom of God/heaven in the New Testament.

Years ago Karl Barth anticipated more recent developments in biblical studies with his argument that covenant is the inner aspect of creation.[18] Already he drew attention to the unusual name of God in Genesis 2–3: "Yahweh Elohim."[19] As we learn from Exodus 3 and 6 in particular, Yahweh is quintessentially the name of the *covenant* God of Israel. The juxtaposition of "Yahweh" with "Elohim"—the name used for the Creator God in Genesis 1:1–2:3—alerts readers to the fact that the God of Israel is the Creator God.

Bill Dumbrell has argued, persuasively in our view, that Genesis 1 is the foundational covenantal text in the Bible and that the subsequent Noahic, Sinaitic, and new covenants in particular all build on and refer back to the creation covenant.[20] "Covenant" is a major word for redemption in the Old Testament, and its grounding in creation opens up the link between creation and redemption. Genesis 12:1–3, for example, makes this clear with its fivefold use of some form of the root "bless," in contrast to the fivefold use of "curse" (*'rr*) in Genesis 1–11; through God's covenant with Abraham, God is at work to recover his purpose of blessing for his whole creation. Thus covenant theology helps us to see, as Ola Tjorhøm says, that creation is the "stuff" of redemption.[21]

17. Oliver O'Donovan, *Resurrection and Moral Order*, 2nd ed. (Grand Rapids: Eerdmans, 1994), 13–15.

18. Karl Barth, *Church Dogmatics* (London: T&T Clark, 1958), III/1.

19. Cf. Jean L'Hour, "Yahweh Elohim," *Revue biblique* 81, no. 4 (1974): 525–56.

20. See William Dumbrell, *Covenant and Creation: An Old Testament Covenant Theology*, rev. ed. (Milton Keynes, UK: Paternoster, 2013); Craig G. Bartholomew, "Covenant and Creation: Covenantal Overload or Covenantal Deconstruction," *Calvin Theological Journal* 30, no. 1 (1995): 11–33; Peter J. Gentry and Stephen J. Wellum, *Kingdom through Covenant: A Biblical-Theological Understanding of the Covenants* (Wheaton: Crossway, 2012); and Scott W. Hahn, *Kinship by Covenant: A Canonical Approach to the Fulfillment of God's Saving Promises*, Anchor Yale Bible Reference Library (New Haven: Yale University Press, 2009). For a contrary view see Paul R. Williamson, *Sealed with an Oath: Covenant in God's Unfolding Purpose*, New Studies in Biblical Theology (Downers Grove, IL: InterVarsity, 2007).

21. Ola Tjorhøm, *Embodied Faith: Reflections on a Materialist Spirituality* (Grand Rapids: Eerdmans, 2009), 36.

Historical criticism has been a mixed blessing in terms of foregrounding the link between creation and redemption as evoked by "covenant." Because historical critics see Genesis 1:1–2:4a as by the priestly author, historical criticism has produced a corpus of rich literature excavating the covenantal link between cultus and creation.[22] Embodied in Israel's cultus as a microcosm, we find the order of creation's macrocosm.

However, in recent decades historical critics have argued that covenant was a late development in the religion of Israel, being read back into its earlier history by the Deuteronomistic movement.[23] Scholars such as Brevard Childs have pushed in the direction of seeing this extrapolation as not anachronistic; yet for most historical critics, covenant is late and therefore excluded from being as central to the infrastructure of the Old Testament as we have suggested.

This is one of those tension points between theological interpretation and historical criticism that has major significance for how we read Scripture as a whole. Can we follow the witness of Scripture at this point, or must we practice a delicate holding operation between historical criticism and theological interpretation? This question alerts us to the importance of the "Historical Criticism" section in the Manifesto and the accompanying exposition. Doubtless there are historical issues in biblical interpretation that are complex and best held open in the face of no solution at hand. Covenant is not one of them. Of course, we would need to give an account of the history of covenant in the Old Testament that differs from that of contemporary historical criticism, which we cannot do here and now. Suffice it to state that the validity of the Old Testament's witness depends on covenant as an early institution in Israel; for that and other reasons, we position ourselves on the side that affirms covenant as emerging early in the life of Israel.

If covenant in the Old Testament opens up the creation-redemption nexus, then in the New Testament the prime contender is the kingdom of God/heaven. This is clearly the central theme of Jesus's teaching, according to the Synoptic Gospels, and John has his equivalent terminology for the same reality. As N. T. Wright has explained, kingdom is about the comprehensive reign of Israel's God.[24] "Kingdom" is never defined in the Gospels, but its meaning is assumed from the Old Testament and intertestamental background and evoked in Jesus's life and teaching. The Jewish background makes it unthinkable that

22. See, e.g., F. H. Gorman Jr., *The Ideology of Ritual: Space, Time and Status in the Priestly Theology* (Sheffield: JSOT Press, 1990).

23. See Ernest W. Nicholson, *The Pentateuch in the Twentieth Century: The Legacy of Julius Wellhausen* (Oxford: Clarendon, 1998).

24. N. T. Wright, *Jesus and the Victory of God*, vol. 2 of *Christian Origins and the Question of God* (Minneapolis: Fortress, 1996), 202–26.

kingdom would relate only to the people of God rather than to the whole creation, as it clearly does. Kingdom is about the recovery of God's purposes for his whole creation, with his people as a sign of the coming kingdom.[25]

More than a century ago, an unhelpful development in New Testament studies was the view that "kingdom" evokes only the reign of God and not *the realm* over which he reigns. For a century or so this view has continued to be perpetuated without close attention to the biblical evidence. In our view, and as some scholars have come to recognize, "kingdom" is a multivocal symbol that evokes different aspects of God's reign breaking in through Jesus, one aspect of which is indeed the realm of his kingdom, meaning the entire creation.[26]

Thus the kingdom of God evokes the integral relationship between creation and redemption; recovery of this theme would go a long way toward helping us to recover the infrastructure of the Bible. While it is true that Paul and the other writers of the Epistles do not make substantial use of the language of kingdom, the same eschatology is found throughout the New Testament: time and again the motif of Jesus as King *is* found.

Recovery of covenant and kingdom in this way would sharpen the lens through which we read the Bible and alert us to the creation-wide implications of the biblical text. Not least is this true of Israel as the Old Testament people of God.

4. We need to attend to the life of Israel as an ancient Near Eastern paradigm of human life under God's rule.

Israel is God's covenant people, called to live in the land under his reign, which is to govern every area of their life. The Old Testament narrates the emergence of Israel as a direct fulfillment of God's promises to Abraham. As David Clines has pointed out, the theme of the Pentateuch is the partial fulfillment of God's promises to Abraham: the promises of great numbers of people, of a special relationship with Yahweh, and of the land. Clines also perceptively explains the retrospective relationship this has to God's purposes with his creation.[27] The emergence of Israel is thus a first stage in the fulfillment of the Abrahamic covenant, through which God plans to bless the world.

25. See Newbigin, *Gospel in a Pluralist Society*, 108.
26. See Bartholomew, *Where Mortals Dwell*, 99–101.
27. David J. A. Clines, *The Theme of the Pentateuch*, 2nd ed. (Sheffield: Sheffield Academic Press, 1997).

Brevard Childs alerts us to the importance of taking the *discrete witness* of the Old Testament seriously,[28] and one area in which this is vital is in terms of reading the Bible for all of life. Israel is a nation with all the dimensions of national life. Israel has a politics, and books like Kings and Chronicles focus on that dimension in particular. Israel's law as embodied in Exodus, Leviticus, and Deuteronomy, which in particular is quite comprehensive, deals with a broad range of facets of human life. The prophets call Israel to account for disobedience in all aspects of life and not just the religious. Or put otherwise, the religious dimension manifests itself for Israel in every aspect of its life: cultic, political, economic, familial, and so forth. Old Testament wisdom is rooted in the doctrine of creation and is comprehensive in its quest for living effectively. Thus Ecclesiastes, in its quest for meaning in life "under the sun," probes pleasure, sex, music, agriculture and horticulture, architecture, work, justice, trade, government, oppression, the cultus, and so forth. What is often not noticed is that if Qoheleth ("the Teacher") finds resolution to his quest, as we think he does,[29] then *all the areas of life* he explores become meaningful. In terms of wisdom's holistic vision, Proverbs 31 is extraordinary in depicting the valiant woman and exploring how her fear of the Lord manifests itself in family life, charity, buying a field and planting a vineyard, trading in high-quality fabrics, and so on.

This *materiality* of the life of Israel must never be lost sight of: we make a major error if we spiritualize it in order to read it christocentrically. Work such as Ellen F. Davis's *Scripture, Culture, and Agriculture*[30] is a rich example in this respect, opening a highly creative and fruitful dialogue among the new agrarians, Wendell Berry in particular,[31] and the Old Testament. Jewish work on the Hebrew Bible remains important and stands out in its engagement with the public dimensions of faith. The Old Testament *is* fulfilled in Christ, but it is *the Old Testament* that is fulfilled in Christ as prophet, priest, king, and sage; hence comes the importance of taking the discrete witness of the Old Testament with utmost seriousness.

28. See, e.g., Brevard S. Childs, *Biblical Theology of the Old and New Testaments: Theological Reflection on the Christian Bible* (Minneapolis: Fortress, 1992), 95–106.

29. See Craig G. Bartholomew, *Reading Ecclesiastes: Old Testament Exegesis and Hermeneutical Theory*, Analecta biblica 139 (Rome: Pontifical Biblical Institute, 1998); idem, *Ecclesiastes*, ed. Tremper Longman III, Baker Commentary on the Old Testament Wisdom and Psalms (Grand Rapids: Baker Academic, 2009).

30. Ellen F. Davis, *Scripture, Culture, and Agriculture: An Agrarian Reading of the Bible* (Cambridge: Cambridge University Press, 2008).

31. See, e.g., Wendell Berry, *The Art of the Commonplace: The Agrarian Essays of Wendell Berry*, ed. Norman Wirzba (Washington, DC: Counterpoint, 2003); idem, *Bringing It to the Table: On Farming and Food* (Washington, DC: Counterpoint, 2009).

As a paradigm of life under God's rule, Israel (the Old Testament) remains normative for Christians today.[32] Two mistakes are often made in this respect. Because the Old Testament is fulfilled in Christ and practices such as sacrifice have become redundant, some Christians think that torah is now of no relevance to Christians. They thereby adopt what Oliver O'Donovan calls an *apophatic hermeneutic*. At the other extreme we find the American reconstructionists who rightly discern the comprehensiveness and ongoing relevance of the Old Testament for life today but ossify God's revelation to Israel as though we can directly translate it into twenty-first-century life. This is an extreme version of what O'Donovan calls a *cataphatic hermeneutic*.[33] Neither approach is helpful or acceptable. The Old Testament *does* provide us with a paradigm of life under God's rule, but it is an ancient Near Eastern historically situated paradigm, one in which Israel is a theocracy. The church remains a theocracy but is now scattered amid the nations and thus operates in pluralistic cultures that are not theocracies.

How then do we read the Old Testament for today in all its comprehensiveness? To do this, we find N. T. Wright's[34] and Craig Bartholomew and Michael Goheen's[35] dramatic approach to the authority of Scripture helpful. If we think of the story of Scripture as a drama in six acts, then we are in act 5, which is continuous with but different from the earlier acts. In act 5 we are, however, called to use all the clues we can find in the earlier acts to work out *responsibly* how to live today and how to relate the Gospel to all of life in our pluralistic contexts. Indeed, we argue that this is precisely what the New Testament authors are already doing.

A good example in this respect is *pilgrimage*. In ancient Israel, pilgrimage to Jerusalem was mandatory. Three times a year Israelites were called to leave their villages and towns and go on pilgrimage to Jerusalem. The Psalms of Ascent (120–34) function in this respect as something of a hymnal for pilgrims. Pilgrimage marked a break in the rhythm of life, a time-out for Israelites to reimmerse their lives in the grand story of which they were part. Refreshed, Israelites were to return to their day-to-day lives, where they were to embody

---

32. See Christopher J. H. Wright's important work in this respect: *Old Testament Ethics for the People of God* (Downers Grove, IL: IVP Academic, 2011).

33. Oliver O'Donovan, "The Loss of a Sense of Place," *Irish Theological Quarterly* 55 (1989): 39–58. Apophatic and cataphatic hermeneutics are two opposite ways of explaining the relationship between the testaments. The former focuses on the negative, seeing discontinuity at virtually every turn, while the latter focuses on radical continuity.

34. N. T. Wright, *The New Testament and the People of God*, vol. 1 of *Christian Origins and the Question of God* (Minneapolis: Fortress, 1992), 121–44.

35. Craig G. Bartholomew and Michael W. Goheen, *The Drama of Scripture: Finding Our Place in the Biblical Story*, 2nd ed. (Grand Rapids: Baker Academic, 2014).

the story of which they were a part. Such ritual was deeply meaningful and an integral part of the life of God's Old Testament people. Repeatedly the rituals called them back to be who they truly were by God's calling.

Although there are examples of pilgrimage in the New Testament, in the light of the Christ event the status of Jerusalem has clearly changed, and pilgrimage is no longer mandatory. Is there nothing, then, that Christians can and should learn from its practice? There are in fact important lessons at stake here. One is the importance of ritual for embedding our most important values in our lives. All cultures and religions and all Christians have some forms of ritual, even if many imagine that they are reacting against all ritual. One of the needs of our day is the creation of healthy, rich rituals that embody, for the church and our cultures, the values we need to cherish in order to flourish. We ignore these at our peril.

But what of pilgrimage itself? In the West we live amid a decline in church attendance and a growth in pilgrimage to destinations such as Santiago de Compostela. What are we to make of this? In our speed-driven cultures, there is surely value in taking time out from our hectic lives and walking at a leisurely pace to a significant destination, giving ourselves time to recenter our lives in the grand story of which we are a part. Pilgrimage thus remains valuable; we agree with Eugene Peterson in positioning it in the arsenal of tools for spiritual formation, yet without making it mandatory, as in the Old Testament.[36]

Many are able to see how the Old Testament is comprehensive in its vision for life but balk at this when they come to the New Testament. In our view the New Testament, rather than reducing the comprehensive Old Testament vision to church life, universalizes it to the life of the people of God now spread among all nations.

5. We need to recognize that the New Testament does not lose the holistic vision of the Old Testament but universalizes it.

In the New Testament the life of God's people shifts from an ethnically centered, geopolitical, ancient Near Eastern nation to a transnational, transgeographical ecclesia ("assembly, church"). This shift in both the makeup and location of God's people has serious implications for how the Christian community appropriates the Old Testament's holistic vision for life under God's reign, and therefore for how theological interpretation can be for all of life. But while the Old Testament and New Testament are in some ways

36. On this subject see Craig G. Bartholomew and Fred Hughes, eds., *Towards a Christian Theology of Pilgrimage* (Aldershot, UK: Ashgate, 2004).

distinct in their articulations of covenant living, they are consistent in their message that citizenship under the reign of God encompasses every aspect of life. Thus from a New Testament perspective theological interpretation for all of life will be a formative task, transforming the reader into the image of Christ so that they can live as Spirit-filled, restored, kingdom citizens in every sphere of life. With this overarching purpose in mind, there are at least two basic contours to the New Testament that help Christians to think about how biblical interpretation can impact them holistically.

The first of these contours is the dramatic change from the old covenant to the new covenant. In the most important sense, of course, the Old and New Testaments are of one accord with regard to the significance of Yahweh's reign and restoration. The new covenant is the reversal of the curse of Adam, the restoration of creation and Adam's task through the Abrahamic covenant, and the judgment and defeat of sin and evil through the Messiah Jesus. Jesus's life, death, resurrection, ascension, and sending of the Spirit all inaugurate the fulfillment of Israel's hopes and expectations for the forgiveness of sin, the restoration of creation, and the defeat of God's enemies.[37] In the Gospels and Acts, Jesus inaugurates the messianic restorative kingdom reign hoped for by Israel in the Old Testament.[38]

But because Christ's advent is for the whole world, both Jew and gentile, it necessarily expands the scope of these accomplishments beyond geopolitical Israel.[39] The people of God are now a global and transnational people, and this transforms how they are to interact with the world and operate as a community. No longer are they defined by being "in the law," but now they are defined by being "in Christ" (e.g., Gal. 3:23–29). No longer do they obey according to the flesh; now all of God's people are given his Spirit so that they might be transformed into the image of Christ Jesus (Rom. 7:1–8:11). Further, Christ is the community boundary marker, not circumcision, food laws, or Sabbath laws.[40] As G. K. Beale explains, "Because Jesus is restoring not only Israel but also all of creation, including gentiles (Matt. 15:21–28; 21:40–44), the true people of God can no longer be marked out by certain nationalistic badges that distinguish one nation from another."[41]

37. In other words, "Jesus' mission was holistic," addressing all aspects of people's lives, declares Samuel Escobar in *The New Global Mission: The Gospel from Everywhere to Everyone* (Downers Grove, IL: IVP Academic, 2003), 143.

38. See, e.g., G. K. Beale, *A New Testament Biblical Theology: The Unfolding of the Old Testament in the New* (Grand Rapids: Baker Academic, 2011), 129–84.

39. Certainly we see universalizing missional tendencies in the Old Testament, but the global purposes of God do not come to full fruition until Christ's coming in the New Testament.

40. N. T. Wright, *Jesus and the Victory of God*, 369–442.

41. Beale, *New Testament Biblical Theology*, 424.

Many of the Mosaic prescriptions related to everyday living, or "all of life," are therefore now universalized for the global church. Ethics is a matter of being fruitful in the Spirit; while the Old Testament law certainly reflects the created order, New Testament life is no longer a matter of obeying culturally specific precepts. This is not to claim that the New Testament says nothing of life's particulars; indeed, Jesus, Paul, and the other apostolic writers have much to teach both for and against specific actions, and for how to journey through life *coram deo* ("in the presence of God"). But rather than doing so mostly in ethnically particular ways, the New Testament authors demonstrate how God's created order is to be reflected in the lives of both Jew and gentile as citizens of Christ's global kingdom.[42] Because of this universalization of God's people and therefore the ways in which they are to live before him, theological interpretation for all of life must take into account the provisional nature of any talk about how the biblical data forms or shapes individuals in areas on which the Bible is relatively quiet.

The second important contour of the New Testament that impacts holistic theological interpretation is its inherent already-and-not-yet structure.[43] Because Christ has inaugurated but not yet consummated the salvation of his people and the restoration of creation, theological interpretation for all of life will necessarily be joyful but not preemptively triumphant. The transformation of the individual, of God's people, and of creation is inaugurated in Christ's first coming but not yet consummated, not until his return. This eschatological tension is perhaps best seen in the depiction of the saints in Revelation. Although they are conquerors in Christ, redeemed by the blood of the Lamb and sealed by his Spirit, they are still led to slaughter all the day long, tested in their faith, and martyred by the dragon's servants. Living as new creations in Christ during the church age is therefore always a life of tension, never one of pure surrender or ultimate triumph.[44] That tension, reflected in the shape of the canon and of Christ's work, ought also to be reflected in our discussion of how theological interpretation affects all of life.

42. In the words of Oliver O'Donovan, reading Scripture and understanding its moral demands gives believers a "frame of reference" for the obedient life in every situation and does so in the universalizing narrative context of Jesus's "fulfillment of history and the redemption of the world." See his essay "The Moral Authority of Scripture," in *Scripture's Doctrine and Theology's Bible: How the New Testament Shapes Christian Dogmatics*, ed. Markus Bockmuehl and Alan J. Torrance (Grand Rapids: Baker Academic, 2008), 170, 173.

43. See, e.g., Hermann Ridderbos, *Paul: An Outline of His Theology*, trans. John Richard de Witt (1975; reprint, Grand Rapids: Eerdmans, 1997), 44–53; Gordon Spykman, *Reformational Theology: A New Paradigm for Doing Dogmatics* (Grand Rapids: Eerdmans, 1992), 524–27.

44. Cf. Scott W. Sunquist, *Understanding Christian Mission: Participation in Suffering and Glory* (Grand Rapids: Baker Academic, 2013).

With these contours in place, theological interpretation ought to bear significantly on the formation and practice of believers outside the corporate gathering of Christ's body. While the Bible is not, as many might put it, a "handbook for life," it certainly shapes and forms Christians to live fruitfully in the Spirit in every aspect of their lives. This Spirit-led life is the goal of biblical interpretation, and it is a life that is defined by participation in Christ and in his restorative work. Christ's renewal of creation includes a restoration of Adam's tasks through his work and by the church's union with him. Christ, in his life, death, resurrection, ascension, and Pentecost, restores what Adam lost—not only dwelling with God, but also doing the tasks for which he was created. Being God's image bearers meant for Adam and Eve that they were to be fruitful and multiply, exercise dominion, cultivate creation, and obey God's word. They failed at obedience and dominion and thus lost the ability to bear fruit and cultivate, as was intended. The promise of the Abrahamic covenant and its fulfillment in Christ restores these tasks. Christ, of course, is the Author and perfecter of believers; he alone is obedient, he alone bears fruit, he alone restores creation, he alone rules supremely with the Father. But by being in Christ and empowered by his Spirit, the church also participates with him in these tasks, as part of the *missio Dei*.

The most obvious participatory element is the church's role as the vehicle through which Christ is fruitful and multiplies, not now through physical procreation but through the verbal proclamation of the gospel (Acts 6:7; 12:24; 19:20).[45] In addition to evangelistically bearing fruit, the church also rules now with Christ, as they too have been seated in the heavenly places with him above all rulers and authorities (Eph. 1:20–22; 2:6). Christ has also given the church his Spirit so that they might, unlike Adam, obey (Acts 2). Finally, while believers and unbelievers can care for creation (and procreate), believers are the only ones who can do so with the proper motivation and spirit. Thus in Christ's redemptive, restorative, and reigning work, he brings his church into participation with him in these tasks, tasks that impact all of life and are done for the Father's glory and in the power of the Spirit.[46]

This brings us to the New Testament authors' vision of all of life: it is life in the Spirit. The New Testament does not articulate directives or processes

---

45. G. K. Beale, *The Temple and the Church's Mission: A Biblical Theology of the Dwelling Place of God* (Downers Grove, IL: InterVarsity, 2004), 266; Matthew Y. Emerson, *Christ and the New Creation: A Canonical Approach to the Theology of the New Testament* (Eugene, OR: Wipf & Stock, 2013), 62.

46. Thus these tasks work together: good works and godly lives contribute to Christian testimony and mission as believers live beautiful lives and serve as "salt and light." See John Dickson, *The Best Kept Secret of Christian Mission: Promoting the Gospel with More Than Our Lips* (Grand Rapids: Zondervan, 2010), 85–110.

for how to daily operate a business in a Christian manner. For instance, there are no instructions on the placement of cash registers in a grocery store or the organization of a board of directors. What the New Testament provides for all of life is, rather, an orientation, a formation of the individual as part of the body of Christ.[47] This orientation can be summed up as "Do everything for the glory of God" (1 Cor. 10:31), do all by the Christ-shaping Spirit, and do all so that they will know you by your love for one another (cf. John 13:35). What distinguishes Christian and non-Christian art, then, is not the lines drawn or the colors used but the telos, spirit, and love in which it is done.

For the New Testament, in other words, "all of life" is primarily about *aims* and *loves*. The redeemed and renewed citizen of the kingdom of Christ is marked off, in every area of life, by his motivations and his affections. Do believers love God with all their mind, soul, body, and strength, and do they love their neighbors as themselves? In the case of neighbor love, the New Testament radically redefines what this means. Jesus hyperbolically calls believers to hate their family in comparison to their love for him (Luke 14:26); Paul turns slavery on its head through the gospel in Philemon; and neighbor love is consistently called for in believers' care for the downtrodden of society (e.g., James 1:27). Right love is a distinguishing mark for "all of life" in the New Testament. The other distinguishing mark is right aims. Is the direction of their actions toward God's glory or for their own gratification? There is thus an antithesis that cuts through every area of life, demarcating God-loving, neighbor-loving, and God-glorifying actions from selfish, idolatrous, and sinful actions.[48]

Additionally, this antithesis runs not only through individual actions, habits, and dispositions, but also through societal structures.[49] Jesus's and the apostles' call to, like Israel, work against the oppression of the poor is not some ad hoc deontological ethic but inherent to the redeemed nature of the church. One cannot help but notice the consistent message on helping the poor and downtrodden throughout the New Testament, from Jesus (e.g., Matt. 5:42) to Paul's call for the assistance of needy churches (Rom. 15:26; 1 Cor. 16:1–4; 2 Cor. 9:1–5), to James's statement on true religion (James 1:27). Paul and Peter's teachings on the family and relationships are also shaped by the gospel. Although all families of the first century would have shared common

47. A. K. M. Adam, "Poaching on Zion: Biblical Theology as Signifying Practice," in *Reading Scripture with the Church: Toward a Hermeneutic of Theological Interpretation*, by A. K. M. Adam et al. (Grand Rapids: Baker Academic, 2006), 33.

48. Al Wolters, *Creation Regained: Biblical Basics for a Reformational Worldview*, 2nd ed. (Grand Rapids: Eerdmans, 2005), 69–86.

49. Ibid., 87–89.

characteristics, the gospel motivation and shape of the family in Ephesians 5:22–6:9 and 1 Peter 3:1–7 are distinctly Christian and subversive. There is likewise a consistent rebuke of economic, political, and social oppression, seen most notably in Paul's gospel-oriented undermining of slavery in Philemon and the downfall of the Babylonian harlot in Revelation 17–18. Although Christians certainly ought to be careful about discussing particular political positions and their relationship to biblical warrant, we ought also not shy away from how, in the New Testament, societal structures and individual relationships alike are impacted by Christ's reign and the example of his sacrificial love.

6. Churches thus need to sound the kingdom note so that believers hear the call to live under the reign of God in all spheres of life.

As mentioned in the Manifesto's section on "Hermeneutics and Philosophy," the New Testament is prescriptive in some areas of life; yet in many areas of modern life, it is not immediately clear what the obedience of faith looks like. With Herman Bavinck, we ought to affirm that although Scripture is not a manual for the sciences, "precisely as the book of the knowledge of God, Scripture has much to say also to the other sciences. It is a light on our path and a lamp for our feet, also with respect to science and art."[50] Indeed, "the authority of Scripture extends to the whole person and over all humankind. . . . Its authority, being divine, is absolute."[51] Bavinck develops a wonderfully nuanced view of biblical apologetics, declaring (inter alia) that "the Christian worldview alone is the one that fits the reality of the world and of life."[52] However, discerning obedience in such fields as politics, economics, business, science, and education requires the hard work of study, observation, and practice as one seeks God's ways in God's world today, all within the context of the orienting worldview provided by Scripture.

In the institutional church, it is important to recognize that all God's people are in holy orders. *Full-time service* is a description of every Christian and not just of pastors and missionaries. What then is the role of the pastor/priest in this context? Amid the full-time servants of God, we set aside gifted individuals to devote themselves to prayer and the Word. The unique role of the pastor is to keep God's people attentive to God and to remind them again and again of the grand story of which they are a part, so that when we leave church, as

50. Herman Bavinck, *Reformed Dogmatics*, vol. 1, *Prolegomena*, trans. John Vriend (Grand Rapids: Baker Academic, 2003), 445.
51. Ibid., 465.
52. Ibid., 515.

it were, another week of worship begins (cf. Rom. 12:1–2). The preacher's role is thus to sound the kingdom note again and again, calling God's people to live every aspect of their lives under God's reign. We cannot and should not expect the pastor to be an expert in what such obedience looks like in all spheres of life. The church has always become enmeshed in trouble when it has tried to prescribe for and govern life in this detailed way. Educators, for example, need to gather together to work out what the obedience of faith means for them today. So too with health practitioners, homemakers, business people, the unemployed, street cleaners, *and biblical scholars*.

An area where the church, biblical scholars, theologians, and other Christian academics ought to work together is in developing *cultural analysis*. John Stott describes how liberals tend to hurl their sermonic missiles right into the contemporary world, but one never knows where the missile came from. Evangelicals, by comparison, launch their sermonic missiles from Scripture but aim at nowhere in particular.[53] What we need is *biblical* preaching and theological interpretation *contextualized* in relation to our cultures today. Such communication will require a sense of what time it is today in our cultures; this, if it is not to be superficial, we will need to learn from deep cultural analysis, or what is commonly called *public theology*.

Our Manifesto was not mandated by a church or churches but is an initiative of biblical scholars to work out what biblical interpretation might look like as an expression of the obedience of faith. Perhaps this is as it should be. Ours is a high calling, with immense implications for the life of the church and the world. If we take seriously ecclesial reception of the Word as primary, then biblical scholars have a vital role in deepening and strengthening that reception. In this context biblical scholars must work together with all the rigor and creativity we can muster, with the goal of reading Scripture to hear God's address. Fewer and fewer of us are trained for such work; this situation justifies the need for a Manifesto to call us and our institutions in this direction.

---

53. John R. Stott, *I Believe in Preaching* (London: Hodder & Stoughton, 1982).

Contributors

Craig G. Bartholomew is the H. Evan Runner Professor of Philosophy and professor of religion and theology at Redeemer University College. He is also the Dean for St. George's Centre for Biblical and Public Theology. He has directed the Scripture and Hermeneutics Seminar since its inception. He is the author of many books and deeply committed to theological interpretation.

David J. H. Beldman is an assistant professor of religion and theology at Redeemer University College. He is a coeditor of and a contributor to *Hearing the Old Testament: Listening for God's Address* (Eerdmans, 2012) and, among other projects, is writing a commentary on the book of Judges for the Two Horizons Old Testament Commentary Series published by Eerdmans.

Stephen G. Dempster is a professor of religious studies at Crandall University. His research and publishing interests are in the areas of Old Testament, biblical theology, and the canon. He is passionate about the theological interpretation of Scripture.

Matthew Y. Emerson is Dickinson Assistant Professor of Religion at Oklahoma Baptist University and a committee member for the Scripture and Hermeneutics Seminar. He is the author of *Christ and the New Creation: A Canonical Approach to the Theology of the New Testament* (Wipf & Stock, 2013) and has published a number of articles exploring theological interpretation of both Testaments.

Denis Farkasfalvy is a Roman Catholic priest and a Cistercian monk in Irving, Texas. He is a native of Hungary and studied in Rome; his dissertation, published in French in 1964, treated the theology of biblical inspiration in the works of Saint Bernard. After having obtained a master of science degree in mathematics in 1965, he taught mathematics in the Cistercian Preparatory School in Irving and theology at the University of Dallas. For twenty-four years he was abbot of the Cistercian monastery Our Lady of Dallas. He served under popes John Paul II and Benedict XVI on the Pontifical Biblical Commission (2005–2014). His latest publication, *Inspiration and Interpretation*, was published in 2012 by Catholic University of America Press.

Mark Gignilliat is associate professor of divinity at Beeson Divinity School, Samford University. He also serves as canon theologian at the Cathedral Church of the Advent in Birmingham, Alabama. He is most recently the author of *A Brief History of Old Testament Criticism: From Spinoza to Childs.*

Michael W. Goheen is director of theological education and scholar-in-residence at the Missional Training Center in Phoenix. He is also a professor of theology and mission at Redeemer Seminary in Dallas. His most recent books are *A Light to the Nations* (Baker Academic) and *Introducing Christian Mission Today* (InterVarsity Press).

Robert (Robby) Holt Jr. is a Presbyterian pastor practicing theological interpretation with a church (North Shore Fellowship) in a place (Chattanooga, Tennessee). By some profound mystery his wife (Chrissy) likes him . . . most of the time.

William P. Olhausen is an Anglican minister in the diocese of Dublin, Ireland. He is also theological adviser to the archbishop of Dublin and chair of the Biblical Association for the Church of Ireland. He has a doctorate in hermeneutics and has been a participant in the Scripture and Hermeneutics Seminar since 2000.

Angus Paddison is reader in theology in the Department of Theology, Philosophy, and Religion, University of Winchester, United Kingdom. He is the author and editor of a number of books committed to advancing and understanding theological interpretation of Scripture. Lately, his work is focused on understanding Scripture's relationship to public theology.

Jonathan T. Pennington holds a PhD from the University of St. Andrews and is associate professor of New Testament Interpretation and director of research doctoral studies at the Southern Baptist Theological Seminary in Louisville. He is the author of several articles and books including *Heaven and Earth in the Gospel of Matthew* (Brill; Baker Academic) and *Reading the Gospels Wisely* (Baker Academic). He is currently writing a book on the Sermon on the Mount and human flourishing and the Pillar Commentary on the Gospel of Matthew.

Murray Rae is professor of theology at the University of Otago in New Zealand. Alongside theological interpretation of Scripture, his research interests include the work of Søren Kierkegaard, theology and architecture, and Maori engagements with Christianity. He is series editor of the Journal of Theological Interpretation Supplement Series.

Aubrey Spears is the rector of the Church of the Incarnation in Harrisonburg, Virginia, and is fellow in practical theology at St. George's Centre for Biblical and Public Theology in Ontario, Canada. He is currently writing a commentary on Esther for the Two Horizons Old Testament Commentary Series (Eerdmans). His book on hermeneutics, application, and preaching is forthcoming from Wipf & Stock.

Jonathan Swales is a tutor in biblical theology at Saint Barnabas Theological Centre in the north of England and is also a pioneer priest in the Church of England, where he heads up Lighthouse, a church for those on the margins due to poverty, addiction, and homelessness. He is married with four children and has a keen interest in the Gospel of Mark, Second Temple Judaism, and the relationship between worldview and a life of passionate discipleship.

Heath A. Thomas is dean of the Herschel H. Hobbs College of Theology and Ministry and professor of Old Testament at Oklahoma Baptist University. He also serves as fellow in Old Testament Studies at St. George's Centre for Biblical and Public Theology in Canada. He is the author of a number of works on theological interpretation of Scripture, Lamentations, and the Minor Prophets and is chair of the Scripture and Hermeneutics Seminar.

Michael D. Williams is professor of systematic theology at Covenant Theological Seminary. Dr. Williams has written particularly in the areas of the nature of theology and theological method as well as history. His publications include *This World Is Not My Home: The Origins and Development of Dispensationalism*, *Why I Am Not an Arminian* (with colleague Robert A. Peterson), and *Far as the Curse Is Found: The Covenant Story of Redemption*.

Christopher J. H. Wright is international ministries director of Langham Partnership, which continues the vision of John Stott for strengthening the ministry of the Bible in the majority world church. He taught Old Testament in India and then at All Nations Christian College, United Kingdom. He has written books on the Old Testament, ethics and mission, and is committed to missional interpretation of the whole Bible.

Scripture Index

Old Testament

Genesis

1 75
1–2 225
1–11 219, 262
1:1 94
1:1–2:3 262
1:1–2:4a 263
1:2–3 147
1:3 12, 13, 143, 148, 248
1:8 225
1:22–28 176
1:26–28 76n14
2–3 262
2:15 92
3:21 142n39
6:1–7 141
6:5–6 227
8:20–22 141
11:8 227
12 181
12:1–3 73, 73n5, 176–78, 262
12:2–3 58, 176
12:3 95, 177
12:3d 177n12
12:4 102
13:14–17 181
15:6 76, 141n35, 157n18
15:7–21 181
17:5 177
18:18–19 179
21:6 225
22:13 225
22:17–18 163n32
26:5 141n35
36:24 140

Exodus

1–18 177, 180
3 262
6 262
7:20 103
12:46 160
16:6 8
19 180
19–23 19, 208
19:1–23:33 93n94
19:3–6 58, 176–78
19:4 177
19:5 177
19:5–6 58
19:6 177
20–23 180
20–24 72n2
24:1–18 93n94
25–40 180
31:18 93n94
33:11 198
34:5–6 143

Leviticus

1:1 72n2
1:2a 93n94

Numbers

6:22–27 93n94, 182
9:12 160

Deuteronomy

4:5–8 180
4:6–8 180
4:9–14 93n94
4:15–31 180
5:1–6 93n94
5:16 157n18
5:26 199
6:3–5 93n94
6:4 179
6:4–9 6, 80, 81, 140
6:5 80
6:6 80
6:6–9 80
8:3 13, 134, 148, 230
24 141
25:4 163n32

Joshua

1:8–9 13, 148

1 Samuel

3:9 13, 148
3:10 197

2 Samuel

5–8 181n25
7:11–16 181

1 Kings

19 19, 208

Psalms

1 90n88
1:1–2 148
1:2–3 13
19 73n3, 140n34
19:1–4 51
22 158
22:1 158
22:7 158
22:18 158
22:22 73n3
25:4–5 107
34:20 160, 161
36:9 134
40:6b 90n87
46:10 86
61:12 225
67 182
69:9 77
72:7 181
72:17 181
88 148
96 73n6, 179
98 73n6
104:31 234
119 90n88
120–34 266
131:1 87n63
131:2 87n63
151 139n29

Proverbs

1:7 11
31 265

Ecclesiastes

5:1 86
5:1–3 87
12:12a 237

Song of Songs

1:2 142n43
2:10–13 93

Isaiah

2:1–5 142
2:2–5 185
5:1–7 140
19:23–25 183

40–55 163
40:1–11 163
40:3 164
40:3–5 161, 163n33
40:6–8 163n32
41:17–20 161, 163n33
42:6 163n34, 186
42:1–4 163n34
42:1–9 73, 73n5
42:14–16 161, 163n33
42:18–22 163n34
43:1–3 161, 163n33
43:9–13 179
43:14–21 161, 163n33
44:6–20 179
44:28 163
45:1–13 163
45:9 163n34
46:12 163n34
48:20–21 161, 163n33
49:1–7 73n5
49:8 163n34, 186
49:8–12 161, 163n33
50 90
50:4–9 91
50:5 91
50:7 91n89
51:9–10 161, 163n33
52:11–12 161, 163n33
53:12 91n91
55 72n2, 73n6
55:11 33
55:12–13 161, 163n33
56:3–8 73n5
60 148
60:3 186
65:17 162
66:22 162

Jeremiah

4:1–3 180
23:16 61
31 205

Ezekiel

2–3 33
5:5 181
36:16–21 182
36:22–23 183
36:24–27 183

Hosea

6:1–3 140
11:1 160n29

Jonah

4:2 143

Micah

2:6–7a 143
5:2 159
6:1–8 140
7:12 186

Habakkuk

2:20 86n59

Zechariah

8:13 183

New Testament

Matthew

1 202
1:1 144
1:3 144n48
1:5 144n48
1:17 145
1:18 144n48
1:21 145
1:22 157n18
1:23 145
2:5 157n18
2:5–6 159
2:15 157n18, 160n29
3:3 160n27
4:4 66, 230
4:12–16 160n27
4:17 233
5:2 231, 231n11
5:14–16 185
5:42 271
5:48 234
6:9–13 235
7:12 218
8:11 228
8:16–17 160n27
8:17 157n18
10:5–6 184

11:10 157n18
12:17 157n18
12:17–21 160n27
13:35 157n18
15:21–28 268
15:24 184
16:15 216n56
16:17 108
16:18 221
19:1–10 141
19:28 64, 165
21:4 157n18
21:25 61
21:40–44 268
22:36–40 233
22:40 218
23:23 140
24:14 73n5
28:6–7 30
28:16–20 186
28:18–20 73, 73n5, 79, 168, 222
28:19–20 221, 228

Mark

1:1 14
1:1–4 164
1:2 157n18
1:10–11 168
1:14–15 183
1:15 163, 233n14
3:32–35 136
4:3–20 72n1
4:26–34 72n1
9:10 221n2
10:45 92
12:29–31 233
15:24 158
15:29 158
15:34 158

Luke

1:1 95
1:1–3 147
2:29–32 146
2:34 187
2:39–52 91
2:51 91
3:1–4:13 91
3:4 157n18
4:14–22:38 91

4:17–21 160n27
9:51 91n89
10:26–28 233
10:39 13, 148
11:2–4 235
12:35–40 91n92
12:37 91, 92
13:29 228
14:26 271
16:15 218–19
21:22 157n18
22:14–20 91
22:37 91n91
22:39–23:56 91
24 19, 74n7, 91, 208
24:13–53 146
24:18 108
24:25–27 8, 52, 73n7
24:27 40, 162, 229, 260
24:44 52, 91, 219n1
24:44–45 229
24:44–46 73n7
24:44–48 73n5
24:44–49 73n7, 91
24:45–47 58, 172
24:45–49 186
24:46 52, 185, 221n2
24:46–47 73n7
24:46–49 147
24:47 186
24:47–48 186
24:50–53 91

John

1 202, 261
1:1 105
1:14 143
1:29 185
1:45 219
3:14 161
4:14 161
5:19 103
5:19–29 168
5:39 32, 52
5:39–40 40
10:16 186
12:14 157n18
12:16 106
12:32 161, 232
13:1–20 92
13:35 271

14 77n17
14:16 60
14:26 70
15:14–15 198
15:26–27 60, 66, 70
16 77n17
16:12–15 8, 108
16:13–15 60, 70, 168
19:14 161
19:24 157n18
19:28 157n18
19:36 160
20:19–23 186
20:31 147
21 19, 208
21:21–23 105

Acts

1:1 186
1:2 222
1:6–7 186
1:6–8 73n5
1:8 186, 188, 222
1:16 66
2 270
2:15–21 160n27
2:17 163
2:42 72n1, 187
2:43–47 187
3:15 24, 258
3:21 64, 165
4:4 72n1
4:8 103
4:32–35 187
6:7 72n1, 270
7:2–53 165
7:42 66
8:4 72n1
8:25 72n1
8:31–35 160n27
9:1–19 102
10:41–42 66
11:27–30 187n40
12:24 72n1, 270
13 187n40
13:1–3 187
13:44–49 72n1
14:10 221n2
14:17 51
15 188
15:7 72n1

17:3 221n2
17:24 161
19:1–7 146
19:20 72n1, 270
20:27 12
20:32 18, 206
27:15 60
27:17 60
28:22–31 72n1

Romans

1:1–6 72n1, 73n5
1:5 188n40
1:7 74n12
1:8 74n9
1:16 61
1:16–17 72n1
1:16–32 140n34
1:17 157n18
1:18–20 51
1:18–25 51
1:18–32 51n6, 73n3
1:19–20 50
3:2 66, 72n2
3:4 157n18
3:10 157n18
4:3 76
4:7–8 164n36
4:22–25 93n94
4:23–24 76
4:25 77
5–8 79
5:5 128
5:14 161
5:19 161
6 122
6:7 74n9
7:1–8:11 268
8 122
8:3–4 185
8:14–17 92
8:18–23 64
8:18–25 76n14, 92
8:19–22 73n6, 79
8:28–30 79
8:29 19, 92, 217
9–11 46
9:15–16 66
9:24–29 160n27
9:27–29 164n36
10:9–10 216
11:17–21 187

11:34 164n36
12:1–2 205, 273
12:2 194
12:17 194
13:14 206
15–16 79
15:4 77, 222, 229
15:8–21 73n5
15:9–11 164n36
15:20 187, 193
15:26 271
16:25–27 73n5
16:26 188n40

1 Corinthians

1:1–4 72n1
1:2 74n12, 77
1:4–9 74n9
1:7 123
1:9 72n1, 74n12, 129
1:10 194
1:12–14 123
1:18 61
1:18–2:5 122
1:18–25 123
1:19 157n18
1:21 72n1
1:26–27 128
1:26–31 72n1, 202
1:31 157n18
2:4 128
2:4–5 61
2:6–7 195
2:6–13 93
2:6–16 128
2:10–11 128
2:12 195
2:16 195
3:3 194
3:18–20 194
3:20 164n36
4:6 66
4:7–14 195
5:7 161n30
6:1–12 195
6:12 195
6:19 128
7:12–16 195
7:17–24 72n1
8:1 194
8:1–2 195
8:6 64

9:9 163n32
9:22 195
10:1–4 163n32
10:1–11 77n18, 93n94
10:1–14 161
10:2 161
10:4 229
10:11 76, 77, 163
10:27–29 195
10:31 64, 271
10:31–11:1 195
12 128
12:12 79
12:21–22 194
12:35–50 221n2
13 128
13:1–4 194
13:12 104, 232n13
14 128
14:3 124
14:25 119, 128
14:26–36 72n1
14:29–33 116
15 123
15:3–5 214, 217, 228–29
15:12–14 221n2
15:34 195
16:1–4 271

2 Corinthians

1:2–11 74n10
1:18–20 91
2:14–17 72n1
3 147
3:1–3 148
3:6 76
3:18 91
4:1–6 72n1
4:11–15 74n10
5 79
5:19 8, 95
6:16 66
6:18 164n36
8:15 157n18
9:1–5 271
9:10–15 74n10

Galatians

1:6–16 72n1
1:11–12 33

2:7 187n40
2:9 222
2:10 187n40
3:1–5 128n68
3:6 157n18
3:8 177n12
3:10 157n18
3:16 163n32
3:17–29 141
3:23–29 268
4:4 163
4:4–5 8
4:19 206
4:24 229
4:25–26 161

Ephesians

1 74n8, 74n11
1–3 79
1:10 40, 64, 165
1:15–16 74n9, 74n12
1:17 75
1:18 74n12, 75
1:18–21 75
1:20–22 270
2:6 270
2:11–3:13 79n20
2:18–20 92
2:20 66
3:1–13 66
3:2–13 73, 73n5
3:7–11 72n1
3:14–19 78n20
4:1 74n12
4:1–6 72n1
4:17 205
4:17–24 122
4:20 205, 205n18, 216
4:20–21 93
4:21–24 91
4:23 205
4:24 206
5:22–6:9 272
5:25 93
5:26 93
5:27 93
5:28–29 93
5:30–32 93
6:3 157n18

Philippians

1 74n8
1:1 74
1:3–6 72n1
1:3–8 6, 74n9, 76
1:6 75
1:9 75
1:9–11 6, 76
1:10 75
1:17 75
1:27–28 194
2:16 194

Colossians

1 74n8
1:3–8 72n1, 74n9
1:6 76, 76n14, 92
1:9 75, 76
1:9–14 78n20
1:9–20 73
1:10 75, 76, 76n14, 92
1:15 198
1:15–17 259
1:15–20 64, 73n6, 79, 202,
    210, 259
1:16–17 7, 105
1:17 253
1:20 64, 165
1:24–29 78n20
1:28–29 79
1:28–3:4 93
2:1–7 78n20
2:16–17 161
2:17 161
3:9–10 91
3:17 64

1 Thessalonians

1:1 74
1:2–10 72n1, 74nn8–9
1:4–7 74n8
2:1–4 72n1
2:9–13 74n9
2:13 66, 72n1, 74
4:12 194

2 Thessalonians

1:3–4 74n9
1:8 217

2:13 18
2:13–15 72n1

1 Timothy

1:15 66, 67
1:17 198
2:5 224
4:1 163

2 Timothy

3:1 163
3:15 5, 18, 57, 206
3:15–17 13, 67, 148
3:16 18, 58, 61, 66, 206
3:16–17 18, 57, 63
4:12 18
4:13 140

Philemon

4–5 74n9

Hebrews

1:1 51–52
1:1–2 12, 50, 143, 224
1:2 52, 163
2:2 66
2:11–12 73n3
4:12 206, 233
5:5–10 161
6:5 77
8:5 161
9:9 161
9:24 161
10:1 161
12:22–23 161

James

1:16–18 72n1
1:22–27 82
1:27 271

1 Peter

1:3–25 72n1
1:16 157n18
1:20 163
1:23 136

1:24–25 163n32
3:1–7 272
4:12–19 217
4:17 217

2 Peter

1:3–4 72n1
1:16–21 72n1
1:19 66
1:20–21 61
1:21 18, 22, 60, 68
3:3 163
3:11–14 162
3:13 162, 165

1 John

1:3 200
2:18 163
3:2 91
4:21 32

Jude

18 163

Revelation

1:3 13, 33, 148
1:9–20 72n1
3:20 90
4–5 203n10

5 161n30
5:4–5 236
5:6–10 236
5:8–10 73n5
5:13–14 73n6
11:15 259
12 165
17–18 272
21 162
21:1 165
21:1–6 216
21:1–22:5 73n6
21:2 161
21:23 12, 143
22:7 148

Subject Index

Abraham, 176–77, 219
Abrahamic covenant, 181,
    183, 264, 268, 270
academic commentaries,
    238–40, 246
academic reading of Scrip-
    ture, 131, 201
academics, and faith, 208–11
academy, and church, 3
accommodation, 250n39
Adam, A. K. M., 96
Adam, curse of, 268
age to come, 77, 185
akolouthia, 22
akribeia, 247
Alexander, T. Desmond, 169
Alexandrian school of inter-
    pretation, 159, 239–41
allegory, 159, 229, 240
all of life, 37, 265, 269, 271
allusions, 157–58
already-and-not-yet, 162, 184,
    186, 269
Alt, Albrecht, 201
analysis of Scripture, 7, 82–84
analytic philosophy, 112,
    119n30, 125n53
ancient exegesis, 229–30
Anderson, Bernard, 163n33
anthropology, 116, 118–23
Antiochene school of interpre-
    tation, 159, 240–41, 244
apocalyptic writings, 220–21,
    222

apologetics, 272
apophatic hermeneutic, 266
apostles, witness of, 69–70
Apostles' Creed, 261
apostolic hermeneutics, 232
apostolic method, and biblical
    theology, 155–64
Archer, Margaret S., 116n18,
    118, 119–23, 127
Aristotle, 44
Arius, 215
Athanasius, 29, 223n4
atheism, 119
Augustine, 32, 45, 81n30, 139,
    204, 223, 231, 233, 241, 255
Austin, John, 125

Babel, 176, 227
Balthasar, Hans Urs von, 33,
    40, 41
Barr, James, 209
Barth, Karl, 1, 28, 29, 33, 34,
    36–37, 38, 86, 114–15,
    132–33, 134, 186, 190, 246,
    252–53, 255, 262
Bartholomew, Craig, 37, 84,
    110n1, 117, 167n42, 169,
    266
Barton, John, 209, 246, 253
Bauckham, Richard, 165n38,
    196
Bavinck, Herman, 51, 51n6,
    52, 57–58, 60–61, 67, 260,
    272

Beale, G. K., 157, 158n22, 167,
    169, 180, 268
Behr, John, 203, 216n56
beneficia Christi, 190
Berkouwer, G. C., 51
Bernard of Clairvaux, 88–89,
    225
Berry, Wendell, 265
Best, Ernest, 205
Bible. *See* canon; Scripture
biblical criticism
    instrumental value of, 211
    "scientific objectivity" of,
        209
biblical imagination, 47
biblical interpretation, and
    obedience of faith, 273
biblical theology, 150–53
    and apostolic method,
        155–64
    and apostolic witness, 155
    and canon, 166–67
    and exegesis, 153
    and narrative approach,
        164–66, 168
    single-center approach to,
        167–68
    and systematic theology,
        153–55
    and theological interpreta-
        tion, 13–15
Biblicism, 62
blessing, 176–77
Blount, Brian, 39

285

Bockmuehl, Markus, 32, 88n68, 206–7, 239n3

Bonhoeffer, Dietrich, 37, 38, 79–80, 144, 203–4, 206, 211, 258, 262

Bourdieu, Pierre, 119n30, 122, 127nn65–66

Bowald, Mark Alan, 28n3

Bowers, Paul, 193

Boyle, John, 34

bracketing of theological beliefs, 208–10, 246, 253

Brazos Theological Commentary on the Bible, 29, 247

Brueggemann, Walter, 25, 201–2

Bruner, Frederick Dale, 246

Bucer, Martin, 244

Calvin, John, 29, 44, 61, 114–15, 154, 244–45

Campenhausen, Hans von, 137

canon, 223
    and biblical theology, 166–67
    and community, 134–36
    goal of, 143–48
    as interpretive context, 139–43
    and mission, 147
    narrower and wider, 139
    ontology of, 135
    and theological interpretation, 11–13, 131–34

canonical intentionality, 256

canonical interpretation, 21

canon within the canon, 141

Capes, David, 164n36

Capetz, Paul E., 107n20

Carroll, John, v

cataphatic hermeneutic, 266

Catechism of the Catholic Church, 154

catena, 242

Catholic modernism, 113–14

Chalcedon, 250, 251

Childs, Brevard, 24, 28, 133–34, 144n47, 154, 155n13, 166–67, 167n42, 199n5, 258, 263, 265

Chrétien, Jean-Louis, 82, 84, 87n63

Christian life, as "on the way," 232

Christian philosophy, 110–11

Christians, narrative of, 200

christocentric interpretation, 9

christological exegesis, 228–29

Christology, 259–60

Christomonism, 213n48

church
    and academy, 3
    and biblical theology, 14
    as home of Scripture, 5–7, 18, 42–43, 72–73, 207
    missional imperative of, 216–17
    as theocracy, 266
    transformed for the sake of the world, 19
    as transnational, 267–68
    use and abuse of Scripture, 211–12
    and Word of God, 214–15, 223

church fathers, as sources, 229–30

church planting, 173

circularity, of historical methods, 8–9

Clement of Alexandria, 240

Clines, David, 264

Coakley, Sarah, 102

codex, 147–48

cognition, 18

commentaries, 237–38. See also academic commentaries; theological commentary

communion with God, 200, 205

community
    as central to Jesus's mission, 184
    church as, 74, 75
    gathering of, 184–85

Comrie, Alexander, 204

Concordia Commentary, 247

confessional exegesis, 235

consummation, 184, 269

contemplatio, 90

content, of Scripture, 52, 58, 61

contextual interpretation, 37–39

continental philosophy, 112, 119n30, 125n53

coram deo, 269

Council of Chalcedon (451), 251n40

Council of Constantinople (553), 251n40

Council of Constantinople (680–681), 251n40

Council of Ephesus (431), 251n40

covenant, 52, 178, 179, 219, 262–64

Cranmer, Thomas, 153

creation, 94, 123, 176, 261
    care for, 270
    ex nihilo, 115–16
    and redemption, 261–64

creation, fall, redemption, and consummation, 165

creational revelation, 3, 51

critical realism, 116–18

critical theism, 99

cross-cultural missions, 173

cultural analysis, 273

culture, listening to, 25

curse, of sin, 176

Cyril of Alexandria, 29, 251

daily office, 85

Davidic covenant, 181

Davis, Ellen F., 265

deixis, 125, 126

Dempster, Stephen G., 169

denominational interpretation, 235

deuterocanonical books, 139

devotional commentaries, 246

dictation theory of inspiration, 68

didachē, 69, 192–93

disciple, 207

disciples of Jesus, 222

discourse analysis, 128

divine address, 134–35, 198

divine agency, 8–9, 98, 100, 102

divine economy, 30–31, 39–42, 100

divine violence, 141–42

docetism, 96

doctrine and praxis, 18
Dooyeweerd, Herman, 117
"double listening," 25
dualism, 51, 62–63, 76n14, 115
Dumbrell, William, 262

ears, 90–91
echoes, 157–58
ecological crisis, 156
"ecology of moods," in
    theology, 35
ecumenical exegesis, 235
egocentricity, 191
election, 178–79, 183
Elliott, Mark, 254
Ellul, Jacques, 25, 85n53
Emerson, Matthew, 37
Emmaus road, 146, 229, 260
Enlightenment, 54, 63, 117,
    119, 131, 171
Enns, Peter, 231, 250
epiekeia, 248
Epistles, 59, 222
Erasmus, 243, 243n21
eschatology, 162, 269
ethnocentric exclusivism, 185
evangelical tradition, 246
evangelism, 173
Evans, C. F., 105
exegesis
    Barth on, 255
    and biblical theology, 153
    and community, 248
    necessity of, 256
    and theology, 21, 23
exodus, and canon, 93n94

faith, 20
fall and judgment, 227
false prophets, 61
Fee, Gordon, 124
fellowship with God, 198, 204
fields, 128
figural reading, 29
figural sense of Scripture, 23
Fiumara, Gemma, 84, 85,
    85n54
Ford, David F., 35
fourfold sense, 40, 234n15, 244
Fowl, Stephen, 31
Fretheim, Terence E., 141n39
full-time service, 272

fundamentalism, 69
Funk, Robert, 105

Gabler, Johann, 13
Gadamer, Hans-Georg, 10,
    116, 124n48, 174
general revelation, 3, 50–51,
    115n14
generosity, 42
genres of Scripture, 49, 59,
    71, 260
gentiles, mission to, 187–88
Gignilliat, Mark, 212
Glossa ordinaria, 242
glossed Bible, 242
gnosticism, 96
God
    calls church into existence,
        73, 75
    at work in the world, 107
    See also divine address; di-
        vine agency; voice of God
"God-breathed," Scripture as,
    57–58, 61
Godfrey of Admont, 90
Goffman, Erving, 126–27
Goheen, Michael, 78n19,
    110n1, 117, 167n42,
    178n20, 266
Goldsworthy, Graeme, 168
good works, 75–76, 270n46
gospel, 6, 217
Gospels, 59, 222
Great Commission, 186, 222
Great Tradition, 214
Green, Joel, 108n22
Gregory, Brad, 97–98
Grice, Paul H., 125
guardrails, in reading Scrip-
    ture, 212–14
Guder, Darrell, 195–96
Guigo II, 88
Gunton, Colin E., 70n51, 261
Guthrie, George H., 205n19

Habermas, Jürgen, 117
Hagner, Donald, 101
Hamilton, James, 167–68
Hart, Trevor, 114n8
Hebrew Scriptures, 218–21
Heidelberg Catechism, 154
Hellenism, 220

hermeneutic of suspicion,
    83, 209
hermeneutic of trust, 71, 86,
    209
hermeneutics, 9–11, 112–13
higher criticism
    destructive power of, 70
    on human dimensions of
        Scripture, 68–69
    naturalism of, 49
    and severing of Scripture's
        properties, 65
Historia scholastica, 242
historical, literary, and ca-
    nonical horizons, 213
historical criticism, 250
    and commentaries, 247
    and covenant, 263
    disenchantment with, 29
    domination of, 104, 106
    fragmentation of, 224
    on history, 95, 97
    loss of hegemony, 132
    naturalism of, 104
    and theological interpreta-
        tion, ix, 7
historical study, as essential,
    201
historiography, 96, 98, 103–4,
    109
history, 8–9, 55n15
    and divine agency, 8–9,
        95–97, 98, 100, 102
    theological reading of, 103–7
history of Israel, 220
holistic theological interpreta-
    tion, 269
Holt, Robby, 31
Holtrop, Pieter, 45
holy nation, Israel as, 177–78
Holy Spirit, 22, 41
    and anthropology, 128–29
    and biblical interpretation,
        260
    and canon, 138
    and Scripture, 4–5
    and transformation, 206
    witness of, 60–62, 69–70
homiletical commentaries, 246
Hoover, Roy, 105
Horton, Michael S., 35, 36
hospitable generosity, 3

hospitality, 3, 42, 90
Hugh of St. Victor, 242
humanism, 242, 244–45
humankind, 224, 226–27, 228
humility, 87n63
Humphrey, Edith, 214

idolatry, 180
Ignatian Examen, 85, 87
image of God, 7, 153
imperative nature of Scrip-
    ture, 34
inaugurated eschatology, 162
incarnation, 225–56
incarnational analogy, 231,
    250–51
"in Christ," 80, 234, 268
individualism, 3, 49
individual use of Scripture,
    207
inductive Bible study, 85
inerrancy, 66
infallibility, 65–66
inspiration, 21, 224
    and incarnation, 230–32
interfaith reading, 45
International Critical Com-
    mentary, 247
International Theological
    Commentary, 247
interpretation, and canon,
    139–40
interpreters-in-relationship, 92
intracanonical intertexual-
    ity, 238
Irenaeus, 164n37, 203–4, 223,
    254, 255, 261
Israel
    as gathered and eschatologi-
        cal, 186
    as God's covenant people,
        264
    mission of, 177–78, 182–83,
        185, 186
    story of, 165
    as theocracy, 266

Jenkins, Philip, 63n38
Jenson, Robert, 43
Jeremias, Joachim, 184
Jerome, 139, 260
Jerusalem Council, 188

Jesus Christ
    as center of biblical
        theology, 168
    as center of Scripture, 172,
        202–4
    death and resurrection of,
        185, 228
    as fulfillment of Scripture,
        77–78
    as goal of canon, 144, 147
    as ideal listener, 90–92
    lordship of, 210
    ministry of, 221
    mission of, 183–86
    as obedient servant, 91
    in the Old Testament,
        162–64
    resurrection of, 225
    as revelation, 3
Jesus Seminar, 101, 105
Jewish theological interpreta-
    tion, 46
Jews
    mission to, 186
    narrative of, 200
John Paul II, Pope, 83
Johnson, Luke Timothy, 35, 47
"Judaizing exegesis," 245
Justin Martyr, 222

Käsemann, Ernst, 96–97
kerygma, 19, 24, 69, 192–93,
    199, 200
Kierkegaard, Søren, 82–84,
    86, 238, 246
king, 181
kingdom of God/heaven, 25,
    56, 168, 183–84, 186, 259,
    263–64
Kipling, Rudyard, 208
knowledge of God, 75–76, 233
Köstenberger, Andreas, 169
Kuyper, Abraham, 204, 260

land, 181
language, 112–13
language philosophy, 124n48
Laplace, Pierre-Simon, 97n3
law, 59, 180
law and the prophets, 218
"learning Christ," 205–6, 215
Leclercq, Jean, 89, 216

lectio divina, 2, 7, 43, 85,
    88–90, 207
Leithart, Peter, 89
Levenson, Jon, 141n35, 201,
    208
Levinson, Stephen C., 126–27
Lewis, C. S., 57, 67
light, revelation as, 134
listening to Scripture, 7, 71,
    82–84, 92n92, 93, 198, 206
literal sense, 23, 231, 238,
    241, 256
Lohink, Gerhard, 185
Lord's Prayer, 235
love
    for God, 46, 233, 271
    and hearing, 93
    for neighbor, 32, 45–46,
        233, 271
Luther, Martin, 88, 244
Lyotard, Jean-François, 151n3

Macintyre, Alasdair, 159n24
MacKinnon, Donald M.,
    107n21
Magrassi, Mariano, 84,
    88n66, 216
Manifesto for Theological In-
    terpretation, x–xi, 1–25
manner, of revelation, 52
Marcel, Gabriel, 87n63
Marcion, 138, 215, 224, 231
Martin, Francis, 122
Martin-Achard, Robert, 180
martyria, 69, 192–93
Matthews, W. R., 113–14, 115
Maximus the Confessor, 261
McCann, J. Clinton, 169
McCasland, S. Vernon, 160n29
McGrath, Alister, 115,
    116n18, 117
meaning, and significance, 23
means of grace, 81–82n32, 190
medieval exegesis, 230, 242–
    43, 244
meditatio, 89
Melanchthon, Philipp, 154
Mendenhall, George, 201
Menschwerdung, 230–31
metanarrative, 14, 55, 64,
    151n3, 173

metaphysical naturalism,
   97–103
methodological naturalism,
   98–103, 109
missio Dei, 17, 174, 270
mission
   and Bible, 16–17
   and canon, 147
   centripetal and centrifugal
      dimensions of, 182, 187
   and theological interpreta-
      tion, 15–17, 172
"missional anticipatory forestructures," 174
missional hermeneutic, 78n19,
   174–76, 189
Mitchell, Margaret, 247
Moberly, Walter, 31, 46
modern criticism, 238, 253.
   See also higher criticism;
   historical criticism
modern hermeneutical theory,
   209–10
modernism, 119–20
   cul-de-sacs of, 31
   reductionism of, 130
modern turn, in theological
   commentary, 245–47
Moltmann, Jürgen, 133, 135,
   262
Monophysitism, 21
monotheism, 178–79, 224–25,
   228
Montanus, 138
moods of Scripture, 35–36
"moral sense" of Scripture,
   234
Mormons, narrative of, 200
Moses, 219
Muller, Richard, 244, 245, 248
Muslims, narrative of, 200
mysticism, 113–14

narrative, and biblical
   theology, 164–66, 168
nations
   blessing in Acts, 186–88
   blessing through arrival of
      kingdom, 183–86
   blessing through Israel,
      176–83
   drawn to God in Christ, 79

naturalism, 9, 97–103
natural theology, 114–15
neoorthodoxy, 132
Nestorianism, 21, 231, 251
Neuhaus, Richard John, v, 110
Newbigin, Lesslie, 24, 49, 54,
   186–87, 258, 260
new covenant, 268
new creation, 175, 205, 206,
   232
new exodus, 161, 163
new heaven and new earth, 21
Newland, George, 41
New Testament, 221–23
   canon of, 12–13
   Christology of, 259–60
   eschatology, 264
   historiographical legitimacy
      of, 106
   as product and tool of
      God's mission, 192–94
   a riddle without the Old
      Testament, 145–16
   use of Old Testament,
      156–64
Nicholas of Lyra, 243, 244
Noah, covenant with, 227
noetic effects of sin, 128
nontheological account of history, inadequacy of, 103–4

obedience to the gospel, 217
O'Donovan, Oliver, 25, 72,
   262, 266, 269n42
O'Dowd, Ryan P., 169
Oecolampadius, John, 244
O'Keefe, John, 241
Ola Tjorhøm, 262
old covenant, 222, 268
Old Testament, 218–21
   canon of, 12–13
   as countertestimony, 201–2
   discrete witness of, 145, 265
   fulfilled in Christ, 265–66
   must be heard with New
      Testament, 146
   as product and tool of
      God's mission, 191–92
   relevance for Christians, 266
   use by New Testament,
      156–64
ontology, 115

opheleia, 248
oratio, 89–90
organic inspiration, 5, 69
organic revelation, 50, 54
Origen, 223, 240
original audience, 148
orthodoxy, 18
orthopraxy, 18
Osborne, Grant R., 203n10
Our World Belongs to God
   (Christian Reformed
   Church), 57

Packer, J. I., 199, 212
palingenesia, 21
Pannenberg, Wolfhart, 97
participation, in God's mission, 173–74
participation framework,
   126–29
particularism, as expression
   of universalism, 175–76,
   184
particular people, 175
patristic exegesis, 229–30,
   234n15, 241
Paul
   Christology of, 76–79, 259
   on the church, 74
   on fulfillment of Old Testa-
      ment, 228
   on hearing God's voice in
      Scripture, 76–77
   letters of, 222
   on missional reading, 79
   mission of, 187–88n40,
      193–95
peace, 156
Pennington, Jonathan, 212
Pentateuch, 93n94, 219, 264
personhood, 121
Peterson, Eugene, 43, 85,
   85n54, 88n72, 89n80,
   90n87, 267
Peukert, Helmut, 126n57
Phillips, J. B., 259
Philo, 240
philosophy, 9–10, 110–11
pilgrimage, 266–67
Plaks, Andrew, 136n18
Plant, Stephen J., 211
Plantinga, Alvin, 118n25

pneumomonism, 213n48
poetry, 59
Polkinghorne, John, 116n18
poor, 271–72
Porter, Stanley E., 28n2
postilla, 242–43
postmodernism, 10, 14, 111,
    119, 120–21, 130, 151,
    173, 210
power, 155
practice, 127
pragmatics, 125, 129
"prayed reading," 216
prayer, 89–90, 215–16, 257–58
preaching, 39
prejudice (prejudgments), 10,
    174
premodern exegesis, 31–
    32n14, 42–43, 245, 248
priests, 181–82
private Bible reading, 6, 18,
    79–80, 85–86
private interpretation, 216
proclamation, and obedience,
    217
production format, 126–27
progressive revelation, 3–4, 53
promise and fulfillment, 141,
    159–60
prophecy, 159–62
prophets, 59, 61, 182–83, 184,
    220, 234
propositionalism, 49n1
protocanonical books, 139
providence, 256
psalms, 234
psalms of ascent, 266
pseudo-epigraphic books, and
    canon, 223n3
public theology, 273
Puritans, 246

quadriga. See fourfold sense
quests of the historical Jesus,
    101
quiet time, 85
quotations, 157

Rad, Gerhard von, v, 138,
    141n35, 143, 201, 261
Rae, Murray, 40, 211
Rahner, Karl, 107n21, 215

rationalism, 3, 10, 19, 49, 112,
    117
reader-response criticism,
    132–33
readers, receptivity and active
    engagement of, 37
reading, macro- and micro-
    levels of, 200, 202
reading communities, 45
realism, 116–17
realist ontology, 121
receptive listening, 7, 84–85
redaction criticism, 250
redemption, 165n38, 261–64
redemptive historical horizon,
    77–78
redemptive revelation, 3, 51–53
Reformation, on theological
    commentary, 243–45
Reformed epistemology,
    118n25
Reginald of Piperno, 257–58
regula fidei, 2, 22, 35, 212,
    253–55
relational epistemology, 124n49
Renaissance, 243–44
Reno, R. R., 241, 249n36
repentance, 233
ressourcement, 31, 32, 229
resurrection, 185, 262
revelation, as organism, 3, 40
Reventlow, Henning Graf, 167
"rewritten Bible," 238
Ricoeur, Paul, 84, 209, 261
Ridderbos, Herman, 57,
    64–65, 67, 192
Ritschl, Albrecht, 113–14
ritual, 267
Roman Empire, 220
Romanticism, 10, 19, 237
Rule of Faith. See regula fidei

Sachkritik, 83
sacra doctrina, 244
sacra pagina, 244
Sacred-secular dichotomy, 5, 62
Sacred Space (Irish Jesuits),
    86–87
"sanctified vision," 241
Sarisky, Darren, 32n14
Sauter, Gerhard, 253
Schleicher, Rüdiger, 211

Schleiermacher, Friedrich, 115
scholia, 242, 243
Schreiner, Thomas, 169
Schriftwerdung, 230
scientific inquiry, in Christian
    theology, 249
Scobie, Charles, 155n13, 167
scriptural revelation 3, 51
Scripture
    academic study of, 131
    as address, 30, 33–39, 48
    attributes of, 3
    authority of, 49, 55, 59,
        62–65, 66–67, 68
    as canon, 134
    centers in Jesus Christ,
        202–4
    central themes of, 167
    as Christian Scriptures,
        171–72
    comprehensive witness of,
        258–59
    as diverse and fragmented,
        14
    divine authorship of, 22
    doctrine of, 3–5
    fourfold sense of, 2
    as God's address, 226
    as God's gift, 198, 204
    in human form, 5, 49, 68
    individual use of, 207
    instrumental authority of,
        66–67
    as living and active, 206
    as means of missional grace,
        190
    as metanarrative, 55, 64
    on mission, 168
    missional purpose of, 58
    and moral teaching, 234
    multivalent testimony of,
        201
    narratives of, 152–53
    as norma normans non nor-
        mata, 214
    as one story, 54–55
    ontological authority of,
        66–67
    organic narrative unity
        of, 71
    as own best interpreter, 23
    power of, 61

as product and tool of God's
mission, 16–17, 189–90
and providence, 252
purpose of, 52, 69
and redemption, 56–60
reductionism and flattening
of, 202
sacramentality of, 232–33
speaks in unsettling ways,
202
as storied, 49
story of, 266
as theocentric, 199n5
as totalitarian in scope, 64
as unity, 4, 80, 150, 223–24,
228
on unity of humankind,
226–27
as Word of God, 48, 150–51,
213
and worship, 207, 234–35
Scripture and Hermeneutics
Seminar, x–xi, 111
Searle, John R., 125
Second Vatican Council, 230,
231n10
Sell, Roger, 121n40
sensus literalis, 22, 241, 243–46
Septuagint, 139
sermon, 237, 238
Sermon on the Mount, 185
Sertillanges, A. G., 217
Shema, 6, 80
silence, 86–88, 90
single-center approach, to biblical theology, 167–68
slavery, 272
small-group Bible studies, 207
societal structures, 271–72
sociolinguistics, 128
Sparks, Kenton L., 250
Spears, Aubrey, 31
special revelation, 3, 50–51,
115n114
speech-act theory, 59n28, 125,
126n56, 126n59
Spinoza, 23
spiritual sense of Scripture,
40–41
Spurgeon, C. H., 202
Spykman, Gordon, 51, 261
Stackert, Jeffrey, 132n2

Stanton, Graham, 106
Stott, John, 25, 273
Sundberg, Albert, Jr., 139n31
supersessionism, 46
suppression, of revelation, 51
Swain, Scott, 33, 42
systematic theology, and biblical theology, 153–55

tabernacle, 180
temple, 156, 167, 180
Tertullian, 225n5
Thatcher, Adrian, 46
theological commentary,
22–24, 237–38
in early Christianity, 239–41
in medieval period, 242–43
and modern turn, 245–47
in Reformation age, 243–45
theological exegesis, 229, 233
theological hermeneutic,
123–29
theological interpretation
and all of life, 24–25, 37,
269, 271
and anthropology, 118–23
articles of faith for, 20–21
and canon, 11–13, 131–34
as ecclesial endeavor, 207–8
formative role of, 32
and historical inquiry,
100–103
history of, 28–29
marks of, 28, 30–32
missional focus of, 217
moral dimension of, 32, 45
as "nonscientific," 19
and philosophy, 112–18
and prayer, 215–16
telos of, 17–19
and theological hermeneu-
tic, 123–29
and transformation, 18,
204–7
theology
disciplinary divide from biblical studies, 1
and exegesis, 21, 23
scientific nature of, 249
theonomism, 213n48
thick and thin interpretation,
210

Thirty-Nine Articles, 154
Thiselton, Anthony C., 111,
113, 116, 125
Thomas, Heath, 30
Thomas Aquinas, 29, 34, 40,
42, 44, 154, 242, 257–58
Thompson, John L., 36, 44,
245, 248
"Thus says the LORD," 226
torah, 180
Torrance, T. F., 115, 249
totalizing theological reading,
201–2
tota Scriptura, 12, 13, 140
tradition, 1, 125, 214, 215n55
transcendent reality, 121–23
transformation
of people of God into new
community, 188
from theological interpretation, 18, 204–7
Trinity, 213, 256
and exegesis, 252
and mission, 175
and Scripture, 4
Turner, Ken, 126n58
Two Horizons Commentary,
247
typology, 2, 141, 160–61

union with Christ, 270
universalization, of God's
people, 267–69

Valentinus, 215
validity, in interpretation, 210
Verschueren, Jef, 125
violence, 156
in the Bible, 141–42
voice of God, 30, 71, 76–77,
199
and canon, 136
Vos, Geerhardus, 52

Waltke, Bruce, 142n40, 169
Ward, Timothy, 66n41
Warfield, B. B., 66n44
Watson, Francis, 36, 241n11
Watts, Rikk, 158
Webb, Robert L., 98–103
Webster, John, 33, 36, 38, 39,
250nn38–39, 251

Wellhausen, Julius, 131–32, 201
Wenham, Gordon J., 177n10
Westcott, B. F., 255
Westermann, Claus, 249n36
Western church, 174
Western culture, assumptions about the Bible, 49
Westminster Confession of Faith, 154
whole-Bible biblical theology, 166–68

whole counsel of God, 12, 140, 170
Wilkin, Robert, 251n40
Williams, Michael D., 49n1
Williams, Rowan, 30, 34, 36, 201–2, 214
Williamson, Paul, 250
Wink, Walter, 29
wisdom, 206
wisdom literature, 59, 220, 234
Witherington, Ben, 165n39
witness, to all nations, 186

Wittgenstein, Ludwig, 88–89n73, 125
worship, 216, 234–35
Wright, Christopher, 78n19, 152–53, 168, 178n20
Wright, N. T., v, 54–56, 116n18, 124n49, 151, 165n38, 189, 260, 263, 266

Yahweh Elohim, 262
Yoder, John Howard, 41–42

Zahn, Molly, 238n2